Disability is Natural

Revolutionary Common Sense for Raising Successful Children with Disabilities

Kathie Snow

Alpha Resource Center
805-683-2145(Santa Barbara)
805-347-2775(Santa Maria)
www.alphasb.org

BraveHeart Press
Woodland Park, Colorado

—Disability is Natural—
Revolutionary Common Sense for Raising Successful Children with Disabilities
By Kathie Snow

Copyright ©2005 by Kathie Snow
Printed in the United States of America

DISCLAIMER
This book is designed to provide information regarding the topics covered. It is sold with the understanding that the author and/or publisher are not engaged in providing legal, medical, or therapeutic services or advice. The purpose of this book is to educate the reader on alternatives to the traditional methods of caring for, providing services to, and meeting the needs of children with disabilities. The author and BraveHeart Press shall have neither liability nor responsibility to any person or entity with respect to any loss or damage caused, or alleged to be caused, directly or indirectly by the information contained in this book. If you do not wish to be bound by the above, you may return this book to the publisher for refund.

Library of Congress Control Number: 2005903920
Snow, Kathie
        Disability is natural: Revolutionary common sense for raising successful children with disabilities / Kathie Snow
        Includes bibliography and index.
        1. Parenting 2. Disability - Social Policies 3. Child care

        ISBN Number 978-0-9707636-6-2

First Edition March 2001
Second Edition May 2005

Bowl of Apples logo and covers designed by Kathie Snow; Bowl of Apples logo polished by Ken Keegan. Clip Art on pages 17, 77, 159,167, 169, 171, 176, 177, 190 and 199 by Adobe InDesign; all other clip art from www.ClipartInc.com.

Published by:
BraveHeart Press
P. O. Box 7245
Woodland Park, CO 80863-7245 U.S.A.
1-866-948-2222, 1-719-687-0735, Fax 1-719-687-8114
www.disabilityisnatural.com

For each child
with a disability
living today,

and for those
not yet born:

may you live the life
of your dreams,

for your
disability is irrelevant.

—Disability is Natural—

One out of five Americans is a person with a disability.
One of the five apples in the bowl is green.

A green apple is more like red apples than different.
A person with a disability is more like people without disabilities than different.

There have always been people with disabilities in the world and there always will be.
Disability, along with gender, ethnicity, age, and other traits, is simply one of many
natural characteristics of being human. This principle is embodied in the
Developmental Disabilities Act and other Federal laws.

The warm rays of the sun shine equally on the five apples in the bowl.

It's time for the warmth of inclusion to shine equally
on people with and without disabilities in our society.

Contents

Cautious, careful people,
always casting about to
preserve their reputation
and social standing,
never can bring about a reform.

Those who are really in earnest
must be willing to be
anything or nothing
in the world's estimation,
and publicly and privately
in season and out,
avow their sympathies with
despised and persecuted ideas
and their advocates,
and bear the consequences.

Susan B. Anthony

Good News!

Your wonderful, precious child who happens to have a disability is *perfect!* And regardless of the type or level of the disability, your son or daughter can enjoy a successful, natural life.

This may be news to you. It may be at the opposite end of the spectrum from what you've heard and/or what you personally believe. If so, I hope you're happily anticipating learning how you can make this happen!

Contrary to what you may have been led to believe, you don't need to change your child—through therapies and interventions—and you don't need to wait for the system to change—to provide more supports, better services, more laws, etc. To ensure your child lives the life of his or her dreams, you simply need to change the way you *see* your child, and then change the way you've been doing some things.

The suggestions in this book have been shared with thousands of parents, people with disabilities, educators, and human services professionals, during seminars I've presented across North America, through the articles on my web site (www.disabilityisnatural.com), and via the first edition of this book. And the suggestions work. I know, because they've worked in our family's life and they're working for other families. Some educators are embracing the concepts, and a variety of human services agencies are beginning to move in this new direction.

The philosophies and suggestions in this book are considered revolutionary by some, because they go against the CONVENTIONAL WISDOM (accepted practices) we're all accustomed to. But they're really common sense—the common sense many of us have lost, but which we can regain.

The premise of this book—that **disability is natural**—may be considered a radical principle, but it is not only common sense, it's also part of several Federal laws (more about this in the next chapter).

How can disability *not* be natural? People with disabilities have been in the world since the beginning of time, and will be until the end of time. Disability is so natural and common, in fact, that it doesn't leave anyone out: it touches people of both genders, and of any age, ethnicity, religion, socioeconomic level, and/or sexual orientation. Disability does not discriminate!

Some parents have said my ideas are "scary;" one mother told me I was "dangerous," adding that I "shouldn't be allowed to speak in public." Later, after thoughtful consideration, soul-searching, and/or allowing these ideas to percolate, many let me know they "did a 180," and enthusiastically joined this

> COMMON SENSE
> IS THE KNACK OF
> SEEING THINGS
> AS THEY ARE,
> AND DOING THINGS
> AS THEY OUGHT
> TO BE DONE.
> *Josh Billings*

gentle revolution. Other parents embraced these ideas immediately, recognizing the awesome life changes they can bring about.

Many professionals who hear my message call it "unrealistic." Others have said, "I love it! Why didn't *we* think of this?" And adults with developmental disabilities—the real experts—call it "the truth," and ask, "Why isn't anyone else spreading the news?" I don't know the answer to that question, but I hope you'll begin spreading the good news, too.

This is not like any other book written for parents of children with disabilities. It's not about learning more about your child's specific condition, how to get more services, or dealing with your child's "problems." As you'll learn, the problem isn't your child's disability at all; the problem is how disability is perceived, and how this perception led to the creation of a Service System that's supposed to help, but which may actually harm.

Too many children and adults spend their lives in DISABILITY WORLD: it's a world where people are called "special," which leads to Special Services, and these, in turn, often result in the segregation of people who use these Special Services. In general, the current practices in DISABILITY WORLD—Early Intervention, Early Childhood Special Education, Therapies, Special Education, Vocational-Rehabilitation, and other programs—aren't working. Our children are not getting what they really need. They're isolated and undereducated in public schools and excluded from community activities. And their futures are uncertain, considering the unemployment rate for adults with developmental disabilities continually hovers around 70-75 percent!

Many of us recognize flaws in the disability service system, so we work to change it, by trying to get more services, more funding, and/or more laws. But we have more of these things than at any other time in history, and our children are *still* excluded and marginalized. The solution is not "more," but "different"—if we think differently and act differently, we'll enjoy different results.

My Journey from There to Here

On January 8, 1987, my son, Benjamin, was born seven weeks prematurely. As "preemies" go, Benjamin had a relatively easy time of things. Being in a "high-level" neonatal intensive care unit (NICU), and based on the "traditional care" provided in NICUs, he received good medical care. But I was generally unhappy with this experience: his tiny feet turned black—and stayed that way—from all the heel sticks to draw blood; the pores in his face repeatedly bled when they pulled off the tape that held tubes in place; the nurses left the lights on 24/7 (until I nagged them to change); and there was more. The neonatologist was one of the most negative people I had ever met. Later, I learned other parents had nicknamed him "Dr. Doom." It all could have been better for babies and their families. (Things are better in many NICUs since then, but there's still room for improvement!)

When baby Benjamin was about two weeks old, he developed hydrocephalus, but it resolved spontaneously, so no shunt was needed. Still, Dr. Doom informed us that Benjamin had "suffered a Grade III Bleed" (the "worst" is a Grade IV) and, as a result, our son would "have something serious," so the pediatrician would need to watch him closely.

At that point, I began bugging Dr. Doom to let me take Benjamin home. He resisted the idea. (I heard later that many "neos" like to keep babies in the NICUs for as long as possible, because they're concerned about parents' abilities to take care of their babies at home!) I bugged him every day, several days in a row, all to no avail. Finally, I didn't ask; I simply told him I would be taking my son home *that day.* Benjamin was in the "progressive nursery" at this time; no tubes, wires, probes, or anything else was attached to his little body. I told Dr. Doom there was nothing they were doing we couldn't do at home, and that Benjamin needed to be home and we needed him to be home. Reluctantly, he finally signed the release papers. With great joy, Benjamin and I escaped from the hospital!

My husband, Mark, got back to his work schedule, and Emily, our 18-month-old daughter, baby Benjamin, and I settled into our routine. Benj slept and nursed, slept and nursed, played a little, cried a lot, slept and nursed. Emily and I played while Benjamin slept. I didn't worry about the "something serious" predicted by Dr. Doom. I was just glad to be home with my precious children. I was tired and happy. Life was good.

At Benjamin's four-month check-up, the pediatrician sent us to specialists, and our son was diagnosed with cerebral palsy. In many ways, it wasn't a big surprise—Dr. Doom had prepared us for "something." The bigger, longer-lasting, surprise came after we entered DISABILITY WORLD.

On the day we were told Benjamin had cerebral palsy, he was given his Passport to Services (the diagnosis); we then took our place in line in the Service System, met the Professional Gatekeepers, and unknowingly entered DISABILITY WORLD. We hopped on the roller coaster ride of Early Intervention Services (EI), alternately flying high and dipping low. The merry-go-round of therapies kept us going in circles; we couldn't seem to get off since it didn't slow down. We were occasionally battered and bruised while making our way through the maze of services, programs, and entitlements. It was a crowded place, where lots of other families were also trying to find their way. But the Gatekeepers kept us in orderly lines and made sure we followed the rules.

I was 37, an "older" mom, with many years of life experience, married to a wonderful husband of eight years, and we were successfully raising our two-year-old daughter, Emily. Even so, our time in DISABILITY WORLD was an experience I was unprepared for. What seemed to begin as "the best of times," became "the worst of times." Later, and as I'll describe, I realized it wasn't my son's diagnosis that led to "the worst of times," it was, instead, the Services that were designed to "help."

The EI service coordinator, "Shelley," visited our home at least once each month, and she always brought articles for me to read, "home programs" to do, and more. The diagnosing physician prescribed physical

In the hospital where my son was born, premature babies and those with disabilities were called "bad babies" by the NICU staff. Years later, I read a summary of a study in which docs and nurses in NICUs were asked how they would feel about having a baby with a disability. The vast majority said it would be a "fate worse than death." So at a time when parents need the most support, encouragement, and positive thinking, many of us are surrounded by Dr. Doom and Nurse Negative. Their attitudes are not based on the facts—that people with disabilities can lead wonderful lives—but on their own personal biases and opinions!

therapy (PT) and occupational therapy (OT) for little Benjamin, and I wanted more. Believing "more is better," I felt we should be doing everything for my son. ("Everything" being all the treatments and interventions recommended by professionals.) So we did more, including therapy at home. I bought the giant-sized orange therapy ball, the yellow therapy benches, and more—turning our living room into a home therapy center. And we bought a hot tub so the physical therapist could give Benjamin water therapy in our backyard.

Shelley, Benjamin's therapists, and other professionals gushed: "You're such a good mother! We wish other parents were like you!" Ahhhh . . . how proud I was of this accolade!

Our lives in DISABILITY WORLD were filled with:

- **New ways of thinking and talking.** I learned about body parts, and could converse fluently with professionals about my son's adductors, abductors, navicular bones in his feet, and more. I put in my two-cents' worth with the orthotist who made Benjamin's AFOs (ankle-foot orthoses). I was quite the expert; quite the "good mother." And I could "hold my own" in the jargon department when talking with professionals of any type!

- **New people.** Benjamin's therapists and Shelley became my new "best friends." I spent more time with these women than with our extended family or friends from our neighborhood and church. None of *them*—it seemed—knew what I was going through. It felt more comfortable to be with people whose focus was my son and his disability. I was unintentionally pulling away from the people who loved us and knew us best.

- **New ways of living.** Just about everything in our lives seemed to revolve around the schedule of therapies, home visits, and other interventions. The kids' nap times, our daily plans (including such mundane but important activities like when to go to the grocery store), family vacations, and more were altered to accommodate the schedule of Services. There were times when baby Benj would have rather been taking a nap or watching *Sesame Street*, times when little Emily needed me, times I was too tired to handle one more thing, and lots of other times—but Services took precedence over everything else. I felt ragged, but also felt the need to continue on this path, regardless of the physical, emotional, or mental cost to our children, my husband, or myself.

Soon, however, discomfort crept in. I didn't like the way our lives were going—didn't like that Services seemed to be running our family. Do you know that feeling?

After bringing two-year-old Emily along to therapy a few times, the therapists recommended that I not bring her anymore. They said her presence was "disruptive:" she wanted to play with all the toys, and I tried to keep her close to me and quiet, so I could focus on what the therapists were doing with Benjamin. With a heavy heart, I followed the therapists' suggestion (baaa, baaa—call me a sheep), and I began taking my daughter to the Mom's Day Out program at church. Emily cried when I dropped her off, fiercely holding on to my leg,

> One symptom
> of being in
> DISABILITY WORLD:
> when your child's
> therapists and other
> service providers
> become your
> "best friends."

while I held her little brother in my arms. Like a "good mother," I acted bravely, even though I also felt like crying.

The on-going assessments of Benjamin also made me want to cry. Even though he couldn't sit up, wasn't walking, wasn't trying to feed himself, wasn't talking, and more, I thought he was a wonderful, precious baby. Our hearts would be filled with joy at some new little thing Benjamin learned to do. But the joy was short-lived. When the next assessment was done, he didn't "measure up" to what was "normal:" he was behind in this, slow at that, and on and on. And, in many cases, the things he *did* accomplish were trivialized, because they weren't "skills" that were part of the professional's tests!

Emotionally, I fought this—hard. In order to protect the hopes and dreams we had for Benjamin, and in order to keep believing in him, I felt I had to choose between the opinions of others and what I saw, felt, believed, and valued in my son. I chose the latter.

This had a chilling affect on my relationship with many of the professionals. They often exhibited serious concern that if Benjamin was "here" on the test, it meant "this" and we should, therefore, consider doing "that." I didn't always react the way I was "supposed to." I often disagreed or, if I didn't have the energy to actively disagree, I passively listened, said little, ignored their recommendations, and did what I thought was best.

I didn't always like Shelley's visits. She was nice, and I know she cared about us, but I felt like our home, as well as my children and I, needed to be "perfect" when she came for the home visits, even though she never gave me any overt reason to feel this way. I was also afraid I might get "written up" if the house was dirty, or if the kids or I weren't "right" somehow. I was sometimes nervous, worried what would happen if SOMEONE found out I wasn't following all their recommendations.

Slowly—as I found my courage—I began actually saying "no" and refused some of the interventions recommended. I also began questioning many of the professionals about why we were supposed to do this and that, and I began to doubt the appropriateness of some of the recommendations. Shelley put a little pressure on, telling me how much Benjamin needed this or that. When I continued to resist, the PT and OT began chiming in. It took me awhile to realize Shelley was blabbing to them, and I guess they thought if they *all* "warned me" I'd get the message. I wondered about confidentiality—did Shelley have the right to share our conversations with others?

During this process, my "good mother" label was changed to "noncompliant parent." So be it. I felt our *lives*—individually and as a family—were more important than professionals and their Services.

I continued adhering to a rigorous therapy schedule for Benjamin—speech therapy had been added—but I did not accept other interventions which professionals recommended with a heavy hand. Despite the pressure I felt, I began to feel a little better about our lives: I felt we were somewhat back in the driver's seat—in charge of our lives and making decisions, even if these decisions were unpopular with some.

20/20 HINDSIGHT

It wasn't until later that I wondered what Emily thought every time I dropped her off before taking Benjamin to therapy. What would most two-year-olds think? She probably felt I was abandoning her—leaving her with others—while I spent time with her baby brother. In Emily's mind, who did I love more?

It's our entrance into the Service System—not a child's diagnosis—that lands us in DISABILITY WORLD.

Our children will always have disabilities, but we don't always have to stay in DISABILITY WORLD!

I began to wonder what Shelley really knew about it all! She was very young and she had an Early Childhood degree, but she had no children! Later, she *did* have a baby and took a short leave. When she came back, she told me how much she had learned from being a parent, and she actually *apologized* for some of the silly stuff she had recommended. At this time, her baby was about 6 weeks old. My, oh my—imagine how much more she had to learn!

I had spent the first two years of Benjamin's life wondering when things would "get back to normal." Then one day the sobering realization hit: this *was* normal for our family. In my head, I reluctantly accepted the facts of life in DISABILITY WORLD. But in my heart, I resisted, believing this wasn't where our family belonged.

Then two things happened over the next few years that confirmed my intuition was correct. We began our journey back to the REAL WORLD, eventually leaving the world of Services behind. Entering DISABILITY WORLD had taken only an instant: the moment Benjamin began receiving Services. It took a little longer to leave it—three years. As Mark Twain once said, "It's easier to stay out than to get out."

The first event that put us on the path out of DISABILITY WORLD was my participation in Partners in Policymaking, a leadership development program for parents of children with developmental disabilities and adults with developmental disabilities, sponsored by the Texas Council for Developmental Disabilities (the same program is offered in many other states). This intense training validated my heart's desires: that my son *could* have the same kind of life we wanted for our daughter—a REAL LIFE, not a life as a perpetual "client" in the Service System.

The Partners training was life-changing, and it put me on a course to take our family's life back. I learned state-of-the-art practices from experienced trainers. And listening to the wisdom of many of my classmates—adults with developmental disabilities—taught me what was really important. I soon realized the original dreams I had for Benjamin (which were the same dreams I had for his sister), that he go to school, have friends, do what other kids do, go to college or trade school, get a job, get married, make me a grandmother, and take care of me and Mark when we get old—*were* realistic.

One of the more important lessons I learned through my Partners experience was that segregating people with disabilities was wrong—*morally and ethically wrong.* The immediate result of my newly-acquired knowledge was our decision to turn down a segregated Special Ed Preschool placement for three-year-old Benj. Instead, I chose to enroll him in a church preschool two mornings a week, where he did just fine with other threes!

Visit www.partnersinpolicymaking.com to learn more about the extraordinary Partners training program.

At age three, Benjamin had just started talking, and the Special Ed Preschool class he would have attended was filled with children who did not yet speak. What might happen to Benjamin's newly-acquired ability to talk if he was with other children who didn't talk? And I wondered: if we want very young children to learn to speak, why do we put them in a classroom with other children who don't speak? Shouldn't they be with others who *can* speak? It wasn't that I didn't want my son with "those" kids; *I didn't think any of the children should be there!* I wished they were at home with their moms or wherever they would be if they didn't have a disability!

By this time, Benjamin was walking in a walker and he also used an orthopedic stroller. He did great in the church preschool! (I did not ask "permission" for Benj to go there, and you don't need to ask permission for your child, either. (More about this in Chapters 7 and 8.) He did not need a "one-on-one" aide. Yes, he needed lots of help, but the classroom teacher, the preschool director, and/or his classmates helped him. He was just "one of the kids"—getting invited to birthday parties and doing other things natural to three-year-olds—but he was also going to several PT and OT sessions each week.

The second event that led us out of DISABILITY WORLD once and for all didn't occur for three more years (I was a slow learner back then). It also involved heeding the wisdom of adults with developmental disabilities, initially, and then later, my own six-year-old son.

During the Partners training, I became friends with adults with disabilities, who were my classmates. Before that time, I had never met adults who had developmental disabilities. These wonderful people helped me become a better parent—in ways no professional ever could—even though *they never talked to me about parenting*. I realized that even though I might be an expert on my son and his condition, these people were the true experts: they had lived with a disability all their lives. I also realized that, in the hierarchy of experts, people with developmental disabilities (including our own children) are first, parents are second, and professionals fall in line behind us.

My new friends told me about their lives as children. I asked many questions, hoping to learn from their experiences. And here's the gist of what they said:

> I wish I could have made my parents happy. They always wanted me to walk [or talk or achieve some other functional skill], so they took me to therapy all the time. But since I was never able to walk [or talk or whatever], I felt like I was a big disappointment to them. *And I really wish my parents could have loved me just the way I am.*

Whoa—I couldn't believe my ears! I had never looked at things this way. Their words made me very uncomfortable: wasn't all the therapy a good thing for Benjamin? And why hadn't any therapists or professionals told me about any potential negative effects of therapy?

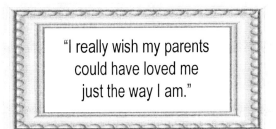

"I really wish my parents could have loved me just the way I am."

This had a profound effect on me—but not profound enough, as it turned out. I considered the words of my new friends carefully, but still believed Benjamin needed lots of PT and OT, and surely the "good" of therapy outweighed any of the "bad." I didn't realize it at the time, but my friends (the true experts) had planted seeds—seeds which would lay dormant for a long while—but which eventually took root.

Over the next few years, I heard stories from other adults with developmental disabilities who had spent their childhoods receiving therapies and interventions. They had "good parents" who followed the recommendations of professionals. Some described what it felt like to spend years being touched, having your body manipulated, how it often hurt, what it felt like for someone to try to make your body do what it couldn't do, and more. They also talked about the indignities of therapy and the loss of privacy—how this "intimate" touching was done by people who were essentially strangers. (Yes, a therapist generally moves beyond the "stranger" role, but think about the level of physical closeness involved between the therapist and the child. Such intimate touching, over a long period of time, usually only occurs between family members.)

This made me think about my son's experiences, especially regarding the issues of intimacy and privacy. In the big therapy room where Benjamin received therapy, other children, parents, and therapists were always present. On many occasions, the therapists took all of Benjamin's clothes off, except his diaper, so they could see what his muscles were doing. I realized that if I had gone to pick up four-year-old, Emily, at Mom's Day Out, and discovered her wearing only her panties, I would have been appalled and angered by the lack of respect for her dignity and privacy. But somehow, it was okay for this to happen to Benjamin because it was therapy.

But there was more. One man told me he and his wife could never achieve sexual intimacy. After being touched by therapists and other professionals for years and years, he couldn't tolerate being touched. He and his wife divorced, and he sought counseling to help him overcome his aversion. The counseling worked, and he eventually married again.

These stories shook me to the core. But I came to the same conclusion as before (I told you I was a slow learner): "All of this is important, but Benjamin needs therapy." This is what I had been told, over and over again, by many professionals. So with seeds planted, but ignored, our lives went on.

In 1991, we moved from Ft. Worth, Texas to Woodland Park, Colorado, a small town in the shadow of Pikes Peak. It was a move of our own making. We wanted a cooler climate; a more beautiful setting; a safer, smaller town to raise our children; and an inclusive school. We began a search and Woodland Park had just what we needed!

In our new home, Emily began first grade at Columbine, one of two elementary schools in our town. (This is not the Columbine made infamous by the school shooting. The columbine is the state flower of Colorado, so many schools share this name.) I once again enrolled Benjamin in a neighborhood preschool, he continued receiving PT and OT, and he began using a manual wheelchair, along with his walker.

A year later, Benjamin started kindergarten. Like the other students with disabilities at Columbine, he was included in Regular Ed classrooms, and received supports and accommodations. He already had friends in his class—children from the neighborhood preschool. Emily was now a second-grader. They both played in the town's Park and Rec T-ball league (more about this later). Life was good for us all.

Summer came, and the physical therapist ("Irene") recommended hippotherapy (horseback riding therapy) for Benjamin. She described it as a weekly class for children with disabilities. I declined, explaining that we did not allow Benjamin to participate in segregated activities. "Oh, this isn't segregated! We

> CERTAIN QUESTIONS
> BATTERED AT HIS
> CONSCIOUS MIND,
> BUT HE WOULD
> NOT LISTEN...
> IF HE HEARD THEM,
> HE COULDN'T HELP
> BUT ANSWER THEM,
> AND, OH GOD,
> HE DIDN'T WANT TO
> FACE THE ANSWERS.
> *Isaac Asimov*

let the siblings ride, too!" she excitedly replied. I wasn't impressed—it was, in my mind, still a segregated setting. But six-year-old Benjamin and eight-year-old Emily were sitting right there, and said they *really* wanted to "ride horses." So we went; insurance would pay the costs for Benjamin, and I figured it was something the kids could do together, after the years of Benjamin going to therapy while Emily was "put" somewhere else.

It didn't last long—after two or three sessions, we were done. Here's what it looked like: beautiful setting, great horses, lots of volunteers. Emily got on her horse, took the reins, and rode slowly around the corral. Benjamin was placed on his horse, surrounded by 4-6 volunteers and Irene. *He* didn't get to ride slowly around the corral, like Emily. This was *therapy!*

One volunteer led the horse; others were on either side of him to stabilize his feet, ankles, and/or thighs; another walked behind; Irene took various positions to perform her therapeutic routine. Benjamin sat on the horse facing forward, being urged to "sit up straight." He was placed on the horse backward and was supposed to catch a big ball Irene tossed to him. (This never made any sense to me: he had trouble catching a ball *while sitting stationary in his wheelchair.* I don't know how anyone thought he'd be more successful trying to do this while sitting backward on a moving horse!) Sometimes Benjamin was placed crossways on the horse, lying on his stomach—his head on one side of the horse's body, his feet on the other. Then he was supposed to raise his head and torso to look at Irene, catch a ball, or perform some other "trick." (Later, I figured if he *had* been able to do all these things, he might have had a career in a circus or a Wild West show!)

I was told hippo-therapy would help Benj: he would be able to "feel" the horse's "reciprocal walking motion" and "weight shift." This, I was told, would enable Benj's body to "learn" these motions, to help with balance and maybe even walking. It all sounded good, and maybe it's true, but was hippo-therapy—and riding on the horse backwards, catching a ball, and more—the only way to achieve this?

After the second or third session, Benjamin said, "Mom, why do I have to do all this stuff on the horse? I just want to ride the horse like Emily does!" At that time, we realized that, in our opinion, Benjamin could get the same benefits (or maybe more) if he *did* just "ride a horse." So hippo-therapy was over for Benjamin—his choice, supported by me. It was glimpse of what was to come, but I didn't know it at the time.

Summer was over and Benjamin began first grade. He was included in Regular Ed classes just like all the other students with disabilities. He had friends and was "one of the kids." Early on, I learned that it's like pulling teeth to get much out of your kids about school: "How was school today?" "Fine." "What'd you do?" "Nothing."

So I became the carpool mom—it was easy to learn what was going on by listening to the kids' conversations on the drive home! Invariably, the talk turned to what they would do when they got home. "I'm going to play Nintendo," said one. "I'm going to watch cartoons," said another. "What are you going to

> *I WONDER...*
>
> How might therapy be different for children if therapists had personal experience—like being on the receiving end of therapy all during *their* childhoods? And what might happen if therapists tried to see things from the child's perspective and/ or learned from the experiences of adults with developmental disabilities? You'll find some answers in Chapter 6.

do, Benjamin," one would ask. Benj would turn to me and ask, "What day is it, Mommy?" When I said, "Tuesday" or "Thursday" he heaved a big sigh and said, "I have to go to therapy."

One Tuesday afternoon, after I had dropped all the other kids off, Benjamin said, "I don't want to go to therapy, Mommy." "I know," I replied, "but you need to go." End of conversation: Mother has spoken! But he was persistent. The scene was repeated several more times over the next few weeks, and Benj became more emotional each time.

Then the dam burst. Through tears, rage, anger, and sadness, my precious, brave, scared six-year-old said, "Mommy, I don't want to go to therapy anymore. I've been going *all—my—life.* I just want to go home and play like the other kids. Going to therapy doesn't make me feel like a *regular person.*" Then his tears ran like a river. And they watered the dormant seeds that had been sitting in my heart and mind. I am, to this day (with my son now 18), eternally grateful for the adults with developmental disabilities who planted those seeds in me years before.

"OK, Benjamin," I replied, blinking back my own tears and hugging his shaking body, "you don't have to go anymore. We'll find other ways to do what needs to be done." But the big day wasn't over. I told Benjamin it was his decision, and I supported him, but we needed to go to the therapy clinic so he could tell the therapists he wouldn't be coming anymore. He wasn't happy at this turn of events and he cried some more, but I told him it was the right and respectful thing to do—and he needed to speak for himself. On the way, we talked about what and how he would tell the therapists. "Okay, Mommy, but I want to sit on your lap when I tell them," he insisted. I agreed.

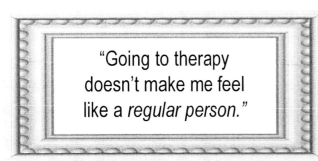

"Going to therapy doesn't make me feel like a *regular person.*"

Once we were there, I told "Mary," the occupational therapist, that Benjamin wanted to talk to her. Irene was there, and I asked if she would listen, too. With Benj sitting on my lap and his arms around my neck, he screwed up his courage and the words rushed out in a single breath, "I don't want to come to therapy anymore and my mom says I don't have to." Then he turned to me and pleaded, "Now let's go!" But it wasn't going to be that easy.

Mary stood about eight feet in front of us; Irene sat at her desk nearby. Benjamin had always "liked" Mary better than Irene because OT seemed "more fun" than PT, and both therapists knew this. After Benjamin's brave declaration, Mary squatted down to be at eye level with Benj—she was still 6-8 feet away—and said, "Oh, I know it's hard sometimes, Benjamin, but I've got some new games we can play today, okay?"

Benj tightened his grip around my neck, buried his head in my shoulder, started crying again, and shook his head "no." Mary moved closer, put her arms out in a welcoming way, and tried again: "I know you *love* those dot-to-dot puzzles—I've got some new ones we can do today, okay? So come on, now—let's go." He shook his head "no," tightened his grip on my neck even more, and pushed against me, trying to get away from Mary's looming presence. I realized Mary was doing the same thing I had done: she wasn't listening to Benjamin—she could not hear the words of a child.

She moved to within inches of Benjamin's face, put one hand on his shoulder and, exasperated, said, "Benjamin! Don't you want to *get well?*" Her response almost put me in shock; *we did not see our son as "sick," and we certainly didn't want Benjamin seeing himself that way!* Mary's words told me more about her than I ever knew. Enough was enough. I put Benjamin in his wheelchair, thanked the therapists, and we left. I don't know who was more relieved to be out of there, Benjamin or me.

That evening, Irene called and read me the riot act: "You're throwing away the last six years of therapy. He's going to get contractures! You don't know how dangerous this is!" I maintained my composure, thanked her for all her help, and added, "It's *Benjamin's* body, it's *his* life, and it's *his* choice."

The sky didn't fall—then or later. In fact, the sun was even brighter!

Instead of water therapy, Benj and his dad got in the hot tub every day, playing "Moby Dick" (guess who was the whale?) and other games to exercise Benj's body. Mark and Benj routinely "wrestled" on the bed, and when Mark "pinned" Benjamin with his arms over his head, Benj's arms got a great stretch, and he was laughing the whole time!

Instead of the OT pulling back on Benjamin's forward-sloping shoulders once a week, we gave him a "shoulder massage" when we got him dressed and undressed morning and night. Was it better for the therapist to do this once a week, or for us to do it twice a day, 365 days a year? Hmm—what do you think? Instead of the PT stretching his legs at the clinic, Benjamin got "leg rubs" and other help from us, at his request, while he watched TV. Later, Benj took karate lessons, and the list goes on today. It's all been easier than you might think, it's more natural, it's better for Benj, and better for our family.

The day Benjamin "resigned" from his Therapy Career was the day we left DISABILITY WORLD once and for all. I didn't realize how much our lives would change. We went back to the "normal life" I thought we had permanently lost. At dinner, we no longer talked about Benjamin's therapy, his goals, or what his body parts were doing or not doing. Instead, we talked about what the kids did at school, new movies coming out, or vacation spots we wanted to visit.

Life—a wonderful life—went on. All of us thrived. I regained the common sense I had lost in the jungle of professional jargon, expert opinions, and intrusive interventions. Our lives were once again our own. We were back to living normal, natural lives. We left clienthood behind and rejoined our community as citizens. *Your child and your family can do the same.*

In kindergarten, Benjamin and his sister played on the Park and Rec T-ball league. In first and second grades, Benjamin was in Cub Scouts. He sang in the choir at school, and his artwork (Picasso-style) was included in the PTA's student art auction fundraiser. He earned two karate belts before deciding to do something else—drama classes.

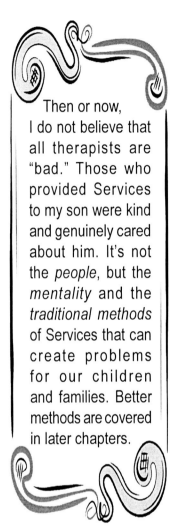

Then or now, I do not believe that all therapists are "bad." Those who provided Services to my son were kind and genuinely cared about him. It's not the *people*, but the *mentality* and the *traditional methods* of Services that can create problems for our children and families. Better methods are covered in later chapters.

One of Benjamin's strengths (a skill which he possessed almost from the time he began talking, and which was never on those pesky assessments I hated) is an incredible auditory memory. When he was four, he could imitate—British accent and all—characters on the *Thomas the Tank Engine* shows. Later, he "learned" to cuss by mimicking Arnold Schwarzenegger movie dialogue.

Also when he was four, we got him started on the computer, anticipating that pencil and paper would not be an effective way for him to write. As he grew, he developed an interest in writing plays. He "rewrote" *Thomas* and other stories into plays, which we—his family—performed in our den. With his great auditory memory and inherent "showmanship," he was a natural ham!

When Benjamin was nine, we finally got him a power wheelchair, and with independent mobility, his life changed dramatically for the better. (If I had to do it over again, Benjamin would have had a power chair when he was 18-24 months—more about this way of thinking in Chapter 6.) When he was about 11 or 12, he said he wanted to be an actor when he grew up. To support that dream, we enrolled him in drama classes. Performances followed. He was the Wizard in *The Wizard of Oz;* a pirate in *Treasure Island;* King Tuba (lording it over the other characters from his ready-made "throne") in a Japanese Kabuki play, and more. "I don't want to be just *any* actor," he proclaimed one day. "I want to be the first James Bond who uses a power wheelchair! Let's make my chair like James Bond's car, with machine guns, an ejector seat, a thing that throws out an oil spill, and..." (And he's still waiting for all those things!)

Contrary to popular belief, it's not *Moms* who don't want to cut the *apron strings*—it's *children* who think the *umbilical cord* is still attached! One day, when Benjamin was about four, his little voice insistently called me from the other room: "Mommy, Mommy, M-O-M-M-Y! Come here!" When I arrived at his beck and call, he asked if I would get him more juice, *and his dad was sitting right next to him!* I wondered who had cerebral palsy, and if my job description included being my son's maid! So we instituted a new rule: Benjamin needed to ask for help *from whoever was closest to him.* Big Sister Emily became an expert at helping her little brother get his coat on, learn new things, and more—just like older brothers and sisters do. (But Benjamin had to help his sister and others, as well. Children and adults with disabilities cannot be *only* recipients of help—that feels awful! They "need to be needed," too, and we should expect them to be responsible and help others.)

Now, back to Benjamin and acting, with the above in mind. At the dinner table one night, 15-year-old Benjamin excitedly said, "I can't wait for my next birthday! Cause when you're 16, you get to date, and then you can kiss girls. And when I'm James Bond, I'll get to kiss all those babes. So, I *really* need to learn how to kiss!" Then he turned to his sister and said, "And Emily, you need to teach me!" His sister just about lost her dinner and wailed, *"Mom!* You're not going to make me help him with *that,* are you?"

"Sorry," I replied to Benjamin, "but you're going to have to learn this on your own." Benjamin didn't like that answer one bit, and whined, "She's gotta' help me, Mom! If she doesn't, how am I going to learn?" I responded, "You're going to have to learn to kiss like everyone else: you can kiss the back of your hand, kiss the mirror, or kiss your pillow, but you don't get to kiss your sister!"

Emily and Benjamin enjoyed a successful elementary school experience in our wonderful, inclusive neighborhood school. But things changed (like they do for so many kids) when it came time for sixth grade at the middle school. In general, middle schools can be very tough for many kids. Emily was somewhat shy; she did better with one or two friends, instead of a group of girls. The competitive atmosphere at this school seemed to increase the tension for Emily (and other students, too). She wasn't happy and I wasn't happy. Emily was on the honor roll, but so were many students: copy-out-of-the-book homework and open book tests made high grades easy. I tried to work with the middle school educators, like I did at the elementary school. I didn't have much luck, but I figured I'd keep trying.

Imagine my surprise when, at the end of her sixth grade year, Emily said she wasn't going back: "Homeschool me, Mom, OK? Please?" *Homeschool her?* I was in the PTA, an active classroom volunteer, and a supporter of public schools! *(What would people think?)* And what did *I* know about homeschooling?

Over the summer, I read several books on the subject, but I thought Emily would change her mind before the next school year. She didn't. Not one bit. So we started homeschooling (more in Chapter 9)—I was scared to death—and loved it. When it was Benjamin's time for middle school, he wanted to follow in his sister's footsteps, so both kids have been homeschooled since middle school.

Emily "finished" high school a year early. This didn't mean she finished a "high school curriculum" (we actually did "unschooling"); she was simply ready to move on with her life. She passed the GED, attended the community college for two years, and received her Associate's degree, in preparation for transferring to a four-year school. As of this writing, she's "taking some time off" from school, and she's moved into her own place with a girlfriend, has a job, and is enjoying her life.

For the last few years, Benjamin has dreamed of becoming a film critic. He wants to be the next Roger Ebert, and have his own web site, newspaper column, TV show, and more. To support this dream, we bought him Dragon Naturally Speaking voice-recognition software so he could dictate his work on the computer, which is more efficient and faster than one-finger typing. As I write this, he's in his last year of "high school." Community college for two years (like his sister) is next, and then Benj wants to transfer to a four-year school to major in journalism. He wants to live in the dorm (his dad has told him lots of "dorm stories"), and to make this dream come true, Benj got a service dog when he was 16. With Riley's canine assistance, Benjamin needs less "human help," and is more self-sufficient.

Our exit from DISABILITY WORLD so many years ago and our determination to not let Benjamin's disability run his life have enabled us to reach this place in our lives. Has it been easy? Not always, but achieving our hopes and dreams is

20/20 HINDSIGHT

Looking back, my husband said he should have realized we were in trouble (in DISABILITY WORLD) during one Thanksgiving, when I asked him to help me put the turkey in the oven, and he asked, "Honey, do you want it in a prone or supine position?" We had both learned to talk like therapists!

worth the effort, and it's actually been easier than you might think. This book provides strategies so you and yours can do the same thing: turn your hopes and dreams into realities!

Is our story over? No, in many ways, it's just beginning since Benjamin is on the threshold of adulthood. He might change his mind—many times—about what he wants to do in his life. (He might decide to join a Wild West Show, after all!) If so, we'll support those new dreams. He'll need accommodations, supports, and assistive technology to achieve his dreams—*but all of us need these same things,* whether a disability is present or not. We focus on Benjamin's interests, strengths, and abilities—this is what REAL PEOPLE do in the REAL WORLD. And you can, too.

I mentioned that my Partners in Policymaking training was a life-changing experience. But it did more than teach me state-of-the-art practices in disability issues. As a result of my participation in Partners—and quite unintentionally—I became a public speaker and trainer in disability issues.

Every Partners graduate was required to complete a project within six months of graduation. I chose to write an article about People First Language and share it with the public, the media, organizations serving people with disabilities, and anyone else! The Partners coordinator wanted me to give a presentation on this topic for the next class of Texas Partners. I was scared to death about speaking before a group, but I was passionate about the topic. Speaking from the heart is far easier than "giving a lecture." The rest, as they say, is history.

Partners coordinators around the country began inviting me to present and I received invitations to keynote at conferences. Over the years, I expanded the number of presentation topics, and I've revised the People First Language article many times since 1991. It's been disseminated to thousands of people around the world. I've been called a "trainer," but I'm also a student, learning from the thousands of parents and people with disabilities I've met over the years.

What's It All About?

I wrote this book for parents. Imagine my surprise—and delight—when a variety of people in the System embraced it, and several universities began using it to train new professionals!

This is not a scholarly manual, filled with citations from research papers and professional studies. It's primarily a collection of stories about real people and their experiences. We can learn so much from one another—none of us needs to struggle so much. Some of the stories are composites, as similar things are happening to many people, and I generally use pseudonyms to protect people's privacy.

Many of the topics I present at conferences are included in this book, and some of it angers parents. Some are both surprised and horrified that I don't believe we should all be clamoring to get every Service our children are "entitled" to—I don't subscribe to the "entitlement mentality." I *could* support today's Services if they were *the best* we could do for our children—if they promoted inclusion, participation, and contribution in all areas of life, and if they significantly improved the lives of our children and our families. But they don't do any of these things for most of us.

Children with disabilities are diagnosed, labeled, and then dropped into one set of Services or another. In general, these Services remove children from the natural environments of childhood to special, segregated settings, where experts work on their bodies and brains, to the detriment of their hearts and minds. While receiving "helpful" Services, our sons and daughters are often dehumanized and marginalized—reduced to a collection of "defective" body parts. They're known more by their labels than their names.

Along the way, Services can wreak havoc in the lives of families. Their natural lives and activities become subservient to the schedule of Services. Moms and dads, following the expert advice provided by professionals, shuttle their children to and from Services, while trying to stay involved in the lives of their other children, maintain some level of family life, and hold themselves together. Families often become fractured while being "helped" by the system.

> THE ONLY WAY TO GET A SIGNIFICANTLY DIFFERENT RESULT IS TO DO SOMETHING SIGNIFICANTLY DIFFERENT.
>
> *Richard Saunders*

We enter DISABILITY WORLD and promptly lose our common sense. It's replaced by the CONVENTIONAL WISDOM of professionals and the Service System. Arriving in DISABILITY WORLD, our reality gets distorted and we begin living unnatural lives. If you're willing to question CONVENTIONAL WISDOM, this book can help you regain your common sense and take your family's life back.

Most parents want things to be better, but we may be resistant to new ways of thinking and doing because it's too painful. For some, acknowledging better ways of doing things seems to equal an admission of wrong-doing in the past. But this just isn't so! All of us—including myself—*have done the best we knew to do, at that moment in time.* In hindsight, I would do things differently. But I was doing what I thought was right at the time, based on what I had learned growing up in American society and what "experts" taught me after my son was diagnosed.

Adopting new attitudes and new ways of doing things should not lead to self-criticism about what we may have done in the past. Think of it this way: for years we cooked with conventional ovens. Then the microwave oven appeared. It's a better way to cook many things. This doesn't mean, however, that using a conventional oven in the past was wrong—it was the only oven we had! The same is true about our thinking and our actions: *we did the best with what we knew at the time.* Learning from the strategies in this book, and listening to your child and what's in your own heart, will enable your "best" of tomorrow to be better than your "best" of today.

Thank You

Because this is different from most books on the subject, I'm making it different in another way. Instead of a formal acknowledgments page that readers often skip, I'm including my thanks here, so you'll know who helped me along the way, for none of us are successful on our own.

On June 1, 1999, I began writing the first edition of this book. Upon its publication in March 2001, the dream became a reality. I began rewriting this second edition in January 2005. It's updated and features a different format, and I've tried to make it easier to use.

This book is the product of the life experiences of parents and people with disabilities I've met across the United States and Canada. Thanks to everyone who has attended one of my presentations. Each person who shared a story, asked a question, and challenged my thinking has helped me.

I've also been helped by the expertise of professionals who have positive visions for people with disabilities—professionals who started as my mentors, and who are now also my friends. I thank them for their wisdom and their willingness to share. I could not list all the names without inadvertently leaving someone out, so I won't make the attempt. You know who you are. I would, however, like to acknowledge those who have too soon passed on to the heavens: Jerry Kiracofe, Herb Lovett, Ed Roberts, Joe Schiappacasse, and Tom Tyree. Their wisdom and goodness live on in me and others whose lives they touched.

I thank and honor Colleen Wieck, executive director of the Minnesota Governor's Council on Developmental Disabilities and *creator* of Partners in Policymaking, and Jopie Smith, the first Texas Partners' coordinator. Colleen and Jopie provided the leadership and vision that started me on this path in 1990. Their generosity, vision, and friendship continue to sustain me.

My deep appreciation and thanks go to those who read the draft of the first edition and shared their valuable opinions: Colleen and Jopie; Laura Buckner, coordinator of Texas Partners; Vicky Davidson, coordinator of Missouri Partners; Christine Pisani, coordinator of Idaho Partners; Joyce Smith, coordinator of North Dakota Partners; and Charmaine Thaner, my best friend. Laura, Joyce, and Charmaine are also parents of children with disabilities and graduates of Partners. These colleagues and friends helped make the manuscript better, but any errors are mine alone.

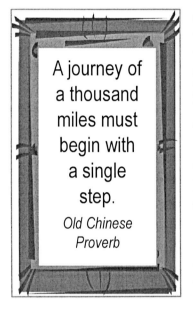

A journey of a thousand miles must begin with a single step.

Old Chinese Proverb

To my mom and stepdad, Iris and Robby Robinson; my dad and stepmom, Felix and Thelma Stoker; my brother, Steve Stoker; and my sister, Sandi St. Claire, and her family—thank you for believing in me and loving me.

To Mark, Emily, and Benjamin, thank you for allowing me to desert you while I cozied up to the computer. Thanks for believing me all the times I said, "I'm almost through!" Thanks for the meals you cooked, the clothes you washed, and the cleaning you did. And thank you for the hugs, kisses, and love that keep me going. I am who I am because of you.

And thank *you*, Dear Reader, for allowing me into your home. Now we'll go back in time to the way things were; it's our first stop on the journey to natural lives for children with disabilities and their families. Confucius said, "Study the past if you would divine the future." Our history is dismal, but it's necessary reading if we're to understand that many of yesterday's ideas—which didn't work *then*—have been repackaged as "new," and they're not working *now.* These recycled practices are, unfortunately, still affecting the lives of many children and adults with disabilities. History *does* repeat itself, but we can choose a different future for our children and families!

Our History: Out of the Shadows, Into the Light

People with developmental disabilities have always been part of the world and they always will be. But from the beginning of recorded history, they have, for the most part, existed in the dark shadows of society. Only during the last fifty years of the twentieth century did they begin to emerge into the light. The history of people with disabilities is as old as the world and it's still being written. You, your family, and your child are now part of this history.

This chapter presents a brief review of Euro-American disability history. In no way is this a complete history. I've tried to include information that is relevant to parenting and the education of children with disabilities.

This overview is not pretty. Much of it is hard to take. Cruelty, paternalism, segregation, prejudice, and gross misunderstanding are intermixed with bits of understanding and a little benevolence here and there. Learning about the past will help you understand how we got to where we are today.

History does repeat itself. Many old ideas and practices are repackaged into twenty-first century rhetoric. I'm ready to put a stop to the cycle—for today's children and for those not yet born—and I hope you are, too.

To convey the mood of previous eras, I sometimes use language common to the time. This is not the language we want to use today. In Chapter 5, we'll explore new attitudes and ways of speaking that are more dignified, respectful, and accurate.

> THE HISTORY OF AN OPPRESSED PEOPLE IS HIDDEN IN THE LIES AND THE AGREED-UPON MYTHS OF ITS CONQUERORS.
> *Meridel LeSueur*

Ancient Greco-Roman Societies

Ancient Greek and Roman ideals profoundly influenced the United States and other Western nations. Today's democracy, law, philosophy, and medicine can trace their origins to these early societies. Unfortunately, their views on people with disabilities, women, children, and slavery also influenced later cultures.

The Ancient Greeks and Romans believed man's goal was the achievement of human perfection, individually, and a perfect society, collectively. They also believed a variety of gods controlled the universe, and things that could not be explained rationally were attributed to divine intervention. Disability, illness, and other conditions were thought to be caused by the gods' displeasure; conversely, good fortune was thought to be a gift from the gods.

Hippocrates (c. 460–c. 377 B.C.), the Greek physician known as the "father of medicine," disputed the conventional wisdom of his time. He proposed natural

"Human Perfection"
in Ancient Greco-
Roman societies.

The perception of
some people with
disabilities in Ancient
Greco-Roman
societies. (Remember
this at Halloween
when you see court
jester costumes.)

causes, not the fickle fingers of the gods, produced different physical conditions. But these new ideas were not integrated into his society's beliefs.

The Greek philosopher and scientist Aristotle (384–322 B.C.), along with other leaders of the time, promoted a social hierarchy in which men (upper-class males) represented human perfection and women represented the first level of "deformity." Below women were children, slaves, and, of course, people with disabilities or other differences.

To create a more perfect society, and to please the gods, parents abandoned babies with disabilities and left them outside to die ("exposure"), threw them over cliffs, starved them to death, or smothered them. In some communities, laws *mandated* the death of sick or "deformed" infants. Occasionally, strangers "rescued" some abandoned children, then purposefully maimed them to increase their value as beggars; others were raised to be slaves, prostitutes, or entertainers. Those who were selected as entertainers (court jesters) were often boys with cognitive disabilities. They were castrated before puberty which prevented them from achieving sexual maturity, so they remained boyish, with high voices, and little or no body hair or muscle development. Their value was not derived from skill in singing, dancing, etc., but because of the laughter generated by their disabilities—what their bodies could/could not do. "Inferior" *parents* were also killed, to ensure they wouldn't create any more of their kind. (This idea was reprised in the United States and in Nazi Germany in the 20th century.)

The Influence of Christianity

With the advent and spread of Christianity, the lives of people with disabilities improved somewhat. Jesus was kind to people who were perceived to be different, and more humane practices evolved. However, many Bible verses reflect the belief that sin caused disability. The person wasn't "whole," creating the myth that people with disabilities were less than human, validating the notion that they should be cured so they *would* become "whole." (This belief lives on in the 21st century.) Faithful and/or repentant people were said to be cured by Jesus, while those without enough faith or who did not repent their sins were not. The open killing of children with disabilities decreased, but death behind closed doors continued. Overall, Christian beliefs resulted in people with disabilities being treated with kindness and mercy. However, these attitudes also led to pity, segregation, and exclusion since people with disabilities were considered unworthy, evil, or sinful.

Early Assistance—Then Incarceration

The fall of the Roman Empire in the 5th century created hardship throughout Western Europe. But the Roman Catholic Church continued to grow, opening the first hospitals, orphanages, and other places to help those in need. Church leaders provided assistance in the belief that good works would earn them a place in heaven.

The Church now prohibited the abandonment and murder of babies, but the practice continued, so the Church opened foundling hospitals where parents could leave their unwanted babies. Only the basics of food and shelter were provided, so many children did not survive beyond their early years.

Leprosy had been a common disease, but as it declined "leprosariums" were no longer needed. Public officials decided to put the empty buildings to good use, and a new form of "care" emerged. The "undesirables"—people with disabilities and differences, those who were poor, and others—were incarcerated in these first institutions.

The "idiot cage" was another form of social control. Undesirables were congregated in a wooden cage in the town center. They were "kept out of trouble," and townspeople were provided free entertainment: gawking at the "creatures." Along coastlines, undesirables were rounded up and placed on a "ship of fools" which sailed from port to port. Residents of the cities where the ship landed could buy tickets to board the ship and stare, ogle, and delight in the antics of the "fools" on board. Later, the "passengers" were unloaded at the last port, where they had to fend for themselves in a strange community.

The Renaissance: Hope for All

The Renaissance, from the mid-14th century to the mid-16th century, once again brought hope that conditions for people with disabilities would improve. The revival of classical learning, the concept of the dignity of the individual, and greater interest in the arts and sciences were hallmarks of the Renaissance. Humanists promoted ideas that led to better health care overall, and a better understanding of disabilities.

The Reformation: Death and Damnation

In the 16th century, priests in Europe protested many of the tenets of the Roman Catholic Church. Amid political, moral, and social chaos, the Protestant Reformation was born as new Christian sects split from the Mother Church.

Martin Luther (1483–1546), John Calvin (1509–64), and other Protestant leaders believed people with disabilities and differences were possessed by the devil. Religious authorities—both Roman Catholic and Protestant—used a variety of methods to drive Satan out: church leaders spat "holy spit" on people, took them to holy places, or performed exorcisms. Parents tried to cure their children by "beating the Devil" out of them. If a child died from the beating, death was considered an unfortunate consequence of a responsible act.

Some authorities took a less accusing position: healing hands could cure the sick if the victim had enough faith and was *deserving* of a cure. An unsuccessful healing was seen as proof the person truly was filled with Satan. Infanticide was outlawed in many countries, but it continued behind closed doors. Because babies were not considered as valuable as adults, it was not considered murder and punishments were light.

Elizabethan Poor Laws & Community Responsibility

The pendulum swung the other way in England under Queen Elizabeth I when she instituted the Poor Laws of 1601. Churches had voluntarily "cared for the needy," but now they were *mandated* to collect taxes from parish residents to expand and pay for this care. Benevolence was mixed with social control: by requiring churches to provide services to those considered needy and/or deviant, the government could exercise authority over those who "polluted good society." The welfare state was born (and this is the road we're still on). But the conditions of workhouses and other "helpful" places were often so harsh that life on the street was preferable to charity.

Two new philosophies were emerging. The first reflected the belief that poverty, regardless of its origins, equaled moral delinquency. The second promoted the notion that people with disabilities should be taken care of by bureaucrats, professionals, and/or others who "know what's best." These erroneous beliefs became entrenched in most Westernized societies, and we're still living with them today.

Radical Thinking

In the late 1600s, the English philosopher and physician John Locke introduced theories that have had a long-lasting and profound influence on society and education. He proposed that all minds were "blank slates"—meaning *all* people could develop intellectual capacities through experiences; this was helpful to many people at the time. Prior to this, the conventional wisdom was that people with cognitive disabilities were unable to learn.

> John Locke's "Blank Slate" theory had a positive impact at the time, but now it's of questionable value: today's educators still use the Blank Slate paradigm, believing students ought to learn everything at the same time (grade level), and in the same way (the way the teacher/school says). Today's *No Child Left Behind* law reflects this mentality.

The French moralist, Jean Jacques Rousseau (1712–1778), believed all people (not just the nobility) had worth and value, and all were basically good and highly sensitive to their surroundings. He recommended a simple life in the country or in small towns instead of big cities. (Later, Rousseau's ideas influenced social reformers in America: many institutions for people with disabilities were built in the countryside.)

Philippe Pinel (1745–1826), a French psychiatrist, made significant reforms in the area of "mental illness." He personally removed the chains from patients in French mental hospitals, where many had been shackled for over thirty years. At the time, society believed sinfulness and immorality led to dementia and madness (the sin/disability paradigm again).

But Pinel proposed these conditions were caused by brain dysfunction. His theories created a shift from physical abuse to humane treatment and "moral management," and he emphasized vocational and work experiences for patients in mental hospitals as a form of therapeutic treatment.

American Colonies, Community, and Institutions

Colonists who crossed the Atlantic for freedom in the land called America brought many customs from the Old World, and they also created new customs and laws. According to the Veteran's Administration website, a 1636 Pilgrim declaration stated, "If any person shall be sent forth as a soldier and shall return maimed, he shall be maintained completely by the Colony during his life." With no central government, residents of the colonies worked together to care for their own.

Since many of the colonists were emigrants in pursuit of religious freedom, they took their faith and its responsibilities seriously. They believed the poor would always be a part of society: the "deserving poor"—those whose poverty was beyond their control, such as widows, orphans, and some people with disabilities—weren't seen as a threat, they were just part of life, and they were often cared for in the local almshouse.

Over time, some almshouses evolved into infirmaries. But as the population in the colonies increased, so did the number of people who needed care, and residents found it harder to care for some people. So in 1773, a new Virginia statute created the first hospital for people with mental disabilities. If, however, a person refused treatment, the only alternative was jail.

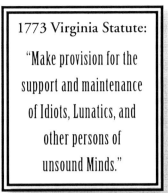

1773 Virginia Statute:

"Make provision for the support and maintenance of Idiots, Lunatics, and other persons of unsound Minds."

The Revolutionary War and Disability

In the early part of the Revolutionary War, cash from the government supplemented (and in some cases, replaced) care from the community. The Continental Congress allocated a benefits package for soldiers who acquired disabilities in battle and for dependents of soldiers killed in battle. This was the beginning of the U.S. government's assistance to people who were considered the "deserving needy."

Industrial Revolution: Technology and Problems

The Industrial Revolution was born in Europe in the mid-1700s, and factory jobs and new products radically changed and enhanced European economies. But people with disabilities did not share in the benefits.

Before industrialization, most common people were self-employed in farming or skilled trades, such as blacksmithing, carpentry, masonry, and other family-run occupations. We can assume that some individuals with disabilities, like other family members, contributed to the family's operations. But the factory jobs—requiring workers to produce mass quantities as quickly as possible—were not available to people with disabilities. Workers who couldn't keep up the grueling pace were excluded.

People left their farms for factory jobs and the population of urban areas increased dramatically. City residents controlled who lived in their communities: undesirable newcomers—people with disabilities, criminals, orphans, prostitutes, widows, or anyone considered deviant or economically dependent—were run out of town.

During this time, European cities saw extreme wealth and extreme poverty, and infanticide was common. By the 1850s, hundreds of dead babies floated on the Thames river in London, filled up ditches, and littered parks. In France, the sewers were full of tiny corpses.

Population Concerns:
Restrict Births, Eliminate Defectives

The grim predictions of the English clergyman, economist, and social philosopher, Thomas Malthus (1766–1834), reflected and reinforced societal concerns about population growth. Malthus wrote *Essay on the Principle of Population* in 1798. His revision of the article in 1803 expanded his theory that population growth would outstrip the food supply.

Malthus noted that natural controls of disease, war, and famine might keep the population size in balance. Further, if couples delayed marriage and then had fewer children, society's economic well-being would improve. Additional reductions in population could be achieved by eliminating the so-called defectives in society: only those who contributed to society should receive its benefits. (This antiquated philosophy is still with us, as demonstrated by educators who are reluctant to invest in the education of students with disabilities, believing they will never contribute to society. But this represents circular logic, for if our children *are not* educated, they *won't* have the skills to become self-supporting!)

The Wild Boy and New Methods of Teaching

In 1799, a ten- or eleven-year-old boy who had been found in the woods of France was brought to Jean-Marc Gaspard Itard, a French physician and scholar. His work with the boy (whom he named Victor) led to advanced thinking about people with developmental disabilities.

Apparently, Victor had been abandoned in the forest when he was three or four and had survived by learning from animals (wolves, it was supposed). Victor did not use human speech and his behavior was more animal-like than human. Philippe Pinel, Itard's mentor, believed Victor was an "incurable idiot." But Itard felt Victor's "retarded" condition was caused by the lack of typical childhood learning experiences. So he took Victor into his home, where he and his female housekeeper used experiential and sensory training to help the boy acquire new skills. After four years, Victor demonstrated impressive strides, but he didn't reach the "normal" level Itard hoped for. Still, Itard's work positively influenced educators during the next century, reinforcing the belief that children with cognitive disabilities could learn.

Dorothea Dix, a New Philosophy, Rise of Asylums

Back in America, social reformer Dorothea Dix (1802–1887) was shocked by the deplorable conditions in prisons, jails, and poorhouses, where many people with disabilities—especially women—were warehoused alongside criminals (usually males). She campaigned for better treatment of persons with mental illness, as recommended by the French physician, Philippe Pinel.

As a result, more than thirty asylums were established across the U.S., to ensure more humane treatment. (At the time, mental illness was a broad category that probably included people with cognitive, learning, or sensory disabilities.) While Dix's efforts were laudable, the success of asylums accelerated institutional segregation and isolation of people with disabilities.

A new philosophy was emerging: deviancy could be linked to problems in the home and community. Thus, if people were taken out of these "troubling environments," deviancy could be cured. By building institutions out in the country, away from communities, patients would reap the benefits of a simple life in the country, *and* administrators could prevent families from trying to visit their relatives. The number of institutions was on the rise.

More Sensory Training—Brought to U.S.

Itard's progress with Victor, the Wild Boy of Aveyron, influenced one of his students in France, Edouard Seguin (1812–1880). Seguin's book, *Idiocy, Its Treatment by the Physiological Method,* was radical for its time, focusing on expert diagnosis, recognition of individual differences, and an emphasis on sensory and motor coordination training. He believed children with cognitive disabilities could achieve higher levels of thinking through these new methods. In 1844, the Paris Academy of Science honored Seguin for solving the problem of "idiot education."

While this language is offensive today, Seguin's theories were valuable and long-lasting. His work influenced many who followed, including Maria Montessori, a pioneer in the education of young children with and without disabilities. In 1850, Seguin arrived in the United States and began working with American leaders in the training school movement.

Training Schools Focus on Education

In 1817, Thomas H. Gallaudet opened the American Asylum for the Deaf in Connecticut, and similar schools were soon opened in other states. In 1864, Gallaudet College in Washington, D.C. became the first institution of higher learning for people with disabilities.

Samuel Gridley Howe (1801–1876), an American humanitarian and physician who was involved in many social issues of his time, directed the Perkins Institute for the Blind, where he pioneered new training techniques. In 1832, he established the Massachusetts School for Idiotic and Feeble-Minded Youth, an experimental boarding school.

> Today, far too many students with disabilities are in segregated schools and/or classrooms which are located "away" from the main student population and/or from their own homes. Just how much have things changed?

Howe and Seguin believed children with disabilities could enter the workforce and lead productive lives if they first received intensive training in residential schools. Students received instruction in academics and self-help skills, as well as physical and sensory training. The schools were thought to be successful, and many hopeful parents clamored to have their children enrolled. (This doesn't seem much different than today, when professionals claim a new treatment "works," and parents enthusiastically follow, putting their children's lives in the hands of "experts.") The humanitarian plan to "cure deviancy" seemed to be working. To meet demand, more schools were built.

From Training to Incarceration

The high unemployment rate in pre-Civil War America dampened the initial success of the training school movement. Young adult students from the training schools could not compete in this job market; many ended up in poorhouses or jails.

Still, reformers continued to promote their schools, parents wanted their children to receive the benefits of training, and enrollment swelled. But the schools were not prepared for the flood of students. Training and education were soon lost in the attempt to accommodate large numbers of new residents. The training schools soon became custodial facilities. Students became inmates. People with disabilities were viewed as economic burdens.

As the population of institutions swelled, administrators grew concerned about operating costs. They devised quite a solution: use the residents as a source of free labor. "Higher-functioning" inmates were forced to do tasks crucial to the daily operation of the institutions, including the supervision of "lower-functioning" inmates. Some institutions grew their own food—inmates provided the free labor, which was regarded as "therapy."

A Voice in the Wilderness Cries for Reason

Samuel Gridley Howe and Edouard Seguin were dismayed at the turn of events. But it was too late to stop the burgeoning new industry. In 1866, Howe was asked to give the keynote address at the opening of a new institution. He shocked those in attendance by criticizing institutions and warning about the dangers of segregation.

He told the stunned audience that people with disabilities should be included in their communities and surrounded by people who didn't have disabilities (see box). Few heeded Howe's wisdom, and his extraordinary wisdom is seldom heeded today.

The Civil War and Disability

When Civil War veterans returned home with permanent disabilities acquired in battle, their families, friends, and neighbors became more aware of people with disabilities. Just like after the Revolutionary War, these veterans received government pensions. In 1866, the National Home for Union Veterans was opened. The care was vastly better than what was provided for those with developmental disabilities in public institutions. Societal attitudes about soldiers with acquired disabilities as compared to people who were born with disabilities were also very different. Veterans were seen as men with personal histories of past successes who had contributed to society; people with developmental disabilities were not seen in the same light.

Doomed to be Cured: The Medicalization of Disability

While earlier reformers were concerned about *social and educational* issues regarding people with disabilities, new leaders in the field were physicians interested in the *medical* aspects of disability. In 1876, superintendents of institutions created the Association of Medical Officers of American Institutions for Idiotic and Feebleminded Persons, which later became the American Association on Mental Deficiency (AAMD), and today it's called the American Association on Mental Retardation (AAMR).

The organization's purpose was to study the causes of, and treatment for, idiocy and feeblemindedness (cognitive disabilities, in today's vernacular).

> "...We should be cautious about establishing such artificial communities... for any children and youth; but more especially should we avoid them for those who have natural infirmity...Such persons spring up sporadically in the community, and they should be kept diffused among sound and normal persons... As much as may be, surround insane and excitable persons with sane people and ordinary influences; vicious children with virtuous people and virtuous influences; blind children with those who see; mute children with those who speak; and the like..."
>
> Howe, S.G. (1866) In "Ceremonies on laying the cornerstone of the New York State Institution for the Blind at Batavia," Genes Co., NY: Henry Todd.

Residents of institutions were viewed as patients who needed to be cured. Despite the warning from Samuel Gridley Howe, residents were categorized and segregated by disability.

The population of institutions continued to grow. Many parents truly believed the institutions could help their children; others simply wanted relief from the financial and emotional burdens of caring for their children at home. Institutional care was thought to be economical and fiscally conservative. By the turn of the century, conditions in institutions worsened. Overpopulation and understaffing, along with low budgets, contributed to harsh conditions at many facilities.

The IQ Test: First Helpful, Then Harmful

The IQ test had benevolent beginnings, but it quickly became a dangerous tool in the hands of Americans. In 1905, Dr. Alfred Binet (1857–1911), a French psychologist, was asked by his government to create a way of identifying "slow" or "retarded" children who might need extra help in school.

The very idea of Binet's test went against the conventional wisdom of his time. Many professionals accepted the theory that intelligence was hereditary and unchangeable, and educators made assumptions about children based on their *parents' achievements or lack thereof.* Concerned about educators' belief that some children could never improve their learning abilities, Binet dictated specific principles for his test (see box). In addition, Binet's test *had no right or wrong answers;* women trained by Binet sat with individual children and asked the questions on the test, then recorded the *oral answers* given by the children. These answers determined how much and what type of extra help a child might need (similar to an informal assessment, which I recommend in Chapter 9).

Binet's test became known as the IQ test (even though that's not what *he* called it). American professionals imported it to the United States, modified it, and began using it to identify and rank persons they believed to be defective. Ignoring Binet's three principles, these professionals set in motion a gross misuse of testing that, as you'll see, has irreparably harmed, and continues to harm, children and adults with developmental disabilities.

Causes of Mental Deficiency: Parents (Who Else?)

In the early 1900s, H.H. Goddard, the director of research at the Vineland Training School for Feebleminded Girls and Boys in New Jersey, studied the causes of mental deficiency and determined it was hereditary. Along with other respected professionals of the time, Goddard believed single genes controlled complex human traits, such as temperament, behavior, and intelligence, and these genes were passed from parents to their children.

Goddard and his peers were relieved that "idiots" and "imbeciles" were locked up in institutions and could not, therefore, make more idiot or imbecile babies. Furthermore, Goddard believed, when these "defectives" in institutions died out, those forms of mental deficiency would die with them, and America would never again be threatened by the "moral menace" of idiots and imbeciles.

> ### PRINCIPLES OF BINET'S TEST
>
> —The test score does not define anything innate or permanent about the child and what is measured cannot be designated as "intelligence" or any other abstract element;
>
> —The scale is a rough guide for the purpose of identifying children who need extra help, not a device for ranking children; and
>
> —Low scores do not mean a child is innately incapable.

But there was still concern about "morons"—mental defectives who could function in society and weren't locked up in institutions, because they "looked normal," but who were still a danger because they could reproduce their own kind. The threat to America, Goddard believed, was great.

Goddard and his peers also decided a person's employment status and innate intelligence were connected. They had developed tests in the institutions to correlate "mental age" with "industrial ability." They took things a step further, using circular logic. If experts could classify typical adults based on the type of work they did—for example, if an adult held a job that a child could do (simple cleaning, for instance)—that adult must have the simple mind of a child—feeblemindedness. While Goddard's theories seem ridiculous today, he was a well-respected professional whose views influenced other professionals, government policies, and societal attitudes.

One outcome of Goddard's work was the rejection of thousands of immigrants on U.S. shores. He convinced government officials that his IQ test should be used to screen immigrants arriving at Ellis Island. Anyone found to be feebleminded would not be allowed into the United States. In 1913, and based on the use of Goddard's test, the U.S. Public Health Service reported that 79 percent of Italians, 80 percent of Hungarians, 83 percent of Jews, and 87 percent of Russians tested were feebleminded. The U.S. Congress then passed legislation severely limiting immigration from countries where "low intelligence" was observed. This was a devastating policy: years later, as Jewish people fled Nazi Germany, the once-friendly borders of the United States were closed.

> Today, we're still living with the remnants of Goddard's practices: many professionals routinely assign a "developmental age" to many children with disabilities, and many people in our society still assume a person's job reflects his intellectual abilities.

More IQ Test Aberrations

Psychologist Lewis M. Terman of Stanford University also modified Binet's test, creating the Stanford-Binet test. While Binet's original test featured open-ended oral questions, Terman's version was a written test, and it included questions that allowed for only one right answer. People who (1) did not have experience or familiarity with the subject of Terman's questions, (2) used a different way of thinking, and/or (3) had a non-English speaking background, did not perform well on the test.

Terman tested average Americans and toyed with the idea of using test results to rank all people into a variety of classifications. He concluded the average mental age of adults in the United States was sixteen, just four "intelligence" years above the moron level established by Goddard. His study also "proved" that intelligence was hereditary and unchangeable, and that lighter-skinned people were inherently more intelligent than darker-skinned people. (Terman, of course, was "white.")

Terman's "success" sparked the beginning of the standardized test industry. Experts believed norms, mental age, and standard deviations could be decoded by the Stanford-Binet test: they accepted testing as an accurate tool for measuring "intelligence" and developed more tests.

The research of Goddard, Terman, and others, in combination with U.S. census figures, showed a dramatic increase in the number of feebleminded

Americans. Hysteria grew. Psychologists, institution directors, and politicians fueled the fire with dire predictions: the increased number of imbeciles, idiots, and morons could ruin America.

The declaration that feeblemindedness was hereditary was devastating to families of children with disabilities: parents were at fault—they were responsible for bringing these defectives into the world. The shame was almost unbearable. For people with disabilities, a new era of cruelty—the eugenics movement—was beginning.

Eugenics: The Ultimate Cure

As originally described in 1883 in Europe, "eugenics" (from ancient Greek, meaning well-born) is the study of scientific methods to strengthen the human race by controlling the mating, and thus the hereditary worth, of people in our society. In the early part of the 20th century, not only was feeblemindedness believed to be hereditary, but people with "low intelligence" were said to also have *low moral values*. Thus, if society controlled who had children and who didn't, Americans could then be assured that future generations of mental defectives would no longer weaken society.

A new method of social control was initiated: legislation in 25 states mandated the *sterilization* of people with disabilities. Young women were given tubal ligations, often without their (or their parents') knowledge or permission. Many were told they were having appendectomies. Doctors castrated men or performed vasectomies, *a brand new procedure created just for this group of people.* Many states also enacted laws banning the marriage of feebleminded persons. Lawsuits were filed to stop sterilization practices, but the Supreme Court upheld the state mandates. In the 1927 *Buck v. Bell* case, Chief Justice Oliver Wendell Holmes, writing the majority opinion, stated: "Three generations of imbeciles are enough."

Over time, the eugenics movement in the United States ran out of steam as the research of Goddard and others was eventually discounted. And little by little, many state laws were rescinded, but not before thousands of people with disabilities were involuntarily sterilized.

Special Ed Starts/Stalls: Educators Not Ready
(Does this sound familiar?)

While many people with disabilities were incarcerated in institutions, the majority were living at home with their families. Some benefited from the work of educators who believed children with disabilities could successfully remain in their communities if they were educated. Rhode Island opened the first special education class in the United States in 1896. By 1923, approximately 34,000 students with disabilities were enrolled in special education classes in several states. But many educators weren't ready to handle these students, so they turned to the "experts" in institutions for help. In response, many institutions incorporated "schools" within their facilities.

> IF THE [AUSTRALIAN] ABORIGINE DRAFTED AN IQ TEST, ALL OF WESTERN CIVILIZATION WOULD PRESUMABLY FLUNK IT.
> *Stanley Garn*

> Today's geneticists know much more than Goddard and his peers 100 years ago. Still, there are similarities: Goddard assumed single genes controlled temperament, behavior, and more. Today's geneticists are on the same path, and they're sometimes able to find "proof" that a particular gene is responsible for certain conditions. And just like Goddard, they believe finding the right gene will, in turn, lead to a cure or prevention. Goddard's "research" was disastrous for people with disabilities. What will today's research lead to? Whether we call it eugenics or genetics, it's still a slippery slope.

Unfortunately, many institutions clung to the belief that cognitive disabilities were hereditary and education would be useless. *The Almosts: A Study of the Feeble-Minded* was a widely-used textbook which demonstrated that people labeled feebleminded were "almost," but not quite, human.

World War I and Vocational Rehabilitation

After World War I, thousands of American soldiers returned home with acquired disabilities. The Federal government's response was different from previous wars. In 1917, Congress passed the Vocational Rehabilitation Act to provide training and education to "restore" veterans with acquired disabilities to employable, productive status. The Act was not passed out of national sympathy, nor because of a moral obligation. It was an economic decision, based on the belief that supporting industry was in the best interest of government and society. Veterans were seen as economic assets: they had been successfully employed before their military service. With retraining and education, they could once again become valuable employees and contribute to the nation's economy.

Educational restoration (rehabilitation) could retrain individuals so their disabilities were not barriers to employment. A veteran who came back from the war with only one arm, for instance, was retrained for a job he could do with the other arm. Physical and occupational therapists were called in to help. (This was essentially the beginning of these two disciplines.)

Invisible Citizens

From the 1920s to the 1950s, most adults and children with developmental disabilities were invisible. At least one public institution was operating in every state, and the population of institutions increased from 25,000 to over 100,000. At their peak, public institutions housed only about four percent of people with developmental disabilities, but the vast majority of public funds earmarked for this population went to institutional facilities.

Even children and adults who lived at home were, for the most part, invisible. The shame of having a child with a disability, the prejudice directed toward the family and the individual, and the lack of community supports and acceptance kept most children and adults with developmental disabilities hidden behind the walls of their own homes. It was not unusual for parents to send their children to the back bedroom when visitors arrived.

Nazi Death Camps: Inspired by American Success

In 1933, the forced sterilization of "undesirables" was one of Adolph Hitler's first priorities. Eugenics was the focus of Nazi Germany: the "superior" Aryan Nation was to be preserved and cleansed of all "inferior" persons. Influenced by the American eugenicists' theory of inherited feeblemindedness and the success of sterilization practices in the United States, Nazi doctors began sterilizing adults with mental illnesses and developmental disabilities, people who were Jewish, and others who they designated as "inferior."

People with disabilities weren't the only ones who were dehumanized during the Eugenics Era. American eugenicists were, in essence, trying to create a Nordic master race (and their work inspired Hitler). Thus, people of certain ethnic backgrounds, and those who were poor or had some other "deficit" were also targeted. Read Edwin Black's *War Against the Weak* for an eye-opening account of this horrific episode in our country's history.

But Hitler's desire to maintain racial purity led him to move beyond sterilization: he decided to eliminate children with disabilities to strengthen the future gene pool, and to free up funding for the war effort. At the urging of Nazi doctors, parents admitted their children with disabilities to medical facilities, under the guise of new treatments and cures. But murder awaited. Nazi physicians methodically poisoned many with drug injections. Other doctors starved the children to death, proud that they saved money: no funds were spent on food *or* poisons. Parents were told their children died during treatment; the bodies were cremated.

Next, adults with disabilities were targeted for death. Once again, the ploy of improved treatment was used to entice them into medical facilities. Once there, all pretense was dropped, and instead of using drugs or starvation, the Nazis gassed and then cremated them. Efficient killing methods were perfected using people with disabilities; six million Jews and others who were considered inferior were next.

Institutional Horrors Exposed

The induction of young men into the military during World War II led to a shortage of staff members in many institutions. Conscientious objectors filled many of these positions, in lieu of joining the service. While long-term staffers were accustomed to the deplorable conditions inside institutions, the newcomers were not. Shocked at the injustices and cruelty they saw, they raised public awareness of the horrific conditions in most public institutions. In 1948, Albert Deutsch published *Shame of the States,* a photographic scrapbook of one of the better institutions. But America wasn't prepared to deal with one of its ugliest secrets.

FDR: A Great Leader, But What If?

In 1933, Franklin D. Roosevelt took office as the 32nd president of the United States. Americans remember Roosevelt as an outstanding and well-loved leader who helped the country recover from the Great Depression, created Social Security, and commanded Allied success in World War II.

Roosevelt had a significant physical disability, the result of contracting polio as an adult. This respected leader could have raised society's awareness of people with disabilities, demonstrating that disability is nothing to be ashamed of and is not a barrier to success. Instead, with the full cooperation of the news media, he successfully hid his disability from the public.

Americans knew Roosevelt had polio, but most did not know how it affected him. In private, he used a wheelchair. In public, however, he skillfully disguised his condition by wearing leg braces to help him "walk" as he was supported (shoulder-to-shoulder) by the arms of a son and a Secret Service agent.

FDR's interest in disability issues was basically limited to research about polio. He lent his support to a fund-raising campaign; children were used to collect donations. The Roosevelt dime was created in his honor, and the campaign became the "Mothers March of Dimes."

Read *FDR's Splendid Deception* by Hugh Gregory Gallagher to learn more about how Roosevelt hid his condition from the American public.

Ordinary people—not the rich or famous—who acquired orthopedic disabilities from the polio virus were not immune from the prejudicial practices reserved for people who were *born* with disabilities. Those who were "crippled" by polio were thought to need *moral training* to ensure they would not develop immoral characteristics which would lead them into the underbelly of society: a crippled body was indicative of a crippled mind.

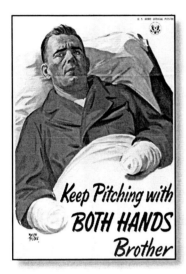

Keep Pitching with BOTH HANDS Brother

World War II and Medical Rehabilitation

By World War II, not only could veterans with acquired disabilities be retrained for new jobs (via vocational-rehabilitation), their bodies could be restored to "normalcy" or "near-normalcy" by physicians using the latest medical techniques. Medical rehabilitation was born as a distinct specialty: the American Board of Physical Medicine was created in 1947.

Shortly after WWII, medical rehabilitation expanded from the military community to general society: first to civilians with acquired disabilities and only much, much later, to people who were born with disabilities.

Precious Babies or Burdens?

In the 1940s and early 1950s, the stigma and shame of disability continued to be an invisible wall that separated families from mainstream society. Some institutions began serving people with disabilities from the cradle to the grave.

When a disability was diagnosed at birth, many physicians urged parents to institutionalize the baby immediately. This would be best for everyone: the child could get the proper care and parents would be relieved of the responsibility. A new mother was advised to say the baby died, and to forget about the child who would be a financial and emotional burden. Some parents followed this advice; most did not. Of those who kept their children at home, some later reversed their positions—the only help available to them *was* in the institutions. Others placed their older children in these facilities when they were no longer willing or able to care for their children at home.

The Parent Movement

The end of World War II brought peace and prosperity to the United States, and Americans were again able to focus their attention on their families and their society. Many parents of children with disabilities turned their energies to creating better lives for their children and families. For many, this meant trying to improve the conditions in the institutions where their children lived. Others wanted their children to be able to attend public school. But how could they make these changes? It was hard to go it alone. Parents realized there was strength in numbers, so they banded together and things began to happen. *They were giving birth to the Disability Rights Movement, but no one—including them—knew it at the time.*

In cities and towns across the country, small groups of parents banded together and started what are, today, disability advocacy organizations: the Arc, United Cerebral Palsy, and others. These peer support groups had one original purpose: to make life better for their children. Today, we look back and call this part of our history the Parent Movement. The actions of these determined parents started us on the path we're on today.

In homes across the country, a variety of forces collided, igniting fires of creativity that burned for the next 20 years. Tired of their children being excluded, parents took things into their own hands.

Their first goal was education. Public schools weren't required to accept children with disabilities, especially those with significant disabilities. Between the efforts of parents and the organizations they founded, some children with disabilities were educated. In churches, basements in public school buildings, their own homes, and other settings, parents found ways to teach their children. There was no set formula on how to do this; groups and individuals decided what they needed and made it happen. Many children were not educated in traditional academics. There was no automatic presumption they would be capable of having real jobs in the community. In many cases, life skills and/or social skills were seen as more important than academics.

Education was important, and so were common childhood experiences. Parents began involving their children with disabilities in sports, field trips, and other childhood activities. For the most part, however, these were segregated. Typical recreational activities were not open to children with disabilities, and simultaneously, many parents didn't believe their children with disabilities would be successful in these typical activities.

More time passed and the children of these enterprising parents were becoming young adults. Employment was next. Jobs in the community were not an option for most at this time, but many parents still wanted their children to have the typical adult experiences of work. Again, they looked to themselves and their organizations: sheltered work environments were created in garages, borrowed facilities, and other locations where young adults could learn skills or engage in work-like activities for part of the day.

Although their children were still not fully included in their communities, what these dedicated parents achieved was nothing short of incredible. While many children and young adults languished in institutions or the back rooms at home, others were learning in home-grown schools, having fun in community activities, and participating in work-like environments. In the context of society's attitudes about people with disabilities at the time, these children and young adults were living the good life. Their parents were motivated, caring, and unstoppable. Much of their success can be attributed to parent-to-parent support, a tremendous resource that's just as valuable today.

> The parents of yesterday didn't know they were planting the seeds of the Disability Rights Movement. Keep this in mind throughout this book; I hope we're planting seeds for a movement in which children and adults with disabilities live natural lives, included in all aspects of society.

Institutions Grow; Medical Model Entrenched

The dire conditions of the institutions in the 1950s led to increased funding for better care. Simultaneously, conventional wisdom dictated that *medical research* would provide answers to the so-called problem of mental retardation and other disabilities. The medicalization of disability had become firmly entrenched. Under the medical model, disability was seen as an illness, a disease,

Rosemary Kennedy reportedly had mental retardation. But some biographers suggest she actually had a mental illness. Evidently, her father chose to portray her as having mental retardation because he felt it wasn't as stigmatizing as mental illness, and thus, would not prevent one of his sons from becoming President. When Rosemary was a young woman, and at the request of her father who was looking for a cure, physicians performed a lobotomy, removing the front part of her brain. Afterward, Rosemary was institutionalized in a private facility, where she lived until her death in 2005.

And that's something I've never understood. With so many brothers and sisters, not to mention family money, why couldn't Rosemary have lived with family members? If her family valued inclusion, and ensured Rosemary was included, maybe the Kennedys would have created "Inclusive Olympics" instead of Special (segregated) Olympics.

an abnormality—a *problem within the person*. Money for medical research often took priority over money for services and care.

The populations of institutions continued to increase. Few meaningful activities took place behind the beautiful facades of the buildings. Most began looking more like hospitals: large sterile wards for "patients;" cribs and beds were lined up end-to-end; tile floors and walls; toilets with no stalls; and white-coated staff members were more like guards than caregivers. Residents—inmates—were segregated by sex, age, and disability. Day rooms were bleak, and adults and children were left to themselves. Many prisons and jails had better living conditions than institutions. Neglect, abuse, and even death were not uncommon.

A Federal Focus on Disability

In the early 1960s, and for the first time ever, the Federal government took an interest in *developmental* disabilities. President Kennedy recognized mental retardation as an *issue of national significance*. Why now? Most believe it was because the President's sister, Rosemary, had been given that diagnosis. Kennedy created the President's Panel on Mental Retardation, which recommended that local communities should work with Federal and state agencies to provide community-based services. In 1963, The Mental Retardation Facilities Construction Act authorized funds for community-based facilities, research centers, and university programs to train professionals.

Inhumanity of Institutions Exposed

In 1965, Senator Robert Kennedy toured the Willowbrook State School in his home state of New York, and was shocked by the deplorable conditions. Some children and adults were naked, sitting in their own excrement. There was little treatment or care. Residents were abused—by staff and other residents.

That same year, Burton Blatt, a professor at Syracuse University, and Fred Kaplan, a professional photographer, used a hidden camera to expose the miserable conditions in institutions. Their book, *Christmas in Purgatory*, documented the overcrowding, filth, hopelessness, and inhumanity. When excerpts were reprinted in a popular national magazine, Americans finally saw the horror of institutions.

"Normalization"

The "principles of normalization" made their way to the United States from Denmark in 1969. "Normalization" did not refer to making people with disabilities "normal." The concept focused on the importance of normal routines (the kind most people experience) for people with disabilities whose lives were controlled in the abnormal settings of segregated, congregate living facilities. For example, people should experience normal rhythms of the day (going to work or school) and the year (enjoying holidays and vacations); normal developmental experiences; the freedom to make choices; and so forth. This philosophy positively influenced many professionals, as well as people with disabilities and their families.

Developmental Disability: A Natural Part of Life

The 1970s saw the passage of the Developmental Disabilities Services and Facilities Construction Amendments (known as the DD Act), which created a Developmental Disabilities Council in each state. DD Councils work toward systems change on behalf of people with developmental disabilities. The term "developmental disability" was coined to describe a significant, permanent disability that manifests itself before a person reaches the age of twenty-two.

The DD Act includes a philosophy that's woven throughout this book, and the following premise is also included in special education and other disability-related laws at the Federal level:

> **Disability is a natural part of the human experience that does not diminish the right of individuals with developmental disabilities to enjoy the opportunity to live independently, enjoy self-determination, make choices, contribute to society, and experience full integration and inclusion in the economic, political, social, cultural, and educational mainstream of American society.**

Read it again, especially the first nine words. Internalize this philosophy. Live it, breathe it, and spread it to everyone you know.

Institutions Continue and Worsen

Even with Federal attention focused on developmental disabilities, the horrific conditions in the institutions worsened. In 1972, television reporter Geraldo Rivera and a film photographer secretly entered a children's unit at the Willowbrook institution in New York to document the deplorable conditions. Children were naked or only partially clothed. They were screaming, crying, silently staring, or sleeping on the bare floor. Some were tied to their beds. While the film recorded the horrible sights and sounds, Rivera told his television audience the camera could not reproduce the overwhelming stench in the building.

Many children were fed by staff members: mush was forced down their throats so fast that some choked to death, while others died of pneumonia after food went into their lungs. Physical and emotional abuse by staff members and other residents was not uncommon. It was a warehouse of human cargo.

Under pressure and facing lawsuits, institutions slowly began to change. Overcrowding was the most critical issue. In 1974, President Nixon issued Executive Order 11776, which reaffirmed President Kennedy's goal of returning one-third of the 200,000 people with developmental disabilities in institutions to community residential placements. The Justice Department was ordered to strengthen the legal rights of people covered by the order.

Amendments to Social Security regulations authorized payments for residential care in Intermediate Care Facilities for the Mentally Retarded (ICF-MR) in the community, and the Supplemental Security Income (SSI) program was established. Other laws and amendments relating to the deinstitutionalization of people with disabilities were enacted at both the state and Federal levels, resulting in reductions in the number of people living at state institutions.

> SAVE US FROM THE HAND OF THE STATE.
>
> SAVE US FROM THOSE WHO WALK IN THE DARKNESS AND THINK IT IS LIGHT.
>
> SAVE US FROM THOSE WHO ARE MEAN AND THINK THEY ARE KIND.
>
> SAVE US FROM THOSE WHO DESTROY US AS THEY CLAIM TO PROTECT US.
>
> From
> *Revolt of the Idiots: A Story*
> by Burton Blatt

Neonatology and Infanticide in the Modern Era

The 1960s and 1970s saw the development of neonatology and medical technology that radically improved the survival rate of premature babies and newborns with significant medical conditions. Still, many babies did not survive. Infanticide was practiced under the bright lights of hospital nurseries.

Some obstetricians and pediatricians shared the beliefs held by society: children with disabilities lived pathetic lives; they were financial and emotional burdens to their families; and their lives were so hopeless that most would be better off dead. These physicians (like most Americans at the time) could not imagine *wanting* a child who had a disability, especially when the parents could replace the "defective" child with a "healthy" child by getting pregnant again, as soon as possible. When a baby with a disability was born, many doctors passed their own *personal* beliefs, couched as "medical expertise" on to the parents: it would be best to let the baby die.

We'll never know how often this happened. It was only when several of these cases were reported in the news that Americans learned newborns with disabilities were being denied life-saving medical care, while others were simply starved to death. Several highly-publicized cases were raging battles fought in hospitals and in the courts. Parents and their doctors were generally on the side of no treatment. Neonatologists and hospital administrators insisted treatment be provided. Sanctity of life vs. quality of life was argued. Legal, moral, ethical, and medical issues collided. (We haven't come very far—witness the Terri Schiavo case in Florida in 2005.)

The Federal government noticed. Lack of treatment was viewed as a form of discrimination based on disability, and hospitals were put on notice: failure to provide medical care was a violation of Section 504 of the Rehabilitation Act of 1973 (described next).

Discrimination Based on Disability Prohibited

With the passage of the Vocational Rehabilitation Act of 1973, people with disabilities—for the first time—were afforded legal protections by the Federal government. The law also expanded rehab services and directed states to give priority to individuals with the most significant disabilities.

While many aspects of the Act were good for people with disabilities, Section 504 was *great*. It prohibited discrimination based on disability in any programs or services receiving Federal funds. Thus, colleges and universities, hospitals, state and local governments, public schools, transportation systems, and any other entities that received Federal funds could not discriminate against people with disabilities. It was a watershed event.

But for several years, Section 504 was unenforceable because the regulations weren't written. Bureaucrats hadn't recognized its powerful implications until after it was passed, and they stalled for time. Disability activists agitated, and the will of people with disabilities prevailed when the regulations were issued in 1977. Section 504 is a cornerstone of equal rights for people with disabilities.

We haven't come as far as we'd like to think. The Ancient Greeks and Romans openly practiced infanticide. During later centuries, Christians and others practiced it a little more covertly. The Nazis starved children with disabilities to death in hospitals, as did American doctors and parents in the '60s and '70s. Today, under the medical guise of genetics, prevention, and selective abortion, many babies with disabilities never get to take their first breaths: we kill them before they're born.

Parents Win Educational Victory

In the early 1970s, parents in many states were advocating for a public school education for their children with disabilities. When these efforts failed, they went to court and filed right-to-education lawsuits on behalf of their children.

One of these was *PARC v. the Commonwealth of Pennsylvania.* The Pennsylvania Association for Retarded Citizens (PARC) sued Pennsylvania for denying children with disabilities access to public schools. The parents prevailed, a consent decree was reached, and Pennsylvania was mandated to educate children with cognitive disabilities in settings similar to other children and to include parents in the planning process.

> "SEPARATE EDUCATIONAL FACILITIES ARE INHERENTLY UNEQUAL."
> *Chief Justice Earl Warren*
> *U.S. Supreme Court*

During the trial, the attorney for the parents, Thomas Gilhool, referenced the 1954 Supreme Court ruling in *Brown v. Board of Education of Topeka.* Remember the lesson from civics class? When the parents of a young "Negro" girl tried to enroll their daughter in the neighborhood school, they were told she had to go to the "Negro school" several miles away. Prior to this time—since the late 1800s—"separate but equal" had been the law of the land.

While the *Brown* case was about racial segregation, the same issues were applicable to the segregation of children with disabilities. The landmark Supreme Court decision in the *Brown* case held that "separate educational facilities are inherently unequal."

At the Federal level, the 1974 Amendments to the Elementary and Secondary Education Act addressed provisions related to the education of students with disabilities. In 1975, a combination of forces (the 1974 Amendments, state right-to-education cases, and parental advocacy) merged, leading Congress to enact the Education for All Handicapped Children Act, Public Law 94-142. The basic tenet of the law is a free, appropriate public education in the least restrictive environment for children with disabilities. In 1986, it was amended to include services for infants and toddlers. The 1990 amendments included a significant change: the law was renamed the Individuals with Disabilities Education Act (IDEA), to reflect the Federal government's commitment to respectful and accurate language. Some of the latest amendments, enacted in 2004, are included in Chapter 9.

Independent Living: Being in Control of Your Life

In the 1960s, during one of our nation's most tumultuous decades, civil rights, war protests, flower power, and free speech issues were all front page news. A quieter revolution was also underway—as evidenced by a California newspaper headline about the "helpless cripple" who was attending college—and it had profound and long-lasting implications for people with disabilities.

In 1962, Ed Roberts was attending the University of California at Berkeley along with thousands of other students. But Ed was the only one required to live in the university's infirmary. Why? Because the school believed this was the

> According to Ed Roberts, independent living is more a psychological idea than a physical concept. In hundreds of presentations across the United States, he taught thousands of people (including me) that being independent is not about being able to walk, talk, or perform functional skills. It's about being in control of your life and making your own decisions.

Ed's unexpected death from a heart attack on March 14, 1995, was an incomparable loss. Also lost is the purity of Ed's dream. For several years before he died, Ed was disappointed and concerned that many CILs were moving away from the original independent living mission. Instead of staying focused on advocacy (and being the watch-dogs of service providers) many had *become* (and continue to be) service providers themselves.

Ed believed CILs had a responsibility to advocate for better voc-rehab services. With an unemployment rate for people with developmental disabilities that continually remains around 70 percent, someone needed to be bird-dogging voc-rehab and other service providers on a regular basis. That's hard to do if you're a provider yourself!

only suitable place for the "cripple." As a result of contracting polio when he was fourteen, Ed had quadriplegia and needed assistance with breathing. He used a wheelchair, slept in an iron lung, and could move only two fingers on his left hand. After successfully fighting for admission to the university, he was an eager student by day and an unwilling "patient" by night.

Ed's determination motivated others who used wheelchairs to enroll at UC-Berkeley, and they began breaking down barriers. Ed believed old attitudes and paternalistic authority (not one's disability) were the greatest barriers facing people with disabilities. The physical obstacles on campus—no curb cuts, inaccessible housing, etc.—were the *products* of these old attitudes.

Ed and his buddies combined good old-fashioned American ingenuity with a little help from their friends to achieve independence. They poured cement (under the cover of darkness) to create the first curb cuts in the nation; set up a 24-hour wheelchair repair clinic; ramped campus housing; hired people to provide personal assistance services; and trained each other in ways to live as independently as possible. Ed and his cohorts now had the freedom and independence to run their own lives. The Independent Living Movement was born.

After college, Ed went to a state voc-rehab counselor for help getting a job. The counselor took one at Ed, told him he was "too handicapped" to work, and recommended he go home and collect his disability benefits. Ed didn't follow this advice. Instead, he got involved in disability advocacy, including demonstrations, and came to the attention of then-Governor Jerry Brown, who appointed Ed the director of the state voc-rehab system!

Under Ed's leadership, the world's first Center for Independent Living (CIL) was opened in Berkeley in 1972, based on the model Ed and others created at the university. Ten CILs in California followed. Soon, thanks to Ed's magnetism and unwavering determination, CILs sprouted from coast to coast.

Ed believed the primary role of CILs was advocacy: doing it (targeting the human services industry) and teaching it (helping others acquire the skills to live independently and advocate for themselves). He wanted CILs to serve people of all ages and with all disabilities. In addition, Ed strongly believed CILs should be run *by people with disabilities*. Who knows better how to help people with disabilities than others with disabilities? Ed's personal experiences had demonstrated that the paternalistic attitudes of most "helping" professionals actually *prevented* success and independence for people with disabilities. Today, hundreds of CILs are in operation all over the world, a moving testimony to the man known as the Father of the Independent Living Movement. The legacy of Ed Roberts and his independent living philosophy continue to grow as new generations of people with disabilities and their families embrace the independent living philosophy of being in control of your own life.

Self-Advocacy: "Speaking for Ourselves"

In Sweden in the 1960s, a few professionals, advocates, and young adults with cognitive disabilities recognized that people with developmental disabilities didn't always need their parents or other adults to speak for them. They were capable of self-advocacy—of speaking for themselves. For the first time, professionals and parents began listening to the young people whose lives they controlled. One of the more important philosophies generated by the young adults was: we are *not* our disabilities, we are "people, first." And with that, the People First Movement was born. (The genesis for People First Language came out of this Movement.)

Like the Parent Movement and the Independent Living Movement, the People First Movement (also called the Self-Advocacy Movement) was another bolt of lightning in the thundering skies of disability rights and advocacy. The first self-advocacy conference was held in Sweden in the 1960s, followed by similar conferences in England (1972), and Canada (1973).

The mantra of many adults with disabilities today is: *"Nothing about us without us!"*

The trailblazing movement spread to the United States when people with disabilities from Oregon attended the Canadian conference. Inspired, motivated, and determined, they spearheaded the first U.S. conference in Oregon in 1974. Expecting a few hundred attendees, conference organizers were delightfully shocked when more than 500 individuals from across the U.S. showed up.

The People First Movement grew and evolved. Today, over 600 self-advocacy chapters in the United States are composed of people with all types of disabilities. Local and state groups are often known as People First or Speaking for Ourselves chapters. Unlike Centers for Independent Living, which are essentially business-like entities, People First chapters are similar to support groups. At regular meetings, members get together for friendship, to learn and share advocacy skills, and to discuss other issues of importance. For many, especially those who grew up in institutions, speaking at their first meeting is often the first time they've ever spoken for themselves and been listened to!

People First meetings and conferences are planned *by* people with disabilities, *for* people with disabilities. The only people *without* disabilities who attend regular meetings are the chapter advisors. The advisor role is to provide direction when asked, but don't try to run the meetings, thank you.

The People First Movement spawned a new organization, Self-Advocates Becoming Empowered (SABE), in the early 1990s. SABE was created to help people with disabilities move from institutions into communities, *and to close down those public institutions.*

Even with Federal mandates from the 1960s and 1970s to reduce the populations in public institutions, today there are still thousands of children and adults in these, and other segregated facilities, including nursing homes!

The Americans with Disabilities Act

With the passage of the Americans with Disabilities Act (ADA) on July 26, 1990, people with disabilities were finally afforded full legal equality. Unlike previous laws that focused on specific entities—programs receiving federal funds (Section 504) and education (IDEA)—the ADA addressed civil rights in all areas of American society. The ADA prohibits discrimination on the basis of disability in employment, public services of state and local governments, public accommodations (theaters, restaurants, child care facilities, and so forth), and telecommunications. While the law is not perfect, most agree it has allowed people with disabilities—and our society—to make progress toward inclusion and the elimination of discriminatory practices.

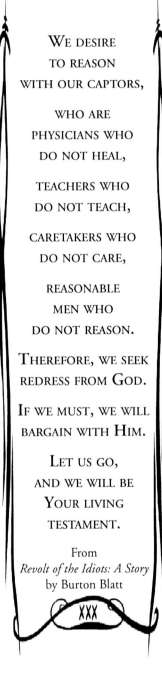

WE DESIRE
TO REASON
WITH OUR CAPTORS,

WHO ARE
PHYSICIANS WHO
DO NOT HEAL,

TEACHERS WHO
DO NOT TEACH,

CARETAKERS WHO
DO NOT CARE,

REASONABLE
MEN WHO
DO NOT REASON.

THEREFORE, WE SEEK
REDRESS FROM GOD.

IF WE MUST, WE WILL
BARGAIN WITH HIM.

LET US GO,
AND WE WILL BE
YOUR LIVING
TESTAMENT.

From
Revolt of the Idiots: A Story
by Burton Blatt

The Olmstead Decision

Even with the ADA and Section 504, thousands of individuals with disabilities have continued to face discriminatory practices, especially at the hands of state institutions (and other congregate living facilities). This was addressed in July 1999 in the *Olmstead v. L.C.* Supreme Court decision.

Two women in a Georgia institution wanted to live in the community. When the institution prevented them from doing so, they filed a lawsuit which made it to the Supreme Court. The Court's decision, based on the ADA, requires states to ensure their services, programs, and activities are provided in "the most integrated setting appropriate to the needs of qualified individuals with disabilities." As a result, states are required to establish procedures to implement the Court's decision (and it's very slow-going) by working with the Centers for Medicare and Medicaid Services and other agencies, whose funding streams and regulations have traditionally been biased toward institutional or congregate living facilities instead of supported or independent living in the community.

The Next Steps

The Parent, Independent Living, and Self-Advocacy Movements, along with a patchwork of Federal laws, helped move people with disabilities from the shadows to the light. More progress has been made in disability issues in the United States in the last fifty years than in hundreds of previous years. We have more laws, programs, entitlements, and services than ever before. Yet individuals with disabilities are still excluded, segregated, marginalized, and devalued. How can this be? Because we can't legislate attitudes or ethical behavior.

There is no doubt that—as Ed Roberts believed—*old attitudes and paternalistic authority constitute the greatest barriers facing people with disabilities,* including your child and mine. Until *attitudes and perceptions change*, little progress will be made toward the inclusion of people with disabilities in all areas of society.

The remainder of this book offers solutions to the dilemmas we face, including ways to change attitudes (our own and others), and strategies to ensure children with disabilities lead real, successful lives, included in all aspects of our society. We can no longer depend on professionals or the government to pave the way. In the past, authorities have led people with disabilities down paths that resulted in second-class citizenship, exclusion, segregation, dependency, abuse, isolation, sterilization, and death. We can no longer let any group—professionals, bureaucrats, educators, physicians, lawmakers, or any other authorities—be in charge of people with disabilities. We cannot let others decide the fates of our children and families. We must not continue making our children and others with disabilities wait for change (as in more money, more programs, more laws, or more anything). We must lead the way toward a more inclusive society. Our children's futures are in our capable hands.

Unfortunately, many of the practices and attitudes of the last 2000 years are still touching the lives of our children. If we don't recognize these negative influences, we won't be in a position to create positive change. That's what we'll tackle next!

Yesterday's Influence on Your Child Today

3

Is the past clouding your child's life? While traveling around the country doing presentations, I've met many parents whose children *do* seem to be living in another century—the result of the attitudes and actions of people who have power and influence over the child's life.

Are you ready to stop history in its tracks? Grab a pencil, get comfy, put on your thinking cap, and answer a few questions about your family's life. Don't worry: it's pretty easy—you're an expert on this subject (but I do want you to think hard). Don't skip it: the questions asked, the situations discussed, and the thinking you'll do can give you a deep perspective and wisdom that can help you create a better life for your child and family. When my son was younger, positive change occurred only after I spent some time thinking about *what* we were doing, *why* we were doing it, and *what impact* it was having on all our lives. Before you start, here are some guidelines:

1. There are no right or wrong answers, so there's no need to try to "cheat" or give the "best" answer! This survey can help you better understand the historical dynamics which may be having a profound (and negative) influence on your child and family today.

2. Some of the questions say, "Have you and/or others . . ." You, *personally,* may not be doing the actions described. But others—family members, professionals of any kind, educators, etc.—might be. And their influence on your child's life may be substantial.

3. Read each question carefully, give each some thought, then circle the answer. Don't worry about the number, focus on the answer ("yes, sometimes, no".

4. These questions may cause sad, angry, or fearful emotions. If so, that's OK. The questions and discussion points can help you gain a clearer picture of your child's life today and help you move to a better place! Just like in a garden, we've got to pull the weeds before planting new seeds. Solutions to the dilemmas presented here are detailed in later chapters, so fear not—bushels of positive change are coming your way!

There's space after each set of questions to write down your thoughts—this can help clarify them. You might also want to begin keeping a journal; I'm going to ask you to write other thoughts throughout the rest of the book. Writing has a way of crystallizing what's in our hearts and minds, and can help us move beyond the status quo. Here we go!

> REALITY CAN DESTROY THE DREAM, WHY SHOULDN'T THE DREAM DESTROY REALITY?
>
> *George Moore*

Your Child's Diagnosis and Prognosis

A. At the time your child was diagnosed and since that time, have doctors, educators, therapists, and/or professionals of any kind (1) described your child's "problems" and/or (2) told you what your child would not be able to do? (Since many of us have had to deal with numerous people in this situation, circle the answer that best represents an average of these experiences.)

B. Have professionals (doctors, therapists, educators, etc.) recommended treatments, interventions, therapies, and/or services to help these "problems" or remedy these "deficits"?

C. Do you and/or others believe your child's diagnosis and/or "problems" are, or will be, barriers to his overall success now and in the future?

D. Based on what you personally know about your child today, do your feel the prognoses (the predictions) about your child, delivered by professionals of any kind, were accurate?

E. *Instead* of treatments, therapies, services, etc., have professionals recommended assistive technology devices, adaptations and/or accommodations to enable your child to be successful?

F. Do you and/or others (family members, friends, professionals of any kind, etc.) routinely discuss your child in terms of his strengths, abilities, talents, hopes, and dreams?

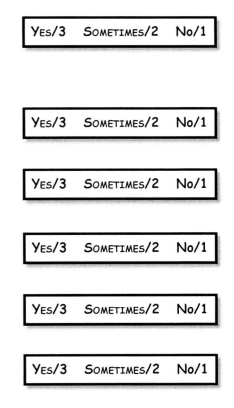

YES/3   SOMETIMES/2   No/1

YES/3   SOMETIMES/2   No/1

YES/3   SOMETIMES/2   No/1

YES/3   SOMETIMES/2   No/1

YES/3   SOMETIMES/2   No/1

YES/3   SOMETIMES/2   No/1

A *Yes* or *Sometimes* answer to Questions A-C indicates the influence of the MEDICAL MODEL: individuals with disabilities are thought of in terms of their "problems/deficits" which need to be "fixed." And these "problems/deficits" are thought to constitute significant barriers to success. (The MEDICAL MODEL will be discussed further in the next chapter, and new ways of thinking about disability will also be detailed.)

A *No* answer to Question D reflects what many parents have learned: "expert advice" is often simply an opinion based on antiquated attitudes, personal bias, or other factors. A *Yes* answer to Questions E and F means your child is living in the 21st century, and this is cause for celebration!

In the space below, or in your journal, write your thoughts about these issues (what you're feeling, what you'd like to change, etc.).

_____

_____

_____

_____

_____

_____

Assessments/Testing of Your Child

A. Have professionals administered IQ and/or other tests to your child, because he has a disability diagnosis?

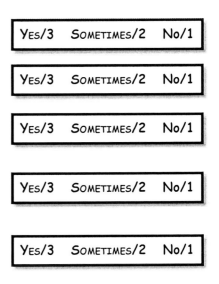

YES/3   SOMETIMES/2   No/1

B. Have these tests been used to identify and measure your child's "problems" or "deficits"?

YES/3   SOMETIMES/2   No/1

C. Have these tests been used to identify and measure your child's strengths and abilities?

YES/3   SOMETIMES/2   No/1

D. Have the test results been used to: (1) define something "permanent" about your child; (2) rank your child, as compared to other children; and/or (3) define your child as incapable, in one way or another?

YES/3   SOMETIMES/2   No/1

E. Based on these tests, have professionals assigned a "developmental age" to your child?

YES/3   SOMETIMES/2   No/1

If you circled *YES* or *SOMETIMES* on Questions A, B, or D, the valuable principles of Alfred Binet have been discarded in favor of the "Americanized" IQ theories (from about 70-80 years ago) that intelligence (1) is something that can be measured and (2) is fixed and permanent. In general, IQ and other standardized tests can be very harmful to children with disabilities. Assessments are supposed to identify and measure a child's strengths and needs. Seldom, however, are a child's *strengths* identified. Instead, test results focus on a child's "deficits"—giving us a lop-sided view of the child. These test results are then taken as "facts/truths," which often leads to the child being segregated in special environments because he's "not ready" for typical environments, which leads to more interventions to help the child achieve an "able-bodied" standard. And these, in turn, have the potential to ruin children's lives.

If you circled *YES* or *SOMETIMES* on Question E, the "Mental Age" paradigm from the Institutional Era (about 100 years ago) is being applied, except it's been repackaged into "Developmental Age." Strategies to move beyond these issues are covered in several chapters. A *YES* answer to Question C is an excellent sign of progressive thinking!

In the space below, or in your journal, write your thoughts about these issues (what you're feeling, what you'd like to change, etc.).

_____

_____

_____

_____

_____

_____

_____

_____

_____

_____

Your Child's "Placement"

A. Has your child primarily been in "special" environments for children with disabilities (such as therapy clinics, special ed preschools, resource or special ed rooms in public school, special sports programs, etc.)?

YES/3   SOMETIMES/2   No/1

B. Do you believe these have been the best placements or environments for your child?

YES/3   SOMETIMES/2   No/1

C. Would you like to have your child in typical, inclusive environments, at school and in the community, with whatever supports, accommodations, and tools he needs to be successful?

YES/3   SOMETIMES/2   No/1

If you circled *YES* or *SOMETIMES* for Questions A and B, the ghosts of many different eras are present, when the segregation of people with disabilities/differences was the rule. Remember: after first promoting the value of special (segregated) educational facilities, Samuel Gridley Howe realized the danger of segregation and publicly appealed for inclusive settings way back in 1866! Strategies to achieve inclusion are in Chapters 6-9. If you answered *YES* to Question C, you're in the 21st century!

In the space below, or in your journal, write your thoughts about these issues (what you're feeling, what you'd like to change, etc.),

Your Child's Responsibilities and Opportunities

A. When an IFSP, IEP, IHP, or other Individualized Planning meeting has been held for your child, had everyone in attendance *actually met and/or spent some time with your child* before making decisions about him during the meeting?

YES/3   SOMETIMES/2   No/1

B. Does your school-aged child *attend and participate* in his IEP meeting (or IHP meeting if your child is a young adult)?

YES/3   SOMETIMES/2   No/1

C. Does your school-aged child *contribute to writing his IEP (or IHP) goals?*

YES/3   SOMETIMES/2   No/1

D. If your child does *not* help write his goals, do you and/or others tell him what his goals are?

YES/3   SOMETIMES/2   No/1

F. Do you and/or others ask your child with a disability (at any age) to share her thoughts and feelings about services, treatments, and/or interventions she receives?

YES/3   SOMETIMES/2   No/1

G. Does your child (age two and above) have opportunities to learn responsibility at home (such as doing chores, taking care of his own room, helping around the house, and so forth)?

YES/3   SOMETIMES/2   No/1

H. If the other children in your family receive an allowance or other "perks," does your child with a disability receive those, too?

YES/3   SOMETIMES/2   No/1

If you answered *SOMETIMES* or *No* to any of these questions, a pervasive and long-standing assumption is a powerful influence in your child's life: people with disabilities are incompetent to make decisions about and/or take responsibility for themselves, so others must do it for them. Strategies to change these practices are included in Chapters 6-9.

In the space below, or in your journal, write your thoughts about these issues (what you're feeling, what you'd like to change, etc.).

Your Family and Community Activities

A. Do you feel your child and/or your family are included in your community (such as participating in typical recreational opportunities, church, neighborhood activities, other children's birthday parties, etc.)?

YES/3   SOMETIMES/2   No/1

B. Do you and/or others feel your child can and should participate in the typical activities of his similar-aged peers (such as Sunday school, community sports, after-school activities, etc.)?

YES/3   SOMETIMES/2   No/1

C. Do you believe your child's disability has created obstacles to your family participating in typical activities together (such as going to restaurants, movies, or church; taking a vacation; etc.)?

YES/3   SOMETIMES/2   No/1

D. Do you feel your child's condition has negatively impacted yourself, your other children, and/or your family as a whole?

YES/3   SOMETIMES/2   No/1

E. Do you feel the services, therapies, interventions, etc. provided to your child have negatively impacted your child, yourself, your other children, or your family as a whole?

YES/3   SOMETIMES/2   No/1

If you circled *No* or *Sometimes* for Questions A and B, and *Yes* or *Sometimes* for Questions C and D, the invisibility, shame, and prejudice prevalent 50-plus years ago is still an influence in your family's life. At that time, physicians and others warned parents how a child with a disability could "ruin" a family's life. Strategies for new ways of thinking about disability and inclusion are included in Chapters 5-7. If you circled *Yes* or *Sometimes* for Question E, your 21st century common sense is kicking in!

In the space below, or in your journal, write your thoughts about these issues (what you're feeling, what you'd like to change, etc.).

_____

_____

_____

_____

_____

_____

_____

_____

_____

_____

_____

_____

_____

Your Child's Future and Potential

A. Do you and/or others anticipate your child will need to be a recipient of Adult Services (for example, live in a group home, work in a sheltered workshop or be in a day program, etc.) when he's grown?

Yes/3   Sometimes/2   No/1

B. Do you and/or others anticipate that your child will go to college, trade school, and/or successfully enter the workforce as a young adult?

Yes/3   Sometimes/2   No/1

C. Do you and/or others anticipate that your child will become a self-supporting, contributing adult member of society?

Yes/3   Sometimes/2   No/1

D. Do you and/or others believe your child will be able to live in the place of her choice in the community, with supports, if necessary, when she's an adult?

Yes/3   Sometimes/2   No/1

E. Do you and/or others believe your child would benefit from an *academic* education (the same type of education children without disabilities receive) and other opportunities for typical growth and development?

Yes/3   Sometimes/2   No/1

F. Do you and/or others routinely talk to your child about his future, and ask him about his opinions, ideas, hopes, and dreams?

Yes/3   Sometimes/2   No/1

G. Do you routinely dream Big Dreams with and for your child?

Yes/3   Sometimes/2   No/1

If you circled *Yes* for Question A, and *No* for Questions B-G, many old ways of thinking are still surrounding your child, including 16th Century Malthusian theories—that only those who contribute to society should benefit from what society has to offer. People with disabilities and/or other differences are victimized by this destructive paradigm which creates a self-fulfilling prophecy: if we don't believe a person can be successful, we see no reason to invest time and energy in him, and then the person is not successful because we haven't invested anything in him, and then we say, "See, we knew he couldn't be successful." Your child, like all children, deserves the best and the most—the best education and the most opportunities—to live the life of her dreams. This cannot happen unless we believe in her unlimited potential. Strategies to address these issues are included in several different chapters. If you circled *Yes* or *Sometimes* to Questions B-G, you're on the right track!

In the space below, or in your journal, write your thoughts about these issues (what you're feeling, what you'd like to change, etc.).

_____

_____

_____

_____

_____

_____

Guilt

A. Have you and/or other family members ever felt that your child's condition is the result of karma, punishment, or something you've done?

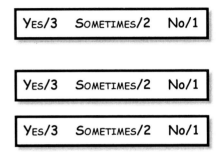

YES/3   SOMETIMES/2   No/1

B. Have you and/or other family members felt you, your partner, or your family lineage somehow "caused" your child's condition?

YES/3   SOMETIMES/2   No/1

C. Have you ever felt guilty that "you brought a child like this" into the world?

YES/3   SOMETIMES/2   No/1

If you circled *SOMETIMES* or *YES* to these questions, the ancient attitudes from the Grecian, Roman, and Biblical times, which lurked in the background for centuries, and then reared their ugly heads during the Eugenics Era, are still a powerful influence. Yes, some conditions are genetic, just as eye color, hair texture, and other characteristics are. If your child's condition is genetic, do you feel guilty that you "gave" your child your eye color, body type, or anything else? No? Then there's no need to feel guilt about anything else you passed on to your children.

Your child's condition—whether it was genetic or not—is not a sign that you/others have done something wrong, that you/others are being punished, or anything else. Reject these notions, once and for all. Recognize how ancient perceptions about disability *were wrong in the past, and they're wrong now!* Strategies to address these issues are included in this chapter and in Chapter 4.

In the space below, or in your journal, write your thoughts about these issues (what you're feeling, what you'd like to change, etc.).

Hoping/Praying for a Cure/Recovery

A. Have you been led to believe that the services, treatments, and/or interventions your child receives will (1) "cure" your child, (2) "lessen the effects" of the disability and/or (3) make your child "more normal"?

Yes/3   Sometimes/2   No/1

B. Have you and/or others hoped or prayed that your child will be "cured" or will "recover" from the disability diagnosis?

Yes/3   Sometimes/2   No/1

C. When/if this prayer/hope isn't achieved, do you/others feel this is because you don't have enough faith or because you/others haven't done enough (via therapies, interventions, or anything else)?

Yes/3   Sometimes/2   No/1

If you answered *Yes* or *Sometimes* to these questions, antiquated attitudes originally from the Ancient Greek and Early Christian eras are again at work. These attitudes, which have been passed from one generation to the next, reflect the belief that people with disabilities are "not whole" (and in some cases, are "less than human") and are not "desirable." This attitude "crossed over" to the medical community, where the "not whole" descriptor was changed to: "unhealthy," "abnormal," "defec-tive," etc. People once worshipped on the altar of religion, but many today also worship on the altars of medicine, services, and/or education, hoping for a cure/recovery to make the person "normal," and therefore, "worthy" and/or "desirable." Strategies to address these issues are included in this chapter and in Chapter 4.

In the space below, or in your journal, write your thoughts about these issues (what you're feeling, what you'd like to change, etc.).

And last but not least: Grief

A. Has your child's disability diagnosis and the prognoses about your child's future from physicians, educators, and others, caused emotional pain in yourself and/or others?

YES/3   SOMETIMES/2   No/1

B. Have you asked yourself, "Why did this happen to me?"

YES/3   SOMETIMES/2   No/1

C. Have you ever felt anguish, that having a child with a disability was not "what you had planned" for your life?

YES/3   SOMETIMES/2   No/1

D. Do you/have you felt hopeless about your child's future?

YES/3   SOMETIMES/2   No/1

E. Have you questioned your child's ability to be a parent when he/she is grown, and wondered if he/she should be sterilized to prevent a pregnancy?

YES/3   SOMETIMES/2   No/1

If you circled *Yes* for any of these questions, the Eugenics Era influence is again present, but it's taken on a new, more respectable name and appearance: genetics. And this influence, along with religious and cultural beliefs, can generate grief.

As you recall from the previous chapter, eugenicists in 20th century America, attempted to "improve society" through breeding, extermination, and other methods (which later influenced Nazi Germany). This led society to make conclusions about:

*   who *should not* be allowed to become parents, and "make more like themselves;"
*   what makes a "good" or "healthy," and therefore, *desirable,* individual;
*   who will/will not have a good quality of life;
*   what type of people will contribute to the overall good of society, and what type will lead to the decline of society, and much more.

As discussed in the previous chapter, the Eugenics Movement in the U.S. eventually died a slow death, as its "research" was proven to be fraudulent. But a tentacle lay dormant for decades, to be reborn in our time as the science of genetics. Like many controversial sciences, much good can come out of the genetics field, if its research is accurate, truthful, and applied ethically. Perhaps a cure for cancer and other diseases that *kill* will be found.

But genetics—like its mother, eugenics—sits precariously on a slippery slope. For with the advances in medical science and technology, genetics can do far more—for good and ill—than eugenics ever could. With the advent of prenatal testing, DNA research, and more, the potential to create a "master race" or a "superior society" once again exists, if scientists, doctors, bureaucrats, couples planning on having children, and/or others have the power and the capability to decide that some individuals:

*   are not "healthy," wanted, or desirable;
*   do not/will not/can not have good lives, so they should not be "allowed" to be born, *or* they should be "allowed" to die;
*   will be a burden to themselves, their families, or society;
*   are inherently incapable of, or should not be allowed to, have children of their own.

These questions don't fall only under the mantle of "science" (eugenics and genetics). They also involve religious, cultural, moral, and ethical domains. These domains often merge—whipped together in a social blender—and what pours out are negative and pessimistic attitudes; scorn and rejection; ignorance, pity, and fear; and so much more, as demonstrated by comments we hear on a regular basis, said by people from all walks of life:

> Someone is asked, "Do you want a boy or a girl?" and the response is, "I don't care, as long as it's healthy." (Meaning as long as the baby doesn't have a disability or other difference.)

In response to thinking about the possibility of having a disability and/or after seeing someone with a significant visible disability, someone says: "I'd rather be *dead* than be like that."

These statements reflect our society's devaluation and marginalization of individuals with disabilities—based on the assumption that people with disabilities live such pitiful, unfulfilled lives, they'd be better off *if they were dead or had never been born!*

What does this have to do with you? Any grief, guilt, angst, or hopelessness you feel about having a child with a disability is not just the result of your *personal* beliefs. We have been set-up—*brainwashed*—to grieve. We have grown up with the belief that the "normal" parental response to a disability diagnosis in a child is grief. Let's take a slight detour to look at the bigger issue.

We seem to be a society at war with ourselves: we "fight" cancer, baldness, wrinkles, gray hair, and more! (Yes, as I already mentioned, I hope we find a cure for cancer and other diseases that kill, but when that happens, "new" diseases will come along—we'll always have *something* to fight.) So when we, as a society, have difficulty accepting "little" differences in *ourselves*—gray hair, wrinkles, a big belly, a bald head—is it any wonder we have difficulty accepting more significant differences, like a disability?

Is today's society substantially different from the Ancient Greeks, whose goal was "human perfection"? (Isn't *that* the ultimate goal of today's genetics?)

In order to deal with one of these significant differences (a child's disability diagnosis), we're expected to grieve the "loss." Yes, we have been programmed to grieve (and you can call me the "Deprogrammer").

Here's what you must know: *your child does not want you to grieve for him. He* did not die; the *dream* of a "perfect child" or a "normal child" may have died. (But, of course, there *is* no such thing as a "perfect" or "normal" child!)

But let's get down to the nitty-gritty: feelings of grief are not really about your *child*; they're about *your* hopes and dreams—for yourself, your child, and your family. I believe, with all my heart, that you can rekindle the dreams you once had—the dreams that were present before your child was diagnosed. Now, your child may never walk or talk or do something else. But were *those specific things* really part of your hopes and dreams? No! Your dreams were bigger than that, weren't they?

In this book, you'll learn that your child doesn't have to walk, talk, feed himself, achieve a certain level of behavior/social skills, or do anything similar in order to live a wonderful life. Isn't *that* what you dreamed? That your precious son or daughter will have *a wonderful life?* He or she can!

Every hour, every minute, every *second* spent grieving is *time wasted!* It's time you could have spent feeling happy, proud, hopeful, delighted, and so much more! If you want to have a happy, successful child who believes in himself *(because you believe in him)*, I have this advice about grief:

get over it for your child's sake!

Your grief will do nothing but hurt your child, one way or another. And don't think your child doesn't know what you're feeling, even if you think you're good at hiding it! Children are very intuitive. Please remember the words of the adults with disabilities who told me, "I wish my parents could have loved me just the way I am." *Those are your child's words, too.*

Frankly, our children have enough to deal with, without us burdening them with *our* issues! Aren't we grown-ups? Let's shape up!

If grief still lives in your heart, let it go, now! And I don't think you need a "grief counselor." (Frankly, I am appalled and disgusted by "grief sermons" for parents like us, that focus on *our* feelings, while never considering the effect our feelings, and our actions based on those feelings, *have on our children!*) Like I said, I'm the Deprogrammer, and the strategies in this book are grief-eliminators. You are not alone. If you ever need to ventilate, write me (kathie@disabilityisnatural.com). I'm a good listener and I'll write you back. (*I will, too,* so don't write if you don't want a reply!)

One antidote to grief is thought to be action: we'll fight the grief. (Here we go, fighting again!) So, instead of sitting around feeling sorry for themselves and/or their child, many parents get moving. And the direction many move toward is a "cure" via therapies, services, interventions, rehab, and more. This, Dear Reader, is not the best direction (and I'll show you a better direction in other chapters). But let's explore this further.

Right now, you may believe a "cure" for your child's condition would be a miraculous wonder, which could restore a sense of wholeness to your hopes, dreams, and family life. But there are several things to consider about this way of thinking.

First, how would your child feel if he knew you felt this way? Can you put yourself in your child's place for a moment and try to imagine what this would feel like? You're a child, and the people who are supposed to love you the most want you to be different, want you to be some other way, want you to be some other child—*but there's nothing you, as the child, can do about it!* You can't make your condition go away. You can't take a magic pill, nor can you wish it or pray it away. How would this make you feel?

What might it feel like (remember, think like a child) if you thought your parents didn't love you the way you are? What can you do to make them love you? How can you please them? And perhaps most importantly, how can you live with yourself, and how

> Grief is the agony of an instant;
> the indulgence of grief
> the blunder of a life.
> *Benjamin Disraeli*

can you love yourself, under these circumstances? As painful as it might be, I urge you to give this serious thought. And it's okay if you're uncomfortable. I've learned that most of us change only when we *are* uncomfortable!

Second, I've never met an adult with a developmental disability who has wished for a cure! On the contrary, they love who they are, they want to be loved for who they are, just the way they are, and the idea of a "cure" insults, demeans, and marginalizes these men and women.

Third, what message does the "cure/prevention" mentality send to individuals with disabilities? It's this: "We don't want people like you in the world." Now, you may be thinking, "No, that's not it. We just don't want people having those conditions (disabilities)." If you think this is a rational, respectful statement, say it to an adult with a developmental disability and see what response you get. If she's a self-confident person, she may tell you to go jump in the lake (or something that couldn't be printed in this book)—*"Who are you,"* she thinks, to tell *her* you wish she wasn't the way she is? If, however, she's a person *lacking* in self-confidence, she'll interpret your words as pity or revulsion, reinforcing her existing belief that she is not OK the way she is.

Finally, here's another perspective for you to consider. If there was a magic pill that could make my son's cerebral palsy go away, I would not give it to him. And, at age 18, he has told me he wouldn't take it (we've talked about this). *Benjamin having cerebral palsy has enriched our lives—mine, Mark's, Emily's, and Benjamin's.* The experiences we've had have taught us so very much, helped us see what's really important in life, and given us a deep understanding of so many other issues.

When Benjamin was 17, an interesting incident occurred while we were visiting my dad and step-mom in another city. We were going out to dinner, and my 84-year-old dad, Benj, and I were chatting in the living room, waiting for my step-mom, daughter, and husband to finish getting ready. Out of the blue, my father said, "You know we pray for all of you every night. Kathie, we pray that your book sells, and we pray for Mark and Emily. And, Benji-Boy, we pray every night that one day you'll get up out of that wheelchair and walk."

In a sense, we were "saved by the bell." My husband, daughter, and step-mom came in at that moment, and it was time to go. On the way to the restaurant, Benjamin and I talked about what my dad said and how he wanted to respond (we were in our van, my dad and step-mom were in their car). We had a nice dinner at the restaurant; Benj didn't want to bring this up during the meal. When we got back to my dad's house, Benjamin wheeled up to my dad and said, "Papa, what you said earlier about praying I would walk—that hurt my feelings. I'm fine the way I am. I don't need to walk; I get around fine in my power chair. I know you love me, but I don't want you to pray for me like that anymore, OK?"

I was hoping my son's words would lead to an important discussion. Instead, my dad grabbed the TV remote and said, "Let's see what's on the boob tube." He didn't know how to respond. I gave Benj a look to indicate, "Let it go..." Later, Benj and I talked again. I explained that just as he wants to be loved the way *he* is, we needed to love Papa the way *he* is. Benj got it. (You might be wondering why I didn't pursue the matter with my dad. Part of me wanted to, but I know my dad, and know some people may *not* ever change. I've learned to pick my battles.)

In many ways, I shouldn't have been surprised by my father's words. Several years before, while visiting at *our* home, he told me about several of his bowling buddies who recently had strokes and/or heart attacks and were now using wheelchairs. With sadness, he said these friends had moved into nursing homes or assisted living centers, and added that he didn't ever want to have to go through that. I hugged my dad and told him not to worry, that if he ever needed to use a wheelchair and his own place wouldn't work, he could move in with us since our home is accessible! He replied, "I didn't mean it like *that*. What I meant was that if I ever get to that point, I hope someone will just *shoot me!*" I pulled him toward the living room, pointed to Benjamin playing a game on the computer and asked, "So you're telling me that because your grandson uses a wheelchair, his life is not worth living?" "Oh, no," he sputtered, "that's not what I meant." "Yes, Dad," I said. "That *is* what you meant." And then he mumbled and muttered, trying to clarify. Part of his attitude, I feel, is a "generational thing"—he's a World War II veteran of Pearl Harbor—and to him and many others, disability represents weakness, being "unable," and worse. (But who's really the "stronger" person here: my dad or my son?)

I've shared a couple of stories to illustrate instances when we've been on the receiving end of ignorance, misunderstanding, pity, sorrow, and negative attitudes. I wish those who are on the *giving end* of these attitudes had opportunities to have

personal and intimate experience with a person with a disability, so they could learn and experience what we have! If Benjamin didn't have a disability, we would have never learned what we've learned, never met the people we've met, and never had the experiences we've had, individually and as a family. I wouldn't change one thing about my son, his life, or our family's life. Our lives are enriched! If you don't already feel this way, I hope you will by the time you get to the last page of this book.

And one more thing: I do not feel like I'm a "chosen" parent, that my husband and I must be "special" or "worthy" or somehow "saint-like" *(Gag!)* because we have a child with a disability. My husband and I are ordinary people, just trying to get along in the world like everyone else. We're human, we try to do good, we make mistakes, we want to be happy, and we want to raise happy, successful, kind

> ### I wish they could only take me as I am.
> *Vincent Van Gogh*

children. We've done no more or no less than millions of other parents. We've just done many things differently, based on our belief that we didn't want our son's disability—a medical diagnosis—to run his life or be the most important thing about him.

It's all about our attitude! And for all of us, the attitudes we hold are *a choice!* Every minute of every day, we make choices about how we'll think and feel about everything! *We can <u>choose</u> how to see our children!*

Let's go back to the attitudes of others for a moment. I'm an eternal optimist, and I believe that most people are basically good. So I don't believe the negative attitudes held by our society regarding disability are the result of people being intentionally cruel or discriminatory (although some are). I think these beliefs stem from gross ignorance and misunderstanding, passed from generation to generation. I also believe that you and I, along with people with disabilities, and others who care about these issues, can help eliminate and/or minimize this ignorance and misunderstanding by educating others (and you'll learn how in other chapters). But it has to start with a change in *our own* attitudes, beliefs, and language.

Leo Tolstoy said, "Everyone thinks of changing the world, but no one thinks of changing himself." Gandhi said, "Be the change you want to see in the world." Can you change yourself? I believe you can; I've changed myself, many, many times! Can you be the change you want to see in the world? I think you can do that, too.

In the space below, or in your journal, write your thoughts about grief (what you're feeling, what you'd like to change, etc.):

> TO BE A GOOD PARENT,
> YOU HAVE TO PUT YOURSELF SECOND,
> TO RECOGNIZE THAT THE CHILD
> HAS FEELINGS AND NEEDS SEPARATE
> FROM YOURS, AND FULFILL THOSE NEEDS
> WITHOUT EXPECTING ANYTHING
> IN RETURN.
> *Howard Kogan*

_____

_____

_____

_____

_____

_____

_____

_____

_____

_____

_____

Flip back through this chapter, add your score, and write it here:_____.

A score between 103-132 indicates ancient histories are having a powerful and most likely, negative, influence on your child's life and your family's life. As a result, you're probably feeling pretty hopeless, angry, and/or frustrated, and your child is most likely not on a path to success as an adult. But this can be changed, so put your fears aside for now!

A score between 73-102 indicates a mixture of old and new influences affecting your child and your family. As a result, you may experience highs, lows, highs, lows, and . . . well, you might feel like you're on a roller coaster; ditto for your child. He may also be in situations in which he takes two steps forward and one step back on a regular basis. This, too, can

be changed: your child can get on the highway to success and move forward!

A score between 44-72 indicates little of the past is affecting your child, but improvements could still be made to ensure you, your child, and your family are all living the lives of your dreams!

If you wrote your thoughts and feelings in the spaces provided and needed to add additional paper of your own, staple those extra pages inside the back cover of this book. We'll come back to them later.

Now it's time to move forward! We've looked at the past, as a whole, and also how it may be affecting your child and your family. Next, we'll focus our attention on today's DISABILITY WORLD to see what's working, what's not, why, and what we can do about it!

Disability World

4

DISABILITY WORLD—it's a world of "special," a world of services, and a world of segregation. It's a world where children with disabilities are seen as "deficient," "unable," or "needy" in one way or another, so a battery of experts are called in, and great efforts are made—sometimes over many, many years—to make a child's brain or body fit someone's definition of "normal."

In DISABILITY WORLD, we focus enormous amounts of time and energy on what children's brains or bodies are doing or not doing, while paying scant attention to their hearts and minds. In this chapter, we'll explore the different components of DISABILITY WORLD and examine how they affect our children and families. In the process, we'll shine the light on practices intended to "help" our children's bodies and brains, which may actually be very harmful to their hearts and minds.

On the day your child was diagnosed, she stood on the edge of DISABILITY WORLD. On the day she began receiving SERVICES—and by that I mean therapies, interventions, or special help of any kind—she, along with the rest of your family, passed through the invisible, mysterious entrance to DISABILITY WORLD. And you probably didn't even know it happened. For many families (like my family, initially), this strange new DISABILITY WORLD replaces the REAL WORLD. Once in this new place, you're expected to follow a new set of rules: CONVENTIONAL WISDOM ("accepted practices" or what we routinely do).

We're going to examine and challenge today's CONVENTIONAL WISDOM and here's why: in my estimation, about 99 percent of the CONVENTIONAL WISDOM of the past was wrong. It was wrong to kill babies in Ancient Greece; wrong to "beat the devil" out of children in the hopes of "curing" them of their disabilities; wrong to prevent children with disabilities from going to public school before 1975; wrong to put people with disabilities in institutions and ignore, abuse, and sterilize them; and—well, the list could go on and on. We look back at history and shake our heads in dismay, wondering how these things happened—*what were people thinking?*

If the majority of yesterday's CONVENTIONAL WISDOM was wrong, *how do we know today's CONVENTIONAL WISDOM isn't also wrong?* Will we continue to wander down the current path, then look back in 20, 50, or 100 years, scratch our heads in wonder and ask, "What were *we* thinking?" Let's look at some of what we're doing today (but there's more, much more):

- For many families, EARLY INTERVENTION becomes Early Interference: a family's daily schedule is dominated by the SERVICES for the child; some

> EVERY GREAT ADVANCE IN NATURAL KNOWLEDGE HAS INVOLVED THE ABSOLUTE REJECTION OF AUTHORITY.
> *Thomas Huxley*

> TAKE THE COURSE OPPOSITE TO CUSTOM AND YOU WILL ALMOST ALWAYS DO WELL.
> *Jean-Jacques Rousseau*

parents tearfully state they didn't feel they could successfully bond with their babies—they were not able to enjoy the simplest pleasures because of the intensive level of Services; and in some cases, parents begin to feel they *must* depend on professionals, and feelings of incompetence are born.

- Many young children who are not yet talking are placed in segregated Special Ed Preschools, where they're surrounded by other children who aren't talking. Over 100 years ago, Samuel Gridley Howe warned against segregating people, and reminded us that children who aren't talking should be with children who *are* talking! If we want a child to learn to speak, shouldn't he be with other children who are talking? *What are we thinking?*

- School-aged children are also segregated—by disability label, intelligence level, or some other factor related to the disability. Many children with autism, for example, are placed in "autism classes," those with emotional disabilities are placed with others "of their kind," and so on. Horrible things can take place in some of these Special Ed classrooms, from low expectations to abuse, and everything in between. (A recent San Antonio newspaper account detailed the investigation into potential abuse after a parent discovered educators had tied her son with Down syndrome to a chair in a Special Ed classroom. In another district, a boy with autism was tied to his chair, and when that didn't work, his chair was bolted to the floor. And I once overhead educators talking about learning the "four point take-down.")

The latest education statistics (covering the 2000-2001 school year, from www.nces.ed.gov, Table 53) show that only *46.5 percent of students with disabilities (ages 6-21) spent 79 percent or more of the day in a Regular Education class.* Yet the Federal mandate for children with disabilities to be educated in the "least restrictive environment" has been in place since 1975! Could the large number of students who are *undereducated* in segregated Special Ed classrooms be a contributing factor to the estimated *70 percent* unemployment rate of adults with developmental disabilities?

- The physical segregation and social isolation many children experience in public schools continue into adulthood: people with disabilities are forced to live with others they don't know, work with others, go bowling with others, and more—whether they want to or not—while being supervised by staff. Sounds a little bit like prison life, doesn't it?

Many of us *say* we want children and adults to be included, but it's not happening. We *say* they are "children, first," but our actions focus on the disability, first—not the child. We *say* we hope they'll be successful, but we prevent them from having opportunities to do so. We talk the talk; we don't walk the walk.

We tend not to see things clearly *while* we're doing what we do; it's like "we can't see the forest for the trees." And *while we're not looking,* the lives of countless individuals with disabilities are laid to waste in DISABILITY WORLD, where children and adults are isolated, ignored, undereducated, congregated in "special" environments with other "special" people, and...this list could also go on and on, and end with the horrific unemployment rate

---

A REAL LIFE

Throughout this book, I talk about the importance of children with disabilities living a REAL LIFE. What does this mean? When a child or adult with a disability is living a REAL LIFE, it means he's doing what he would be doing if he didn't have a disability. This doesn't refer to functional skills like walking, talking, etc., but to having age-appropriate experiences and opportunities in typical, inclusive environments. In later chapters, you'll learn about the importance of providing your child with the assistive technology devices, supports, accommodations, and modifications to enable him to live a REAL LIFE— the life of his dreams.

of adults with developmental disabilities. This shameful unemployment rate doesn't just mean people with disabilities aren't working. It means most are still living with their parents, in a group home, or in some other congregate facility; working for sub-minimum wages in a sheltered workshop or spending endless hours in a "day program;" collecting "disability welfare" (Supplemental Security Income-SSI, Medicaid, and maybe food stamps); and existing below the poverty line.

If we think about the millions of adults with developmental disabilities who are currently unemployed (many have *never* held a REAL JOB), we have to wonder: when these individuals were children, was this the dream of their parents? Did their mothers or fathers lie in bed at night and think, "Oh, I hope my son grows up to live in a group home, work for sub-minimum wages in a sheltered workshop, collect his paltry government benefits, and exist below the poverty line..."? Was that *any parent's* dream?

More importantly, though, *was this the dream of the children?* Did any of them think, "I hope to grow up and never have a REAL JOB, live with other people with disabilities I don't know, be managed by staff, and have others write plans and programs for my life..."? Was that the dream of *any child?*

So it wasn't anyone's dream, *but it happened anyway,* to millions of people! Why? There's no pat answer, but I'm guessing it happened to many because they followed CONVENTIONAL WISDOM! So here's my proposition: if we don't make significant changes in what we do and how we do it, 70 percent of the children with disabilities alive today will end up unemployed and living on the margins of society when they're adults. Is this what you want for *your child?*

Instead of looking at what we do (CONVENTIONAL WISDOM) *at the time we're doing it,* we've depended on hindsight. We have 20/20 vision when we look backward. And look where it's gotten us.

What if we step back from the forest so we *can* see the trees. What if we use *foresight* instead of hindsight or no sight? No one can predict the future. But if we learn from the big history, as well as our personal histories, and the experiences of others; if we think critically and creatively; if we ponder and ask ourselves lots of questions; if we listen to our children and other people with disabilities; and if we rediscover our common sense, we'll acquire foresight—a valuable tool that can help us change the course of our children's lives.

The majority of children and adults with developmental disabilities today are usually viewed as not being successful, meaning they're not living REAL LIVES: achieving or enjoying the traditional milestones most Americans take for granted, like having friends, being involved in their communities, doing well in public school, going on to college/trade school, being employed in the job of one's choice, living in the home of one's choice, getting married, having children, taking vacations, and more. For many children and adults with disabilities, *the American dream is a myth.* And this makes me sad and angry.

Why *don't* more people with disabilities achieve success? The answer will depend on who you ask, but for some, the reason seems so obvious the question

Every state has a Vocational-Rehabilitation department and there are other "employment agencies" whose responsibility is to help people with disabilities achieve gainful employment—and we still have a 70-75 percent unemployment rate. Does this seem odd?

Do you know what the unemployment rate is for people *without* disabilities? It hovers between 5 and 6 percent, and when it changes even a tenth of a percent, it makes the news!

But when was the last time the news media reported on the "shockingly high" unemployment rate of people with disabilities?

shouldn't even have to be asked: people with disabilities aren't successful *because* they have disabilities. And this attitude also makes me sad and angry! It's another prejudicial assumption that's based on opinion, not fact. For there *are* children and adults with developmental disabilities (some with very significant conditions) who are leading successful lives—REAL LIVES.

I propose that the presence of a disability is not a barrier to success. Instead, the barriers lie within today's CONVENTIONAL WISDOM—our attitudes and perceptions about disability, combined with a SERVICE SYSTEM (therapies, interventions, Special Ed programs, etc.) that:

- makes the disability the most important thing about that person;
- focuses on correcting a person's so-called deficits;
- sends a powerful, demoralizing NOT-OK message;
- congregates people with disabilities in "special" programs;
- reduces people with disabilities to clients/recipients, who have little or no control over what happens to them;
- robs people with disabilities and families of privacy, autonomy, self-direction, and self-confidence;
- presumes people with disabilities are incompetent;
- ignores or minimizes a person's strengths and abilities.

Before making the assumption I'm attacking therapists, educators, service providers, or anyone else, take note: I am not saying people who work in the SYSTEM, in any capacity, are bad, evil people. Most are kind, caring people who work hard to help the individuals and families they serve. They're just doing their jobs (and yes, some could probably do their jobs better, but that's another story). It's not the *people,* but the SYSTEM itself, that's not working. Why? Because it's based on flawed logic: that the "problem" of disability is within the *person* with a disability. When we see the locus of the problem as being within the person, our efforts are focused on fixing, curing, teaching, training, coaching, analyzing, and/or medicating the person.

The "problem" of disability is *not within the person.* The real problem is our *attitudes* about disability. And attitudes (our personal perceptions and our collective societal perception) are vitally important, because they:

- determine how we personally treat children and adults with disabilities;
- influence the laws and social policies which create the SERVICES that touch the lives of children and adults with disabilities.

Some people work to "solve the problems" of individuals with disabilities by *advocating for more:* more services, programs, interventions, therapies, laws, and so forth. But we have more of those than ever before, and more than any other nation in the world, and people with disabilities *still* don't have what they really need: inclusion, friends, a good education, real jobs, and all the other *ordinary* things most Americans take for granted.

WALK IN THEIR SHOES

Some people are angered by my message—and feel like punching me in the nose (but they just write nasty letters, and that's OK). Based on what they tell me, it seems they hear my criticism of today's CONVENTIONAL WISDOM and its SERVICES as an attack on them, *personally.* I believe this happens because they're seeing things from their "position"—as a parent, therapist, educator, etc. From that position, I can understand why my words might get their dander up.

But if they looked at things from the perspective of a child or an adult with a disability, they might see things differently. And isn't that how we'll do *our* best—by trying to walk in *their* shoes? Isn't *their perspective* the most important of all? And shouldn't we care how *they* feel?

So as *you* read this book, I hope you'll try to see things from the perspective of a child or adult with a developmental disability—then you'll see things with new eyes.

Others work to *change the SYSTEM*—and it does need changing! But even the most progressive, responsive SYSTEM cannot ensure inclusion, friendships, and other ordinary activities and events that create wonderful lives. Those things are available only in our communities.

I propose that we need to change our attitudes and how we do things. This book is not about changing the SYSTEM. If it changes—and it *is* in some quarters (some agency directors have told me they're making changes because of my message)—that's great. The solutions I propose, however, are actions we, as parents, can take, irrespective of what the SYSTEM is doing. In a moment, we'll examine CONVENTIONAL WISDOM, beginning with the MEDICAL MODEL. First, however, let's compare the parallel lives of children and adults in the REAL WORLD and in DISABILITY WORLD.

REAL WORLD	DISABILITY WORLD
Eighteen-month-old child stays home with Mom, plays a lot, naps, explores, learns, enjoys typical babyhood.	Eighteen-month-old spends most of his time receiving therapy (at clinic and at home), schedule of Services runs child's and family's daily schedules.
Three-year-old goes to preschool/daycare with other three- and four-year-olds while Mom works part-time, goes to birthday parties, plays with other kids.	Three-year-old goes to Special Ed Preschool with other children who are labeled, receives many hours of therapy each week, does not go to birthday parties or play with other children in the neighborhood.
Ten-year-old has friends, participates in community sports and other activities, hangs out with friends, is excited about middle school.	Ten-year-old is in ungraded Special Ed Classroom, does not participate in school or community activities, has no friends, isn't invited to birthday parties, will go into ungraded Special Ed Class in middle school.
Sixteen-year-old is learning to drive, dates a little, is in Debate Club and plays tennis, is thinking about college.	Sixteen-year-old is in segregated Special Ed Life Skills class, has few friends, doesn't participate in school or community activities, is unsure of what the future holds.
Twenty-five-year-old lives in her own place, has attended college, is engaged to be married, loves her job.	Twenty-five-year-old lives in a group home, works part-time in sheltered workshop, spends other time in adult day program, has two "friends" (paid staff) in the group home.

The Medical Model

In Chapter 2, you learned how the concept of disability changed over hundreds of years. Throughout history, those in power—religious leaders, training school directors, or whoever took responsibility—"constructed" a concept of the "problem" of disability and then developed a "solution." It has been seen as a "spiritual problem," so religious authorities set the tone for "treatment" (beatings, abandonment, prayer, healing, and more). In England in the 1600s, "needy" people fell under the "social problem" umbrella, and tax dollars paid for their care. The MEDICAL MODEL of disability evolved during the Institutional Era (late 1800s-early 1900s) when physicians "took control," and it's what we're living with today.

The MEDICAL MODEL is one we're all familiar with. Here's an example: you have a sore throat and a fever. You go to the doctor to be cured of your illness. The good doctor examines you, delivers a diagnosis (strep throat), prescribes the cure (antibiotics, bed rest, plenty of fluids), and announces his prognosis (you'll be fine within a week or so).

> PERFECTION
> IS WHAT IS
> ABNORMAL.
> *Lou Marinoff*

For most of us, the MEDICAL MODEL works just fine—and we like it. We like it so much, and we're so accustomed to "cures on demand" (because that's what many in the medical community promise), that we insist on a cure for just about everything!

But what happens when conditions we call "disabilities" are under the MEDICAL MODEL? There are no magic pills, surgeries, or potions to "cure" cerebral palsy, Down syndrome, spina bifida, autism, or the wide variety of conditions we call "developmental disabilities." Nevertheless, the physician's response is the same: prescribe a treatment (therapies, surgery, drugs, etc.). None of these can provide a cure, but we may be told they can "improve" the person's condition or provide some other benefit. "So what's wrong with that?" you might be wondering. Lots, as you'll see. But the negative outcomes aren't limited to the health care field. The different components of the MEDICAL MODEL of disability—described next—influence government policies (and drive the entire Service System, including Special Education) and society-at-large.

Not-OK

The basic premise of the MEDICAL MODEL is that the problem is in the person, and the person is NOT-OK. Let's go back to the strep throat example. When you feel sick, you're NOT-OK, you want the doctor to make you OK again, and after treatment (or sometimes with no treatment), you *are* once again OK ("back to normal"). Let's compare a strep throat diagnosis and prognosis, with the diagnosis and prognosis of a developmental disability:

STREP THROAT: Being NOT-OK is temporary.

DEVELOPMENTAL DISABILITY: Being NOT-OK is *permanent.*

STREP THROAT: Cure available—works fast and restores the person to "normal."

DEVELOPMENTAL DISABILITY: No known cure; a variety of treatments will be used to try to restore the person to "normalcy;" these efforts may take decades or the person's entire life.

STREP THROAT: Treatment interferes minimally in person's daily schedule and overall life; little or no effect on family's life.

DEVELOPMENTAL DISABILITY: Treatments, interventions, and services may *dominate* the person's daily schedule and overall life; most likely has significant impact on *family's* daily schedule and overall life.

STREP THROAT: No presumptions are made about the individual, or his value as a human being, his potential, or his ability to lead a "normal" life.

DEVELOPMENTAL DISABILITY: Numerous negative presumptions made about the individual, his value as a human being, his potential, and his ability to lead a "normal" life.

STREP THROAT: No long-term negative effect since people with strep throat are not marginalized and devalued.

DEVELOPMENTAL DISABILITY: Serious long-term negative effects, since people with developmental disabilities have been marginalized and devalued since the beginning of recorded history.

Think for a moment how most of us feel about getting medical treatment, and I'll use myself as the example. I don't really look forward to going to the doctor: being poked and prodded and questioned, and having things stuck in me or on me, and more. But I want to "get well," so I put up with it all, hoping I won't have to do that again, any time soon.

But what about a child with a developmental disability who receives interventions and therapies on a regular basis, for years and years? Every time a child receives therapy or some type of intervention, we're sending the message: "You are NOT-OK the way you are, and we're going to keep giving you these treatments until you *are* OK, *according to our standards.*" And this is, of course, the "able-bodied" standard. If a child cannot walk, talk, feed himself, sit on the toilet, use his hands or other body parts the "right way," behave, or do other "normal" things in a "normal" fashion, he does not meet this standard. "You're NOT-OK, you're NOT-OK, *you're NOT-OK...*" A child hears it over and over and over again. *What does this do to a child's heart and mind?*

We can see evidence of the NOT-OK mentality across society and across the lifespan of people with disabilities. For adults, it's evidenced in the high unemployment rate of people with developmental disabilities ("We only hire people who are OK; *not* those who are NOT-OK"), as well as in a variety of Special Programs in Adult Services that focus on making the person OK.

In the educational arena, the influence of the NOT-OK paradigm is even greater and is often taken to extremes: children who are judged to be NOT-OK are "placed" in segregated Special Education classrooms. Many are "allowed" into Regular Ed classrooms only if they *become* OK, by someone's standards.

The NOT-OK mentality is evident in many Regular Ed classrooms, as well. There are a variety of skills we expect children to achieve in school. In kindergarten, these include cutting with scissors. So when my son, Benjamin, was in kindergarten, the teacher expected him to master this "critically important skill." During Benjamin's therapy career, the OT had worked on this, but Benj never achieved "success" per the OT's standard. I wasn't sure what would happen in kindergarten with scissor-cutting, but we always wanted Benjamin to have the same opportunities as other children. He had surprised us many times by doing things no one thought he could—things he didn't (or chose not to) do in therapy, but which he *did* do at home or in other environments.

> "But my child *loves* therapy—it's fun," you might be thinking. That may be true. When my son was young, he often had fun at therapy. Even so, our children may still experience long-term negative consequences from feeling they're NOT-OK.
>
> Isn't it possible that even a very young child feels "different" or "not as good" because therapists work with him and not his brother or sister? Even if therapy is "fun" today, what will his feelings be when he's 20, and he looks back on his childhood?
>
> Our children are very smart, and the sooner we give them credit for being fully-aware of what's happening to them, the better!
>
> On the off-chance you think your child is "not aware," what if you're wrong? Are you willing to take the risk? Shouldn't we err on the side of caution?

(The same might be true about your child.) Children don't seem to be highly motivated to "perform" for therapists, or even their own parents, but many *are* highly motivated to do what their peers are doing!

It didn't take long to realize Benj could not cut with "kindergarten scissors," and the teacher was dismayed. I wasn't; I just gave him different types of scissors to try. Motorized, battery operated scissors came first (the kind that cut by vibration). No good: the teacher said they were "too loud" and disrupted the class. With typical scissors, Benjamin could squeeze the handles closed, but he had difficulty opening the blades, so I bought a spring-loaded pair that opened automatically. No good: the teacher said the blades were too sharp.

She wanted a better solution, but at that point I told her Benjamin was not going to grow up to be a tailor—scissor-cutting was not high on our list of priorities. And I added, "Let's not make Benj spend time on something that's irrelevant and unimportant, at the expense of things that *are* important to him. *You* can cut the paper for him, a classmate can do it, or Benjamin can tear the paper with his teeth, but let's get on with his real education!"

In the school arena, the *way* children with disabilities do things is often judged to be NOT-OK. Unless Benjamin could cut paper the "normal" way with the "normal" scissors, his way was NOT-OK.

This attitude often extends to children who don't have disabilities, too. When my daughter, Emily, first began scribbling, she held the crayon a certain way. It didn't bother me; I figured she held it in a way that was most comfortable for her. But one teacher told her she held her pencil the "wrong way," and tried to make her change! I politely told her to leave Emily alone. *What difference did it make how she held her pencil?* In college and at her job today, this is of no interest to anyone. So how important is this, really?

Regardless of where it's practiced—at home, in school, or in other environments, the NOT-OK mentality represents an arrogant mindset that Someone-in-Authority can decide there is a "right" way to do things and, by extension, a *right way to be*.

What does this do to a child? Is there any greater loss a child can suffer? To be judged, and to never measure up to the grossly artificial definition of "normal"? To be thought of as "less than" by others, simply because your hands, legs, brain, or other body part is different from others? How does a child deal with this, when there is nothing he can do about it? What does this feeling of powerlessness do to a child? *Think like a child,* and wonder about all this.

I hope the words of the adults with developmental disabilities in the first chapter are still fresh in your mind. Today, you can visit a variety of web sites hosted by adults with developmental disabilities, where you can get a feel for their perspectives, as they describe their sadness, anger, and frustration at efforts to "fix them." You can also connect with adults with disabilities through People First Chapters or Independent Living Centers in your community who can share their own personal stories about what it feels like to be on the receiving end of years of treatments orchestrated to "normalize" them.

THE MOST APPALLING CRUELTIES ARE COMMITTED BY APPARENTLY VIRTUOUS GOVERNMENTS IN EXPECTATION OF A GREAT GOOD TO COME, NEVER LEARNING THAT THE EVIL DONE NOW IS THE SURE DESTROYER OF THE EXPECTED GOOD.

Katherine Anne Porter

"I wish my parents could have loved me just the way I am."

I've met numerous adults with developmental disabilities who have shared the following sentiment with me: "The reason I'm not as successful as I'd like to be is not because of my disability, but because of the way I feel about myself." *If you've been treated as if you're Not-OK throughout your childhood, how can you feel OK about yourself when you become an adult?*

We can do better. In Chapters 6 and 7 you'll learn how we can ensure our children receive the help they need without "therapizing" their lives and making them feel they're Not-OK.

Not-Ready

The Not-OK paradigm often leads to the Not-Ready mentality, which lives and breathes within the health care arena, disability services, in public schools, and in some places in our communities. Sadly, many parents have embraced this mentality. Here are some examples of the Not-Ready mentality (also known as the Readiness or Get-Ready paradigms):

TREAT PEOPLE AS
IF THEY WERE
WHAT THEY
OUGHT TO BE
AND
YOU HELP THEM
TO BECOME
WHAT THEY ARE
CAPABLE OF BEING.
Johann von Goethe

- a child with a disability is Not-Ready to attend a neighborhood preschool because she can't feed herself;
- a student with a disability is Not-Ready for a Regular Ed class because he's not at grade level, so he'll stay in the segregated Special Ed classroom;
- an adult with a disability is Not-Ready to move from a group home into a place of her own because she doesn't make her bed, cook, balance her checkbook, and/or perform other daily living activities to the standards imposed by the group home staff.

Yet there *are* children in age-appropriate neighborhood preschools, even though they can't feed themselves. There *are* students with disabilities who are in age-appropriate Regular Ed classrooms, even though they're not at grade level—the curriculum is modified, per Special Ed law. And adults with disabilities who only make their beds once a week or don't balance their checkbooks perfectly (like the rest of us) *are* able to live in their own places!

Like the Not-OK paradigm, there's an arrogance in the Not-Ready mentality when Someone-in-Authority has the power—misplaced and illegitimate power—to determine a child or adult with a disability is Not-Ready, and to then exclude, segregate, and/or devalue the person. This is Grand Theft Robbery: opportunities for the person to live a Real Life have been stolen.

Ultimately, the entire Service System—from Early Intervention to Vocational-Rehabilitation—is based on the premise that children and adults with disabilities are Not-Ready. But have no fear: Services will get them Ready! But do they? For decades, we've had "birth-to-death" Services for people with disabilities, with what outcome? Undereducation in public schools and a shameful unemployment rate. Think there's a connection?

The Not-Ready mentality puts many children on the slow track to nowhere. If they're diagnosed when they're very young, they receive Early Intervention (EI) Services—based on the theory that if we "get 'em while they're young," we can fix them or at least minimize the effects of the disability, so the kiddos won't need Special Ed Services later (more about this in Chapter 8).

But what really happens is this: after EI Services, many children are *still* considered NOT-READY, so they're "promoted" to Special Ed Preschools. After that, they're *still* considered NOT-READY, so many go into segregated Special Ed classrooms for the remainder of their school years. After that, they're *still* considered NOT-READY for post-secondary education or a real job, so they go into Adult Services, where (unless we start doing things differently right now) 70 percent will remain—unemployed and living a less-than-desirable existence.

Children and adults with disabilities *are* READY, right now, to lead REAL LIVES: included in their schools and communities, participating in the activities of their choice, and enjoying all the rights and responsibilities of citizenship!

In the REAL WORLD, children and adults who *do not* have disabilities are not held hostage to a READINESS standard in everything they do. Preschool-aged children do not have to GET-READY to ride a bike; they're deemed READY simply because they're four or five and they want to ride a two-wheeler, and they *learn by doing*. School-aged children do not need any type of specialized help to GET-READY for adulthood; they learn by doing—at home, in public school, in community activities, and in other environments. Young adults strike out on their own *(you and I did)* whether they're proficient in cooking, balancing their checkbooks, or any other skill—and most of them make it, one way or another!

There's another aspect of the NOT-READY paradigm that often has a negative influence on our children. Growth and development are (mistakenly) thought to be linear and/or sequential. You're probably familiar with these widely-accepted examples:

—a child must crawl before he can walk;
—a child must read before he can write;
—a child cannot learn unless he can read.

These, and many other scenarios, represent this concept: one must first accomplish steps "A" and "B" before getting to point "C." This is such a basic and pervasive concept that we seldom question it. This SEQUENTIAL/LINEAR concept represents order, and we like order—it makes sense. The numbers on a ruler are linear; the letters in the alphabet are always in the same order; the seasons always occur in the same sequence; and so forth.

The opposite of SEQUENTIAL/LINEAR could be called "random:" "B" happens without "A" occurring first. We're not as comfortable with this, it doesn't always seem to make sense, and we may even question whether "B" is really true or valid.

For example, "Julia," a six-year-old who has autism, had a passion for looking at books from the time she was two. But no one ever expected her to learn to read because she didn't talk: books are full of words and if you don't use words (talk), how could you read? Although Julia didn't talk, she *was* learning to "speak" through Facilitated Communication (FC).

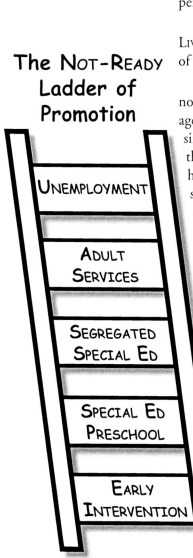

The NOT-READY Ladder of Promotion

UNEMPLOYMENT

ADULT SERVICES

SEGREGATED SPECIAL ED

SPECIAL ED PRESCHOOL

EARLY INTERVENTION

At her birthday party when she turned seven, her grandparents gave her several new books, but there was no time to read them to her that day. "Tomorrow morning," her parents promised. That night, she took her new treasures to bed with her, looking at them intently until her parents kissed her good-night and turned out the light. Imagine their delightful shock the next morning when, through FC, she asked detailed questions about the characters in one of her books—questions that indicated Julia had done more than look at the pictures! Her parents were flabbergasted, so they "tested" Julia by showing her other books which she had never seen before. Sure enough, Julia was really reading!

Julia's achievement turned the READINESS and SEQUENTIAL/LINEAR models upside-down. What she did was not *logical*: she achieved "C" (reading) without first mastering "A" (talking) and "B" ("sounding out" written words). Our children's experiences have taught many of us that growth and development are not always linear or sequential, but it's often very difficult to convince some educators and other professionals to believe what they're seeing because their view is clouded by SEQUENTIAL/LINEAR logic!

In DISABILITY WORLD, the NOT-READY model restricts our children's growth and development, limits their opportunities to be included in typical activities and environments, and holds them hostage to artificial standards of READINESS. We can do better, as I'll detail in later chapters.

Developmental Age

Hand-in-hand with the NOT-READY mindset is the DEVELOPMENTAL AGE concept. Using one assessment or another, professionals, educators, and/or others test the child and assign a DEVELOPMENTAL AGE to one or more areas of the child's life. Not only is this *not* helpful, it can be very harmful.

First, using the DEVELOPMENTAL AGE concept causes many of us to think about and treat a child differently—and inappropriately. For example, a variety of parents have approached me after a presentation to ask a question about their children, and have said something like, "Jason is 11, but he's really more like a five-year-old." When we think this way, how do we treat him? Like a five-year-old! And then we're frustrated or disappointed when he doesn't "make progress." (We *should* be disappointed—in *ourselves* and *our* actions!) If we *treat* Jason like a five-year-old, we don't allow him to have the *opportunities and experiences to be an 11-year-old!*

A DEVELOPMENTAL AGE is usually specific to *one area of a child's life*, but it may mysteriously expand to define everything about a child, with terrible consequences! When professionals assigned this DEVELOPMENTAL AGE to Jason, it probably applied to emotional development, cognitive abilities, or something else, but professionals and his mother have generalized it to *all* of Jason. He has lived six more years than a five-year-old, and has *six more years of experience!* So how can we say he's more like a five-year-old? And when a parent so easily tosses this descriptor around, there's no doubt her son has heard these words! What does he think about how his mom sees him? More importantly, *what does he think about himself?* How can we do this to our wonderful children?

FC—FACILITATED COMMUNICATION

I'm no expert on FC, but I've known several parents who have helped their children learn to communicate using this method. How does it work? In brief, the person with a disability (the Typist) uses a keyboard, and a Facilitator (the parent or someone else) provides tactile support to the child's wrist. Over time and/or as the Typist's ability grows, the tactile support moves up—to the forearm, the elbow, the shoulder, etc., so that the support can, at some point, be removed and the Typist types by herself.

FC *is* controversial: some say the Facilitator is actually doing the typing by "leading" the Typist's hand. But many vigorously dispute this, noting that Typists have written things only they could know. FC has been used by children and adults with cerebral palsy, autism, and other conditions. More info is available from books and on the Internet.

Embracing the DEVELOPMENTAL AGE mentality can also cause us to treat a child "like a baby" or younger than she is. We may not expect her to be responsible or to "act her age," and we may even use "baby talk" with her. In a segregated Special Ed Preschool environment, a four-year-old child with a cognitive disability, who has been assigned a two-year-old DEVELOPMENTAL AGE, may be allowed to "get away with" behaviors that would not be acceptable in a four-year-old *without* a disability. Instead of expecting the child to behave like a four-year-old, and *giving her the help she needs to do so*, the child's teachers and parents may accept such behaviors, because, "She has Down syndrome and that's the way those kids are."

Second, a child's DEVELOPMENTAL AGE is often used to justify exclusion in chronologically age-appropriate environments—in public school and other settings. When my son, Benjamin, was five, the whole family went to school for Benj's kindergarten IEP (Individualized Education Program) meeting. (Yes, our kids should be at their IEP meetings; it's *their* education, not ours—more in Chapter 9.) The meeting was held in the kindergarten room, and Benjamin and Emily sat at one of the little tables, while the members of the IEP Team sat in a circle a few feet away. At the time, Benjamin was not reading, but people thought he was. With his great auditory memory, he had memorized 60 or 70 books, which he recited out loud, while turning the pages at exactly the right time. It sure *looked* like he was reading, and I didn't tell anyone any different!

Even at this inclusive school, things weren't perfect: the kindergarten teacher was a little nervous about having a child with a disability in her class. But just look over there at that cute little five-year-old apparently reading a book! What's not to love about that kid? What's there to be scared of?

Based on recommended practices, I had invited Benjamin's physical therapist, Irene, to attend the meeting. As you're probably familiar with—or will be, if you haven't yet attended your child's first IEP meeting—the IEP Team members share their "reports" about the child. When it was Irene's turn, she began: "Benjamin Snow; spastic diplegia cerebral palsy; age five years, four months; functions at the level of an eight-month-old..."

The kindergarten teacher just about fell out of her chair! She jerked her head toward Benjamin, then back at the therapist, and back to Benjamin, and then had a dazed look on her face. It all happened in a flash, but it seemed like slow motion to me, and I could imagine what the teacher was thinking: "This is kindergarten! I can't have an eight-month-old in my class!"

I jumped in with, "Irene means that on a *gross motor developmental scale,* Benjamin is at an eight-month level because he never crawled." At that, the teacher relaxed a bit. But there's no doubt some damage had been done: that bit of information would most likely stay with the teacher forever, and would have a negative impact on her opinion of my son. Benjamin would not have the opportunity to define himself, to show who he really was; in her mind, my son would always be "like an eight-month-old." (And to this day, as he prepares to attend college, Benjamin would still described as "functioning" at the eight-month level according to a *gross motor scale.* That *is* gross, isn't it?)

Have you noticed that when a child *without* a disability is five, for example, he's five, period! But a child *with* a disability is, "5 years, 4 months, 1 week, 3 days, 6 hours..."

OK, so I'm exaggerating a bit, but this is a ridiculous consequence of Developmental Scales and the DEVELOPMENTAL AGE mentality. If professionals describe your child this way, tell 'em to drop it! If your child is five, he's five, just like other kids!

But what might have happened if Benjamin had *not* been at the meeting that day? What if all the teacher had to go on was the information in Irene's report? If she hadn't had the opportunity to see Benjamin with her own eyes, the meeting would have probably been over at that instant, with the teacher refusing to allow Benjamin in her classroom!

Benjamin, and other students with disabilities at this inclusive school, did just fine with the help of curriculum modifications and other supports. But too many children with disabilities are not even *given the opportunity to try* because of the DEVELOPMENTAL AGE that's been assigned. The child may be "guilty as charged," and given a life sentence of incarceration in segregated Special Programs. There's virtually no chance for parole, but the Authorities may let the child "earn her way" to less restrictive settings if she achieves goals that move her closer to her CHRONOLOGICAL AGE, as determined by the Authorities. Even if she *does* meet with some success, such as being "allowed" to participate in some Regular Ed classrooms, she's watched like a hawk, and any missteps will land her back in the segregated Special Ed setting.

Third, when we use the DEVELOPMENTAL AGE concept, we tend to focus on isolated skills or functional abilities instead of the whole child. When Benjamin was 18 months, I thought he should have the opportunity to try using a walker. He couldn't get into a sitting position by himself or stand unassisted, but sometimes he moved his legs in a "walking motion." When I asked the physical therapist (PT) about it, she said, "No, developmentally, he's not ready." (There's that NOT-READY mentality!) But I felt he was, so I asked the orthopedic doctor, and told him what the PT said. He agreed with *me*, wrote the prescription for a walker, and then gave me an extraordinarily wise piece of advice: "Kathie, Benjamin is a year-and-a-half, and his *body* might not be like other kiddos his age, since he's not walking independently. But I believe some part of Benjamin knows that kids his age are upright most of the time, moving their bodies through space—not sitting or lying down like babies do. Even though his *body* might not technically be ready—like the therapist said—*he's ready in his mind.* So we need to listen to Benjamin: he wants to be treated like an 18-month-old."

> LOGIC:
> AN INSTRUMENT
> USED FOR
> BOLSTERING
> A PREJUDICE.
> *Elbert Hubbard*

In this instance, the therapist was influenced by the DEVELOPMENTAL AGE, NOT-READY, and SEQUENTIAL/LOGICAL concepts. According to a gross motor chart, Benjamin was probably at the level of a three- or four-month-old. Therefore, in the therapist's mind, he was NOT-READY to walk: three- or four-month-old babies don't walk. And from the SEQUENTIAL/LOGICAL perspective, children crawl before they walk. But Benjamin never crawled in the typical fashion; he "commando-crawled" (his body was flat on the floor, and he pulled himself forward using only his arms). In essence, the therapist was saying we should not *allow* Benjamin to try a walker since he had not mastered the skill of crawling! The therapist looked at Benjamin's body parts with logic; the doctor and I saw him as a whole child.

Educators often make the same mistake as my son's therapist: they use the DEVELOPMENTAL AGE concept when making important decisions about what the child should learn and/or what activities he should be doing. This can lead to gravely erroneous thinking that can cause harm to the child.

While doing a presentation for a conference of Special Ed Preschool teachers, I started by reviewing parts of Special Ed law (IDEA), focusing on how parents are integral members of the IEP Team, especially when writing goals for a child. To make sure we were all on the same wavelength, I asked, "So this is how you do it, right? Any questions?" Every teacher in the audience had the deer-in-the-headlights look. Finally, one shared her thoughts: "We don't do it that way. Parents don't help write the goals; they don't know how. So *we* write them, then the parents come to the IEP meeting, we show them the goals, and they sign the IEP." I replied that this practice didn't follow the requirements of the law (detailed in Chapter 9), and then had the following disturbing interchange:

Question: You write the goals without talking with the parents first?

Answer: Yes.

Question: Hmmm—then you must have spent some time with the child before writing the goals, right?

Answer: No, we don't see the child until the first day of school.

Question: I don't understand. How can you write *individualized* goals if you haven't talked to the parents and you don't know the child?

Answer: We just look at his assessments to see where he is. Then we look at the Developmental Scale to see what's normal for a three- or four-year-old, and we write goals that will make him more like a normal child.

I was beyond flabbergasted, and almost couldn't get any words out (unusual for me), but finally sputtered, "What if the goals you're writing aren't relevant, meaningful, or important to the child or his parents?" The deer-in-the-head-lights look was back. They had no answer. Even more amazing was that these teachers believed it was their job to make three- and four-year-old children with disabilities "more normal."

Later, I tried to imagine what might have happened if educators had done that to my son when he was four. Based on the results of developmental tests, they would have determined that Benjamin had great difficulty writing with a pencil, wasn't walking independently, couldn't do some simple things like wash his hands or face, nor a long list of other "developmentally appropriate typical four-year-old" activities, and *these* are what they would have focused on, *whether or not they were important to Benjamin or his dad and me.* And those things were not! For example, we knew handwriting would be laborious and difficult for Benjamin; we already had him on the computer! At the age of 18, he still has great difficulty cleaning his face and hands "appropriately," but this hasn't stopped him from having a wonderful, successful life. His service dog, Riley, does a fantastic job of licking Benj's hands and face clean—better than Benj *or* I could ever do it!

As it was, Benjamin's inclusion in a neighborhood preschool helped him learn "how to be four" by being around typical four-year-olds. He learned that when you pick your nose, four-year-old girls turn into little mothers and say,

A message from a child:

Listen to Me WITH YOUR EARS, YOUR EYES, AND YOUR HEART.

"That's yucky! Don't do that!" And no one had to write a goal or a "behavior plan" to address this issue. Did he achieve all the milestones on a four-year-old developmental scale? No, but then some of his classmates didn't either, and they didn't have disability labels! And *they* were not excluded, treated differently, or expected to attend GET-READY classes (segregated Special Ed Preschool), so why should Benjamin or any other child with a disability?

The DEVELOPMENTAL AGE concept might have good intentions. In the best-case scenario (and it ain't so good), professionals use it to determine what kind of help a child might need, so that—one day—his DEVELOPMENTAL and CHRONOLOGICAL AGES might match. In the worst-case scenario, it's used as justification to exclude and segregate. The bottom line? The DEVELOPMENTAL AGE concept devalues children! If your child's DEVELOPMENTAL AGE is not the same as his CHRONOLOGICAL AGE, he's already in the doghouse—he's "not good enough" and doesn't "measure up" to other children. We probably don't use these words, but that's what we mean. What does this do to a child? Between this and all the other hurtful consequences, can we continue to support the DEVELOPMENTAL AGE paradigm?

> A CHILD CAN NEVER BE BETTER THAN WHAT HIS PARENTS THINK OF HIM.
> *Marcelene Cox*

Presumption of Incompetence

The NOT-OK, NOT READY, and DEVELOPMENTAL AGE concepts are often wrapped up together in a neat little package that creates the PRESUMPTION OF INCOMPETENCE mentality. And to a large degree, the PRESUMED INCOMPETENT paradigm infects all areas of the Service System, including Special Education.

Young children with disabilities are PRESUMED INCOMPETENT to attend typical preschools; school-aged children are PRESUMED INCOMPETENT to be in Regular Ed classrooms; and adults with disabilities are PRESUMED INCOMPETENT to live on their own *or* find a job on their own (they're supposed to get help from Voc-Rehab or others who provide employment assistance).

The PRESUMPTION OF INCOMPETENCE is not limited to individuals with disabilities, however. It can also extend to family members and others. For example, "Deena," a friend and neighbor, had a baby within days of my own son being born. Why didn't an Early Intervention Service Coordinator visit *her* home once a month? Because *Deena* was PRESUMED COMPETENT, while I was PRESUMED INCOMPETENT: *I* didn't know anything about having a baby with a disability, so I needed the expertise of professionals.

CONVENTIONAL WISDOM dictates that young children with disabilities should attend a Special Ed Preschool. But "Linda" wants something different for her daughter, "Bethany." She wants to keep three-year-old Bethany at home with her. When Bethany turns four, she plans on enrolling her in a neighborhood preschool which her other children attended.

Professionals and others might discourage these ideas, stating that Bethany *really* needs the help that's provided at the Special Ed Preschool. But underneath it all is another PRESUMPTION OF INCOMPETENCE: Linda, as well as the teachers at the neighborhood preschool, are PRESUMED INCOMPETENT to help Bethany because they have no professional expertise in developmental disabilities.

> TWO THINGS ARE TERRIBLE IN CHILDHOOD: HELPLESSNESS (BEING IN OTHER PEOPLE'S POWER) AND APPREHENSION— THAT SOMETHING IS BEING CONCEALED FROM US BECAUSE IT WAS TOO BAD TO BE TOLD.
> *Elizabeth Bowen*

This PRESUMPTION is unspoken, of course, for if a professional stated it out loud, it would provoke the anger and wrath of the person so described. In many situations, we don't even *use* this particular descriptor. Instead, we use the NOT-OK, NOT-READY, or DEVELOPMENTAL AGE concepts. Nevertheless, when we get down to the nitty-gritty, the PRESUMED INCOMPETENT mentality is pervasive and harmful, resulting in the continued devaluation, marginalization, exclusion, segregation, and isolation of children and adults with disabilities—not to mention the loss of opportunities!

The Disability Double Standard

The concepts described thus far all contribute to the creation of the DISABILITY DOUBLE STANDARD. It, too, is unspoken, but its existence is visible in the lives of children and adults with disabilities in a variety of settings.

The DISABILITY DOUBLE STANDARD reflects that we have one set of rules for people *without* disabilities, and another set for people *with* disabilities:

How *did* my grandchild fail preschool?

- Parents of babies with disabilities who receive EI Services are expected to have goals for their babies. But in the REAL WORLD, parents of babies without disabilities are not. Most just hope their babies are happy. But "having a happy baby" would not be an "appropriate goal" according to EI Services.

- The majority of parents who have three-year-old children *without* disabilities would never put their children on a school bus for a 30-minute ride to a preschool across town. But somehow it's considered "normal" to put three- and four-year-old children with disabilities (some of whom may be very vulnerable because they don't yet have mobility or communication) on a school bus for a half-hour ride across town to the Special Ed Preschool. In addition, many parents of children *without* disabilities expend a great deal of effort to investigate child care centers in order to find the one that's best. But parents of children with disabilities are not expected to do the same with Special Ed Preschools. Often, there's not a choice to begin with—so there's nothing to compare. Even when there's only one option, however, few parents check out the preschool before sending their children. Why do we presume it's a good place for our kids? Just because Someone-in-Authority says so? And then there's the whole issue of children with disabilities who are "retained" in Special Ed Preschools. *How does a child fail preschool?* How many children who *don't* have disabilities fail preschool? (More about this in Chapter 8.)

- Preschool-aged children with disabilities are often excluded from age-appropriate Sunday School classes and other typical activities because they're still wearing diapers. Do these same churches and other entities exclude middle-aged and older *adults* who *don't* have disabilities who need to wear *Depends?*

- Children and adults with disabilities who need an assistive technology device often have to "prove" they can use it before they're allowed to have it. Yet children and adults who *don't* have disabilities routinely buy things before *they* know how to use them. How many people buy PDAs and other devices before they know how to use them?

- Before they're "given permission" and "allowed" to move into their own places, many adults with developmental disabilities in group homes must meet goals like: "makes up bed within 20 minutes of getting up;" "washes dishes within 30 minutes of eating;" "balances checkbook;" and many more. Yet the Service Providers who write these goals admit that they don't always meet these "goals" *in their own lives.* Under what authority can they impose standards on others which they don't meet themselves? When I moved out of my parents' home, I didn't meet such goals, but no one prevented me from getting on with my life (and the same is true for most of us)!

In the REAL WORLD, people *without* disabilities go to a dance whether they know how to dance; buy things they don't know how to use; spend money they don't have; strike out on their own whether they've mastered "adult skills" or not; get married, buy a house, and have kids before they're ready; and engage in a variety of other activities and growth-oriented experiences without a Seal of Approval from Someone-in-Authority.

We put children and adults with disabilities in a no-win position: we hold them to higher standards while simultaneously having lower expectations for them. The simplest, most equitable, and most respectful way to put an end to the DISABILITY DOUBLE STANDARD is for us to adopt this maxim:

If it's not right for people *without* disabilities,

it's not right for people *with* disabilities.

Quality of Life

If you haven't heard this phrase used about your child, you probably will at some point. QUALITY OF LIFE is a big part of today's CONVENTIONAL WISDOM, and it's used as one of the justifications for many of the Services provided to our children. This concept may also be applied to a person who has had a serious illness or injury: if family members and/or doctors don't believe the person will have a "good" QUALITY OF LIFE, the decision is made to "pull the plug."

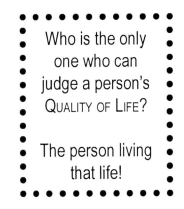

Who is the only one who can judge a person's QUALITY OF LIFE?

The person living that life!

In society's collective mind, QUALITY OF LIFE equals a "normal life." This generally means a person can walk, talk, see, hear, feed himself, wipe his bottom, etc. And many in our society seem to believe *only* a "normal life" (whatever that means) is worth living. More frightening is the idea lurking behind this mentality that only those who *can* lead a "normal life" *should* be allowed to live. The idea that a good QUALITY OF LIFE is dependent on a person having "normal" functional skills is another concept that's so ingrained we seldom question it.

But Ed Roberts (you met him in Chapter 2) and others with disabilities have challenged this old way of thinking. They showed that QUALITY OF LIFE has *nothing* to do with functional skills, and *everything* to do with being in control of your life by *making decisions* about your life. Ed needed someone to dress him, feed him, and more, yet he had an extraordinary and wonderful QUALITY OF LIFE: he was successfully employed, had married and fathered a child, taught the Independent Living philosophy around the globe, was honored with a MacArthur Genius Award, and did so much more. In many ways, Ed lived a fuller life than many people who *do not* have disabilities!

Ed readily admitted in radio and television interviews that many people looked at him and thought *(and sometimes said),* "I'd rather be dead than be like that." Again, this attitude reflects the belief that you can only live a "normal life" if you have a "normal body." But this gross ignorance can be remedied when our children, and others with developmental disabilities, are out and about in society, participating in typical community activities, and living REAL LIVES. When my son, Benjamin, was the Wizard of Oz on stage, when he played T-ball and took karate lessons, and when our family goes to the movies, to restaurants, and other places, Benjamin's presence helps others see and think about people with disabilities differently. The same is true about your child.

There's another component of the QUALITY OF LIFE paradigm we need to consider. When we and/or professionals talk about our children's QUALITY OF LIFE, what we may actually be describing is "quality/quantity of care or services." And I embraced this mentality when Benjamin was very young and I wanted more therapy for him, believing this would make him have a better life. (I was also still under the delusion that Benjamin had to walk to have a good life. It wasn't until I met Ed Roberts, Tom Tyree, and others who used power wheelchairs *and* had great lives that this mentality was finally erased from my brain.)

But as I found out (and maybe you have, too) the Services that are supposed to help can actually have a harmful and negative impact—on the child, individually, because of all the negative unspoken messages, and on the child and the family when the schedule of Services runs everyone's life, and the family's *real* QUALITY OF LIFE declines. I hope we'll be more careful with the words we use and the meanings we attach to those words.

When people talk to us about our children's QUALITY OF LIFE, we need to remind them that the only one who can define QUALITY OF LIFE is the person living that life! And, ultimately, the way to ensure a child has a good QUALITY OF LIFE is to ensure he lives a REAL LIFE!

> THERE ARE PEOPLE, WHO THE MORE YOU DO FOR THEM, THE LESS THEY WILL DO FOR THEMSELVES.
>
> *Jane Austen*

The Entitlement Mentality

At some point, once our children begin to receive Services—Early Intervention, Special Ed Preschool, or Special Ed Services in public school—many of us acquire the ENTITLEMENT MENTALITY. It usually happens this way: Someone-in-Authority informs us about the Rights or Services which our child/family is entitled to, *or* we find out on our own, through other parents, support groups, etc. From then on, some parents decide to actively pursue each and every Right, Benefit, Service, and/or Entitlement available—and then some.

There are several reasons why parents choose this route. Some believe MORE IS BETTER, as previously described, so why not go for the whole pie? Others, it seems, feel they're incompetent, and are ready to relinquish much of their parental responsibility to professionals, believing they know best. Some are too busy with other things—so they allow professionals to assume responsibility. And some may be very angry at the "cruel blow" that's been inflicted on them (having a child with a disability)—there's got to be a way to "make up for this" and/or they feel someone "owes them," so Services and Entitlements are viewed as a form of compensation. There may be as many reasons for going down this path as there are parents who choose this path.

Long ago, when I was just starting out as a public speaker and way before I wrote my first book, my husband was laid off and was unemployed for about a year. Our children were about seven and nine at the time. For the first time ever, and based on our low (zero) income, Benjamin was "qualified" to receive Supplemental Security Income (SSI) and Medicaid. It was the worst year of our lives. It wasn't awful because we were poor. It was awful because of the invasion of privacy, the loss of our family's autonomy, and the feelings of helplessness and incompetence generated by dependence on the government. At any time, social service workers or officials from Social Security could come into our home, examine our bank and other financial records, and ask all sorts of questions about our lives, our money or lack thereof, and more.

When I had a problem or needed to "check in" with the Social Services office in our county, I felt we were being judged. Because we had nice, but not expensive, clothes, I felt the Social Services people thought, "They don't look poor enough or pitiful enough to be receiving government help." I felt I had to watch how I spent "their money" lest I get in trouble: was it okay to buy a nice roast now and then or should I only buy the cheapest ground meat? It was like walking a tight rope. After my husband found another job, we were no longer "qualified," the SSI checks stopped coming, and the joy and relief I felt was equivalent to winning the lottery!

While our family's experience may or may not be typical, there are other common outcomes that are not anticipated and not pleasant. It doesn't take long to become dependent on the System, and I'm not just referring to being dependent on cash from the government (like when we receive SSI on our children's behalf). We can also become financially dependent—whether we know it or not—when our children receive "free therapy" (through Early Intervention), "free Special Ed Preschool," or other "free" Services.

Many parents acknowledge they're not totally happy with a segregated Special Ed Preschool for their children, but they rationalize the decision to keep their children there by saying, "It's free." And my response is twofold: "You get what you pay for," and "So what if it's free? Is this what's *best* for your child?" Embracing the ENTITLEMENT MENTALITY causes many of us to lose our common sense about what's really important for our children. If it's "free" and/or if it's "easy," we often do it, whether or not it's really what's best. And who, ultimately, pays the price for our decisions? Our children.

We can also become *emotionally* dependent on people who work in the Service System: therapists, doctors, service coordinators, educators, and a whole host of others. Because we are "entitled" to their help, we take it—accepting their opinions, following their recommendations, and/or doing what they tell us to do, even when we're uncomfortable and even if it's not what's best for our children and families. Many of us come to believe we're incompetent, that

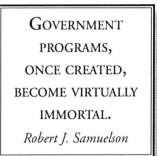

GOVERNMENT PROGRAMS, ONCE CREATED, BECOME VIRTUALLY IMMORTAL.
Robert J. Samuelson

A GOVERNMENT THAT IS BIG ENOUGH TO GIVE YOU ALL YOU WANT IS BIG ENOUGH TO TAKE IT ALL AWAY.
Barry Goldwater

I've met a number of parents who have either quit their jobs or not taken a promotion so the family income would be low enough for their children to quality for SSI/Medicaid. I understand the frame of mind that would lead to such a decision: "If this is the only way to get my child what he needs, I'll do it." But it's a short-sighted decision that can have very long-term negative outcomes. Once you're in the clutches of government assistance, it's very hard to get out. And, again, the System is not the best we can do for our children and families.

Why don't we explore getting a different job—one with good health insurance benefits? Articles on web sites and in magazines often detail a list of companies that are "good for families." These companies have generous benefits, including insurance, family leave provisions, and more. Shouldn't we be good role models for our children in this way, and use the System as a last resort, only after all other efforts have failed?

we're not the experts on our children, and that others surely know "best." And, again, our children pay the price.

One solution to move away from the ENTITLEMENT MENTALITY is to see the Service System as a *last resort,* instead of the *first choice.* I believe most parents want to do what's best for their children. And we're led to believe that the Service System *is* the way to go. We are, it seems, too easily seduced by the promises, benefits, and other goodies offered to us by the Service System. Once we're told about the Services our children are entitled to, that's all many of us see. We're led to believe this is The Path—the only path. Many of us quickly realize the promises are false, and the benefits are of questionable value, but it can be hard to extricate ourselves from the System. Moreover, if *parents* embrace the ENTITLEMENT MENTALITY, odds are the children will, too, and they'll grow up to be dependent on the System.

There is a way out, however! As I'll describe in Chapters 6 and 7, we can find much of what our children and families need in our very own communities. If we look there, first, we'll ensure our children lead REAL LIVES, included in their communities. In addition, when Services are cut (and they always are, at one time or another), we won't run around like Chicken Little, thinking the sky is falling. The natural supports and generic services we've identified in our communities can sustain us. More importantly, this will help our children grow into self-reliant, successful adults who have important connections and supports in the community. Many parents are worried about what will happen to their children after they're gone—leaving our sons and daughters in the hands of the Service System isn't a comforting thought. When your child is connected to his community, you can set many of your worries aside.

Having said all this, I have great empathy for families whose children are dependent on SSI, Medicaid, and/or similar Services—been there, done that. For a variety of reasons, some families may not be able to "get off" SSI in the near future. With waivers, many children do not receive SSI, but do receive Medicaid. This is very helpful—lifesaving, in some instances. But these Services come with rules and regulations which may be intrusive and downright ridiculous. So we may be relieved (and even grateful) that our children have these benefits, but we may also chafe at all the rules and regulations, and hate where we are! If you're in this position, I hope you'll examine other options (see box on facing page)—and there are always other options if we look hard enough.

Insurance/Medicaid is a huge concern, of course. There is still a great deal of discrimination in the insurance industry (but insurance executives call it "good underwriting practices"), so that people who are self-employed (like my husband and me), or those who are not covered for health insurance by their employers, cannot find an individual health insurance policy that will include children with disabilities, because they have pre-existing conditions. But many states offer individual insurance policies for the "uninsurable." So, for now, my husband and I have an individual health insurance policy for the two of us, and Benjamin is on a separate policy through the "uninsurable" health insurance agency. And, yes, we pay for it ourselves.

We are, however, always on the look-out for other options: one of us going to work for a company with good benefits, joining an organization ("for the self-employed" or something similar) which might enable us to be covered by a group policy, and/or other options. Under Federal law, people with pre-existing conditions (like our children) cannot be excluded from a *group* health insurance policy. It's not perfect, however: there can be a time-limited (6-12 months) exclusion on coverage for the *condition*, but the person is covered for everything else. For example, if we were able to get group health insurance that covered Benjamin, anything related to Benjamin having cerebral palsy could be excluded for six months. After that, anything related to his condition *would* be covered (within the limits of the policy).

"I Have to Follow the Law"

Many parents know that states are mandated by law to provide specific Services, but some also believe this mandate *requires* them to use these Services! More parents than I can count, in states all across the country, have said to me, "I thought I *had* to send my child to the Special Ed Preschool. *I thought I had to FOLLOW THE LAW.*"

Yes, laws *do* mandate that specific Services and/or programs be offered, but we, as parents, are not mandated to accept them. *It's our choice:* we can say "yes," "no," and/or "yes" to some and "no" to others! I have a big bone to pick with professionals who do not make this abundantly clear to parents. When parents tell me they believed they *had* to enroll their children in Early Intervention or Special Ed Preschool Services, I ask, "Did the professionals tell you these were an *option?*" The answer has always been "no," and this makes my blood boil! Professionals *know* these Services are optional, but many don't act like it. Are they *intentionally* keeping parents ignorant of the facts?

At a time when many parents are confused, vulnerable, and/or looking for answers, "helpful" professionals swoop down with "solutions" (Services). It is, of course, their *job* to provide this help to parents, and most may believe their Service or Program *is* "what's best" for the child and/or family—and this creates many dilemmas.

First, many professionals are heavily invested in the overall MEDICAL MODEL ("cure/fix/treat" the child's disability), so they may believe the Services they offer (which are usually based on the MEDICAL MODEL) are "the only" way to go. Thus, they may not be very likely to present these Services as an *option.* Many professionals do not or will not see the inherent dangers of Services which may (1) send NOT-OK messages to children, (2) segregate children, and (3) lead to the dependence of families.

The following mentality seems pervasive: "As a professional, I'm going to do what's best for your child, and if you're a good parent, you'll do what's best for your child, and what's best are the Services I provide (or recommend)." Many parents have been made to feel guilty if they didn't follow the experts' advice in this area. And when we feel guilty in regards to our children, many of us are easily led around by the nose!

> THOSE WHO KNOW THE LEAST OBEY THE BEST.
> *George Farquhar*

THOSE WHO MAKE
SOME OTHER
PERSON
THEIR JOB
ARE DANGEROUS.

Dorothy Sayers

Many conferences about children with disabilities include workshops about "Transition from Early Intervention to Early Special Education" or "Transition from High School to Adult Services." It's apparently a foregone conclusion that the *only* path for children with disabilities is the Ladder of Services (and this book disputes that notion). Our children get "promoted" from one level of Services to the next. Is this the best we can do for our kids? Is this what will help ensure their success? Will this help them lead REAL LIVES? It hasn't so far, has it?

Second, when professionals believe their Services are the "best," they may not believe the child will be in "good hands" anywhere else. For example, if a parent indicates she wants to enroll her child in a typical neighborhood preschool or try alternatives to traditional therapies (PT, OT, etc.), professionals may discourage these plans. They probably don't outright torpedo the parent's ideas. Instead, using subtle persuasion, they describe how the Special Ed Preschool has "so much to offer" in the way of Services and professional expertise—and it's all free! Or professionals may invoke the "guilt trip," as in, "We don't know what might happen [something bad] if your child doesn't continue with_____."

A professional may go so far as to describe how much better everyone's life will be if the child attends the segregated Special Ed Preschool: little Mary will get all help she needs and Mom will finally get some rest when Mary is out of her hair! How many of us could refuse such an offer? Sounds too good to be true, doesn't it—and it probably is.

Third, some professionals *may* be aware of the dangers of dependence and segregation that are often part and parcel of Special Services, but they may not be aware of any other options. Why would they? To some degree, they "live" in DISABILITY WORLD, too. For example, a physical therapist may not see that the whole family going swimming on a regular basis could be just as valuable as providing "water therapy" to the child with a disability. In this situation, the therapist would be a consultant instead of a "hands-on" provider, and she could help the family learn how to incorporate beneficial "therapeutic-like" activities during the family's weekly "swim day" (more about this in Chapter 6).

Fourth, in many professional quarters, *it is a foregone conclusion* that children with disabilities will enter the Service System and stay there forever. When my son was five, the school district psychologist returned from a meeting at a Service Provider agency in our area, then told me and another parent, "There's a very long waiting list for Adult Services, so you better get your children's names on the list immediately!" When we both said we had no plans for our children to use Adult Services (group homes, sheltered workshops, etc.) when they were grown, he was almost speechless: "What do you mean? If your children don't use Adult Services, what will they do?" We replied, "They'll go to college or trade school, and get a real job—just like our other children." He shook his head in amazement and said, "You're not being very realistic..."

Finally, our children are, in essence, commodities. I doubt if any professionals in the field—therapists, teachers, service providers, or anyone else—stand around the water cooler and discuss this, but the fact is that children and adults with disabilities are "cash cows." Yes, most of the Services they receive are funded by taxpayer dollars, and in that sense, they're considered "consumers" of Services (and taxpayer dollars). But these same Services employ hundreds of thousands of people *who would not have jobs* without children and adults with disabilities.

Think about it! If all of us said "no" to Early Intervention, Special Ed Preschools, therapies, Vocational Services, and more, these providers would be out of work! If they want to keep their jobs, they have to continue adding new "clients" to their "caseload." In some cases, this explains why children or adults are still labeled NOT-READY: if an agency "releases" too many people because they no longer need Services, the Powers-That-Be will cut the agency's budget, along with a few jobs! In all fairness, many professionals are overworked and have too many "clients," and would like nothing better than to have a smaller "caseload." Still, children and adults with disabilities are the raw material of the multi-billion dollar "disability business."

Far too many parents, for whatever reason, are influenced, coerced, and/or led to believe they must FOLLOW THE LAW (or the recommendations of the experts) or they will be "in trouble." Others feel they should be "grateful" for all the help their children are receiving, and to refuse Services and/or professional advice might make them seem ungrateful. Under Federal and state laws, professionals are supposed to tell us about the rights and entitlements guaranteed to children with disabilities and their families. And some do this better than others. In so doing, however, most seem to omit that parents can *choose* whether or not to accept Services. Shame on them!

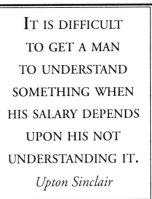

IT IS DIFFICULT TO GET A MAN TO UNDERSTAND SOMETHING WHEN HIS SALARY DEPENDS UPON HIS NOT UNDERSTANDING IT.
Upton Sinclair

It is, therefore, up to us to educate ourselves, and to share what we learn with other parents. And I see nothing wrong with letting professionals know when they can do better.

The "Worse Off" Hierarchy

In order to receive some Services, parents may behave in ways they might normally find repulsive. This generally occurs in the areas of Respite Care and/or Family Support programs (which provide cash and/or specific Services based on a family's needs).

Let's say in my home state of Colorado, there's funding to provide Respite Care Services for a certain number of families. And let's say I want Respite, and I know other families want it, too. But there's not enough money in the budget to provide it for everyone who wants it. In general, the criteria is based on "need." So what do I have to do to make sure that *my family* gets respite care?

That's right: I have to make my family look more needy by (1) making my son appear to be more "difficult" or "hard to care for" and/or (2) making my husband and myself look more "stressed out" or "incompetent." In other words, I have to make *my* child and family look "worse off" than others. *Gag!*

On any given day, our family might actually be in pretty good shape. But if I want to make sure we get Respite Care (just in case we might need it or because my friends have it and say it's great) and/or if I've embraced the ENTITLEMENT MENTALITY, I'm willing to paint a very different (and negative) picture of my son and my family! How can we live with ourselves when we do this?

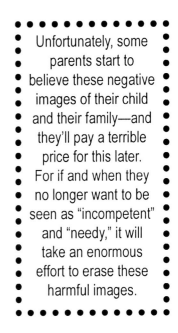

Unfortunately, some parents start to believe these negative images of their child and their family—and they'll pay a terrible price for this later. For if and when they no longer want to be seen as "incompetent" and "needy," it will take an enormous effort to erase these harmful images.

In some states, Respite and Family Support are considered one and the same. In other states, they're two different programs, with Family Support dollars paying for therapies which are not covered by insurance, home modifications, and/or other benefits. In any case, we still may play the WORSE OFF game to ensure we receive the Services we want.

Originally—decades ago—Respite was a service for families whose children were "at risk" of being institutionalized. It was believed these families needed extra help to ensure their children could remain at home. The general idea was that raising a child with a disability was extremely difficult, the parents couldn't do it all and/or were incompetent, the child was having a negative impact on the family as a whole, and more. Not a pretty picture, is it?

The solution was Respite: give the parents a break from the rigors of parenting this child, and odds were good that the child would not be institutionalized. So Respite Care could have been provided in different ways:

- A Respite Care Provider could come into the home to take care of the child with a disability while Mother spent time with the other children and/or did other important tasks needed by the family.

- A Respite Care Provider could come into the home and stay with the child while the family went out to a movie, took a vacation, etc.

- The child could be sent to facility (group home, for example) for a specified period of time (weekend, one week a month, etc.) while the family enjoyed some "peace and quiet" at home or on a vacation.

As time went by, and as a result of changes in laws, social policies, and attitudes, fewer and fewer children were "at risk" of being institutionalized. But there was *no corresponding decrease* in the need for Respite Care. The need actually *increased*, as the next generation of parents—whose children were not, for the most part, in danger of being institutionalized—insisted they also needed Respite Care Services. So today, most states have some form of Respite/Family Support. In some programs, parents are entitled to a specific number of Respite hours per year, offered by an "approved/certified" provider. In others, parents can choose a relative or friend to provide Respite, and this person receives payment from the state or agency. Look how far we've come: we can get government-funded baby-sitting at taxpayer expense!

All parents need a break from their kids at one time or another. Some need it more than others, for whatever reason. I know many parents whose children *do not* have disabilities who need more breaks than I ever did!

Why should the government be responsible for paying for this? What makes us think we need Respite when other people just need a baby-sitter? And what message does this send to our children? How would your child with a disability feel if you shared the following:

> My Darling Daughter, you and your disability make life so difficult for me and the rest of the family that we just can't deal with it! And our government leaders agree with us, so they've created this social policy—which parents have advocated for—that will use taxpayer dollars to pay for someone to come in to take care of you to give us a much-needed break.

Or maybe we would take this approach:

> My Darling Daughter, I am such an incompetent, overworked, stressed-out nincompoop, that I can't handle you without help. So

From:
The Arc's Q & A on Respite Care
www.thearc.org

'Respite' refers to short term, temporary care provided to people with disabilities in order that their families can take a break from the daily routine of caregiving...[it] may sometimes involve overnight care for an extended period of time.

One of the important purposes of respite is to give family members time and temporarily relieve the stress [of] providing extra care for a son or daughter with [a disability]. This, in turn, can help prevent abuse and neglect, and support family unity (US/GAO, September 1990). Respite care enables families to take vacations, or just a few hours of time off.

I've applied for Respite Care, and they agree that I'm in pretty bad shape, so they're sending someone to help.

If you think Respite Care is the greatest thing since sliced bread, you'd probably like to beat me over the head with this book, and I understand why! Respite Care is something many parents have worked very hard to get; we lobby our legislators to fund it; and we might even think we can't live without it. But what does it do to our children and our families?

Some families take a trip to Disneyland, and leave the child with a disability at home (or in another location) with a Respite Care Provider. The justification is that such a trip would not have been possible otherwise. Well, maybe that's true. But there are lots of families who, for a variety of reasons, will never get to take a vacation to Disneyland (or anywhere else) and there's no extra help provided to them. That's life in the big city! They deal with it, don't whine about it, and move on!

Is such a trip worth the potential negative outcomes?

- The child with a disability feels left out, devalued, ignored, hurt, and.... unloved. "But my child wouldn't have enjoyed Disneyland; it would have been too much stimulation and he doesn't like amusement rides," is the response. *It doesn't matter.* He still feels all those things; he's still left out of an important family activity.

- The other children in the family learn that the child with a disability is unimportant and his feelings don't matter. They might have a good time at Disneyland, but in the back of their minds they might also be wondering what would happen to *them* if, for some reason, they were "hard to deal with" like the child *who has been left behind.* They've also learned that people with disabilities don't deserve what others deserve.

- The other children in the family have learned that it's OK to abandon another family member if including them is not easy and/or convenient. So we, as parents, better be aware of this when we're older and need help. Our adult children will remember this lesson from their youth, and will feel no compunction about leaving us in the care of others instead of helping us themselves.

Where are our "family values" in these circumstances? Where is our loyalty to *all* our family members? Where is our belief in the importance of family togetherness—of working out our difficulties together, so we'll all be stronger, individually, and as a loving family, as a whole? Whatever happened to that tried and true maxim, "We'll sink or swim together."?

Some parents have said they don't feel their other children should have to "put up with the burdens" imposed by the child with the disability, so using Respite Care is one way to give their *other children* a "normal" life. But what about the child with a disability? *Doesn't he also deserve a "normal" life?*

These are some of *my* concerns about Respite Care. For many parents, the issues are more mundane, like some of the ridiculous rules and regulations. In some programs, for example, the Respite Care Provider can only take care

> IF YOU CANNOT TRUST YOUR FATHER AND MOTHER TO LOVE YOU AND ACCEPT YOU AND PROTECT YOU, THEN YOU ARE AN ORPHAN, ALTHOUGH YOUR PARENTS ARE UPSTAIRS ASLEEP IN THEIR BED.
>
> *Elizabeth Feuer*

of the child with a disability. So if a husband and wife want a night out, they have to separate their children! The child with a disability may have to go to the Respite Care Provider's home, while a baby-sitter comes into the family's home to take care of the other children (or vice-versa). Even under these harmful circumstances, many parents still embrace Respite Care. They don't like it, and they may recognize the harm, but they still do it.

Parents who are able to choose a relative or friend as the Respite Care provider seem to be the happiest with this Service. But I have reservations about this method. In the REAL WORLD, most parents don't pay Grandma or Aunt Sally or Best Friend Mary to baby-sit their children when they go out for an evening. Grandma or Aunt Sally does it for free because family members take care of one another! And Best Friend Mary does it because you take care of her kiddos when she and her hubby need a night out—that's called "friendship"! To me, it is revolting that something which is freely given in the REAL WORLD becomes a financial commodity in DISABILITY WORLD.

"But Respite Care is the only way I can get a break," some respond. No, it's not. We can get the help we need in more natural ways—ways that don't hurt our children, fracture our families, or cause other negative outcomes—when we look to the abundant supply of generic services and natural supports that exist in our communities (covered in Chapter 7).

Sibshops

If you're the parent of a very young child, you might not have heard about Sibshops (sibling support workshops/groups). If your child with a disability is older, you might be familiar with these, and your other children might be involved in one. Like many other components of CONVENTIONAL WISDOM, this is one with good intentions, but less than desirable outcomes.

On a variety of different web sites, Sibshops are described as fun-filled events that include games, activities, guest speakers, and more, geared to help children who have "siblings with special needs" deal with the issues they face and interact with others like themselves. In addition, it's noted that Sibshops are "not therapy, but their effects may be therapeutic" for some children. Sibshop literature details that siblings don't always get the attention they need, because their parents are too busy with the child with the disability. Evidently, Sibshops can help solve a problem which has been created by parents. I'm not crazy about that theory—what about you? The idea of Sibshops might sound good, but what's the message to our children with and without disabilities?

First, what shall we say to the brother or sister?

> Susan, your brother having a disability has caused lots of problems for you—and the same is true for lots of other kids who have a brother or sister with a disability. So this Sibshop group will help you deal with all these problems.

How might Susan translate this message? Here are some possibilities:
- "Gee, I didn't *know* I was so screwed up, but I guess I am..."; *or*

A SISTER & HER BROTHER

My husband and I have tried to raise Emily so that she loves and values her brother just the way he is. Yes, we were on the wrong path during the early years, but we learned from our mistakes and moved on.

When Benj needed more of our help or time than Emily, I tried to help Emily see the Big Picture: sometimes I needed help from her Dad, he needed my help, and we all need help—sometimes more, sometimes less. Life *isn't* always fair—or as my sister says, "The 'fair' comes to town once a year!" We've tried to keep things "even," in the sense that sometimes we *did* tell Benjamin, "I'll help you in a minute—right now I'm helping Emily."

When our children were very young, Emily once wistfully told me she wished she had CP, because then she could, "go to therapy and have fun." That was an eye-opening comment! I talked to her about what therapy really meant, that sometimes Benj wished he didn't have to go, and that it wasn't always fun. This seemed to help, but I also increased the level of fun for Emily and the whole family!

(cont. on next page)

- "So all the problems I have are all my brother's fault!"; *or*

- "We already have to do enough for him, and now Mom's making me do *this!* I *hate* him!"

Or, to make it more appealing to Susan, maybe it would be better to lie about it. We could tell her we're taking her to a fun activity, and hope she finds the Sibshop meeting so much fun and so helpful that she'll forgive the lie when she discovers the true purpose of the group. On the other hand, what do we tell the child with a disability?

> Honey, you and your disability have caused some problems for your sister. It's not really your fault—you didn't mean to do it, but she's really having to deal with some issues. So she'll go to these meetings with other kids who also have problems because they have a brother or sister with a disability, and this will really be helpful to her.

It's too painful to even consider how the child with a disability might interpret this message. But maybe, recognizing the danger of the message, we would lie to him, too, and tell him his sister has joined a new club of some sort. Then we can hope and pray he never finds out the truth.

Some of us *might* put the needs of our children with disabilities first, and this *can* create dilemmas for everyone in the family. But in my opinion, the solution is not Sibshops. Instead, we can change how we do things (and that's what this book is about) so our children *don't need Sibshops!*

Some parents argue that Sibshops are just like parent support groups, so what's the big deal? First, as parents, we make the conscious decision to attend a support group based on *our* needs. Children do not; we make the decision for them, based on our assumptions about their needs. Second, no one (I hope) *tells us* to go to a support group because we "have problems" related to our child having a disability. Again, the same is not true for our children.

In addition, many parent support groups start out with the best laid plans: to provide support. But some degenerate into glorified "pity parties," where parents whine and complain about how awful things are. At this point, some parents leave the group, while others stay. Those who stay may get quite a pay-off from attending such meetings: they validate the "ain't it awful" belief. These parents may, in turn, project this attitude onto their other children, and believe *they* need a place to complain and whine. If so, they're setting their children up for "victim status"—a sometimes life-long condition that leads to misery.

According to the literature, Sibshops are facilitated by social workers, special education professionals, psychologists, and other experts, as well as "adult siblings of people with special needs." Personally, I would not want to expose my daughter, Emily, to the influence of others—people who don't share the same attitudes and perceptions we have about disability. Wouldn't this send a confusing—and potentially harmful—message to her?

I'm sure many children who attend Sibshop meetings have fun, learn new things, and have the opportunity to share their feelings and experiences. But

(cont. from previous page)

When the kids were older, Emily once *sarcastically* said she wished she had CP, but this time her reason was different: "Cause then I wouldn't have do to all these chores." Once again, we talked: Benjamin had chores to do, but they were different from Emily's. I explained that all of us were expected to do what we could, and then described that I'm good at some things, so I do them, and there are things her Daddy does better, so he does those things, and so forth.

Emily sees Benjamin as "her brother," period. Yes, he has a disability, but he's more *like* other "younger brothers" than different: sometimes she feels he's a pain in the butt and other times he's her greatest admirer!

Benj unintentionally helps Emily know more about new acquaintances: she can tell a lot about them by how they react to her brother. What a wonderful gift!

A child's relationship with, a brother/sister with a disability will reflect the attitudes and actions of the parents. Our children will model our behavior and attitudes.

at what cost to them, their brother or sister with a disability, and the family as a whole? If the brothers and sisters of children with a disabilities are having "problems," it's not because they have a family member with a disability. It is, instead, because we've followed CONVENTIONAL WISDOM, and this may have created uneven lives for everyone in the family. We can change this. We can work to build a balance in the family so our children who do not have disabilities have no need of such groups.

Telethons, Walkathons, Special Sports, Etc.

While these activities are not part of the Service System, they're part of DISABILITY WORLD, and many include some of the worst components of the MEDICAL MODEL (NOT-OK, NOT-READY, and PRESUMED INCOMPETENT mentalities, and more). In addition, they may also reinforce prejudice.

Many parents—as well as many adults with developmental disabilities and others—recognize the danger of disability-related telethons: pity is used as the motivator to encourage donations from the viewing audience. These events may raise money for research for a "cure" or "prevention," or to provide help or treatments, but most also perpetuate negative stereotypes and attitudes. As previously mentioned, the unspoken message of "cure/prevention" is, "We don't want people like that in the world."

So every time a disability-related telethon airs, the general public gets another large dose of pity: "Those poor, poor things...they need our help (but not our respect or equal treatment or equal opportunity). Aren't we lucky we're not like that..." which, in turn, reinforces and even expands the devaluation and marginalization of children and adults with disabilities.

Walkathons and similar activities are usually billed as fundraisers. I know parents who enthusiastically lend their support to these events, and they feel these are positive, energetic, wonderful activities. I have no doubt that the people *attending* have a great time. But the more important outcome we should consider is the *public's perception*. If the fundraising is for research for a cure or prevention, or for treatments to make the person "normal," the same negative perceptions generated by telethons may be the outcome.

Some events focus on increasing awareness, promoting inclusion, or some other goal. But, again, let's look at the outcome *in the eyes of the public*. For example, what unspoken message does the public receive if the event is about having a "buddy"? Could the public interpret the message to mean that "those kids" are "so pitiful" that no one will be friends with them, and this event is necessary to help them find a friend? The event may raise a ton of money, and everyone may have a delightful time, but if—in the end—it perpetuates less-than-positive images, does the good outweigh the bad? (And I'm not trying to pick on any one event/organization—there are many that need to be changed—this is just one of the more visible examples.)

If we want to have a fun party to celebrate our children, we can do so without press coverage. If we want to increase an organization's budget, we can go after foundation or grant money, privately, instead of vying for the public's

---

CORPORATE SUPPORT?

The Wal-Mart TV ad in support of the Buddy Walk bothers me. It shows parents and their children with Down syndrome, along with Wal-Mart employees, having fun at a Buddy Walk. One mom, who seems close to tears, says something like, "They [Wal-Mart employees] *like* our kids..."

Here's the thing: it's easy for a corporate sponsor (or anyone else for that matter) to support *anything* when it involves *children.* But just how genuine is Wal-Mart's support? Does the store "like" *adults* with Down syndrome? Does the store hire them, or others with disabilities, and not just as a "greeter"?

Why don't we ask any corporate supporters to do what's *really important:* like hire people with disabilities in REAL JOBS, make their stores accessible, donate money to support *inclusive* community activities and schools, and so much more?

"pity dollars." And if we want to demonstrate that children and adults with disabilities are "regular people" who ought to be included, we should consider that an event built around the disability defeats the very purpose of the activity, and can perpetuate negative attitudes. From the public's perception, "those people" must *not* be "regular people" if we have to have an event to prove it!

We can demonstrate that children and adults with disabilities are "regular people" who can and should be included by ensuring our children participate in inclusive activities—their *presence* can send more positive messages and destroy more stereotypes than any "special event" can. We're not doing our children any favors by supporting events that have the potential to perpetuate pity and reinforce old attitudes. Our children will have to live with these outcomes long after we're gone. Is this the legacy we wish to leave our sons and daughters?

Special Sports teams for children and adults with disabilities—Special Olympics, Challenger Baseball, Miracle League, and others—also perpetuate negative images. Have you heard as many derisive jokes about Special Olympics and similar activities as I have?

In organized activities which pair a child/adult with a disability with a "helper" who does *not* have a disability, the person with the disability is automatically PRESUMED INCOMPETENT, as well as needy and unable. What does *that* feel like? Yes, our children may sometimes need lots of help. But why don't we ensure they're in activities where they're not PRESUMED INCOMPETENT?

Let's think about this for a moment. What if the Park and Rec department in my town announced that it was creating a softball league for 50-something women who are out of shape and have no talent for the game (like me), but the game will be modified so every player will be successful: (1) each unathletic older woman will be paired with a helper who is in better physical shape; (2) other people will be recruited as cheerleaders and huggers, so every player will get lots of attention, regardless of their ability to play the game; and (3) every player will win a ribbon, and the woman who receives 23rd place will feel like a "winner," even though she knows she actually came in last.

How many women would sign up? Few, if any. Why? In the REAL WORLD, most of us gravitate to activities in which we have an interest and for which we have *some* ability or talent. But in DISABILITY WORLD, it's OK to put people in situations they would otherwise never choose to participate in.

"But my child *loves* his Special Sports team," you might be thinking. I'm sure he does. If you've only been given vanilla ice cream, you probably think vanilla is the best and you love it! But if you've been given a choice of vanilla, chocolate, or strawberry ice cream, you might decide vanilla's *not* your favorite. Once again, we can learn from adults with developmental disabilities. Many who were once involved in Special Sports, but have since moved on, have said, "You know what I learned from special sports teams? That everybody wins! But in real life, everybody *doesn't* win!" Many gained a false perspective of how the world really works, which they later had to painfully unlearn.

In addition to Special Sports, there are summer camps and other activities that are *only* for children with disabilities. And, yes, these might be fun for our

---

CHANGING ATTITUDES OR REINFORCING STEREOTYPES?

The stated purpose of many "special" events is to change attitudes—but do they?

The 2003 Special Olympics (SO) Annual Report (from its web site) states: "We...recognize [SO] for what it has evolved into: the single most powerful vehicle for changing attitudes, promoting acceptance and overcoming prejudice and ignorance of every kind." *What?*

The SO web site also includes data from SO's 2003 international study of attitudes about people with cognitive disabilities. The results were dismal, showing that "...stereotypical views [are] the greatest barriers to better quality of life" for people with cognitive disabilities. The study noted that attitudes were better among people without disabilities *who were S.O. volunteers.*

SO's solution to change attitudes? "...Expand the SO experience to new generations of athletes and volunteers..."

I don't get it! In my opinion, the growth of SO and similar activities have

(cont. on next page)

children. But every time we enroll our children in such activities, we've passed up opportunities for our children to be included in typical community activities; we reinforce that segregated settings are OK for people with disabilities; and DISABILITY WORLD continues.

Many parents moan that they will not even *attempt* to enroll their children in typical activities "until the community is ready." But the community *is* ready, and our children *are* ready. If the activities in your area are not yet inclusive, it's probably because no one has asked them to make the change and/or no one has helped them learn how to do it. The directors of many Park and Rec departments think they don't *need* to offer inclusive activities because Special Sports teams handle "those people"—and they may also think we don't *want* our children to attend "regular" activities.

Some parents recognize the dangers of special, segregated activities, but they justify their actions by saying, "This is the *only way* my child can be involved in sports." But there are plenty of children with disabilities who *do* participate in inclusive sports activities in their communities. In some cases, these children are the *first* to do so, because their parents spent time and energy in positive ways, (1) helping coaches and/or others understand the importance of inclusion and (2) teaching others how to provide accommodations or supports.

In some cases, these accommodations *do* include a "change in the rules" to enable the child with a disability to play on a more-or-less equal footing as players who don't have disabilities. Unlike the changes made in Special Sports, however, such changes aren't made for the purpose of allowing the child with a disability "to win." Isn't it important for our children to learn about winning *and* losing, as well as the risks, benefits, struggles, and opportunities inherent in team sports, just like other players?

Having said all this, I do not believe children with disabilities should be pushed into organized sports ("regular" or "special") under the guise that all children "deserve the chance" to play team sports. We need to *listen to our children!* Some children are *not interested* in sports. Parents who push their children into these activities often do so because they're important to the *parents,* not the child! In addition, we probably wouldn't want our children to participate on a sports team that is "driven to win" at all costs. Many parents recognize that such teams aren't the best for *any* children. There are, instead, softball, soccer, and other typical sports teams that are led by rational coaches who focus on teamwork and skill development, and who ensure all players—not just those on the "first string"—get to play. If such teams don't exist in your community, start one—there are other parents and children who will join you! My friend, Mark Ohrenberg, heads an inclusive recreation project at the University of Missouri/Kansas City; visit www.moaccessrec.com to learn more.

Your child might prefer to participate in an art or drama class, or take ballet or karate lessons. Let's find out what's available in our communities so we can offer our children a variety of options. We can help create inclusive communities when we *make the choice* to ensure our children and our families are included. In Chapter 7, you'll learn more about how to make this happen.

(cont. from previous page)

probably generated *more* negative attitudes, not *less*, sending the message that "those people" belong only in segregated activities. Derisive jokes about SO abound! But SO thinks the solution is to *expand* its programs since *volunteers* have better attitudes than the general public!

What might happen if SO used its *$88 million* (2003 revenues) to *educate communities on inclusive recreation*, instead of spending it on segregated sports? Ditto similar organizations.

I believe "special" events of any kind, which focus on the disability, *reinforce existing negative attitudes.* Real change in attitudes will come when people with disabilities are included in their communities. The sheer *presence* of one person with a disability in an ordinary setting—which demonstrates *similarities* between those with and without disabilities—can change more attitudes than all the public relations generated by "special" events that focus on the disability.

And so...

As parents of children with disabilities, we entered Disability World without even knowing it. Once there, we were indoctrinated in some of the components of Conventional Wisdom covered in this chapter. In the process, many of us adopted the medical, therapeutic, and educational jargon of professionals; learned everything about the latest therapies and interventions; and assumed the responsibility, many times in partnership with professionals, to make our children's bodies or brains "better" through a variety of means. We truly have done the best we knew to do, based on what we knew at the time.

But during all of the hours and days spent working on our children's bodies and brains, we might not have paid enough attention to their precious hearts and minds. In too many cases, we've been unaware of, or inattentive to, our children's feelings about *what was being done to them and how it made them feel about themselves.* In Disability World, "benevolent services" often result in unintended negative consequences.

When physicians prescribe treatments, when therapists and others provide Services, and when educators teach our children in segregated settings, do any of them *tell us* there might be unintended negative consequences? Perhaps we should back up and ask, "Are they even *aware* of potential unintended negative consequences? If so, do they care?"

Several years ago, after doing a presentation for a Service Provider agency in New Hampshire, Roy Gerstenberger, the caring, innovative director of the agency, wrote an article about this situation, based in part on what he learned from my presentation. In the article, Roy noted that when we receive a prescription from a doctor, we're also told about the side effects. In the excerpt below, he describes why this is important, and relates it to disability Services:

> We know that this information is valuable: it allows us to learn about unintended consequences and about other options. Then we're able to choose which option is the most tolerable. And, once we choose a remedy or a procedure, we know how to ameliorate the known side effects... Maybe we haven't done this in the human service industry because there hasn't been legal action to force the disclosure of side effects or other options. However, I like to believe it won't take legal action to force people in the human service industry to do things that are helpful to others. At the same time, it does seem that—to the extent that such disclosures tend to weaken the image of the professional as confident and powerful—there might be a natural tendency to avoid the disclosure of side effects and the presentation of other options...To use John McKnight's words, this would represent the removal of the "magic cloak" of therapeutic help. The human service professional will resist it. Disclosure will also be resisted by those who are convinced *there is value in being a consumer* of the human service industry product; they will make no request for disclosure of side effects or other options. Parents like Kathie are not among them...

THE NONPROFIT SERVICE SECTOR HAS NEVER BEEN RICHER (IN TERMS OF SHARE OF THE GROSS NATIONAL PRODUCT AND JOBS), MORE POWERFUL, OR LESS ACCOUNTABLE. IT IS THE ONLY SIGNIFICANT POWER BLOC THAT IS ESSENTIALLY UNREGULATED, IN SPITE OF THE FACT THAT MOST OF ITS MONEY COMES FROM THE GOVERNMENT, THROUGH EITHER DIRECT SERVICE CONTRACTS OR TAX EXPENDITURES... TAXPAYERS FOOT THE BILL. POOR PEOPLE SUFFER THE CONSEQUENCES.

Theresa Funiciello

> RESTLESSNESS
> AND DISCONTENT
> ARE THE FIRST
> NECESSITIES
> OF PROGRESS.
> *Thomas Edison*

Like Roy, I'm hopeful people in the Service System will embrace the idea of "disclosure," but also like Roy, I feel many in the System may resist it. *We,* however, can remove the "magic cloak" that covers *our eyes* and see things as they really are. Then we can make choices that will ensure the protection and nourishment of our children's hearts and minds. I hope we can begin to view the System as a last resort, and not our first choice.

Not all Services are horrible; some are better than others, and positive change *is* happening in pockets here and there. Some Early Intervention agencies are moving away from "direct services" to a "coaching model," in which parents are "in charge," and the focus is on more natural methods of help, in inclusive, natural environments. Inclusive education is becoming a reality for more children. And people like my friend Cary Griffin are showing that not only can adults with disabilities be successfully employed, they can become self-employed business owners!

In addition, there are some extraordinarily wonderful PTs, OTs, and other therapists, Special Ed Preschool teachers, Special Ed teachers, Regular Ed teachers, Service Coordinators, and others, who believe children with disabilities are children, first, and they do their best to ensure children feel great about themselves and lead REAL LIVES. There are also some professionals who probably shouldn't be in this field at all, and there are a whole bunch in between these two extremes.

After reading this chapter, if you're feeling frustration at me, because I've criticized a Service you like, that's all right. Keep reading, anyway. Wait to Email me until you've finished the whole book, OK? On the other hand, if you're feeling frustration at yourself or someone in the System because you think some "bad things" have happened to your child, I have one thing to say: learn from it, let it go, and move forward. As I said before, each of us (including me) has done the best we knew to do at the time! So don't spend one more moment feeling angry, guilty, or sad. Don't waste your valuable time on this—there's too much "good" that needs your attention! And your child's life is not ruined—I promise! My son, Benjamin, has survived all my mistakes; your child is resilient, too!

> IF ONE ADVANCES
> CONFIDENTLY IN
> THE DIRECTION
> OF HIS DREAMS,
> AND ENDEAVORS
> TO LIVE THE
> LIFE WHICH HE
> HAS IMAGINED,
> HE WILL MEET
> WITH A SUCCESS
> UNEXPECTED IN
> COMMON HOURS.
> *Henry David Thoreau*

As Benjamin has grown into a wonderful, self-confident young man, I've realized that his decision to resign from his therapy career at age six, and our decision to not let his disability run his life, were the right decisions—they protected his heart and mind and enabled him to lead a REAL LIFE. Benjamin believes in himself and his future; he's proud of who he is; he's very aware that he has a disability and he also knows he's perfect just the way he is. By the time you finish this book, I hope you realize that your child is perfect, and that the well-being of her heart and mind are far more important than the functional abilities of her body or brain.

I am ever hopeful. Changes in my own attitudes and actions altered my son's and my family's life for the better. I've watched as similar changes have occurred in other families. Awesome outcomes are within our power when we adopt new attitudes and actions—and that's where we'll go next.

New Attitudes and Actions

5

The extraordinary American philosopher and psychologist William James said: "The greatest discovery of my generation is that human beings can alter their lives by altering their attitudes of mind."

Yes, you can alter your own life, and the lives of your child and other family members by altering *your attitude!* Are you ready to change things for the better? Then let's begin: it all starts with an attitude adjustment!

Grab a pen or pencil (and a piece of paper or your journal if this is a library or loaner book) and:

◆ Print your child's name:

(in BIG letters—first name or nickname)_____

◆ List four things your child loves to do:

1. _____
2. _____
3. _____
4. _____

> EACH ONE SEES
> WHAT HE CARRIES
> IN HIS HEART.
> *Johann von Goethe*

◆ List three of your child's favorite foods:

1. _____
2. _____
3. _____

◆ List two of your child's most-loved possessions:

1. _____
2. _____

◆ List one thing your child does really well:

1. _____

This is who your wonderful, precious child really is!

Your child is not his/her disability. He/she is not a Down's kid...a CP kid...LD...autistic...PDD...hyperactive...ADD...retarded...ADHD...Rett's...FAS...high- or low-functioning...ten, but functions like a five-year-old...slow...non-verbal...wheelchair-bound...confined to a wheelchair...ventilator dependent...tube fed...or anything else.

Your child is a unique person with many strengths, abilities, talents, gifts, hopes, and dreams, and your child is perfect, just the way he is.

Too many of us have only seen our children through the lens of a disability diagnosis. One mother transformed herself in an instant. You can, too.

During one of my presentations several years ago, a parent in the audience (Kim) didn't agree with everything I said. I never take this personally—I know my message can be shocking and everyone has his or her own opinions! Afterward, Kim and I talked privately, and she shared her concerns: my ideas might work for my son and others, but *her* daughter, Lisa, had autism, so my strategies didn't apply. (I hear this frequently from parents of kids with autism.)

I replied that I didn't think it mattered what *type* of disability a person had; what mattered more was what attitudes and actions we adopted in response to having a child with a disability. I asked Kim when her daughter was diagnosed. "When she was two," Kim answered. And then I posed the *Big Question*, "Kim, on the day after Lisa was diagnosed, was she any different than the day before?" Kim shook her head "no." "You're right," I agreed. "So who *was* different?"

"...it was me.
***I* was the one**
who was different!"

Kim's eyes widened for a moment. She took in a deep breath and said, "Oh, my gosh—it was me. *I* was the one who was different! Oh, Kathie! I can't believe this! Ever since that day, every time I looked at Lisa I saw the word 'autism' branded on her forehead—*and that's the way I've been treating her!*" And then Kim burst into tears. We hugged, and when Kim dried her eyes, she proudly announced, "Kathie, I'm taking the word 'autism' out of my vocabulary. From this point on, my daughter is *Lisa* and her life is going to be different." And it was. Kim stayed in touch, and sent the following Email:

You challenged my thinking, and when this happens, I'm uncomfortable. I need to look inward and find out why. I am humble enough to know change is good. When Lisa was diagnosed at two, I believed my "normal" daughter died. I literally grieved for her. If only someone had said the things you said when Lisa was a baby, it wouldn't have taken me a decade to get back the daughter that was there all along. Since learning from your message, I look in Lisa's eyes and presume competence. We highlighted her hair this weekend. She loves it. In the past, I overlooked typical activities and did them only for her sister. I'm going to enroll Lisa in a Red Cross babysitting class. I'm now treating her like a 14-year-old and she responds! The best part? I'm seeing her for who *she really is*. I always thought I had done that, but the A-word was always in the way. I threw it out the window, and will not use it in my home. A mountain is off my shoulders.

And that mountain can be lifted from *your* shoulders when you see your child for who *he* really is. Lisa's *life* changed when her mother's *attitudes and actions changed.* Lisa still has autism, but she no longer lives the life of "a child with autism." She's living the life of her dreams, and *the same can be true for your child.*

Like Kim, myself, and millions of other parents, you've been told your child has a disability. But—

What *Is* a Disability?

As you learned in the previous chapter, the MEDICAL MODEL is the current social construct of disability in the minds of many. This paradigm of disability reigns within the Service System (including Special Education). If we *deconstruct* disability, we'll see that it can mean many different things.

A Medical Diagnosis and a Passport to Services

First and foremost, a disability is a medical diagnosis that becomes a Passport to Services—that's all! Contrary to what you may have been told, a medical diagnosis is not a valid predictor of your child's potential or future, and we cannot allow others to use a child's label to squash his hopes and dreams!

The diagnosis should never be used to determine *where your child spends his time* at school, in the community, or in any other setting. Nor should it be used as the primary factor in determining what *Services, therapies, or interventions* your child might need. Instead, only your child's *individual, unique, and specific needs* should be considered.

When my son, Benjamin, was diagnosed with cerebral palsy (CP) at the tender age of four months, the physician prescribed physical therapy (PT) and occupational therapy (OT). At the time, I didn't question this—what did I know about it? As time passed, however, I began to do a lot of wondering. What were the therapies supposed to accomplish? (I never got very good answers from anyone.) Why did the doctor prescribe something without telling me more about it? Why didn't the doctor ask *if we wanted it?* Were there other options? If so, why weren't those discussed? I didn't know to ask the doctor all these questions at the time; I just did a lot of thinking, later.

After some time had passed, I met other parents. Through conversations with them, I realized PT and OT were the routine prescriptions for children with CP, just as Ritalin is a routine prescription for children with ADD, OT is routinely prescribed for children with Down syndrome, and so forth.

This is the norm in a doctor's office: prescribe treatments or interventions based on the *diagnosis.* This works fine with strep throat: the antibiotic kills the strep germs. But it doesn't work for diagnoses of developmental disabilities! And as you learned in the previous chapter, the MEDICAL MODEL influences the educational arena. So when children with disabilities begin receiving Special Ed Services, educators may imitate doctors: deciding "treatment"—where a child should be "placed" and/or what Services he needs—based on the *diagnosis,* not on his actual needs. Are all children with Down syndrome alike? Are all children with ADHD alike? Are all children who have the same medical diagnosis—whatever it is—alike? No, they're all different!

Let's go back to the strep throat example from the previous chapter for a moment. If two people visit a doctor because they both have sore throats, the physician (we hope) would run some tests and talk to the patients before deciding these two people *need the same treatment because they have the same condition—a sore throat.* After the physician's investigation, he discovers one patient has strep throat, but the other has sinus drainage—so the same treatment is not appropriate!

The way the disability affects a child, the level of disability, the child's individual personality, what's important to the child and family, and many other factors should all be considered before deciding what medical or educational Services, treatments, or interventions are needed. Every decision should be based your child's *individual needs,* not the diagnosis.

Think about the Services, therapies, and interventions your child is receiving (or has received), in the medical and educational arenas, and circle your answers to the following questions:

- Did anyone ask you and your child (depending on her age) about what's really important for your child's life and success?   Yes   No
- Were your child's *unique and specific needs* discussed?   Yes   No
- Were a variety of options discussed?   Yes   No
- Were you told specifically *why* the Services/therapies were recommended, as well as *what* they're supposed to accomplish, and *by when*?   Yes   No
- Are/were the Services, therapies, and/or interventions *designed* to meet your child's *specific needs?*   Yes   No

stands for
individual!
Your child is
a unique
individual
like no one else!

Think about these issues, and think some more about Roy Gerstenberger's comments at the end of the previous chapter. Talk with your child and other family members about these issues. Then, in your journal (or on a separate sheet of paper), list (1) your recollections of how and why the Services, treatments, and interventions for your child came about and (2) how you'd like things to be different. Continue reading this book to learn about alternatives to the traditional ways we've been doing things. Then go back to your list of how you want things to be different and make any revisions. When you're ready, make plans for you and your child (depending on her age) to talk to your child's doctor, therapists, educators, and others about the changes you'd like to make.

Now, back to the issue of disability being a medical diagnosis. In polite society, a medical diagnosis is considered private, personal information. Most of us have one diagnosis or another at any given moment in time, and we keep this information to ourselves, discussing it only with a very few people we can trust. *But the same is not true for our children!* This is another manifestation of the DISABILITY DOUBLE STANDARD, described in Chapter 4: we frequently share our children's medical diagnoses with every Tom, Dick, and Harry, under the misguided notion that people need to know! *Wrong!*

Here's a question for you if you're a married woman: when you attend a parent group meeting, a Sunday School class, or a family gathering, would you announce, "My husband started taking Viagra last week." I hope your answer is no! And why *wouldn't* you announce this? Because it's *private,* and you wouldn't violate your husband's privacy or his trust in you. But think *how many* people you've told about your child's diagnosis. And think *who* you've told: your hairstylist, neighbors, other parents, and probably even strangers in the grocery store! (Been there, done that myself, at one time...)

It doesn't matter *why* you've done this ("To explain about my child's be-havior," "Because someone asked," "So people would know what my child needed," and more....), *your child doesn't want you to do this anymore!* Just like your husband wouldn't want you telling everyone he takes the magic pill!

The lives of children with disabilities *are not for public consumption!* We've been led to believe otherwise, since our children's diagnoses are hot topics among those who provide Services. (This is another way we've been brainwashed. So don't beat yourself up about this—you did what you were taught to do, but now you can do things differently.)

No one has a "right" to know personal information about your child and his diagnosis. Yes, in *some* instances, *some* people may need to know *some* specific things about your child, and this will be detailed later in this chapter and in Chapter 7. For now, however, eliminate the DISABILITY DOUBLE STANDARD: if *you* don't tell everyone your own diagnosis or your husband's personal information, *do not reveal private, personal information about your child.*

In addition, knowing that you *will* need to discuss certain things about your child with others, anticipate what details you'll need to share, keep them to a minimum and on a "need to know" basis, and then ask your child's per-mission before talking about him to others. *Yes, ask his permission!* (I asked my son's permission before sharing his personal information with you). When you *do* need to talk about your child, *do so with the greatest respect and dignity.* He deserves no less than that!

Disability: A Natural Part of the Human Experience

You learned this in Chapter 2, but it's so important, I want you to look at it again. The Federal Developmental Disabilities Act states, in part:

> Disability is a natural part of the human experience that does not diminish the right of individuals with developmental disabilities to enjoy the opportunity to live independently, enjoy self-determination, make choices, contribute to society, and experience full integration and inclusion in the economic, political, social, cultural, and educational mainstream of American society.

Read it again, especially the first nine words. They helped me see things in a totally different way—I hope they have the same effect on you! (You can tell how important these words are to me: they inspired the title of this book!)

There have *always* been people with disabilities in the world and there *always will be.* One of every five Americans is a person with a disability. People with disabilities make up the largest minority group in the United States, and it's the only group that *anyone can join at any time*—like in the split second of birth, in an accident, or through an illness. And it's the most *inclusive* minority

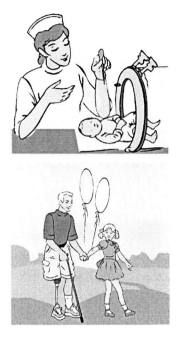

group: disability does not discriminate! People of both genders, and from any age group, ethnic background, socioeconomic level, religious faith, and sexual orientation may experience disability. And the incidence of disability is on the increase, because of advances in medical technology. Not too many years ago, premature babies often died shortly after birth. Today, they survive, but may have disabilities. Once upon a time, many children and adults died from accidental injuries or serious illnesses; today they live, but may have disabilities. And many of us will live to a ripe old age, but with some type of disability. Contrary to CONVENTIONAL WISDOM, *it's as natural or normal to <u>have</u> a disability as it is to <u>not</u> have one.*

Your child's condition is as natural a part of life as teenagers getting pimples, women going through menopause, men going bald, and many, many other experiences common to us all. As I hope you've figured out from previous chapters, it's not your child's diagnosis that's created difficulties in his life, it's how he's been perceived—*and treated*—by others. Yes, you may think he's had difficulties because of something his body cannot do—like walk, talk, etc.—but as you'll learn in the next chapter, when our children have the tools and accommodations they need, functional limitations are no longer barriers to success!

Can you get your arms around the idea that disability is natural? If so, you'll start seeing your child and her condition in a different, better light, and this will lead to many more positive outcomes!

One of Many Human Characteristics

Like gender, ethnicity, religion, age, and other traits, a disability is simply one of many different characteristics of being human. "Joe" is a 42-year-old man, with dark brown hair and hazel eyes. His ancestors have Austrian, Polish, and Spanish roots. He works as an electrician, attends services at the nearby synagogue several times a month, is a self-described "rabid" college basketball fan, and is the married father of three children. One of Joe's knees gets stiff and painful, and he wears a compression bandage and takes prescription medicine for this condition. He considers himself an "easy-going" guy. Joe cannot be defined by any one of these characteristics. The same is true for all of us.

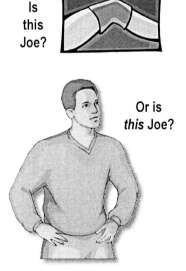

Is this Joe?

Or is *this* Joe?

Unfortunately, a developmental disability *is* often seen as *the single defining characteristic* of many children and adults who have been labeled. This is certainly a consequence of today's CONVENTIONAL WISDOM (because of the influence of the MEDICAL MODEL) and the DISABILITY DOUBLE STANDARD. While Joe's stiff knee is seen as a condition related to the bones and cartilage in his leg, a developmental disability is seen as a condition *of the person as a whole.* Few *choose* to see beyond the diagnosis—even those who are supposed to be helping our children.

But we share some of the responsibility. Many of us have followed the lead of physicians, therapists, Special Ed professionals, and others: *we* have seen—and frequently *publicized*—our child's diagnosis as the defining characteristic. You might not *think* you do this, but how often is your child's diagnosis one of the first words out of your mouth when you talk about your child?

We can minimize and maybe even eliminate this terrible injustice by changing our own language and behavior, and encouraging others to do the same. And the first step is easy: go back to the first page of this chapter and read what you wrote about your child. Do you see his diagnosis anywhere on that page? It's not there, is it? If you describe your child using *these* characteristics, *you'll* see him differently, *others* will see him differently, and most importantly, *he'll* see himself differently!

A Body Part That Works Differently

If disability is a natural part of life, is there anything "wrong" with you if you have a disability? I say no; I hope you agree. But we use that word—"wrong"—over and over and over again when talking about our children. How many times have we heard or said something like, "We knew there was something *wrong* when our baby didn't [roll over, make eye contact, or whatever]." And, doctors, educators, and/or others may ask us, "When did you first notice something was *wrong?*"

This is another antiquated attitude from the past that's still living and breathing throughout our society today, and because it's so deeply ingrained we seldom question it. Worse, it's a concept children pick up from their parents at a very young age, as I'll describe.

From the time of his diagnosis as a baby, I never thought there was anything "wrong" with Benjamin—that word was not part of my thought processes or my language. (I did other bad things that you're going to hear about, though.)

When Benj started using a pediatric walker at 18 months of age, we were stared at wherever we went—at the mall, the movies, the grocery store, and many other places. Adults and older children pretended they weren't staring—you know, when they act like they're looking at something else, but their eyeballs are about to slide out of the sides of their eye sockets?

But younger children—with their unfettered curiosity—took one look at Benjamin, came right up to *me* (they didn't speak to Benjamin—the Presumption of Incompetence mentality is ingrained in children very early) and asked, "What's wrong with him?" (Where did these four-, five-, and six-year-olds learn to think and talk like this? See how pervasive this attitude is?)

My reply was always, "*There's nothing wrong with him;* he has cerebral palsy." At the time, I didn't realize how important that response was *to my son*. What if I had left the first part out, and the interchange was this:

> *Child:* What's wrong with him?
>
> *Me:* He has cerebral palsy.

What would my son have learned? Read it again if the answer doesn't come immediately—bingo! My son would have thought I believed there *was* something wrong with him, and worse, I would have been blabbing it to perfect strangers! But this story isn't over yet.

I was proud of myself for not using the word "wrong" about my son. But my response didn't really work, because the curious children didn't know what I

was talking about. They couldn't say "cerebral palsy," much less understand what it was. They *really* wanted to know why Benjamin used the walker. So I came up with a "spiel for children." I had one for adults—you probably do, too—a one or two sentence reply that I could whip out without thinking to answer nosy questions. Here's how the interchange went with my new answer:

Child: What's wrong with him?

Me: There's nothing wrong with him; he has cerebral palsy. His legs don't work as good as yours, and the walker helps him walk.

This answer worked. The children seemed to understand, and after taking another good look at Benjamin, they scampered off. It seems like a pretty good answer, doesn't it? I thought so, and I was pretty proud of myself. I gave this response dozens of times over the next 18 months (until Benjamin was three)—to all the different children who approached us.

About this time, I participated in the Texas Partners in Policymaking leadership development program, which I described in the first chapter. I was learning all kinds of great information from the presenters, as well as from the adults with developmental disabilities who were my classmates. Perhaps because I was in the company of these new friends and was learning so much from them, my brain was moving in a new and different direction—a clearer direction.

So the next time I gave my "spiel" to another little inquiring mind, *I really heard myself for the first time:* "There's nothing wrong with him; he has cerebral palsy. His legs don't work *as good as yours,* and the walker helps him walk."

What had Benjamin heard me say for more than a year? That he wasn't "as good" as other kids! Do you think he separates his legs from who he is as a person—are his legs some strange appendage that are not part of him? I was horrified! Here I was (I thought): a caring mother who works diligently to make sure no one hurts her child, and yet who was my son's worst enemy? *Me!*

I knew I had to change, immediately. I went through all the notes from my Partners classes, and found the answer. I don't know who said it—it was part of pages and pages of notes I had scrawled in my almost illegible handwriting: *a disability is a body part that works differently.* It rang true for me and it seemed like an accurate descriptor. (I hope you feel the same way.) The first thing I did was apologize to my son for saying things the wrong way. Then I told him what I'd be saying in the future:

There's nothing wrong with him; he has cerebral palsy. His legs *work differently* than yours and the walker helps him walk.

At the time, Benjamin had just started talking, but when he was in his walker, every ounce of concentration was focused on walking—he literally couldn't walk and talk at the same time. But not long after, he *could* walk and talk at the same time, and then he started speaking for himself.

Using this new paradigm of disability, how will you change the way you and/or your child describe his condition? A child with Down syndrome (or other cognitive disability) "learns differently." A child with autism "communicates

—*PATIENCE!*—

Years ago, I realized we need to be a little patient with others. We have the benefit of personal experience with disability—others don't. I had never seen a child using a walker before my son started using one! So if Benjamin hadn't been my son, I probably would have stared at him, too—not with prejudice or cruelty, but with curiosity. So let's not take everything too, too personally!

differently" and/or "learns differently." Think about the body part that's affected and describe it as "working differently" or something similar. In the space below (or in your journal), write your new descriptor:

_____

_____

Remember, if anyone asks something like, "What's wrong with her," always respond, "There's nothing wrong with her; she has _____ and she _____ differently," or something similar. Please, please, *please*, take the word "wrong" out of your vocabulary as it relates to your child—and tell everyone in your family to do the same! As soon as possible, your child needs to speak for herself! You won't always be around—*you do know that, don't you?* The sooner your child can speak for herself—whether it's with her voice or an alternative method—the better. (Later in this chapter, I'll share other strategies on how to deal with uncomfortable situations.)

A Consequence of the Environment

In many respects, what we call a disability is more a consequence of *social and physical environments* than what a person's body or brain can or cannot do. As I've mentioned before, the "problem" of disability is not within the person, it's in societal attitudes, and our attitudes shape the world we live in.

First, societal attitudes can create environmental barriers. For example, a store owner says people who uses wheelchairs don't/won't shop at his business, so he sees no need to make his business wheelchair-accessible (despite the ADA which prohibits discrimination based on disability). What the store owner fails to recognize is the *reason* he has no customers who use wheelchairs is because *they can't get in the front door!*

If the store was accessible, people who walked and those who used wheelchairs would enjoy equal access. But the lack of accessibility is an environmental barrier (generated by the store owner's attitude) for those who use wheelchairs or other mobility devices.

When my son, Benjamin, wheels into our kitchen; gets a bag of microwave popcorn from the modified (accessible) pantry; tears the wrapper off with his teeth; sticks the popcorn sack in the easy-to-use microwave and pushes the over-sized "popcorn" button; and then pours the yummy, fluffy kernels into a bowl with a handle that's sitting on the lowered counter top; he does not have a disability! Yes, he has cerebral palsy, *but he does not have a disability in that environment—there are no barriers to his success.*

The same could be true for countless others, including your child: if she has the tools (assistive technology devices or other equipment) and the modifications, supports, and/or accommodations she needs to accomplish what she wants to do, she doesn't have a disability! She still has a medical diagnosis, but she does not have a disability in that environment.

This concept is extremely important when it comes to our children's education. Many students with disabilities are not allowed to attend Regular

When Benjamin was four, our family went out to dinner with another family that included two young children who were also playmates of our children. The younger of the two, Brittany, was five. As we left the restaurant, she walked next to Benjamin (who was using his walker), and asked, "Benjamin, why can't you walk?" Without breaking stride, he indignantly replied, "I *AM* walking!" And I think he *really* wanted to say, "I *am* walking, *stupid!*" but he knew better than to talk like that!

FROM
PLATO NOT PROZAC!
BY LOU MARINOFF:

In 1987, the American Psychiatric Association voted in attention deficit hyperactivity disorder (ADHD) as a mental illness—science by ballot. In that year, 500,000 American children were diagnosed with ADHD. [By] 1996, it was estimated that *5.2 million children—* 10 percent of American schoolchildren—were diagnosed with ADHD. The "cure" for this "epidemic" is Ritalin...this is good for the drug business; not so good for the children. There is not one shred of medical evidence that ADHD is caused by any specific brain disease, but that is the claim that justifies pronouncing millions of American schoolchildren mentally ill, drugging them by coercion, and recording these "diagnoses" of "mental illness" on their permanent records...The pharmaceutical industry and the psychiatrists who prescribe their drugs are committed to identifying as many "mental illnesses" as they possibly can. Why? For the usual reasons: power and profit.

Ed classrooms because they're not "at grade level," can't talk, or are not able to perform some other functional skill—so they're segregated in Special Ed classrooms. But these students could be very successful in a Regular Ed classroom if we *changed the environment,* by modifying the curriculum; providing assistive technology, supports, or accommodations; and so forth. The barriers to success faced by many children are not caused by their medical diagnoses, but by the inaccessible and unfriendly environments of public school classrooms.

There's another important consideration about disability being a consequence of the environment. From birth, many children *without* disabilities have learned just fine, thank you, in their own homes, at day care, or in other typical environments. *They learned in ways that were best for them!* But at some point after entering public school, the *unspoken* message of a teacher was: "You don't *learn* like I *teach,* so you can't be in my class anymore." The actual *spoken* message may be something like, "Jeremy can't seem to settle down and concentrate," "Chloe isn't reading at grade level," "Tim's behavior is too disruptive," "I think Serena should be tested for..." or some other justification for *referring a child to Special Ed Services.* (This is a convenient method Regular Ed teachers use to remove children who don't "fit" in their classrooms.) At this point, the child is tested; found to be "deficient" in some way; labeled with a sensory integration disorder (SID), a learning disability (LD), attention deficit disorder (ADD, ADHD), or some other alphabet soup mix. The student is then either pulled out of the Regular Ed class for help in the Special Ed Resource class or is placed full-time in a segregated Special Ed classroom.

These are, in my opinion, *"environmentally-induced"* disabilities! In general, these conditions are not diagnosed until a child enters public school. In addition, many children have these conditions *only when they're in public school!* Are these "true" disabilities? It depends on which social construct of disability we use. The soccer coach doesn't think Jeremy has a disability, but the teacher at school does. *It's all about the environment!*

Federal Special Ed law (discussed in Chapter 9) mandates schools to provide assistive technology, supports, curriculum modifications, and other accommodations to enable a student with a disability to be involved in and make progress in the general curriculum. But few Regular Ed classroom teachers do any of these things. Some throw up their hands and say they weren't "trained" to teach children with disabilities *(but we weren't either, were we?),* others say there's not enough time, and still others are resistant to moving out of their comfort zones because of personal feelings, teacher union issues, or something else.

These types of diagnoses, and the ensuing Special Ed Services, can put students at great risk. "Luis" was a 10-year-old whose world was turned upside-down by the LD label.

Luis had always been a happy, well-adjusted son, who did well in school, according to his mother, "Mariana." But a couple of months into the fifth grade, Mariana was informed by the school that Luis should be tested, because he was having difficulty with core subjects. With concern for her son and gratitude to the educators for their offer of help, Mariana agreed to the Special

Ed assessments. After, educators told her Luis had a learning disability, but not to worry, the Special Ed teachers knew just what to do. (This was the IEP meeting, but Mariana didn't know it. No one explained the process to her, including her right to help write goals for Luis, as a member of the IEP Team. She remembers signing papers, but didn't know what it all meant until things went sour and she learned about the Special Ed process from other parents. How many other parents has *this* happened to?)

A week after the IEP meeting, Luis was suspended from school. It all started the first day Luis began receiving the "extra help" promised by educators. Mariana had no idea Luis would be *pulled out* of his fifth-grade classroom, nor did Luis. His mom told him what *she* had been told: Luis would get the help he needed.

On that first day—a Monday—the Special Ed teacher arrived in the classroom after lunch, during one of Luis' favorite subjects. He didn't know who this strange woman was, but his teacher told him he should go with the stranger. When Luis and his brother arrived home that afternoon, he couldn't hold back the tears of shame and frustration. "She took me to the *retard* room!" he cried out. "I don't belong there!"

Mariana didn't know what he was talking about; she didn't know that's what the students called the Special Ed room. She assured Luis she would straighten everything out; she thought a mistake had been made and a simple visit to the school would put things right. She was told, however, that the Special Ed room was the *only place* Luis could receive the "special help" he needed, and the Special Ed teacher said Luis would "get used to" his daily visits to her classroom. Mariana told Luis this information, believing with all her heart that the Special Ed teacher and others were kind people who had her son's best interests at heart. She did not know, however, what this experience was like for Luis, and when she told me this story, she cried softly, wishing she had been aware of what was really happening.

As it turned out, Mariana received a phone call from the school on Friday afternoon—the fifth day of Luis receiving "special help"—and was told her son had been suspended for "aggressive behavior." By the time she got both sides of the story—from educators and Luis—she felt sad, guilty, and angry. Evidently, when the Special Ed teacher went to get Luis each day, he resisted a little more. By Friday, things had escalated to the point that the Special Ed teacher had to forcefully take Luis by the arm to get him down the hallway into her room. On that day, Luis had enough; he pulled away from the teacher, and when she tried to take hold of his arm again, he pushed her arm aside and tried to get away. The teacher attempted to "restrain him" in a bear hug, and Luis again tried to get away. Another teacher joined the commotion, and the two adults "took control" of Luis and deposited him in the Principal's office. For Luis, this was a relief—better to be in the Principal's office than in the hated "retard" room. And that's when the call was made to Mariana.

I can't tell you how this sad story ends. Mariana was considering a variety of options: homeschooling Luis and his brother for the foreseeable future; looking for a private school; or keeping them home for the remainder of the school year, anticipating a move to a different city. What she *did* know, however, was that Luis was *traumatized* by the entire event: getting a label, being pulled out of the classroom, and being manhandled by an overbearing Special Ed teacher. No one at school was sensitive to what Luis was feeling. Mariana wished she had known what was really happening, but Luis was afraid to tell her. He never wanted to go back to that school, nor did his younger brother, and Mariana felt she could never again trust anyone at that school.

Contrary to the educators' beliefs, Luis *could have* received the help he needed in the classroom. If more of us (parents and educators) would try to see things through the eyes of the child, many difficulties could be avoided, and we wouldn't put a child's heart and mind at risk.

So be aware of "environmentally-induced" disabilities—those conditions which are usually "apparent" only within a public school classroom. And also be aware that many children, like Luis, aren't "identified" by educators until the upper grades in elementary school. Why? Because many kindergarten through third grade classrooms are very different than higher grades. The daily environment in primary classrooms might include children learning at "centers," where they can make choices about what activities to do; lots of movement and/or hands-on activities; and so forth. Contrast that environment with a fourth- or fifth-grade classroom in which students are expected to sit quietly at their desks, moving very little, and a teacher stands at the front of the room and lectures. Because many children *do* learn better through movement, by doing activities, and so forth, everything's okey-dokey in the earlier grades. But these same children are the ones who may be labeled in the upper grades, simply because sitting at a desk and listening *is not how they learn best!*

We don't need to change children or adults with disabilities; we need to change the environment. And there are an infinite number of ways we can adapt, transform, and/or remodel the environment—we're limited only by our imaginations. But *will we* work to change the environment? Or will we continue to insist that we need to *change the person?*

Disability as Social Oppression

In his book, *The Politics of Disablement*, author Michael Oliver notes that in Western societies, a disability is seen as a PERSONAL TRAGEDY. Pity and sorrow are outcomes of this perception:

- A doctor says, "I'm sorry to have to tell you that your child has_____."
- After informing others of their child's diagnosis, parents hear family members, friends, and even strangers say, "How sad..." or "I'm so sorry..."
- Disability organizations frequently use pity-laden fundraising approaches and words like "the tragedy of birth defects."

Another outcome of the PERSONAL TRAGEDY paradigm is a focus on the person—if it's a "personal" tragedy, the problem is obviously in the person,

---

DID LUIS *REALLY* HAVE A DISABILITY?

ONLY IN SCHOOL.

Have you noticed that many children with ADD, for example, do not have any difficulty "staying on task" when they're doing something they love—like playing a computer game? If a child learns best by using a computer, why can't he be provided with a computer that's loaded with fun and interesting academic programs, in the Regular Ed classroom, instead of being pulled out of class and taken to the Special Ed room for "special help"?

right? Many Providers in the Service System may not use the words "PERSONAL TRAGEDY," but they embrace this concept since they try to "improve" the person. And much of CONVENTIONAL WISDOM—the NOT-OK, PRESUMED INCOMPETENT, and other mindsets—are consequences of the PERSONAL TRAGEDY paradigm.

Oliver notes, however, that the concept of disability actually represents SOCIAL OPPRESSION, and comparisons with other groups of people provide valuable examples. We once looked at some people in our society and said, "You can't ride in the front of the bus, or drink out of that water fountain, or have that job because of the color of your skin." The problem was seen as being *within the person* because of his skin color. The Civil Rights Movement taught us that the problem was never in the person; the real problem was in society—the SOCIAL OPPRESSION of people of color. As a result of the Civil Rights Movement, attitudes, language, social policies, and laws have changed (although we still have a long way to go).

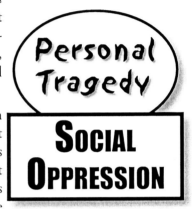

We once looked at another group of people—half the population, in fact—and said, "You can't have certain jobs, behave in a certain ways, or expect to be treated like an equal, because of your gender." The problem was seen as being within the person, because she was female. The Women's Movement helped us learn that the problem was never in the person; the real problem was in the SOCIAL OPPRESSION of women. While no law was passed as a result of the Women's Movement (it was defeated, unfortunately), attitudes, language, and social policies changed (and we still have a ways to go there, too).

Oliver notes the same is true about people with disabilities. We see the problem as being *in the person*—because he can't walk, talk, see, hear, behave, read a book, wipe his own bottom like others, etc.—so we focus on changing *him.* But just as the problem was not a person's skin color or gender, the problem is not disability—it's the SOCIAL OPPRESSION of people with disabilities.

Is this SOCIAL OPPRESSION obvious to you? Societal attitudes identify the "problem" as being in the person; this results in *social policies* that focus on changing/fixing the person, through Special Services (therapies, rehabilitation, etc.); we make people "go to the Services," which results in their segregation. Then circular logic sets in: if people *need* to be in those Special Places, they're obviously NOT-READY and/or NOT-OK to be in general society, because the problem is within them—and we're back to where we started.

When you think about SOCIAL OPPRESSION and your child, recognize that the difficulties he's faced, including social isolation, physical segregation, and other issues, are not a *direct result* of his medical diagnosis. Instead, they're the result of the oppression brought on by societal attitudes about disability. And, unfortunately, the attitudes of parents may contribute to this state of affairs, if we promote the beliefs that our children are INCOMPETENT, NOT-OK, NOT READY, and so forth.

People of color and women didn't need to change; society needed to change—and it did. People with disabilities don't need to change; society needs to change—and it can and will. The first rung on the ladder of change is attitudes—starting with our own!

We're in the midst of the Disability Rights Movement, and as detailed in Chapter 2, laws passed since the early 1970s now guarantee equal rights and prohibit discrimination based on disability. But progress in the disability arena—as compared to the Civil Rights and Women's Movements—seems painfully slow. This snail's pace of change is probably the result of many factors, but to my mind, one of the more significant factors is the continued absence of children and adults with disabilities, and their families, in the movement toward inclusion and full citizenship. It's almost like someone scheduled the Disability Rights Movement, and no one came!

Yes, there are disability-related groups who work to change laws and social policies, by trying to influence Congress and our state legislators. I'm glad they do what they do—and I write letters to *my* elected officials. But it seems little effort is directed toward promoting inclusion and participation in our communities—the places where we live, where our children are growing up! I don't know whether this is a result of apathy, reticence, fear, or something else, but sometimes it seems that there's not enough of us who want change to happen—or perhaps not enough of us are *willing to work* to make it happen.

Inclusion
Participation
Responsibility

COMMUNITY

Belonging
Activities
Friends
Fun

I'm old enough to have lived through the Civil Rights and Women's Movements: they were not easy. Just because laws and policies changed, people of color and women were not automatically welcomed and included into all domains of American life. There were struggles and setbacks, but those who wanted to change the landscape of our nation kept the faith and kept trying (and they continue to do so). They knew they couldn't depend only on laws and social policies to effect change. The dreams of inclusion and participation became realities because people made the effort to become personally involved in their communities.

We need to do the same. We can change our own attitudes and actions, and get ourselves and our children involved in our communities, our schools, and other places. Our children's presence in inclusive settings can influence change in others' attitudes and actions—faster and more effectively—than anything else.

Do you think it was scary and lonely to be the first person of color employed at a particular company? Ditto the first woman in a new environment? It probably was—but those courageous, determined people dismantled attitudinal and environmental barriers, and paved the way for others. We can do the same.

I'm issuing a call to arms to all children with disabilities and their families, and all adults with disabilities: get into your community to create positive change! In the process, you'll help deconstruct disability, eliminate SOCIAL OPPRESSION, and create inclusive communities where everyone belongs!

The Power of Language

The words we use about people with disabilities; the meanings we attach to those words; and where, how, and when we use those words can have a profound effect on the people being described. It's time we more fully understand, and take responsibility for, the power of language.

As I mentioned in the first chapter, participants in the Partners in Policymaking training program I attended were required to complete a project of their own choice within six months of graduation. I chose to write and distribute an article about the importance of People First Language (PFL). During the Partners training, we learned a little bit about People First Language—how it was "created" by individuals with developmental disabilities during the People First or Self-Advocacy Movement way back in the 1970s, when individuals with disabilities (primarily cognitive disabilities, at the time) said, "We can speak for ourselves, and we are not our disabilities! We are people, first."

I chose to write about People First Language because I felt it was vitally important. At first, it was very personal: I didn't like the words used about my three-year-old son. I didn't see him as "handicapped," "crippled," "lame," "a spastic," "a CP kid," or anything else! He was a precious little boy, and those descriptors made him into something else. But I also didn't like the pejorative and hurtful words used to describe individuals with disabilities, in general. And I was often saddened by the words parents used about their children and dismayed by the words some adults used about themselves.

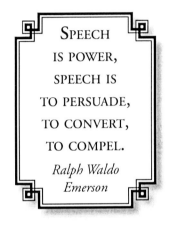

SPEECH IS POWER, SPEECH IS TO PERSUADE, TO CONVERT, TO COMPEL.
Ralph Waldo Emerson

At the time I wasn't aware of any specific research about the importance of language. Even though I had grown up hearing "handicapped" and other descriptors, I had never thought much about these words. But I learned a great deal from the adults with disabilities in my Partners class about how they felt about the words used about them. The way people with disabilities were described just seemed wrong to me—morally and ethically wrong.

As I mentioned in Chapter 1, the Partners coordinator asked me to return to Texas to give a presentation on PFL to the next class of Partners. That led to my becoming a public speaker, and then, later, an author.

In March 2001, the first edition of this book was published. In December of that year, our family was spending the Christmas holidays in San Antonio with my mom, step-dad, and older brother, Steve. During this visit, my brother brought up the subject of General Semantics (GS). I told him I didn't know what he was talking about. *"What?"* he asked incredulously. "That's what part of your book is about—that's when you *do* in your presentation about People First Language! I thought you must have studied GS and applied it to what you do! I can't believe you didn't know about it!" I responded with a confused look on my face, so my brother launched into a mini-lecture about General Semantics and told me about books on the subject, which I later lapped up with enthusiasm.

My study of GS helped me understand that the *feelings* I had about the dangers of Disability World language were valid. There *are* very good reasons—based on research, not just feelings—why we should change our language and attitudes. I'm sorry I didn't have this information to include in the first edition of this book, and am delighted to share it in this edition.

While parts of General Semantics can be very deep and require a great deal of thought and discussion, GS is, to me, simply a study of how our *use* of language *creates* the world we live in. We can learn much by applying lessons from General Semantics to our own lives: the attitudes we have and the actions we take *based on the words we use.*

One of the primary principles of GS is: "The word is not the thing." In other words, the *word* "apple" is not the *actual* apple: you cannot eat the *word* "apple." It is a *symbol* for a thing that is a certain shape, has a certain color, tastes of a particular flavor, comes from a particular type of tree, and so forth. And, of course, there are many different types of apples, aren't there?

None of us would *try* to eat the *word* "apple" because we *know* the word is not the thing. But with other words or descriptors, we often engage in "primitive" thinking in which we *do* confuse the word with the thing. In *Telling It Like It Isn't: Language Misuse and Malpractice/What We Can Do About It*, author J. Dan Rothwell writes about this confusion:

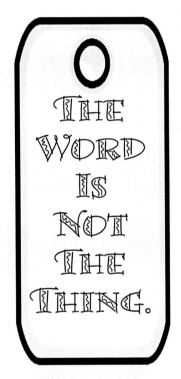

> ...despite our linguistic sophistication, much of our language usage reveals a striking ignorance of this fundamental characteristic of language...The meaning of a word resides in a person's head, not in the word itself...

Rothwell says the meaning of a word is determined by *how* it's used, as in this example: "He felt a tear in his eye and a tear in his pants." He adds:

> Unless we become aware that people determine the meaning of words...we will fall prey to the illusion that meaning is intrinsic to the word itself and assume meaning is immutable... Korzybski [the creator of General Semantics]...was correct when he said..."Whenever we describe, we distort." When we classify by placing a person, event, phenomenon, and so forth, into a category, we have not identified the substance of reality. Classifications reveal our view of the world, our perception of what reality seems to be, not what exists in nature... In such a case, the word assumes an existence of its own... The word becomes a thing unto itself.

The practice of confusing the word with the thing is "reification," and Rothwell writes:

> One of the most serious consequences of reification is the dehumanizing negative evaluations we attach to people when they have been plastered with a damning label. Because we have slapped a label on them, we assume we have identified the essence of this person semantically branded... Thomas Merton (1948) coined the term "self-fulfilling prophecy" which has become the focus of numerous studies.

Rothwell described several of these studies, including one which involved a third grade teacher who was helping her students learn about the "consequences of discrimination and prejudice." He writes:

> ...she abruptly announced to her class one day that brown-eyed people were more intelligent and better people than blue-eyed people. Blue-eyed children were labeled *inferior* and brown-eyed children were accorded the privileges of the "ruling class" befitting their label.

The results of her statement were devastating, as the children with blue eyes (who were in the majority) revealed feelings of sadness and hopelessness, and the children with brown eyes felt powerful and successful.

The teacher then "reversed the process to show the arbitrariness of prejudice," (blue-eyed students were said to be better than brown-eyed students). And the self-fulfilling process was again manifested, as Rothwell writes, "Behavior of students reflected a *superior* or *inferior* self-concept." He concludes:

> The power of labels to stigmatize, create self-fulfilling prophecies and reduce or enhance self-images is awesome... Until we learn to appreciate the power of language and the importance of using it responsibly, we will continue to produce negative social consequences for those victimized by dangerous language habits.

How many of our children (and millions of other people with disabilities) have been stigmatized in public schools and other environments because of the label assigned to them? How many have been perceived as "failures" because of the self-fulfilling prophecies espoused by physicians, educators, other professionals, and sometimes even parents?

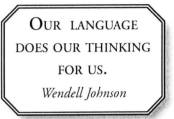

OUR LANGUAGE
DOES OUR THINKING
FOR US.
Wendell Johnson

Many educators (and some parents) say, "Students with _____ could never be successful in a Regular Education classroom!" In too many cases, children with disabilities have never been given the *opportunity* to participate in a Regular Education classroom, so *how do educators know this?* They don't really "know," they're only sharing their *opinion*—based on the *child's label*—but they state it as fact and it's believed to be true.

Let's look at a specific example. "Mrs. G," a Special Ed teacher, doesn't believe "Ethan" could be successful in a fourth grade classroom because of his disability. But under pressure from the parents—and against her better judgment—Mrs. G reluctantly "allows" Ethan to join the Regular Ed classroom. But she's sure he won't do well, and when a slight difficulty arises in the fourth grade class, Ethan is yanked out of there and shipped back to the Special Ed room—probably forever. This "failure" proves that Mrs. G was right all along, and it will be noted in Ethan's file for everyone to read in the future, so no further chances to be in Regular Ed classes will ever be offered. Mrs. G's *self-fulfilling prophecy* came true.

Many educators and parents have said, "Children with _____ cannot go to college." This *attitude*—based on a label, and taken as fact—is acted upon: the child is not provided with the public education he needs to go to college. Thus, he is *unable* to go to college, and the self-fulfilling prophecy comes true.

A TORN JACKET IS
SOON MENDED;
BUT HARD WORDS
BRUISE THE HEART
OF A CHILD.
*Henry Wadsworth
Longfellow*

More lessons about the dangers of erroneous thinking are included in one of my favorite books, *Living with Change: The Semantics of Coping* by Wendell Johnson. He writes:

> We talk about kinds because that is the way our language is built....We hardly ever talk about individual persons...[but each of us is] first of all a human being... If we label a person we tend to see the label, not the person. We put a label on him and then proceed to react to him as if he and all the other people so labeled were the same. That takes care of that...*Our language does our thinking for us.* [Italics added.]

Johnson provides additional information about the harm in classifying people, because we generally use a "two-valued" system in our thinking: black/white, either/or, yes/no, right/wrong, and so forth. Put another way, something is or isn't—there's no in-between. This way of thinking is so common, and so deeply-rooted, that we seldom think about it or question it—but we should.

Here's how it applies to DISABILITY WORLD: we decide that some individuals have a disability and some individuals do not have a disability (there's no in-between in the minds of many). A person who is said to have a disability is then *treated like he has a disability.* Remember Kim's story from the beginning of this chapter? She realized that even though her daughter, Lisa, was no different the day after the diagnosis, she began treating Lisa "like she had autism" (until she learned to think and act differently).

This is, sadly, all too common. Has it happened in your family? Do you treat your child like "a child with _____"? Imagine what could happen if you stopped this harmful practice—which leads to a self-fulfilling prophecy.

Think about what happens to our children within the framework of Services. Children with autism, for example, are treated like "children with autism:" they receive "autism treatments" and are put in environments with other "children with autism." Ditto many children with other conditions. Can you see how, in many ways, these situations make a child have "more autism" (or other condition)? The self-fulfilling prophecy is complete.

In *contrast* to two-valued thinking—a person does/does not have a disability—are the *different paradigms* of disability I detailed earlier in this chapter. What we call a "disability" can be many things, depending on one's perspective, one's social construct of the word, the environment, and so much more. When we adopt new attitudes about disability, we can share them with others, and the lives of our children will be changed in the process.

In *Language in Thought and Action (Fifth Edition)*, by S.I. and Alan R. Hayakawa, the authors discuss "how judgments stop thoughts:"

> A judgment ("He is a fine boy," "It was a beautiful service," "Baseball is a healthful sport," "She is an awful bore") is a *conclusion...*

Once such statements are made, there is little left to be said. If, however, more information is added, it must all be in agreement with the conclusion already stated.

So when we say, for example, "Mark has Down syndrome (mental retardation)," this is a diagnostic judgment that's a *conclusion.* Then we mistake the word for the thing ("Mark is retarded.")—so what more is there to say or know about Mark? We think we know everything about him, and we also think we know—immediately and completely—what needs to be done to or for Mark (treatments, interventions, education, etc.).

The Hayakawa father/son team also write, "When we name something, then, we are classifying. *The individual object or event we are naming, of course, has no name and belongs to no class until <u>we put it in one</u>...*" [Underlining added.]

SELF-FULFILLING PROPHECY

Most of us are aware of the idea that if we call a child "stupid" or "lazy" or other descriptors, the child will "become" that. Isn't that true for disability descriptors, as well?

What if we create wonderful self-fulfilling prophecies, by talking about how "smart" or "talented" or "strong" our children are? And what if we add to that by helping our children dream Big Dreams about college, or jobs, or being married, or other typical characteristics of a successful adult life? Aren't *these* the prophecies we hope will be fulfilled?

They then discuss how we classify people by race, noting that at one time in the United States, the definition of a "black" person was:

> ...any person with even a small amount of "Negro blood"... *It would be exactly as justifiable to say that any person with even a small amount of "white blood" is "white."* Why say one rather than the other? Because the former system of classification *suits the convenience of those making the classification.* (The classification of blacks and other minorities in this country has often suited the convenience of whites.) Classification is not a matter of identifying "essences." It is simply a reflection of social convenience or necessity—and different necessities are always producing different classifications... As soon as the process of classification is completed, our attitudes and our conduct are, to a considerable degree, determined.

> DO YOU KNOW WHAT IT'S LIKE TO FEEL *WRONG* 24-HOURS A DAY? DO YOU KNOW WHAT IT'S LIKE TO BE DISAPPROVED OF, NOT ONLY FOR WHAT YOU DO AND SAY AND THINK, BUT FOR WHO YOU *ARE?*
>
> *Joyce Rebeta-Burditt*

Education is the focus of Chapter 9, but in this chapter on new attitudes and actions, it's important to recognize the power of language in Special Education. As I mentioned, a disability is a medical diagnosis which is then used as a Passport to Services. In the process, however—especially within Special Education and other Services—our children are classified. Here is the definition of a "child with a disability" from Section 602 of IDEA (2004 Amendments):

> The term "child with a disability" means a child with mental retardation, hearing impairments (including deafness), speech or language impairments, visual impairments (including blindness), serious emotional disturbance (referred to in this title as "emotional disturbance"), orthopedic impairments, autism, traumatic brain injury, other health impairments, or specific learning disabilities...

The decision to include these specific diagnoses seems to make sense: Congress used disability labels as the criteria to determine which children were entitled to Special Ed services. However, many educators take *actions* based on these labels that generate extremely negative consequences for our children.

First, students are classified according to the label, and many educators assume children with the same label need the same type of education, by teachers trained in that specific area of expertise. This, in turn, causes educators to set up "programs" based on these classifications. So in different schools across the country, you'll find "autistic programs," "EBD classrooms" (EBD-Emotional/Behavioral Disorder), "OI programs" (OI-Orthopedic Impairments), and many more. As Hayakawa and Hayakawa wrote, "As soon as the process of classification is completed, our attitudes and our conduct are, to a considerable degree, determined." And as Johnson wrote, "Our language does our thinking for us." Many educators certainly let their language do their thinking for them, and once a child is classified, the attitudes and conduct of many educators are determined!

Additionally, two-valued thinking sets in: Special Ed is for "those kids" and Regular Ed is for everyone else. So in many schools, if a child is thought to need Special Ed Services, it's believed he has no need for Regular Education.

In many schools, (1) a child's educational "placement" is determined; (2) assumptions are made about a child's educational needs and potential; and (3)

IEP goals are written, based on the child's Special Ed classification, *not* on the child's unique and individual needs. In essence, children with the same diagnosis are treated the same—like they're all peas from the same pod!

This is not the intent of IDEA. *No where in the law are schools instructed to "set up programs" based on classification categories.* Instead, IDEA says the purpose of the law is to ensure that children with disabilities have a free appropriate public education "designed to meet their unique needs." [2004 Amendments, Section (d) (1) (A)] And Section 602 (29) defines special education as "specially designed instruction...to meet the unique needs of a child with a disability."

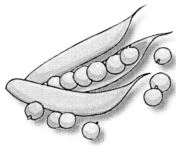

Some kids with disabilities, in the minds of some educators.

So the creation of Special Programs is based on the (erroneous) belief that children who share a characteristic (diagnosis) are the same, and therefore, need the same type of education, environment, and so forth. But there's more to it. As Hayakawa and Hayakawa described, a system of classification *"suits the convenience of those making the classification."* While Congress determined which medical diagnoses "defined" a child with a disability for *eligibility purposes,* it is *educators* who have turned these diagnoses into classifications *to suit their convenience!*

For example, it's easier to put students with autism and similar conditions in the same place *so the teachers, materials, and/or equipment will only have to be in one place!* If these students were in Regular Ed classrooms in their neighborhood schools, the Special Ed professionals would have to go where the students are (and in high quality inclusive schools, this is what happens, and it's not as difficult as people think—more in Chapter 9).

The *practices* of schools have made Special Ed a "place" instead of a "service." And, again, this is not the intent of IDEA. Sadly, many educators do not know the law—they've never read it. School districts, in general, do not follow Special Ed law; they follow school policy. And how is this allowed to happen? Because there are no "IDEA Police" running around the country enforcing the law, issuing citations, or throwing law-breaking educators in jail. Instead, the Federal Department of Education surveys schools every few years, and if major violations are found, schools *may* be taken to task. Simultaneously, parents often have to take responsibility for ensuring the law is followed. Some are more successful than others, for a variety of reasons, not the least of which is that schools are "bigger" than parents and they have more money and power.

I've shared only a minuscule amount of what I've learned about the absolute connection between *the words* we use and *the worlds* we create for ourselves and others. (To share it all would require a separate book, which is on my "To Do" list.) But I hope the lessons here will help you think more clearly, and help you understand the constraints that are put on our children based on the *language* we (and others) use and the *actions* we (and others) take as a result of our words. I hope you'll take some time to think about how you, personally, think about and treat your child, and how the language, thoughts, and actions of your family members, therapists, doctors, and a variety of other people affect your child's life.

Disability Words:
Looking Backward, Moving Forward

We've taken a brief look at the power of language in general. Now we'll examine some words of DISABILITY WORLD specifically—and we'll do a little time-travel in the process.

Old Language

In the early part of the 20th century, people with disabilities in institutions were given intelligence tests and assigned a score and a label. The generic term for people who were considered to have low intelligence was "feebleminded." But within that broad category were three classifications:

- Moron: A mental deficient who may take a normal place in society, but needs constant supervision.

- Imbecile: A mental deficient who may learn to communicate with others, but is incapable of earning his own living.

- Idiot: A mental deficient who is incapable of learning and understanding, is completely helpless, and requires constant care.

These were the original definitions from the Institutional Era. Do you notice a word is missing in each of these? Look at the three definitions again, closely. What's missing? The word "person." If you were diagnosed with one of these, you weren't a person, you were a mental deficient—*you were your label.* (This represents the erroneous thinking from a couple of pages back, confusing the "word with the thing.")

Current dictionaries show slight variations in the definitions above. Some actually include the IQ score associated with the different labels, and almost all include a secondary definition of "a stupid or foolish person."

Moron, imbecile, idiot, lame, spastic, cretin, deaf and dumb, mute, and many other words were all medical diagnoses *in the past.* For purposes of this discussion, I'll throw in blind, deaf, retarded, and handicapped, although they are still in current use. What these, and other words, have in common is that they are currently used *as insults or in some other pejorative way.* Medical diagnoses of people with disabilities have become insults. What does that say about our society's attitude toward people with disabilities? It represents the extreme marginalization and devaluation of these "categories" of individuals.

When my daughter was in sixth grade, she came home from school one day and told me a story about something that happened in class, ending the story with, "It was so *lame!*" "Whoa!" I replied. "What do you mean by 'lame'?" She didn't have an immediate answer, so I pressed her. Finally, she said, *"I don't know, Mom!* I guess it means stupid or dumb or something...." I turned her toward the kitchen doorway so she could see her brother in the living room, playing a computer game, while sitting in his wheelchair, and said, "Emily, many people in the past—and some even today—would look at your brother and say he is 'lame.' So when you say 'lame' means 'stupid' or 'dumb,' what are you saying about your brother?" She got the message, and I told her to go back to school and teach her friends the lesson.

Watch TV; read a newspaper, magazine, or book; listen to the radio; or simply think about conversations you've heard or participated in yourself, for more examples of how disability descriptors (including mental health diagnoses) have become "bad words:"

- *Newspaper story:* "The company will be handicapped by the strike."
- *TV news report:* "They turned a blind eye [or deaf ear] to the request."
- *Casual conversation:* "That guy is a moron [or cretin, imbecile, or idiot]!"
- *Radio talk show host:* "Congress has another idiotic plan."
- *Child on playground:* "You're a retard; you can't play with us."
- *Parent to teen:* "No, you can't go out tonight in this storm! Are you insane?"

None of these examples, of course, actually refer to a person with a disability. Our society has embraced these words as insults or derogatory terms because they seem to be good, accurate, and/or easy-to-use descriptors. And, again, what does this say about our society? If we, as parents, are to make positive changes, it's imperative that we understand the pervasiveness of the inherent prejudice and devaluation of people with disabilities.

Lessons from a variety of different authors, including those mentioned in this chapter, have taught me that the devaluation or marginalization of any person or group *begins with language.* If we use a label that describes a person in a negative way—sub-human or less-than—we then feel *justified in treating him* in a negative way. Slurs used to denigrate individuals or groups because of their religion, ethnicity, gender, sexual orientation, etc., have been common in our society, and many of us have *recognized the harm of these insults and have eliminated these from our vocabularies.*

But there are two disturbing differences between insults based on gender, ethnicity, religion, etc. and disability descriptors as insults. First, an insult using a slur based on religion or ethnicity, for example, is an insult only if it's "used properly." If "Tom" wanted to insult his boss, "Mary," because she gave him a mediocre performance review, calling her a "kike" would have no effect *as an insult* because Mary is not of the Jewish faith. Similarly, if Mary wanted to insult Tom because he doesn't do his share of work, calling him a "spic" would have no effect *as an insult* because Tom is not of Hispanic heritage. So when using slurs based on religion, ethnicity, gender, sexual orientation, etc., there must be a connection to the person being insulted for such a slur to be considered an insult.

But the same is not true for disability descriptors used as insults. Tom could call Mary an "idiot" and Mary could call Tom a "retard" and both of these would be perceived as insults, even though neither Mary nor Tom have disabilities. Unlike other categories of slurs, disability words used as slurs have been *generalized*—they're insults, no matter what!

Second, while the use of slurs based on ethnicity, religion, etc. has *diminished* as people are more sensitive to the dangers of using such words, the use of

---

MORON

IMBECILE

IDIOT

WERE REPLACED BY

MILD

MODERATE

SEVERE

PROFOUND

(They added a category!)

For cognitive disabilities, these descriptors are tied to IQ scores and they can be very harmful. A teacher might be willing to include a child with a "mild" cognitive disability, but not one with a "severe" descriptor. But what if the assessment was wrong? What if the stupid IQ test is inaccurate?

These are used with other disabilities, too. When my son's therapist told me he probably had "severe" CP instead of "moderate" CP, I wondered what the big deal was! Did he win a prize for this or was there some benefit? If not, who cares? One person's mild is another person's moderate...and so on. These descriptors have no value in telling us anything about a person—and they're dangerous!

disability words as slurs seems to be *increasing,* as the general public becomes more familiar with different medical diagnoses. For example, I heard someone ask in a sarcastic manner, "What are you—*ADD,*" as a way of insulting someone who was not paying attention. I've heard others refer to someone as "bipolar" because the person was having an up-and-down stressful day.

Let's deconstruct one example. When your next door neighbor doesn't return the tools he borrowed, you call him an "idiot." But his behavior actually reflects that he is thoughtless, rude, inconsiderate, and/or forgetful. Why, then, is "idiot" the insult of choice?

Remember that disability descriptors are medical diagnoses. Why aren't other medical diagnoses used as insults? When your neighbor doesn't return your tools, you don't say, "That guy is such a *diabetic!*" Why? Because people with *diabetes* (and other conditions) have not been devalued and marginalized since the beginning of recorded history, unlike people who have conditions we call "disabilities"! This is a sad state of affairs—one that we should thoroughly understand so we can address it in our daily lives.

In recent years, some people have begun to use descriptors like "physically-challenged" or "mentally-challenged." I don't care for these. For the most part, people *without* disabilities have promoted these terms as "polite" disability descriptors. But consider what's happened with these: their use has been corrupted and ridiculed as evidenced by people saying things like, "vertically-challenged," "directionally-challenged," and so forth. These are not used as respectful terms, but as sarcasm or demeaning jokes.

I hope you'll talk with your family about the use of disability descriptors as insults, and eliminate the words in this section (and many others) from your vocabulary. And when you hear others using these words, I hope you'll gently educate them about this issue.

People First Language

You know that individuals with disabilities "created" People First Language (PFL) in the 1970s when they said, "We are not our disabilities. We are people, first." It has taken many years for their wishes to be recognized by society—and we still have a long way to go. The same has been true for other groups when language has changed. We can be very slow to change, can't we?

People First Language is just that: it puts the person first. Its use is critically important if we want our children (and others) to be seen as individuals—as people—rather than their diagnoses. Saying, "People with disabilities," is more respectful and accurate than "the handicapped" or "the disabled." But when you're talking about your own child, you might want to say something like, "My son has a diagnosis of _____." This make the point that the condition *is* a diagnosis, not who your child is!

The chart on the next page shows some examples; a few of these will be discussed in greater detail. Be aware this is only a partial list—there are many more descriptors we need to change!

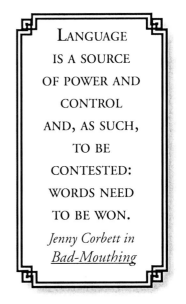

LANGUAGE IS A SOURCE OF POWER AND CONTROL AND, AS SUCH, TO BE CONTESTED: WORDS NEED TO BE WON.
Jenny Corbett in Bad-Mouthing

Say:	Instead of:
People with disabilities (or disability diagnoses).	The handicapped or disabled.
He has a cognitive disability (or...diagnosis).	He's mentally retarded.
She has autism (or a diagnosis of autism).	She's autistic.
He has Down syndrome (or diagnosis of...).	He's Down's; a Down's kid.
She has a learning disability (...diagnosis).	She's learning disabled; she's LD.
He has a physical disability (...diagnosis).	He's a quadriplegic/crippled.
She's of short stature/she's a little person.	She's a dwarf/midget.
He has a mental health condition (...diagnosis).	He's emotionally disturbed/mentally ill.
She uses a wheelchair or mobility chair.	She's wheelchair bound/confined to/in a wheelchair.
He receives special ed services.	He's in special ed; sped kid; special ed student.
She has a developmental delay.	She's developmentally delayed.
Children without disabilities (...diagnoses).	Normal or healthy kids.
Communicates with her eyes/device/etc.	Is non-verbal.
Customer.	Client, consumer, recipient, etc.
Congenital disability.	Birth defect.
Brain injury.	Brain damaged.
Accessible parking, hotel room, etc.	Handicapped parking, hotel room, etc.

I hope you already embrace and use People First Language. If not, you may have a variety of reasons for not using it—such as "it doesn't matter what we call people," "it's too many words," or something else related to how you personally feel. But here's what's important to know: it really doesn't matter whether *we* like it or not because the words aren't being used to describe *us*. PFL is important to people with disabilities—they're the ones being described—and shouldn't we care how *they* feel? Would *you* want to be described in ways that might be hurtful or demeaning, are inaccurate, or which represent what someone else thinks about you instead of what you know about yourself?

Some people *say* they use PFL, and they *think* they're using PFL, but they only use portions of it. For example, I've been with parents who say something like this, "Yes, my child has a physical disability—he uses a wheelchair [so far so good]. But when we go to the mall, it's so hard to find a handicapped parking space." Egads! This parent has learned not to use "handicapped" about her child, but she doesn't realize PFL means not using it at all, even if the parking sign at the mall has that ugly word on it! If we want others to stop using antiquated, pejorative words, *we* have to stop using them! And the more accurate term is "accessible parking"—because it's an accommodation that provides access.

News reporters are often resistant to using PFL. Some use "new" and "old" language (handicapped, disabled, and person with a disability) within the same story, believing these words are interchangeable. Some chafe at being told "what to say." Others say PFL is "too long" or "too PC." But "African-American" is "longer" than the N-word or "black" and reporters adopted new language, didn't they? We have to be persistent, and they'll eventually get it right.

Use Labels Only in Disability World

In addition to *what* we say, we need to be very careful about *where and when* we use our children's disability diagnoses/labels. Disability *words* belong only in DISABILITY WORLD. We may need to use them in an IFSP/IEP meeting, and with physicians and health care providers. If so, use them once, then move on and stay focused on your child's strengths and needs.

Labels have no place anywhere else. Remember: your child's disability condition is a medical diagnosis that's private information. So don't take it to church, the playground, your mother-in-law's home, etc. As I'll explain in Chapter 7, sharing your child's diagnosis or his "problems" can set your child up for exclusion, low expectations, and other negative consequences.

The H-word (handicapped-yuck!)

This is such an awful word that it's hard to say it or write it, so I'll use "H-word" instead. To many people with disabilities and their families, this word is as offensive as the N-word is to others. It is, in my opinion, in the same "class." It's a word that was once commonly used, it was *imposed* on one group of people by another group of people, and it has never meant anything positive.

The history of the word has nothing to do with people with disabilities. Word origin books indicate it is an Old English word referring to a game of barter: two men took their caps off and held them in their hands, then placed money and/or an object for sale/barter in the caps. The game involved seeing who would "win" the object, and the person who did not win was said to have his "hand in his cap," and was thought to be at a "disadvantage."

At some point in history, the phrase was shortened to a word, and was applied to people with disabilities since they were seen as having a "disadvantage." But having a disability, in and of itself, does not constitute a disadvantage. The disadvantage—if there is one—is in how a person with a disability is thought of, talked about, and treated.

The original meaning of the word was also applied to other games or contests: golf, bowling, horse racing, etc. Players who are "not as good" (this is a "disadvantage") are given a "handicap" (extra points or some other benefit) to level the playing field or to indicate a player's status or level of ability.

A *legendary* version of the word indicates its use came out of the Crimean War in the mid-1800s. When French soldiers returned home with acquired disabilities, they asked their government for help. They were told no help would be given, so they should go out and beg with their caps in their hands. The translation from French to English resulted in the H-word.

The H-word is antiquated, pejorative, insulting, and—like the N-word—it belongs in the trash heap. It is no longer used in any Federal legislation; People First Language is used instead. Some state laws and services, many school districts, and other entities still use it, however. On the positive side, a few state legislatures, after powerful efforts by people with disabilities and family members, have passed legislation mandating the use of PFL in new laws. We can and should do everything in our power to eliminate this word.

PC OR GOOD MANNERS?

Contrary to popular belief, PFL is not political correctness (PC). It's just good manners and reflects the Golden Rule: treat others the way you want to be treated.

Have you noticed that many people who object to using People First Language or other more respectful descriptors are often those who have, themselves, seldom or never been on the *receiving* end of derogatory labels and descriptors?

My response to these folks is to ask, "Would *you* like to be known as, 'the big-butt teacher,' 'the bald accountant,' 'the wart lady,' or similar descriptors?"

"Disabled" (The D-word)

Some people eliminated the H-word and replaced it with "disabled." I used this word a long time ago—it did seem to be an "appropriate" replacement for the H-word. But consider how it's used by general society today:

- *Traffic Reporter:* "We have a disabled vehicle blocking the left lane." *Translation:* car is broken down. Reporters used to say "stalled car."

- *Flight Attendant:* "It is against Federal law to tamper with, disable, or destroy the smoke detector in the lavatory." *Translation*: don't break it.

- *Sports Reporter:* "After last night's big game, John Smith has been placed on the disabled list." *Translation:* Smith is unable to play and he is of *no value* to the team until he is "able" again. Reporters used to say "injured reserve."

- To make something on your computer inoperable, you "disable" it.

The D-word has come to mean "broken," "doesn't work," "non-functioning" and more. Because the general public is accustomed to *those* definitions, what might someone think if you say, "My child is disabled."?

This can be confusing to some people; they think I'm saying we should not use "disability" in any form. So I'll explain. Saying, "people with disabilities" puts the person first, and describes what a person "has," not what a person "is." Furthermore, remember when we deconstructed and redefined disability? *It's a body part that works differently.* Having a disability is nothing to be ashamed of, so the word "disability" is fine. But since "disabled" is commonly used to mean "broken," "inoperable," or "nonfunctioning," is it an appropriate word to describe our children and others?

Some adults with disabilities—especially those with *acquired* disabilities—disagree with me about this. "I'm disabled," some say, "and there's nothing wrong with that word." I respect and honor the wishes of an individual in how he wants to be described. But I won't use this word—and many others—when speaking about people with disabilities, in general, and when trying to educate others about the importance of PFL. And I always want to respect my "teachers:" adults with *developmental* disabilities who created PFL!

"Disability" and "disabled" look similar, and they come from the same root word. But remember what I included earlier in this chapter about the *meanings* of words. *How* words are used can make a world of difference. Think, also, of the difference it can make when you say, "My child has a *diagnosis* of [whatever]." See Mark Twain's wonderful bit of advice on this subject in the box (left).

"Mentally Retarded"

This word just has to go! It is one of the most pejorative of all the medical diagnoses, and one that's become a favorite insult! Some organizations are making a change, and recommend the use of "intellectual disability" instead. This is better than the MR descriptor, but it's not my favorite, as it's too closely connected to "intelligence" as in "Intelligence Quotient" (IQ). It can still be disparaging, indicating a person's "intelligence" is somehow deficient. I know many people who are said to have "low IQs" who are smarter than the

> THE DIFFERENCE
> BETWEEN
> THE RIGHT WORD
> AND THE
> ALMOST RIGHT
> WORD
> IS LIKE THE
> DIFFERENCE
> BETWEEN
> LIGHTNING
> AND THE
> LIGHTNING BUG.
> *Mark Twain*

professionals who tested them! I prefer "cognitive disability"—meaning the person may learn differently.

"Autistic"—"Deaf"—"Blind"

Many people use PFL when it comes to the majority of medical diagnoses, but for a variety of reasons, some labels seem to be "immune." For example, many parents say, "My child is autistic," instead of "My child has autism." My guess is that physicians say "autistic" when they diagnose, and many parents follow. Here's something to consider: have you ever heard a parent say, "My child is cancerous?" No! She says, "My child *has* cancer." Again, a disability is a condition one "has," it's not who one "is."

There are, however, *some* adults with autism who are vehement in their proclamation: "I do not *have* autism; I *am* autistic." They also express anger and frustration at efforts (by their parents and others) to "cure" them. I agree with this latter sentiment 100 percent, and hope all of us will learn from adults with developmental disabilities.

As I mentioned earlier, I will always respect one individual's wish about how he wants to be described, but I do not support the idea that everyone with this condition should be called "autistic." I feel the preference to be called "autistic" is a "generational" thing—this is what these adults were called when they were growing up, before People First Language had taken root. Also, however, it seems some want to be called "autistic" as a way of distancing themselves from others and/or to carve out a unique identity. Many, in fact, don't believe they have anything in common with people who have other disabilities.

Similarly, some people say they are "Deaf" (with a capital D), and are part of the Deaf Community. Like some adults with autism, they don't feel a connection to people with other disabilities. Some say being Deaf *isn't* a disability—it's a "culture" and/or a form of communication. Others say they have a hearing impairment, and do not like the Deaf label. Similarly, some people say, "I'm blind," while others say, "I have a visual impairment."

In contrast, there are many people who have been called "retarded" all their lives, and they feel the opposite: they say they are not their disabilities; they want to *be—and be seen as*—ordinary people; and they understand and value the commonalities they share with those who have other disabilities (such as facing discrimination and prejudice), so they feel a connection.

I know there will never be consensus among the estimated 54 million Americans with disabilities (and millions more who are family members) about everything disability-related, and it's important to respect individual preferences. If, however, every person with a disability (and their family members) recognized that they're more *like* people without disabilities than different, the attitudinal barriers could more easily be dismantled. Some people with disabilities, and their family members—individually or as a group—have erected barriers around themselves, yet they routinely complain about how they're misunderstood, excluded, and more. If they want to be part of society, they have to first tear down these self-imposed attitudinal barriers.

—MEMORIES—

While doing a presentation about historical perspectives of people with disabilities, 50-something Howard raised his hand. "I have two brothers. All the time I was growing up, when my father introduced us, he said my brothers' names and then he always said, 'And this is our retarded son, Howard.' *Why did he do that, Kathie? It always made me feel so bad."* Then Howard broke into shoulder-heaving sobs—the years of pain pouring out. Several of us comforted him as best we could.

Howard's pain was clear evidence that words—especially the words used by parents—hurt very deeply and the pain is long-lasting. His father's actions took place about 40 years ago, but the pain of Howard's recollections made it seem like it just happened.

Wouldn't you think things would change in four decades? Well, a few months later, the coordinator of a conference where I was presenting was doing her "welcome." Imagine my shock when she said, "And I want all of you to meet my 13-year-old son, Robby, who's there in the back of the room. Robby's autistic." It makes me sad to think that 40 years from now, Robby will probably still recall this pain, just like Howard.

HIERARCHY OF DISABILITIES

With justification, parents are concerned about disability-driven prejudice and discrimination. But we must first look inward, for there's a great deal of this among parents! There is, in essence, a "disability hierarchy," and it runs both ways.

Some parents, for example, say, "Oh, my child *only* has [such-and-such,]" as if that's "better" than some other conditions. Then there are parents who wear their children's diagnoses like badges of honor: "Your child *just* has [*that*]? Well my child has *severe [this]*, and *moderate [that]*, and *mild [this]*."

I guess this is supposed to indicate her child deserves more pity and/or she deserves more respect for having to put up with this "pitiful" child!

Maybe things will get better if we could just agree that a disability is a disability is a disability—and get rid of the hierarchy once and for all!

"Special Ed Student"

Yes, many of our children are "in" Special Education classrooms. But remember that Special Education is not supposed to be a "place," it is supposed to be Services brought to the student. Let's speak in ways that indicate what "should be," not just how things *are*. This can help us move in a different direction.

When we call a child a "special ed student," "sped kid," or something similar, we're not using People First Language. More importantly, these labels can automatically generate low expectations, prejudice, and segregation! The more accurate, respectful descriptor is, "student who receives Special Ed Services."

"Non-Verbal"

When we tell someone a child is "non-verbal," are we aware of what the listener might infer from that descriptor? That the child doesn't speak, doesn't understand, and has nothing to say (making them totally incompetent in some people's minds)! This is an inaccurate perception, of course. Furthermore, many children who do not have oral speech are communicating all the time: with a communication device (or cards), FC, or sign language; or with their eyes, actions, behavior, or in some other way. We must not routinely give people the idea that our children are incompetent by using this descriptor!

I met a young woman who signs with one hand, uses a communication device, and also has some speech. "I have *three ways* of communicating, Kathie," she said, "and people call *me* non-verbal!" She hates the term, and I do, too. Let's describe what our children *can* do, not what they cannot, so a parent can say, "My child communicates with/by [a device or whatever]."

"Birth Defect"

How can *any* baby be defective? Every baby is perfect, regardless of any condition. How dare we label a new life this way! If you buy a new toaster and it doesn't work, you take it back to the store and say it's "defective." Is this what we should do with babies who have "birth defects"—send them back for a "perfect" baby? Some organizations use this term because it generates a ton of "pity" donations. *Gag!* This descriptor also needs to go in the garbage can, and be replaced by "congenital disability."

"Brain Damaged"

If a car is damaged, we get it fixed. If there's a great deal of damage, the car is considered a total loss. Ditto other products. So if a person has "brain damage," he needs to be "fixed," and if there's "severe brain damage," he's probably considered a "total loss." *Ugh!* The respectful and accurate term is "brain injury."

More New Paradigms

Now we'll explore some paradigm shifts that can help reduce rampant disability discrimination and prejudice. Adopting these methods will also help put our children on the path to living REAL LIVES!

"Special Needs"

This descriptor also belongs in the dumpster. When I do presentations on People First Language, many parents are in agreement until I get to this part—and then they're in shock! Hear me out...

When you tell someone, "I have a child with special needs..." what's the reaction of the other person? In general, it's probably a sympathetic pat on the arm and a sad, "Ohhhh....." In the worst-case scenario, the person might even add, "I'm so sorry...." and *your child might be standing right there!* This descriptor generates *pity!* (And that makes this term another effective fundraiser! Yuck!) But there are even more reasons to bury this descriptor.

Way back in 1993, William Henderson, the principal of an inclusive school in Boston, Massachusetts and a person with a disability, wrote an article entitled "Handicapism" (in *Equity and Choice*), which stated, in part:

> Handicapism is manifested in schools in many ways. Simply categorizing children as "special needs" causes some educators to focus on deficits and view [the children] as essentially incapable. These educators tend to lower expectations and abrogate their responsibility for these children. Others feel discomfort or fear around persons with disabilities. They are inhibited from engaging in and promoting positive interactions. Consciously or not, educators sometimes act in ways that stigmatize or patronize children with "special needs." Some have refused to be involved even with the provision of services and accommodations.

So there's an *educator's perception* on the damage this descriptor does to our children in school. And there's more.

When we say a child has "special needs," we don't *allow* him to be "regular" or "ordinary." Saying a child has "special needs" can automatically cause parents, teachers, or others to believe the child needs to be in "special" places, with other "special" people like him, taught by "special" teachers, and...ad nauseam. In other words, *we limit his opportunities based on this descriptor!*

Equally important, adults with developmental disabilities have told me, "I *hated* being called that when I was a child, and I still hate it as an adult." Shouldn't we listen and learn from their experiences? Some parents have said, "But I like this term better than 'child with a disability'." As I mentioned before, our feelings aren't as important as *the feelings of the person being described, and the impact the words have on the person's life.*

Some parents say they like the term because they believe "all children are special." But this descriptor essentially sends the opposite message: children with "special needs" are unwanted, devalued, and marginalized. If society *really* thought children with disabilities were "special," no one would say, "Ohhhh.... I'm sorry" to us; children with disabilities would be the first to be adopted, not the last; and doctors wouldn't recommend abortions to mothers whose fetuses have been diagnosed with congenital disabilities.

I hope you'll take this descriptor out of your vocabulary. In addition to harming your child with a disability, it can also have a negative effect on your

> *IT'S JUST A WORD!*
> My friend, Trina, was talking to her daughter's kindergarten teacher about her daughter's education. During the conversation, the teacher repeatedly said, "But kids with autism..." Trina responded, "It's just a word! Why are you letting a *word* get in the way of you seeing who my daughter really is?"

other children! At first, they might feel jealous or unloved if a brother or sister is described as "special." Later, however, many come to realize they don't *want* to be called "special"—they've seen how their brother or sister is treated because of that word!

"Special needs" is a descriptor that might have been "good" at one time; but like other descriptors, *its useful life is over.* Many people ask: what do we replace it with? In some cases, nothing (sometimes saying nothing is the best thing to do). In other cases, we can simply say "children with disabilities" or "my child has a diagnosis of _____."

"Problem" vs. "Need"

My unscientific study reveals that "problem" is most likely the #1 word used about children and adults with disabilities. I think we learn to use this word from physicians, educators, and others who are in positions to diagnose and/or provide Services to our children. It may also be a concept some of us have grown up with, another paradigm that's pervasive in our society: within the MEDICAL MODEL, everything that's not "right" about one's body is a problem. And, boy-oh-boy, does this word ever cause *real* problems!

First, what does it make a child feel like to hear his parents, extended family members, teachers, and/or others talk about his problems all the time? Many of us talk about our children in front of them *like they're not even there!* Is there anything a child can do about all these problems caused by the disability? No! She's powerless, and that's a terrible feeling! Worse, the child comes to believe that *she* is the problem. And what's a child supposed to do with *that* feeling?

Second, we often use the word with the best of intentions, at IEP meetings and in other settings, not realizing it may cause a huge backfire! For example, at her son's IEP meeting, "Joanna" describes all of her son's problems (and she also uses some professional jargon, instead of plain language): "Jack has problems with reading and math; he also has problems talking—severe articulation problems; he's always had a few behavior problems—socially, he's 'behind' the other kids; and lately we've noticed he's having problems with organizational skills—he can't remember to put his lunch in his backpack, he forgets his backpack at school—he's just pretty disorganized."

Joanna shares this information with the best of intentions: she believes if she details all of her son's *problems* at the IEP meeting, this will ensure Jack will receive all the help he needs from educators. But if she wants Jack included in an age-appropriate, Regular Ed classroom, or even if she's content with a Special Ed Classroom placement, but wants him to go to Regular Ed art, PE, and music classes, Joanna's description has just convinced educators that Jack has "too many problems" to be anywhere but in the segregated Special Ed room (or an even more restrictive placement) 100 percent of the time!

A similar outcome can occur if we want our children to participate in typical community activities. We may think we're doing the right thing by sharing a child's problems with a Park and Rec coach, Scout leader, or other person-in-charge, but we're really setting up the child to be excluded.

"Problem" is used about people with disabilities all the time (we even disclose such information to new acquaintances and perfect strangers!); yet seldom do we use it about *ourselves*. Why? Because most of us know that talking about our problems or what we can't do *does not paint us in the most favorable light!* If you and I became new friends and I started telling you about all my problems, you might decide I'm not the friend for you! (On the other hand, some new friends might decide to have a contest to see who has the *most* problems! *Ugh!)*

I don't talk about all of *my* problems on a regular basis, and I hope you don't either. Specifically, however, I don't say I have a "problem" seeing—I say I *wear* or *need* glasses. So if I talk about myself that way, shouldn't I also do the same for my son? Here's a description about Benjamin which might come out of the mouths of many professionals (and mine, before I knew better), based on the "problem" paradigm:

> Benjamin can't walk, he has problems using his hands, he can't write with a pencil, he has problems feeding himself, he can't go to the bathroom by himself, and... [I could go on, but I think you get the picture.]

Now here's a descriptor of Benjamin using the "needs/uses" paradigm:

> Benjamin uses a power wheelchair to get around, he uses a computer to do his school work, he needs big-handled utensils so he can feed himself, and he needs a little help going to the bathroom.

> IF THOUGHT CORRUPTS LANGUAGE, LANGUAGE CAN ALSO CORRUPT THOUGHT.
> *George Orwell*

Compare the two. Some people have said it appears these actually represent two very different children! Now consider this: which description is more likely to result in Benjamin being included in a Regular Ed classroom? As a young adult, which is more likely to help him get a job? Now here's the *most important consideration:* which description enables Benjamin to *feel better about himself?* If you answered "the second one" for all three questions, yell "Bingo!"

The chart below illustrates some more examples of reframing. As you look at it, think about *your* child and the different ways you and/or others have described him by his so-called problems or deficits.

Problem	*Needs, Uses, Does, etc.*
Greg has behavior problems.	Greg needs behavior supports [in the classroom, or on the playground, etc.].
Maria has reading problems.	Maria needs large print [or books on tape, etc.].
Stephen is nonverbal/can't talk.	Stephen uses a communication device [or signs, or communicates with his eyes, etc.].
Emma can't use her hands.	Emma uses a mouth stick [or needs help with...].
Tarek can't remember things.	Tarek does best when he has a planning notebook [or when someone helps him remember things].
Josie can't feed herself/has a G-tube.	Josie needs help with eating.
Michael has problems listening.	Michael needs things repeated [or needs an FM system].

You're probably familiar with, "Is the glass half-empty or half-full," question—it's all about perspective and how we *choose* to see things. This is the same thing! It's about reframing—looking at things from a different perspective. We need to focus on what our children *can* do, instead of what they can't. This is also about good manners, and treating others the way we want to be treated. You don't want to be known by your problems, right? Your child doesn't either!

In the spaces below (or in your journal), write what you or others have described as "problems," briefly, in the left-hand column. Then reframe them using "needs, uses, does" etc., in the right-hand column, starting each one with your child's name.

Problem	*Needs, Uses, Does, etc.*
_____	_____
_____	_____
_____	_____
_____	_____
_____	_____
_____	_____

Does your child look differently to you now? Think he'll look differently to others? Most importantly, how might this change *how he feels about himself?* If, by any chance, you think this isn't important, remember (1) how *we* feel about language isn't as important as how our *children* feel about it and (2) how your child is "presented" affects how others treat him! So, *please*—for your child's sake—take the word "problem" out of your vocabulary, when it comes to describing your child.

"Deficits/Problems" vs. "Gifts/Assets/Strengths"

There's even more you can do to present the most accurate and respectful image of your child. Again, it involves reframing and looking at things from a different perspective. But first, a little story.

As a young girl, I was called Chatty Kathie and Motor Mouth. When I share this story during presentations, it evokes lots of laughter, and I tell the audience that it's OK to laugh about it *now,* but I didn't think it was funny when I was a child. Because people saw this as a problem/deficit, they were always trying to change me—to make me stop talking so much. Sometimes I got in trouble or was punished, other times I got "bad grades" in "conduct," or notes were sent home to my parents. It was hard to like myself during these times.

I share this not for anyone to feel sorry for me—you may have experienced something similar in your own childhood—but as a comparison. What *I* experienced (and maybe you, too), was probably *1/100th* of what happens to many children and adults with disabilities: so many people identify *so many problems* in the person, and then great efforts are made to change and/or fix the person.

But what if things had been different? What if, instead of seeing my Motor Mouth as a problem, someone had reframed it and said, "Kathie has the *gift of gab?*" In addition, what if they *built on it,* instead of trying to change it. For example, if they had realized that talking, words, expressing myself, etc. were important to me, they might have suggested I get involved in drama, a debate club, reading to younger children, or something similar. (Did any of the adults who chided me for talking too much when I was a child ever consider that one day people would *pay me to talk?*)

Think about what you and/or others have seen as a problem and/or deficit in your child, and consider how you could reframe it into a gift, asset, or strength. If your child loves the sound of her own voice like I do mine, see her chattiness as a gift and build on it—instead of trying to change her!

This can be a hard exercise for many parents; it's not something we've spent much time thinking about, and many of us have been brainwashed by professionals into seeing our children primarily through the lens of deficits/problems. So here's a little more help to get you started.

Some parents tell me their children are "runners"—the child likes to bolt when he's not supposed to (and this *can* be dangerous, depending on where the child is and where he wants to run). This is seen as a problem or deficit. But it probably meets a need for the child, or *he wouldn't do it!*

Who do we value in our society that runs? Track stars, other athletes, delivery people who hustle, etc. Perhaps some children who like to move fast will grow up to be athletes, or maybe couriers: riding bicycles in metro areas, racing lickety-split, hopping off the bike, running into an office, running out again, and then back on the bike!

So if your child has been considered a "runner," and that's been seen as a deficit, reframe it and build on it. Set up a running course in your home (or at school or in other places) using traffic cones or other devices, so your child can run safely. Or consider giving him a trike or bike to ride (in the house or in the school, if that's what works—down a long hallway?). Maybe *movement,* not just running, is what he craves. If so, make sure he has free access to a swing set in your yard and/or at school. You could also install a net swing (or whatever works best for your child) inside your home (and at school). What else might work? A mini-trampoline or...?

Many children with autism and other conditions are called "rockers," and this is seen as "inappropriate behavior." Again, it must meet a child's needs or she wouldn't do it. She's probably good at doing this, so build on it! You can turn an "inappropriate behavior" into an "appropriate" one: buy her a rocking chair, a rocking horse, a ball with a handle she can bounce on, or some other toy/device she can rock on, and let her rock whenever it meets her needs.

My brother, Steve, has always been known as a "loner." In our society, we have a tendency to look down on loners—they're seen as different, not socially apt, or whatever. I believe it's this general societal disdain for loners that causes us to expend great efforts to "socialize" some children with autism and other disabilities. But let's widen our perspective a bit. Once I started looking at things differently as regards disability, I started seeing almost everything differently. Specifically, I realized there was another way to see my brother: socially, he's very *self-sufficient—he doesn't need a lot of people in his life!* He's well-mannered and friendly when he's with others, but he's happiest in his own company. So is this a deficit or is it actually a strength?

I hope these ideas get your creative juices flowing. Sit and think—don't worry if the ideas don't come immediately. Again, this is a new way of thinking, so be patient with yourself, and tap into the creative minds of others in your family, friends, or other parents—many minds are better than one! In the space below, or in your journal, briefly list what you or others have seen as problems/deficits in the left-hand column, then reframe these into strengths, gifts, or assets in the right-hand column and include how you and others can build on these.

Problems/Deficits   *Strengths, Gifts, Assets*

_____   _____

_____   _____

_____   _____

_____   _____

_____   _____

Once again, think how this reframing can help you and others see your child in a new and positive light. Most importantly, your child will see and think of herself in a wonderful new way!

Not Every Characteristic is Part of the Disability

We do this a lot! In a later section, I'll share a story about a young child with autism going ballistic in the grocery store. For now, just keep that picture in your head and think about this: many of us will assume the child went ballistic "because he has autism." How do we know that? Maybe he went ballistic because he's mad at his mommy because she didn't buy him the candy he wanted—*just like any other four-year-old!*

Great harm can come to children when we assume every characteristic is part of the disability, because we feel we must "work on that" through therapies or interventions. When this happens, our efforts amount to trying to scrub away part of a child's personality! How can we do this?

Let's go back to my brother again. His preference to spend time in his own company is part of his personality. How do we know this same trait in a child with autism or similar condition isn't also part of the *child's personality,* and not the result of having autism?

"Kate," the mother of a 10-year-old boy with autism lambasted me for my criticisms of intensive therapies for children with autism. She said I "didn't understand anything about autism," and proceeded to detail a laundry list of her son's "problems caused by autism." She was rendered practically speechless when I related that my son, who has cerebral palsy, not autism, did many of the same things her son did! For example, her son would bite the back of his hand; my son did, too, when he was younger. For both our sons, this was a sign of frustration, *which had nothing to do autism or cerebral palsy!*

Isn't it time we learned to look beyond the label, and realize that our children are children, first and foremost, with unique personalities and distinct personality traits, many of which have nothing to do with their condition? Maybe a child who "doesn't have good social skills" is just shy. Maybe a child behaves this way or that because he takes after his dad, or because he's three, or for a myriad of other reasons.

When we begin to see our children as wonderfully-unique individuals, we'll be more respectful, we'll let them be who they really are, and we won't impose the Disability Double Standard on them. A story from my friend, Trina, illustrates this point. I met Trina while presenting at a conference in Idaho several years ago. I was sharing much of what's in this chapter and Trina "got it" right away. A few days after I returned home, I received a delightful Email from Trina in which she wrote:

> I learned so much from your presentation on Saturday! On Sunday when we were at church, my daughter started "flapping," and I was about to reach over and put my hands on her arms to remind her not to do this. But then I happened to look down and realized I was shaking my leg back and forth. It hit me: if *I* can do *that,* my daughter can flap her arms! Thanks for helping me see things differently!

Each of us has certain traits or characteristics that might be unusual or unique *in the eyes of others.* But does that mean they're wrong or that *we* should be changed? We give ourselves the freedom "to be," don't our children deserve the same?

> IT IS A MYSTERY WHY ADULTS EXPECT PERFECTION FROM CHILDREN.
>
> FEW GROWNUPS CAN GET THROUGH A WHOLE DAY WITHOUT MAKING A MISTAKE.
>
> *Marcelene Cox*

Developmental Age vs. Chronological Age

This topic was covered in the previous chapter, but I include it here as a reminder! Always, always, always refer to your child only by his chronological age. If he's been assigned a developmental age, *ignore it*—do not accept its validity. If a report showing this information is in your child's file, consider adding your own document to the file that includes something like, "I/we are not in agreement with this assessment, and I/we do not want this information shared with others." Under Special Ed law, you have the right to see what's in your child's school file, and to add your own information.

Never Compare to Others

Parents, teachers, grandparents, and others may routinely compare a child with a disability to other children: classmates, brothers and sisters, etc. This is not helpful to parents, and it's certainly not helpful to the child if she never

. . . .

*PLAIN LANGUAGE,
PLEASE!*

If we want to have better communication, we need to use plain language. Many parents have adopted professional jargon, believing this puts us on an equal footing with professionals. Unfortunately, this practice results in our seeing our children in terms of "body parts," "deficits," and other descriptors that are part and parcel of the MEDICAL MODEL. So at IEP meetings, and with therapists, doctors, and others, *we* need to speak plain language and insist that others do the same. This will help us understand each other better, and will hopefully keep us focused on the child as *a real person,* not a diagnosis, body part, deficit, etc.

In addition, I'd like to see professionals change some of their *own* labels. "Case manager" is one example. I never saw my son as a "case" and I surely didn't want him to be "managed." Aren't descriptors like "service coordinator" and "supports coordinator" more accurate job titles? What would *you* like to see changed?

. . . .

"measures up" to other children. This, along with other ways we describe children, can be very hurtful to them, and can lead to self-fulfilling prophecies.

When my son, Benjamin, was in kindergarten, I had to address this issue with his teacher. As in many classrooms, the students' artwork was hung on the walls. I could pick out my son's picture from 30 feet away, while most of the other parents had to get up close in order to find their children's names on the sheets of construction paper—which featured a cow, house, or something similar. I *liked* that I could immediately recognize my son's Picasso-style artwork, and I was proud of it!

But his kindergarten teacher was apologetic. "I'm sorry Benjamin's work isn't like the others," she said. I think what she *really* wanted to say was "not as good as the others." I replied, "Please don't ever compare Benjamin to other kids. If you do, *you'll* always be disappointed: in your mind, he won't measure up to the other kids, and you'll see him as a failure. But if you compare Benjamin *only to himself*—what he was doing six days or six weeks or six months ago as compared to today—you'll be able to see how he's growing and learning."

We can break our own hearts when we compare our children to others, and this can cause us to see our children in a less-than-positive way. More importantly, this can cause us to overlook or minimize the wonderful things our children *do* accomplish. Most importantly, *we can break our children's hearts* when we do this—it's very, very harmful to our sons and daughters. I hope you'll resolve today to stop comparing your child to others—even to the other children in your family. And if other people—grandparents, teachers, etc.—compare your child to others, ask them nicely to stop and model the behavior and language you'd like them to adopt.

Formal Special Ed Assessments vs. Informal Assessments

In addition to the casual (but harmful) "comparing" described above, our children are formally measured, assessed, and/or evaluated by professionals when they receive Early Intervention, Special Ed Preschool, and Special Ed Services. As I mentioned in Chapter 1, I was always dismayed when Benjamin was assessed. The results of the tests did not match up with the child I knew. The same might be true for your child. I was also somewhat amazed by these tests—at how ridiculous some of them are. I'm going to share several stories about my son's experiences with these formal assessments, and will go into detail to expose some of the processes—and the harm—of these tests.

When Benjamin was two-and-a-half, I was told to bring him to the therapy clinic (which was part of a bigger center) for an assessment. At the clinic, we were shown into a very small room—just big enough for a desk and a little space for me to position Benj in his orthopedic stroller. A woman neither of us knew was sitting behind the desk. I told her who we were and her first words were, "You can wait in one of the chairs out in the hall."

I couldn't believe it! My son didn't know this woman—why would I leave him alone with a stranger, and how well would he do on a test under these circumstances? I told her I would stay, and she admonished me not to interfere with the test! (How can this woman live with herself? Is she Attila the Hun reincarnate?)

The test began, and things seemed to be going OK until she asked Benjamin to start stacking blocks. She instructed: "Please stack two blocks..." Then three, then four, then five, and so on. Because of the spasticity in his hands, it was difficult for Benj to relax his grip on the blocks in order to get them squarely on top of each other. So by the time he had the seventh block in his hand, the stack looked like the Leaning Tower of Pisa, and when he tried to place the last block on top, the whole thing fell down.

I watched in horror as Ms. Attila marked a zero on this part of the test! "Wait," I said, almost in a scream. "What are you testing? Is this a test of his fine motor skills or an intelligence test [I knew it was the latter]? If it's an intelligence test, he understands what you want him to do and you shouldn't penalize him just because his fingers can't do what he wants them to do!" She was unmoved; the test instructions were clear: if the child didn't complete the task, the score was zero. Things went from bad to worse.

A couple of questions later, Ms. Attila whipped out a piece of paper and some crayons, and ordered, "Draw a straight line and a circle, Benjamin." At home, when Benj wanted to color or paint, he used a desk-top easel, which sat on a piece of non-slip fabric on the kitchen table. Then, a piece of paper was taped to the easel. Benj held on to the easel with his left hand, for support, and in his right hand was the fattest, longest crayon we could find! Only with all these things in place could Benjamin color. But none were available for the test.

Benjamin *knew* the routine for coloring, and since these things weren't in place he ignored her command. So Ms. Attila prodded him by shaking some of the crayons out of the box. They were regular size crayons that had been *worn down to no longer than an inch or so long*—he couldn't even get a grip on one! Another zero on the test.

At the end of this tortuous experience, Ms. Attila said I could request a copy of the test results. I politely responded that the results were invalid, because she scored Benjamin on his fine motor skills—not his ability to understand and follow directions—and he was not provided with the accommodations he needed. I wrote these comments on the test, and we left.

A few months later, when Benjamin was "exiting" Early Intervention Services at age three, the Service Coordinator (Shelley) arrived on our doorstep one last time, test kit in hand. I sat Benjamin at the little table and chairs he and his sister used all the time. Shelley sat down opposite him, and then said, "You and Emily need to leave the room now." "No," I replied politely, "we'll say where we are, on the couch." I couldn't believe it! Why should I leave the room *in my own home and leave my son alone with her?* She responded by instructing Emily and me to be quiet and not interrupt. (Shelley must have gone to the same Test-Giver School as Ms. Attila.) It was all I could do not to laugh out loud! What did she think we were going to do? Dance to *Sesame Street* music during the test, give Benjamin all the answers, or what?

SOMETIMES YA' GOTTA' LAUGH !

Do you ever get tired of educators or others telling you, "But your child *does* have _____."

Next time someone tells you this in an IEP meeting or wherever, say, "Yes, and I knew it before you!" Then chuckle a bit.

Or try this: look the person in the eye, slap your hands to your cheeks (practice this right now), open your eyes and mouth as wide as possible in absolute shock, and say, *"He does? Why didn't anyone ever tell me?"* And try not to laugh out loud!

No interruptions! Or else!

So Emily and I sat as quiet as two little mice on the couch, just like we were told, listening to Shelley asking the questions, and Benjamin responding. Until...

I heard Shelley asking the same question repeatedly. Benjamin, meanwhile, was picking his nose and staring at the ceiling—ignoring her one way or another. Here was the question: "Benjamin, is your mommy a boy or a girl?"

Now, Benjamin has always loved words, and he is also a very "literal" child—a word means what it means! He had only been talking for a few months, but he had a big vocabulary. Benj had gone from saying, "Ma-ma-ma-ma-ma...." (which didn't mean me—it was just the only sound he made) to practically speaking in paragraphs! It was like everything he heard since he was born was "in there" and once he started talking, it all came out!

So when Shelley asked him, "Is your mommy a boy or a girl?" he didn't answer because *the question didn't make any sense to him!* I got up off the couch—breaking the rule, yes, I did—kneeled down next to Shelley and whispered in her ear, "Benjamin knows I'm not a boy or a girl—ask him if I'm a *man or a woman.*" She whispered back, "I can't; that's not what the test question is! If I ask it that way, it will invalidate the test!" I whispered back, "If you want him to give you an answer, you've got to ask the question the right way!" She relented, followed my suggestion, and Benjamin answered, "My mommy's a *woman!*"

As it turned out, Benjamin did well on the test—according to Shelley, he did "better than expected." I didn't know if this was a compliment or an insult. Regardless, I wasn't enthralled with my son being tested. But I tried to be a "good parent," so when staff from the next rung in the Service System (Special Ed Preschool) called a few days later, Benj and I made the trip to their offices for a battery of tests: intelligence, PT, and OT.

The intelligence test was first. This tester didn't ask me to leave—I don't know if she had read Benjamin's file to see *my* "history" or if it wasn't a big deal. We were in a large room where all the tests would take place: one area was filled with OT/PT mats, while another part was more office-like.

The tester began: showing Benjamin pictures, photos, and other things, asking him to identify them. At one point, she showed him photos of cartoon characters and he couldn't give her any answers. Why? Because when my children were very young, I didn't let them watch cartoons! So he earned some zeroes on that part of the test. Later, the tester showed him photos or drawings of household goods. He did fine on this part until she showed him photos of an iron and an ironing board—0 and 0 again! Who irons anymore? Benjamin had never seen me iron. The few times I did—during the three years he had been alive—were after our kids were in bed!

I've mentioned that one of Benjamin's strengths is his great auditory memory. He also has extraordinary hearing—he can hear things the rest of us don't! And he's always been ultra-sensitive to sounds: he often stopped what he was doing to listen to a sound, and an unexpected sound could throw him for a loop. (As a baby, he cried frequently because of this, and to this day, he has a very sensitive "startle reflex" to unexpected sounds, as do others with disabilities.)

Toward the end of the test, Benjamin was shown a picture of something (I don't remember what), and the tester asked him what it was. He practically screamed with joy, "Garbage truck!" and gave me a big smile. Well, it wasn't a garbage truck and the tester gave him another zero. "Wait," I implored. "He said that because *he heard a garbage truck drive by!*" I proudly added details about Benjamin's great auditory abilities: the mini-blinds of the wall-to-wall windows in this room blotted out any vision of the outdoors, but Benjamin heard a sound *from very far off* and knew it was a garbage truck! The tester wasn't impressed; the zero stood. I asked, "Can't you give him another chance to answer that question?" "No," she replied, "that would invalidate the test."

Next were the PT and OT assessments. Everything went fine with the PT, but not with the OT. She wanted me to put Benj on the floor so he could stack donuts and do other "OT stuff," but she had *no* positioning chairs. I told her Benj could sit up by himself on the floor, but *he wouldn't be able to do anything with his hands or arms*—it would take every bit of concentration for him to maintain his posture. She repeated her instructions, I restated my position, and she finally agreed he could stay in his orthopedic stroller. Then she searched for something to use as a table surface. I attached Benjamin's stroller tray, and she grinned in apparent embarrassment and appreciation.

This episode disturbed me. What happened with other kids who might not have had an orthopedic stroller with a tray? If they weren't positioned properly, how well would they do on the OT assessment? And why didn't the OT have the right equipment? How many children had been assessed inaccurately because she didn't provide the appropriate accommodations?

Well, that was it. I made the decision to never allow Benjamin to be tested again. If anyone wanted to know about him, they could "informally" assess him by spending time with him, playing with him, talking to him, coloring with him, talking to me and his dad, interviewing others who knew Benjamin, or something else. But no more *formal* assessments—and informal assessments *are* permitted under IDEA. Now, for what it's worth, some school districts might say they can't do informal assessments, just because that's not what they usually do. But Federal law says they *can* be done, as detailed in Chapter 9.

During Benjamin's elementary school years at the wonderful, inclusive neighborhood school, no formal assessments were ever done. But one day, "Tina," a wonderful Special Ed teacher told me she had just received a new test, and asked if she could give it to Benj—not to test *him,* but to determine if she liked the test. (The testing industry is Big Business, and these companies vie for educators' business.) Tina and I were friends, Benj loved her, so I agreed. Afterward, she was confused about something and asked me about it. There were several pictures on the test Benj couldn't identify, and Tina knew Benj knew what they were. Why couldn't he identify them on the test? When she showed me the pictures, I immediately knew why: they were black and white drawings, and Benj has always been able to see things better *in color* than black and white—his dad and I figured this out early on. Again, this made me wonder about other children. What if a another child had vision like Benjamin's, and she received a bunch of zeroes on an intelligence test simply because she saw color better than black and white? How accurate would that assessment be?

There's one more story that illustrates the harm that is often part-and-parcel of Special Ed Assessments. During his first grade year, we thought Benj could learn to read easier if he had large print. Before we could access large print Services from the state's office "for the blind," a qualifying diagnosis was needed. So an ophthalmologist gave one to Benj: "visual cerebral defect," meaning there's sometimes a disconnect between the signal from the brain to the eye. Benjamin's teacher was then able to send his first grade books to Denver, where they were enlarged. I didn't know it at the time, but this information—the paper trail of the diagnosis and the fact that his teacher was using these state Services—was passed on to our region's Board of Cooperative Educational Services (BOCES). Our small school district—like many others—didn't have its own roster of different specialists, so the BOCES specialists provided certain Services.

A few months passed, and when I picked Benjamin up one afternoon, Kim, the teacher's aide said, "Benjamin doesn't like that vision lady very much." I didn't know what she was talking about and told her so. She went on to explain, "It was the same lady that was here last week, you know?" I still didn't know what she was talking about! Here's the long and the short of it: the week before, "some lady" walked into Benjamin's classroom, told the classroom teacher and Kim that she needed to do a vision assessment, took hold of Benj's wheelchair and began pushing him down the hall. Kim stayed with him, but when they arrived at a little office off the library, the Vision Woman told Kim she needed to wait outside while she tested Benj (she, too, went to the same Test-Giver School as Ms. Attila!). Evidently, Benjamin—much to his credit—"did not cooperate," so the Vision Woman gave up, chalked it up to Benjamin "having a bad day," turned him over to Kim and left. She came back the next week—this time allowing Kim to stay with Benjamin during the assessment—and was able to give him part of the test before he again "refused to cooperate." *(Yay, Benj!)*

As Kim told me this story, I was in shock. I had no idea who this woman was, I didn't know there were any plans to give Benjamin a vision assessment, and I had not given my permission! Kim and the classroom teacher assumed I was on top of all this and had just forgotten to tell them. I was furious! I wasn't mad at Kim or Benj's classroom teacher—they thought they were doing what I wanted them to do. And they were as appalled as I was that someone from BOCES could just waltz into the school and do what she wanted! They were also embarrassed and felt bad that they hadn't protected Benjamin better.

I called the BOCES office to find out what was going on and advised them I had not given my permission for Benjamin to be tested. Their response? When I signed the original IEP forms, giving my permission for Benjamin to receive Special Ed Services, I was also giving permission for assessments! It was news to me! Is it news to you?

Here's the outcome: I told the BOCES people that I would not allow my son to be taken from his classroom by anyone without my permission and his teacher's permission, and they must give me prior notification before attempting

Time for your test, Benjamin!

to assess my son for anything. I felt a lot of anger, but I was very polite and calm on the phone. We can be firm and polite without stirring up a hornet's nest that will result *in our children being stung.* They were polite in return, and agreed to my request.

Next, I told his teacher and the teacher's aide that when Benjamin was at school, *they were in charge,* and they were not to let him leave the room with anyone unless I had given my written permission. They were happy with this "authority," and they didn't like the Vision Woman either.

I had no idea what these experiences were like for Benjamin, and I felt guilty that I had not been able to protect him. He was very shy at the time, but if he felt comfortable and safe, he was a happy, friendly little boy. The fact that he "did not cooperate" with the Vision Woman told me so much. He must have been scared to death to be pushed by a stranger, into a small room he was unfamiliar with, where he was bombarded with questions on an assessment! At this time in his life, when he was scared or nervous, he just shut down: he'd drop his chin to his chest, slump his shoulders, and become nonresponsive. And at that time, he couldn't propel himself in his wheelchair very well, so there was no way to get away from this scary woman!

It breaks my heart to think about the millions of children with disabilities —maybe yours—who have similar experiences every day in a public school where they're supposed to feel safe, and where *we think* others are taking good care of them. Think about how many children are being assessed by strangers, in strange environments. Think about how the results of these assessments are used to make important decisions about our children's lives and their education. And this information is likely to *stay in the child's permanent record!* If all of us—parents and educators—tried to walk in our children's shoes, maybe we would do things very differently. I hope we will, because the results of these assessments can be inaccurate and cause harm:

- Assessments may be given by a strange person, and in a strange environment. How does anyone expect a child—especially a very young child—to do well in this situation? The result? An inaccurate assessment.

- If the child is a "morning person" and the test is in the afternoon, the test results may be inaccurate, since they don't reflect the best the child can do.

- Too many testers do not provide the appropriate accommodations to children with disabilities, which can lead to inaccurate test results.

- For the most part, assessments compare our children against the "norm" (an "average" child), and our children never "measure up." Seldom do assessments compare the child "today" to the same child six months ago, to determine progress and accomplishment.

- Assessments are supposed to measure a child's *strengths,* as well as his needs, but seldom are the strengths identified and/or measured—the focus is on a child's "deficits"!

Finally, I think we should consider the words of an experienced Special Education teacher (25+ years), who once told me, "Educators are supposed to

> THOSE WHO ARE
> ONCE FOUND
> TO BE BAD
> ARE PRESUMED
> SO FOREVER.
> *Latin Proverb*

use assessments to discover something new about a child—his strengths and needs. But assessments are often used *to prove what an educator already believes to be true.*" What could this mean for your child? A tester might choose a particular test in order to get the results he wants. In other cases, what happened to Benjamin might happen to your child: accommodations aren't provided and/or a test intended to assess intelligence is *scored* based on a child's fine motor skills!

During the IFSP or IEP process, the Services a child will/will not receive, *where and how* a child will be educated, and other potentially life-altering decisions are made, *based on the results of assessments.* What if the assessments are wrong? I hope you'll consider staying "no" to formal assessments and "yes" to *informal* assessments for your child. I also hope you'll do whatever it takes to make sure you know what's going on at your child's school. Is your child being tested without your knowledge and permission? Do *you* know the person who is giving the test? Does your *child* know the person? *Where and when* will it be given, and under what circumstances? Do you know *what* tests are being administered and *why?* Do you ask to see the tests beforehand, and/or inquire about the different tests available, in order to discover which is appropriate for your child? Our children's lives are too precious to be scarred and wounded by uncaring professionals who subject our children to the tyranny of formal assessments. There are better ways to get the needed information, which I'll detail in Chapter 9.

Stop Apologizing!

If we want our children to be successful in any environment, now and in the future, we need to stop apologizing! We don't always use the words, "I apologize" or "I'm sorry"—but we speak and/or behave in ways that are apologetic. And this is very harmful to our children!

I'll share one of my favorite examples—favorite because so many parents can relate to it. Many parents do this, or some variation, but parents of children with autism seem to do it more than others.

The scene: four-year-old child with autism goes ballistic in the grocery store check-out line. He screeches, flaps his arms, and more. Everyone within earshot has stopped in their tracks to stare. Mom grabs her child's hand, looks at the gawkers, and says, "He has autism..." When she does this, she's apologizing for his behavior.

Let's say you're this mom. Most likely, your response is, "No! I'm not apologizing, I just want people to know that his behavior is part of his disability." Well, that sounds good, but what's really going on in your head is that you don't want people to think you're a lousy parent, because you know some of the gawkers are thinking *(or saying),* "If that were *my* kid, when I got him home, I'd..."

So you're *really* apologizing for your own benefit, but that's not what your child hears. Your child is hearing, in essence, that his behavior is OK because it's part of having autism (or whatever). You might disagree, but keep reading—there's more.

Have you ever seen a four-year-old child *who does not have autism* go ballistic in the grocery store check-out line, and everyone within earshot stops to stare? I thought so. When *he's* screeching, flapping his arms, and more, does *his* mom grab him by the hand and say to the gawkers, "He takes after his father!" I hope you're chuckling—audience members during my presentations usually chuckle at this point, and I'm glad. Because sometimes it takes humor to get a serious point across!

Back to the story: the second mom probably does *not* give that response—she probably says nothing. Why? Because it's nobody's business! *And the way your child behaves, walks, looks, eats, or does anything is also no one's business!* As I've mentioned before, our children's lives are not for public consumption—they have a right to privacy! Have they ever given us permission to talk about them? We do not owe anyone an apology or an explanation about our children—and consider how our children feel when we do this!

If we're not offering unsolicited explanations, as described above, we may feel obligated to respond to the questions of Ms. Nosy. Many parents answer Ms. Nosy's questions in the belief that they're helping to educate or inform others about their child's disability or people with disabilities, in general. But put yourself in the shoes of Ms. Nosy: do you really want to learn something important or *are you just trying to satisfy your curiosity?*

Many of us may be offended by nosy questions, but we still answer them. Why? I think it's because from the time our children are diagnosed, we spend lots of time talking to many different people about our children: physicians, therapists, educators, and many others. So even though we might not *like* the nosy questions, providing answers or explanations about our children—even to people we may not like or know very well—becomes second nature. In addition, when strangers, acquaintances, or even other family members ask personal questions, we may automatically answer them so as not to cause offense. But this is very offensive and harmful *to our children*—shouldn't we care more about *their feelings* than the feelings of others?

You may still feel it's important to try to educate others when the opportunity arises—like when someone asks you something about your child. If so, let's be realistic: how much information can you really provide while standing next to someone in a store's check-out line, or while you and Ms. Nosy are squeezing the tomatoes? Not much, so don't bother. If, however, a longer period of time is available and you're still determined to educate on-the-fly, tell Ms. Nosy about your child's condition, *but never about your child.* In other words, if it were me, I could explain that cerebral palsy is not genetic; not progressive; and it's similar to a person having a stroke, but it occurs before, during, or just after birth. I would not use my son as an example and talk about "his" cerebral palsy. He's not a medical school mannequin; he's a living, breathing person with feelings!

Being accosted with questions or comments from Ms. Nosy and Mrs. Curious (men seldom do this), can cut us—and our children—to the bone. And it gets old and tiresome! To save our hearts and souls, many of us (including

1-800-Blah-Blah

Some parents have shown me business cards they carry in their wallets that say something like, "My child isn't misbehaving; he has autism." The card includes a phone number people can call to "learn more." This is another idea that's backed by great intentions, but which probably leads to less than desirable outcomes!

Pretend you don't know anything about autism; you see a young child going ballistic in the grocery store check-out line and the mother hands you this card. Are you *really* going to run right home and call that number or are you going to hope you don't ever see a kid "like that" again?

These cards can do more harm than good. Since Ms. Nosy probably won't call for more info, she'll be left with a negative impression of autism. Better for her to think your kid is just having a bad day than to perpetuate negative, stereotypical images about people with autism!

me) develop a little tougher skin, along with a one- or two-sentence spiel we can reel off without thinking, and then go on our way. But I've got some ideas that may work better.

First, however, give some thought as to *why* nosy questions or rude comments make us feel so bad. On the surface, we might think it's about our children. But I think it's really because these invasions of our privacy leave us feeling violated—vulnerable and powerless. Many of us have spent enormous amounts of time dealing with a great number of people (physicians, therapists, Service Providers, etc.), and we're accustomed to handling what amounts to routine *invasions of privacy.* But being *accustomed to something* doesn't always make it easier to deal with—it's almost like a wound that doesn't heal, and each time we have to share personal information about our child's history (and our *own*, sometimes), it's equivalent to reopening the wound. So, again, we're left feeling powerless and vulnerable.

Was he born like that, Dear?

One way to take the power back is to answer a question/comment with a question. So if someone asks, for example, "Was he born like that," you can respond, "Why would you ask that?" When *you* ask a question, you've shifted the "obligation" back to Ms. Nosy, and your question will most likely make her realize how rude *her* question is.

Doing this might seem inconsiderate—many of us are so accustomed to being nice and answering everyone's questions (even though we're then being rude and cruel to our children!), that doing anything else might seem less than polite. But you can answer a question with a question with a gracious smile on your face and in your most pleasant, kind voice. *You* will look well-mannered, and Ms. Nosy will be the one who looks (and is) rude!

Our children are counting on us to protect them. Their feelings and their privacy are precious and should not be violated to satisfy someone's spontaneous curiosity. Remember that our children learn from our actions. How *you* handle these situations is how *your child* will one day handle them. As an adult, do you want him feeling obligated to respond and explain to every Ms. Nosy who crosses his path?

I'll share other strategies to use when unwanted questions arise, in the next section on humor. But there's more to cover on the subject of apologizing.

Whining and sharing too much information (TMI) about our children aren't exactly apologies, but they're in the same class of actions which are harmful to our children. *Our* whining isn't the same as when our children whine—a parent's whine is more in the form of explaining and giving TMI.

For example, "Judy's" six-year-old daughter, "Michelle," has been invited to a classmate's birthday party. Judy is as excited and happy as she could be—it's the first birthday party Michelle has been invited to. But she's also worried: Michelle has cerebral palsy (but you can substitute any disability and the accompanying details), and she uses a walker, feeds herself with her fingers, wears diapers, and can't transfer from her walker to a chair by herself. Judy wonders if she should expect the birthday girl's mother to help Michelle with these things?

What if Michelle's messy eating habits grosses everyone out? What if she has a bowel movement while she's at the party? Judy considers going to the party with Michelle, but she might be "in the way" or that might be embarrassing to Michelle. Oh, there's too many problems—maybe Michelle shouldn't go...

But Michelle wants to go so badly, and Judy wants her to go! So she calls the birthday girl's mother (who she only knows very casually) and says:

> Michelle is so excited about coming to the party! And—well, you know she has cerebral palsy and uses a walker, and I thought about coming with her to help, but that probably wouldn't feel too cool to her—and so I hope you don't mind helping her—I mean she can't transfer into a chair by herself. And you know she's a pretty messy eater—I hope that won't be a problem—I mean she still eats with her fingers, but she's not like a baby—you know she just can't hold a fork. And, well, she's still in diapers and...

Zip it, so you don't give

Too

Much

Information

Judy continues explaining and gives Too Much Information. She thinks she's being helpful, but her words have made Michelle look awful, *and* they've scared the pants off the birthday girl's mom! Judy doesn't realize she's whining, but she is; she knows Michelle is going to need help at the party, and she feels a little guilty about it, so she's also pleading.

Here's a different way Judy could share the information:

> Michelle is so excited about coming to the party! She said your daughter loves Barbie dolls, but let me know if there any other toys she loves...we're going shopping tomorrow. You know Michelle uses a walker, and she'll need a little help transferring into a chair or to the floor. I thought it might be helpful if I brought her to the party a few minutes early so she and I can show you how to help her get into a chair. Would that be okay?

That's all Judy needs to say *for now*. When they arrive early for the party, Judy can show the birthday girl's mom (and any other adults who are there—grandparents, etc.) how to help Michelle transfer. Next, if Michelle can speak for herself, she can tell the other mom that she'll eat the birthday cake with her fingers, and she might need someone to help her eat the ice cream, but maybe some of the other kids can help, since they probably already do this at school. If Michelle cannot speak for herself at this time, Judy can share this information in a casual, light-hearted way, giving only the information that's needed (no talk about how Michelle's hands don't work, etc.). And Judy won't bring up the diaper issue unless there's a good possibility Michelle might have a bowel movement during the party (many of us know our children's "schedules"). Judy doesn't need to worry about a wet diaper; Michelle can be changed after she gets back home. If Judy *does* need to discuss the BM/diaper issue, she can do so a positive, respectful way with a minimum of fuss. Michelle needs to be involved in this, as much as possible, explaining how it's best to change her on the bed, or whatever.

If you're gasping, thinking Michelle is too young to do this, or this would be embarrassing to Michelle, think again. The sooner Michelle can speak for

A DAD'S EPIPHANY

After I spoke on this subject at a workshop, David, the father of a four-year-old daughter who has Down syndrome approached me and said: "I have a confession to make. People come up to my daughter and me in grocery stores, malls, and other places and say, 'Oh, your daughter is so cute!' And she really is—we're so proud of her. But when people say that, I answer, 'Thanks, but she has Down syndrome.' *I don't know why I do that!* I guess I'm apologizing for her disability and I shouldn't!"

David was quiet for a moment, then added, "I guess it wouldn't be much different than if someone told me I had a great mom, and I said, 'Yeah, but she has a lot of flatulence!' *That* wouldn't be right, so what I've been doing to my precious daughter isn't right either! *I'm not going to do it anymore.* When someone says my daughter is cute, I'll proudly say, 'Thank you!' No more apologizing!" And I suggested that he talk to her about it, apologize (this is the time when an apology *is* appropriate), and assure her it won't happen again. I feel it's important to own up to our errors. Others will forgive us and help us do better.

herself and take responsibility for getting the help she needs, the better. And which would be less embarrassing for Michelle: to take part in explaining what she needs and how she needs it, or to be talked about like she's not there, and then to be changed by someone she has no relationship with? By taking part in the details of how it should be done, Michelle is more in control and grown up—instead of being like a passive baby having her diaper changed.

Many parents have said they feel the need to explain about their child and her condition when strangers or new acquaintances speak to the child and the child doesn't respond—because she doesn't hear or she doesn't speak. At that point, the parent launches into an explanation about *why* the child didn't respond *(TMI!!!).* In too many cases, the Stranger then expresses pity or sympathy: "Ohhhh, poor little thing..." or "Ohhhh, that's too bad..." or something similar. People mean well, *but such comments can be terribly hurtful to our children!* There are a couple of solutions to handle this situation, which require the participation of the child. This needs to be discussed with the child ahead of time, and practicing/role playing at home will help both you and your child feel comfortable with these new methods.

If the child doesn't hear and uses sign language, the parent can sign to the child, saying that the Stranger spoke to the child and telling the child what the person said. The child can then sign back a response, and the parent can interpret. If the Stranger's comment was something like, "What a pretty dress..." the child's response could simply be, "Thank you." So the parent would say, "My daughter says 'thank you'." If the Stranger's original comment was something like, "Hi, how are you today?" The parent can sign that to the child, and the child can respond (and the mother translates to the Stranger), "I'm fine, thank you. I use sign language to communicate."

There are different solutions if the child didn't respond to a Stranger's comment because she doesn't speak and doesn't have a communication device. If the Stranger said something like, "You're such a nice strong boy..." The parent can speak for the child and respond, "My son says 'thank you.' He communicates with his eyes [or whatever]." If the Stranger simply greeted the child ("Hi, how are you today?"), the parent needs to teach the child to wave and/or smile/nod in response. The parent might also want to add, "My son says 'hello,' too. He communicates with his eyes [or whatever]."

In these situations, *no more explanations are needed.* If the Stranger follows-up with, "What's wrong with him," or something similar, the parent can respond, "There's nothing wrong with him, he simply communicates differently," or she could use some of the techniques in the next section on humor.

Sometimes we *do* actually say, "I'm sorry," and then our children learn to say it, too. Several years ago, I became friends with Jim, a man who has cerebral palsy and uses a power wheelchair. While spending time together at a conference, I opened the door for Jim, picked up something he dropped, and helped him transfer from his chair to a sofa. Each time, he said, "I'm sorry..." and I got sick of hearing that! So I asked him why he kept apologizing every time I helped him with something. At first, he was surprised—he didn't even realize he did this! Then he had to think about it for a moment, and replied, "I guess it's because I've needed so much help all my life that I feel like I'm a bother to other people. And I don't like to *ask* for help, because I feel like people already have enough to do for me..."

I told Jim I helped him because we were friends, it was the right thing to do, and it was not a "bother." I added that when I can't get the door open because my arms are full of groceries, and someone opens the door for me, I don't say, "I'm sorry," I say, "Thank you." He promised he would work hard to change his vocabulary!

I felt bad for Jim—what must it feel like to think you're a "bother" to others? But I also had a feeling Jim might have inadvertently learned some of this from his parents. When he was younger and being pushed by them in a manual wheelchair, they might have said, "I'm sorry," many times, like when people had to "make way" to let Jim's wheelchair through, or when an elevator became more crowded by Jim's wheelchair, and similar circumstances. So we need to be aware of our language and our actions, knowing our children will most likely imitate us, sooner or later.

In all situations, we need to care more about our children's feelings than the feelings of those asking the questions! With that rule in your heart, respond in ways that protect your child's feelings, privacy, and dignity. If words fail, communicate with your body language: (1) be silent, but friendly, maintaining eye contact, putting the burden of continuing the conversation on the other person; (2) turn your back to end the conversation; or (3) walk away. Remember, we owe more courtesy and respect to our children than to strangers or other nosy people.

We may apologize, whine, explain, and give TMI in many different ways and for many different reasons. But we can change and do better. And because our children will have to deal with similar situations the rest of their lives, it's important they learn to speak for themselves—and the sooner, the better!

The Power of Humor

When we're accosted by nosy, curious, and/or rude people, we can use humor to take the power back *and* protect the privacy and dignity of our children and families. Following are several examples you can use as is, or modify them for your particular circumstances. In most cases, you'll need to discuss these ahead of time, with your child and/or other members of the family so everyone is in "on the act." Many of these scenarios are written with the parent doing the talking—when our children are very young and can't yet speak for themselves. But as soon as possible, our children should speak for themselves, so these can be modified and/or you and your family can create your own humorous responses. Keep in mind that if your emotions are ragged, for whatever reason—your child is very young, you're still dealing with lots of new feelings, or you're just not up to using humor at any given time—fall back on a suggestion from the previous section: respond to Ms. Busy-Body with, "Why would you ask that?"

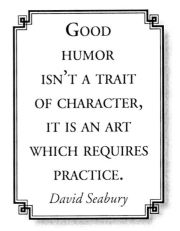

GOOD HUMOR ISN'T A TRAIT OF CHARACTER, IT IS AN ART WHICH REQUIRES PRACTICE.
David Seabury

Since my son, Benjamin, got his service dog, Riley, he's stared at even more than before! Sometimes Riley wears a "haltie"—it's like a horse halter, which helps Benj control Riley better. But many people think the haltie is a muzzle, so they ask, "Does she bite?" Benj learned how to handle this question from "Dave," a man who also uses a wheelchair and has a service dog. When strangers approach Dave and ask, "Does your dog bite," Dave replies, with as much seriousness as he can muster, *"How do you think I ended up in this chair?"*

BADDA-BING!

GENERIC RESPONSE TO ALMOST ANY INTRUSIVE QUESTION

You and your child are in the grocery store, at church, or other location. Ms. Nosy asks you a question about your child. You don't need to grit your teeth, hold back tears, or anything else. Instead, begin digging through your purse, pull out a pen and paper, and say, "Gee, we're really busy right now, but I'll be happy to discuss this with you later. Give me your name and phone number and I'll call you this evening. It won't take more than an hour or so—what would be a good time for you?"

At this point, Ms. Nosy will probably back-pedal away from you as fast as possible! But if she's determined, and says something like, "Well, I just wanted to know [whatever]," be a broken record and repeat yourself. But if she *does* give you her name and number, toss it in the first garbage can you come across.

RESPONSES TO: "WHAT HAPPENED TO HIM?"

Become very serious and respond, "You know, we're not sure! A meteor landed in our neighborhood last night, and all the children in the neighborhood were affected. Do *you* know anything about it?"

Or, if parents are together when this question is asked about their child, they can simultaneously point to one another and exclaim, "He/She did it!" And then laugh uproariously as you move away.

RESPONSES TO: "WAS SHE BORN LIKE THAT?"

With as straight a face as you can manage, and with pride oozing from your voice, say, "Why, yes! She has the Albert Einstein syndrome." (You could substitute any famous name: Marilyn Monroe, Zorro, Barbie, etc. or use a silly word—Pine Needle Syndrome or Senatorial Syndrome!) Most nosy people won't bother to ask any further questions; they'll usually nod in agreement (they don't want to feel stupid) or mumble, "I've never heard of that..." If so, you don't need to say anymore, just look at the person and smile, and put the burden on them to continue the conversation. Most will simply go their way and leave you alone.

Alternatively (and this was shared by another parent), if someone asks, "Was she born like that?" you can hold your hands about fifteen inches apart and respond, "No, she was about like this when she was born."

Here's a different strategy to use with any type of question: you and your family members, including the child with a disability, can create your own gibberish language—practice it at home. When Mrs. Curious asks you a question, begin simultaneously jabbering in your new language. Try not to laugh too hard in your native language as Mrs. Curious walks away from you.

And here's one my son and I came up with after a stranger approached us in an airport. Ms. Busy-Body walked up to me, pointed to Benjamin who was behind me, and asked, "Is that your son?" When I said "yes," she mumbled some pity-laden drivel and quickly walked away before I could respond. Benj asked me what happened, I told him, and he asked, in his biggest 18-year-old voice, "When is this pity crap going to stop?" So we agreed on a new game plan next time someone points to Benjamin and asks, "Is he your son?" I'll say, "Who?"

and when Ms. Busy-Body points again and says, "Him," I'll respond, "I don't know who he is, but he's been stalking me for the last 18 years!"

RESPONSES TO STARES:

If it's a stare "in-passing," at the mall or somewhere else, smile the biggest, goofiest smile you can, wave like you're Miss America, and say, "Hi! How are you?" as you keep moving.

If it's a "standing-still-stare," like when you're in parallel check-out lines, your technique will be a little different. Make eye contact with the Starer and then look to your right and left, as if trying to determine if you're actually the *Staree.* Make eye contact again and point to yourself as in, "Me?" followed immediately with a big grin and an even bigger wave, as if you've been recognized for being a famous person!

There are other ingenious strategies—you might already have some of your own. "Jayne," the mother of a beautiful two-year-old daughter told me:

> My daughter has very pronounced Down syndrome facial characteristics, and because of our family's skin tones, Megan looks like she could be Chinese. In the grocery store one day, Megan was talking a blue streak—but we couldn't understand her speech pattern at the time. A lady who was within earshot came closer and said, "My goodness! I've never heard anyone so young speaking Chinese!" And I replied, "Oh, that's nothing! She's starting French lessons next week!"

Again—as soon as possible and to the greatest degree possible—our children need to speak for themselves and handle these situations on their own, including dealing with children at school or in other settings.

Many parents express deep concern when their children are teased about their disabilities. But it's important to remember that children tease other children because they have big ears, small ears, short hair, long hair, and a myriad of other reasons. And, frankly, many children tease other children because they *like* them and/or want their attention. So in one sense, if a child with a disability is being teased, it can mean he's being seen as "just like the other kids"—and that's a good thing! In many instances, children who are genuinely disliked are ignored. Of course, cruel or persistent teasing and bullying are harmful and adults should be called in at that point.

In a perfect world, no teasing of any kind would ever occur. And some schools do a better job of monitoring and discouraging teasing among students. But in all likelihood, our children will be teased at some point, so we better help them learn how to handle it. With my own children, role-playing was helpful: my daughter would play the role of the Teaser and I would pretend to be Emily to show her different responses.

How to handle teasing ultimately represents a family's values. Some families teach their children to walk away and tell an adult. This might work temporarily, but it might also set the child up for even more teasing as soon as the adult is out of earshot. Humor can also be used by our children. "Sandra" was concerned about her eight-year-old daughter. One side of "Amber's" face was different

Ed Roberts (from Chapter 2) used a power chair and breathed through a portable ventilator tube. He made a *conscious* decision that when people stared at him, he would believe they were staring because *he was a star*—not a "helpless cripple." Ed's mental technique took the power away from the Starer and put is squarely in Ed's lap. The strategies I've shared—and those you create—can do the same for you, your child, and your family.

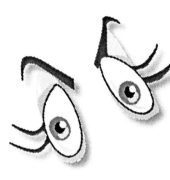

from the other side: one eye was smaller and didn't "match up" evenly with the other, and she was being teased about it. Here was my suggestion to Sandra: "When another child asks Amber about her eye or makes a comment about it, she can say, 'Don't you know? It's a bionic eye and I can see right through you!'" Some children will believe her and some will know she's pulling their leg. Regardless, the outcome is that Amber is back in charge of the situation; she's not at the mercy of others.

Three Questions for Better Relationships

In *Living with Change: The Semantics of Coping*, author Wendell Johnson shares some of the best advice ever on improved communication. He first detailed the difficulties we have in relationships because of faulty communication between speaker and listener: we misunderstand each other, your words don't mean the same to me, and so forth. So he shared three questions we can ask that can move us to better understanding and better relationships:

1. What do you mean? [for clarity]

2. How do you know? [for validity]

3. What then?—or—What's next? [what do we do with this information, where do we go from here, etc.]

Imagine how using these questions can change things! Your child's teacher says, "Johnny isn't doing so well in math..." You ask, "What do you mean?" Your question forces the teacher to be specific, to provide more details, to explain further, to give you information that's really helpful. After she's provided this information, you ask, "How do you know?" Now the teacher needs to show you proof, explain her opinion, and so forth. Once she's done that, you ask, "What then?" or "What's next?" What should be done about this, how can we better help Johnny, and more.

Imagine using this technique with therapists, physicians, the IEP Team, and others who touch your child's life. These questions can help us get to the nitty-gritty, at one end, and the Big Picture, at the other. Asking these questions can help us discover the details that are crucial when making decisions, thinking about what's really important for our children's lives, and so much more.

Johnson suggests teaching this strategy to everyone in the family, too! Think of the family dilemmas that could be avoided with improved communication. And he thinks it's ever so important for children to learn to ask these questions—this is a truly valuable life skill. Don't be surprised (or offended) if your child asks *you* these questions! Be proud—you're teaching him how to gather information and have improved communication and better relationships!

Who Has the Disability?

When Benjamin was seven, I was concerned about him being taken to the bathroom at school by a female teacher's aide. I thought it might be time for the school to hire a male aide. To get someone else's perspective, I called my friend,

Tom. We had met years before and had become fast friends. I considered him a mentor: he had cerebral palsy, used a power wheelchair, lived on his own, and had a great life. I had already learned a great deal from Tom.

When I made the call and asked Tom for his opinion, I was surprised by his response: "What does Benjamin say about it?" I swallowed hard and sputtered and said I hadn't asked Benjamin.

With love and firmness, Tom replied, "Kathie, you go ask Benjamin. This ought to be his decision, not yours. And in the future, before you ask me or anyone else for advice about your son, you need to ask him, first. It's his life." Got the message—it came through loud and clear.

Part of me knew this. After all, I had let Benjamin make the decision to resign from his therapy career the year before. But I wasn't *acting on* what I knew in my heart. Tom's words stayed with me—they still live in my heart. So I asked Benjamin about the situation, and he said, "It doesn't matter—a lady helping me is fine." Whaddya' know? What I thought was a dilemma—one of my own creation—wasn't a dilemma at all.

In too many families, parents assume the responsibility for, as well as the "identity" of the disability. It's as if *we* had the diagnosis, instead of our children. As a result, we give our children few opportunities to participate in decisions about *their lives*. This, in turn, leads to our children growing into adults who have *learned helplessness*; they're unable to be in charge of their lives, so others take charge in group homes, sheltered workshops, and other segregated, special programs. And the dream of living a REAL LIFE goes up in smoke.

There are many bits of "evidence" to indicate that a parent is taking full responsibility, while giving the child little or none. And the easiest to spot is the way a parent talks, as when a mother says, "My IEP meeting is tomorrow," or "My therapist..." or "Our therapist..." when she's actually talking about her *child's* IEP meeting or her *child's* therapist. Saying, "Our Service Coordinator..." within Early Intervention Services makes sense, because those services *are* "family/child services." But in the other examples, we need to be accurate and precise, and say, "My child's [whatever]."

A child needs to "own" his disability and his life. *It is his life!* A child cannot take ownership unless and until his parents relinquish their ownership *to* him. He cannot have power and control over his life unless his parents cede *their* power and control *to* him. And there are two basic considerations of this issue.

First, your child needs to know he has a disability, including the name of it, and he needs to be able to tell someone if he's asked. I've met educators from the disability services department at universities as well as coordinators of youth conferences, who have said they routinely meet young adults with disabilities who are not even aware they have a disability! When this occurs, how in the world do we expect the young person to speak for himself and be in charge of his life?

Second, our children need to be involved in decisions about their lives, including the Services they receive (and how those Services are provided), their education, and more. If we hope our children will grow up to be self-directed

> ### KEEPING SECRETS
>
> The parent of a three-year-old told me her son didn't know he had cerebral palsy, and she had no intention of telling him. I told her *she* better tell him before someone else did!
>
> This is similar to parents who do not tell their children they were adopted, and the child finds out years later from someone else! Imagine the betrayal the child feels: "If my parents lied about this, what else did they lie about? Is my whole life a lie?" Most parents do not keep a condition like cancer or leukemia a secret from their children, do they? Why should we?

adults, we have to listen to them when they're children and be respectful of their wishes. Self-directed children become self-directed adults.

There are countless adults with developmental disabilities who were given few or no opportunities to make their own choices or decisions about their lives as children. Their parents didn't talk to them about therapies and other Services they received, and their parents and educators didn't involve them in discussions or decisions about their education. As children, they were expected to comply; their feelings didn't matter—and, again, many learned to be helpless. Sadly, adults often value a child's compliance more than his self-direction.

As adults, many of these people are at the mercy of the Adult Service System: they don't feel they can do anything without the authority, permission, or direction of someone else. Twenty-five-year-old "Jeff" complained that he had been waiting six years for his Vocational-Rehabilitation counselor to get him a job. "Why don't you try to get a job on your own," I asked. He responded, with a perplexed look on his face, "You mean I could *do that?*" Like many parents who think they must FOLLOW THE LAW, Jeff thought he had to do whatever someone in authority told him to do.

If we respect our children, if we listen to them, if we trust them, and if we have high expectations for their success, today and when they're adults, we'll make sure they're in charge of their lives. There's no better gift we could give our children.

> CHARACTER—THE WILLINGNESS TO ACCEPT RESPONSIBILITY FOR ONE'S OWN LIFE—IS THE SOURCE FROM WHICH SELF-RESPECT SPRINGS.
> *Joan Didion*

Regardless of where we've been or what we've done, we can change the direction of our children's present and future through our attitudes and actions. Remember: everything you've done in the past was the best you knew to do at the time—and the same is true for me. My "best" tomorrow will be better than my "best" today.

I hope you feel differently about your child now, than when you began reading this chapter. I hope you'll communicate these new feelings so your child will know what a wonderful, precious, able person she is! I hope she knows how proud you are of her, and I hope she's proud of who she is!

With the new attitudes and new actions described in this chapter, you're on your way to helping your child live a REAL LIFE. The next step involves examining the therapies and interventions that have been provided for your child, and considering alternatives.

A New Therapeutic Landscape and Tools for Success

6

Many, many children with disabilities spend much of their lives receiving one type of therapy or another: physical, occupational, speech, behavior, art, horticulture, horseback riding, music, etc., etc., etc.—we really know how to therapize children's lives. Because therapy is one of the components of CONVENTIONAL WISDOM that affects children in their private lives, as well as within Early Intervention, Special Ed Preschools, and Special Education Services, it deserves "first place" in the discussion of alternatives to CONVENTIONAL WISDOM which can enable our children to lead REAL LIVES. This chapter also details strategies for providing our children with the TOOLS they need to succeed, and the chapters that follow incorporate the philosophies included in this chapter.

Traditional Therapy could be generally described as: one or more adults working directly with a child—in a clinical setting or at home—for the purpose of helping a child achieve one or more specific functional skills, based on an able-bodied standard. Depending on the type of therapy, the adult may place her hands on the child's body, instruct the child to perform tasks, and/or spend time talking to the child. And there could be many other scenarios in between.

Traditional Therapy has been provided to children with disabilities for decades. And we first have to ask a really Big Question: if intensive therapies for children with developmental disabilities were really the "cure-all" they're promoted as, *why are there still adults with significant developmental disabilities?* These are adults who, as children, received intensive therapies for years and years, and many have painfully revealed some of the unintended, negative outcomes of traditional therapy—*which are now inflicted on many of our children.* That's a troubling scenario: decades of expensive therapy sessions with questionable effectiveness which may cause more harm than good. We can do better.

> IF THERE IS ANYTHING THAT WE WISH TO CHANGE IN THE CHILD, WE SHOULD FIRST EXAMINE IT AND SEE WHETHER IT IS NOT SOMETHING THAT COULD BETTER BE CHANGED IN OURSELVES.
>
> *C.G. Jung*

Unintended Consequences of Traditional Therapy

Like many other components of CONVENTIONAL WISDOM, the intent of Traditional Therapy is good (to help the child), but there are a variety of unintended, negative consequences that can be harmful to children and their families. Unfortunately, parents are not told about these consequences. I don't know if it's because providers of therapeutic services are *unaware* of these consequences or if, as Roy Gerstenberger noted at the end of Chapter 4, professionals are reluctant to reveal the side-effects of therapy.

Many parents of children who *do not* have disabilities make extraordinary efforts to protect their children from harmful or negative influences and environments. For example, some take their young children to school, instead of letting them ride the bus, because they don't want them being influenced by older children on the bus. Others homeschool their children, have strict guidelines about who their children spend time with, and do a variety of other things in an effort to reduce their children's exposure to harmful or potentially harmful influences and experiences.

Shouldn't we do the same? Because therapy has been promoted to us—by physicians, therapists, Early Intervention and Special Ed Preschool Service Provider, and others—we've been seduced by a cacophony of voices extolling the virtues of Traditional Therapy. In some instances, its importance is made the equivalent of a life-or-death decision. In other instances, practitioners peer into their crystal balls and predict dire consequences if our children do not receive therapy. We've only heard one side of the story, but there *are* two sides—and sometimes many more—to every story, as detailed below.

I'm Not-OK

One powerful and long-lasting lesson a child learns from Traditional Therapy is that he is NOT-OK. This was covered in detail in Chapter 4, but it's included here as a reminder. Please remember how adults with developmental disabilities felt they could not please their parents (because they couldn't walk or talk or achieve whatever goal the therapy attempted to fulfill), and they wistfully wished their parents could have loved them just the way they were.

I'm Not Important

What does a child learn if he cries, feels pain, or experiences some other discomfort at the hands of a therapist? What *more* does he learn if his mother doesn't protect him from the person causing the pain or distress? What does a child learn if these experiences occur when his mother *is not even present?* Some parents drop their children off at therapy and run errands. And, unbelievably, there are still clinics that insist parents sit in the waiting room while the therapist takes the child "into the back" for the therapy session. In all cases, the child learns that he is not important.

In addition, the same mother who would scoop her child into her arms to protect him from running into the path of a car or from the fist of another child may sit idly by while a therapist makes her child cry. The child learns that life is uneven—some people are allowed to hurt him, but others aren't. Perhaps he learns that it's OK for someone to hurt him if it's "for his own good" (even if he'll never understand what was good about the therapy).

What about this scenario: "Eric's" conscientious mother stays with him during therapy and steps in to rescue him if he becomes distressed. But Eric routinely sees and hears *other* babies and young children crying. What does Eric learn from this? He might believe something bad could happen to him, and *that fear* might cause him to cling to his mother, and he appears to "resist" the therapist (the consequences of resisting are detailed in the next section).

ADULTS RESPOND

When speaking about therapy during my presentations, I ask the audience, "What's the message of Traditional Therapy to a child?" And parents, after thinking for a moment, respond with, "That there's something wrong with you..." or similar answers.

But if adults with developmental disabilities are in the audience when I pose this question, they call out different answers—the most common are "pain" and "torture."

I hope we can learn from those who have personal experience.

Achild may learn he's not important in other, equally harmful, ways. Much of the therapy done "to" a child is to help him achieve a functional skill that's important to parents and/or therapists, *but which may or may not be important to the child!* This seems to happen far more than it should, with terrible repercussions for the child.

If the goal is not *meaningful and relevant* (memorize those two words) to the child, he will be disinterested in it, at best, or resistant to a therapists's efforts, at worst. In either case, and far too often, the child's disinterest or resistance is seen as "manipulation," "noncompliance," or "inappropriate" somehow, which causes many therapists to redouble their efforts. The therapist digs her heels in, determined to make the child comply so he'll achieve the skill. The child, meanwhile, is *demeaned and marginalized*—his wants and his comfort are ignored (by the therapist *and* the parent who has allowed the therapist such power over her child). In defense of his own personhood, the child may resist even more and this increased resistance may be matched or exceeded by the therapist's increased determination. And so a "helpful" therapy session degenerates into a Battle of Wills—and guess who loses?

I honor and respect the child who resists. He is demonstrating what we hold most dear as human beings: a sense of self and self-protection, and the desire to be self-directed and in control of his life. We revere these traits, *except* when it comes to a child resisting an adult who's doing something "for his own good." I hope we will listen, very, very carefully, to a child who resists, and respond in ways that respect and honor the child as a valuable human being.

If we do not listen and respond with respect, we risk much, including the creation of a child—yes, we will have *created* such a child—who has learned that he and his life are unimportant, so *he will do whatever he feels is necessary to feel important.* And then we, of course, will throw more labels at him and give him more therapies, interventions, and maybe even medication to enforce his compliance to our directions.

Conversely, some children in the Battle of Wills give up and give in to a therapist's control. Their disinterest or resistance is replaced by passivity. "Victory!" a therapist or parent might think, "He's recognized how important this is and he's going to comply." And rather than feeling victorious, we should be both ashamed and afraid—ashamed that we have used our superior power to beat a child's spirit into submission. How are we any different than a bully on the playground or a bully nation that forces another to submit?

And we should be afraid for the child's future. The number of adults with developmental disabilities who have been the victims of sexual or physical abuse at the hands of their "helpers" (including family members; paid, personal care assistants; staff members of group homes; and others) is astounding. I know of no official statistics, but sit in a meeting of adults with developmental disabilities and ask who has been sexually or physically abused, and watch as over half the people raise their hands. Then watch the hurt on their faces, see the tears flow, and listen to the anguish in their voices as they describe how, as children, they felt they had little or no control over what happened to them at the hands of

> THE "GOOD" CHILD MAY BE FRIGHTENED AND INSECURE, WANTING ONLY TO PLEASE HIS PARENTS BY SUBMITTING TO THEIR WILL, WHILE THE "BAD" CHILD MAY HAVE A WILL OF HIS OWN AND GENUINE INTERESTS, BUT ONES WHICH DO NOT PLEASE HIS PARENTS.
> *Erich Fromm*

> DISOBEDIENCE IS THE TRUE FOUNDATION OF LIBERTY. THE OBEDIENT MUST BE SLAVES.
> *Henry David Thoreau*

people who were supposed to love and care for them, including family members, therapists, and others. As children, they learned that trying to exert control over their own bodies or lives in whatever form—passive disinterest to active resistance, including actually saying "no" or "please stop"—never worked.

As adults, many feel they have little or no power to stop sexual or physical abuse. Their self-direction was stripped from them when they were children; as adults, some now attend classes to learn how to become self-directed so they have the power over their lives the rest of us take for granted.

Is Therapy at Home Much Better?

Some parents and therapists have recognized the danger of turning a child into a "therapy kid" who spends hours each week in a therapy clinic. Their solution is to move the therapy from the clinic to the child's home or other natural environment. Revisions to Special Ed law (IDEA 1997) mandating that Early Intervention Services be provided in natural environments has accelerated this change for many children of all ages. Some therapists have been providing therapy in the home long before this latest trend (therapists provided hour-long therapy sessions in our home way back in 1990). But in many cases, Traditional Therapy at home may not be much better than therapy in a clinical setting.

While I was presenting at an EI conference on this subject, "Sally," the parent of a very young child who was receiving Early Intervention Services, bravely spoke up (she said this while surrounded by EI professionals and therapists):

> Kathie, I know therapists are supposed to provide services in natural environments, but I don't want them coming in my home. If a therapist comes into our home and makes my son cry—or does something else that makes him unhappy—how can he feel that our home is a safe place? I wouldn't let anyone else come to my home and make my son unhappy. Why is it different just because it's a therapist? So I have the therapist meet us at the park or the McDonald's playground. Then, if my little boy gets upset during therapy, we just leave and go home—where he knows he's safe.

I think we can learn something from Sally's wisdom. Her story reminded me of how my children's pediatrician operated when it was time for immunizations or other injections. He insisted that a nurse hold the child while the shot was given, then the nurse would hand the child to the parent. When it was time for Emily's first shot, I initially objected to his "rule" until he explained further: "If *you* hold Emily while we give the shot—and you know you'll have to really hold her tight and manhandle her so she can't fight us—she'll think *you're* hurting her, too. But if the nurse holds her during the shot, and then we hand her to you to comfort her immediately afterward, she'll know we're the 'bad guys' and you're the 'good mom' who can kiss the hurt away."

Isn't it the same when it comes to our homes? Shouldn't our children always feel safe there? If, in the eyes of a child, we, as parents, are in concert with a therapist or other in-home service provider who causes the child distress, how can the child feel secure in his own home? If he can't feel safe and secure there, where *will* he feel safe?

LISTEN...

I've told you I'm a slow learner. I didn't listen to my son until he was six—when he cried and raged not to go to therapy anymore. But there were signals before then...like at age three when he cried as we drove into the parking lot of the therapy clinic.

Why did I not "hear" my son's messages? Perhaps because there were bigger, more powerful voices sending me the opposite message. While others voices might have been bigger and more powerful, *the most important voice belonged to my son.*

When your child receives any type of Services from a therapist (or any other professional) in your home, make sure you and your child are "in charge." It's your home, it's your child's home, and anyone who comes into your family home needs to abide by your "rules." Under the auspices of "doing what's best" for your child, do not allow anyone to hurt your child, physically or emotionally, in his own home! *How can that ever be "what's best" for any of our children?*

If there is any potential for harm to your child at the hands of a "visitor" to your home, follow Sally's advice and meet the therapist or other professional in a neutral location. But keep in mind that if someone makes your child cry at the playground, he might learn to see the *playground* as a horrible place. Be aware—use your foresight—and plan accordingly. (And we should hold to this same rule wherever our children receive Services, although it's much more difficult to impose our rules in other environments. In some circumstances, the only solution is to leave that environment.)

> I DON'T SEE AS IT MATTERS MUCH HOW WELL YOU *MEAN*, IF IT'S HARM YOU'RE DOIN'.
>
> *Martha Ostenso*

A Skewed View of the World

The unnatural environments of therapy clinics and similar settings can lead to children acquiring an unnatural or unusual view of the world. As I've previously described, when my son, Benjamin, was three and four, he attended a neighborhood preschool, not the Special Ed Preschool. Still, for the first four years of his life, he had been around children with disabilities at the therapy clinic more than he had been around children without disabilities.

My sister, who lives in another state, has a son, Colin, who is a few months younger than Benjamin. The two little boys saw each other infrequently—primarily when they were babies at family get-togethers during the holidays—but they talked on the phone sometimes, and I always "gave a report" about Colin and the other cousins when I talked with my sister. Benjamin always loved hearing about Colin, loved helping pick out birthday and Christmas presents for him, and thought of his younger cousin as a little brother. When Benjamin was four, he asked, "Mommy, does Colin still use *his* walker?" I didn't know what he was talking about and had to ask several questions before I understood: Benjamin thought *all* children learned to walk *by going to therapy and using a walker,* because that's what he experienced during his first four years of life!

What unusual perceptions of the world has *your* child acquired from being in the unnatural environment of a therapy clinic? Few parents have considered this question before, and it takes some a number of hours and a great deal of intensive thought to arrive at an answer—then an "Ah-ha" moment explodes out of their heads and things that didn't make sense before become clear.

Disruption of Childhood

The schedule of Traditional Therapies can significantly disrupt a child's daily schedule, effectively robbing her of her childhood and the ordinary opportunities of play ("children's work"), spending time with other family members; and doing all the wonderful, typical activities that represent real learning, growth and development, and a REAL LIFE. As previously mentioned, there are times

If I ever have a stroke and am unable to speak or walk, I have no plans to go into "rehab." Instead, I'll get a power wheelchair, a communication device, and any other supports I need, and will get on with living my *Real Life!*

Did I always feel this way? No. Thankfully, my attitudes have been shaped by people with disabilities, including my own son, who demonstrate that the presence of a disability is not a barrier to living a successful, happy, fulfilled life! I am a fortunate and appreciative recipient of their wisdom and experiences.

when Services to "improve QUALITY OF LIFE" (functional skills) may actually have a harmful effect on a child's *real* QUALITY OF LIFE—and a childhood filled with therapy sessions is one of those times.

In addition, children with disabilities who receive lots of therapy and other interventions spend much more time with adults than do children without disabilities, and this can have unusual consequences. When my son began talking at age three, he went from saying, "Ma-ma-ma-ma-ma..." (and he didn't mean me—that was the only sound he made) to practically speaking in paragraphs, way above his chronological age. It was like a supply of words and sentences had been in his head for a long time, and when a "switch" was flipped, everything that had been stored in his head came out. I was delighted at this turn of events. But later I wondered if the reason he didn't go through the traditional pattern of speech development (talking baby talk, stringing a few words together, then a few more, and so on) was a result of him being around adults (therapists) most of the time. Many parents have shared similar stories about their own children, so my son's experience is not an isolated incident.

In the same vein, some parents report their children seem to "get along great" with adults, but have difficulty knowing how to interact with children. This, too, seems to be a consequence of children spending so much time with adults in therapy (at the clinic or at home). It's possible that the *extent* of this difficulty can be correlated to the *amount of time* a child spends with adults. Ironic, isn't it, that getting "help" for a child in one area of his life can create problems in another area?

Disruption of Family Life and Loss of Autonomy

As previously detailed, the schedule of Services can disrupt a family's life—including family privacy, autonomy, and self-direction. Because therapy is often one of the primary Services provided to children—eating up hours of a family's time each week—we need to be aware of its impact on families.

As a whole, our society tends to have an over-dependence on professionals of any kind. When it comes to therapy and other disability-related Services, many of us tend to over-rate professional help, and under-rate ourselves as experts who know our children best, and can therefore help and teach our children better than anyone! But our faith in our own abilities can often be undermined. This can happen if therapists are overbearing and/or if they behave in ways that indicate they, as professionals, are superior, and we, as parents, are inferior—and the therapist essentially takes control of the child. On the other hand, there are many therapists who are respectful of parents' expertise, and want to work in equal partnership with us, but some of *us* don't want this responsibility, so we willingly cede control to the therapist.

Regardless of how this happens, the outcome is the same: feelings of helplessness that bleed into other parts of our lives. We may begin to question our own competence in other areas of parenting the child with a disability, as well as other children in the family. These consequences can have serious side-effects on the whole family, including the marriage.

It's vitally important that we retain (or reacquire) our self-confidence. It's important for us personally, as well as for the overall health of our families. Helpless, dependent parents are at risk of raising helpless, dependent children.

We *are* our children's best teachers! Yes, in some instances, we might need guidance in specific areas in order to best help our children, but this help is easily obtainable. In the case of therapy, many parents have already learned how to be "amateur therapists:" we've learned how to do home programs and we may have watched and/or participated in hundreds of hours of therapy sessions provided by professional therapists.

When my son resigned from his "therapy career" at age six, my husband and I simply took what we had learned from the years of therapy and put it to work in our home and other environments in more natural ways. We had learned a great deal from my son's therapists. Other parents are doing the same.

But there were other important outcomes to my son's decision: our family's life was once again our own, and we regained the autonomy and self-confidence that had been bruised and battered during the years therapy sessions ruled our family's life.

Later in this chapter, I'll share alternatives to Traditional Therapy. Therapists can be valuable partners with parents. Their professional expertise coupled with our personal and intimate knowledge of our children can create a powerful combination. And as you'll learn a little later, when we create a new therapeutic landscape, our children can lead more natural lives.

Life Lessons to Consider

Before offering alternatives to Traditional Therapy, I want to share some lessons for your consideration. There are lessons from your own life that could be beneficial to you, but you might not see them for what they are at this moment in time—but perhaps you will by the end of this chapter.

Here's what I'm talking about: there have been times when I didn't feel right about something, as well as times when I learned new information, but I took no action. It was like the Little Voice in my head or the new information was not "big enough" to counteract the awesome power of CONVENTIONAL WISDOM and/or the professional advice that influenced my thinking. So I would live with a certain amount of unease, a gnawing in my gut that something wasn't right and/or a feeling that I should be doing something differently. And early in my son's life, when I could no longer stand the emotional tug-of-war going on inside me, I pushed the feelings deep down or ignored the new information.

One example of this has already been shared: the stories told to me by adults with developmental disabilities about what it felt like to be taken to therapy all the time. I heard those stories when my son was three, but I didn't act on them. It wasn't until my son was six, and he cried that therapy didn't make him feel like a "regular person" that the buried information rose to the surface.

Another piece of new information I received *prior* to hearing the stories described above *should have provoked me to act,* but it didn't. When Benjamin

We assume a "cause and effect" relationship when it comes to therapy. If a child is receiving therapy and he learns how to do a new skill, we assume this is the result of therapy. But we don't know that for a fact! It's only a guess. The child might have done it whether or not he was receiving therapy. Later in this chapter, you'll hear from therapists on this issue.

At the therapy clinic my son attended for the first three years of his life, I was disturbed that many of the therapists totally ignored a child's tears. While sitting by my son during his therapy sessions, I watched in disbelief as children screamed, cried, and/or whimpered while therapists rolled them on the therapy ball, stretched their body parts, and so forth.

I badgered the director to let me speak to the therapists at their next in-service. She reluctantly agreed, and invited a couple of other parents to attend. (It was a set-up.)

In a nutshell, my spiel was this: if kids cry during therapy, something's very, very wrong! The two other parents disagreed, saying they didn't care if their children cried, since therapy was "for their own good." Of the 5-7 therapists present, most said nothing, but one seemed to speak for the majority when she said, "You don't understand, Kathie. Kids with disabilities learn to be manipulative very early—sometimes as early as six months. *They cry to get out of doing therapy—that's all!* We have to learn to ignore them in order to do our jobs and help them."

And so the tears and fear and pain continued.

was about eighteen months old, one of his doctors informed us that we should anticipate many surgeries for Benj over the next 12-15 years—operations performed on many children with CP to lengthen the hamstrings and other tendons in the lower body which usually tighten as children with spasticity grow. At the time, I knew several school-aged kids who had undergone these surgeries, so I had a little knowledge of what they involved. After these operations, the child was usually in a body cast from torso to ankles for several weeks, more intensive therapies were needed after the cast was removed, and additional surgeries were needed every few years until the child stopped growing in early adulthood.

I didn't look forward to my son going through all this, and when I inquired about alternatives, I was told about a relatively new procedure—a selective dorsal rhizotomy—in which a surgeon identified the sensory nerves that led to spasticity in the muscles, then cut them. We were told that most children who had the rhizotomy surgery would probably never need multiple orthopedic surgeries. "One" surgery sounded better than "many." At that time, most surgeons would not perform the surgery until the child was three, so when Benjamin was two, I began a year-long research effort to learn all I could. As it turned out, Benj had the surgery at age three, and we were extremely pleased with the results.

But during the year of research at medical libraries near our home in Texas (this was in 1989, way before the Internet!), I came across a variety of *other articles* about children with CP, one of which *should have* spurred me into action. This particular article (and I'm sorry to say I didn't have the foresight to record the date, source, or other pertinent information, so you'll just have to trust my memory) detailed research about the effects of physical and occupational therapies in preschool-aged children with CP. Two groups were compared: one group received extensive PT and OT, while the other group received only typical exercise-type activities provided by the parents, at home. The result of the study showed there was *no significant difference in the two groups!* As "Therapy Mom" of the year (if they gave such an award), I was astounded by these results!

I was shocked and dismayed by the research paper, and a dialogue in my head went back and forth about what I should do with this information. But in my mind, at the time, the study only represented black ink on a piece of paper which could not compete with the face-to-face directives and recommendations of a physician, Early Intervention professionals, and two therapists who all insisted—without a doubt—that PT and OT were the only way to go. So I did *nothing* with the new information, except bury it in my brain so it wouldn't interfere with the daily routine of therapies, which had become part of a "normal life" for us. I *had* to bury it—if I kept it in the front of my brain, it would have created too much conflict!

There were other instances during those early years when I ignored my own feelings or buried other new information, and this led to a persistent, nagging, overall discomfort about our daily lives. When I took no actions to resolve these issues, the discomfort became a normal part of my psyche—sort of like a slight headache that never goes away, which one learns to live with, despite the pain.

You, too, may have a Little Voice in your head that you're ignoring. You, too, may have learned new information that you've put aside. You, too, may be experiencing today (and for the past several years), a generalized discomfort about your child's life and your family's life that you've come to accept and have learned to live with, even though you don't like it. But contrary to the common perception, *none of this is a result of your* child's condition. It is, instead, a consequence of the different components of Conventional Wisdom which have portrayed your child as Not-OK, Not-Ready, and more, and which, in turn, have led to therapies to resolve your child's "problems," which have, in turn, impacted and/or taken over your child's life. And all of this may have made you feel incompetent, overwhelmed by responsibility, and fearful of the future.

Whew! It's a mess, isn't it? But as I'll describe next, if you follow your heart and listen to your child, life will be smoother. A word of warning: some of what I'll share about listening to your child may make you uncomfortable or even angry. That's OK. You're strong—you can handle it. And as I mentioned in an earlier chapter, sometimes we don't change *until* we're made uncomfortable.

Follow Your Heart

You have more wisdom than you know—let it come forth and blossom. Know that even if that Little Voice in your heart is the *minority* opinion, your instincts are right and should be followed. If it's hard to find the courage to go it alone, get an ally on board: your spouse, a friend or other family member, or write to me (kathie@disabilityisnatural.com), and even though I can't be with you in person, I'll be with you in spirit. One mother wrote to me after buying the first edition of this book. She decided to make significant changes but was met with criticism and resistance from therapists and other providers. So she began carrying the book with her to meetings that might be contentious—she encircled the book with one arm, and held up against her chest, just like a shield. If that works for you, go for it!

When I've gone against Conventional Wisdom, I, too, have been on the receiving end of criticism from (1) therapists and other professionals who tried to scare me by warning me about the "dangers" of my decisions; (2) parents (who I thought were my friends and acquaintances) who implied I was either "crazy" or a "traitor" for not following professional advice in lock-step they way they did; and (3) others who accused me of being "in denial." But who always supported and encouraged the changes I made? Adults with developmental disabilities. Again, they are the true experts.

It often took great courage to follow my heart in the face of opposition coming from many directions, and I do not see myself as a very courageous person. I was guided not by a personal desire to be brave or bold or different, but by a heart-wrenching, gut-gnawing desire to protect my son's life and my family's life from forces that were harming us.

When a mother bear rushes headlong into danger to protect her cub, she is not operating from *intellect,* but from *instinct.* As members of the human species (the supposedly highest form of life on the planet), we

---

NO BODY IS PERFECT!

When Benjamin was two or three, the PT tried to get him to "sit up straight." She positioned him on a bench, placed his palms flat on the bench next to his thighs, then she pulled his shoulders back to get his head to come up—but his palms came off the bench. "No, no, Benjamin," she said, as she replaced his palms flat, and tried again to sit him "straight." This went on and on, and I could see Benj was frustrated—I asked her to do something else!

That night, I tried to figure out why Benj couldn't do what the therapist was working on. So I had my husband and my daughter sit on our piano bench and mimic the "sitting-up straight-with-palms-on- the-bench" routine. No problem. Then I tried it—and couldn't! I was not able to raise my head and shoulders up straight *and* keep my palms flat on the bench. Why? My arms aren't long enough, and neither were Benj's!

When I demonstrated this to the therapist, her jaw dropped! And I wondered how many other children and adults had gone through fruitless hours of therapy because of similar circumstances!

demean animal-like behaviors as primitive, and we *extol* the virtues of human intellect. But there are times when instinct—listening to your heart—is a wiser course than any intelligent thought-process. While saving her cub from danger, the mother bear may put herself at risk and even be injured, but the desire to protect her cub is greater than any fear for her own well-being.

If you decide to protect your cub and are at risk of being "attacked" by others, any verbal scratches or injuries you may receive will not only heal, but they'll make you stronger. The first time I said "no" to professional expertise was hard; the second time was easier; the third time easier still; and so on. So be like a mother bear! (If you're a dad, be like a *mother* bear, too, not a father bear—some of them *eat* their young!)

Listen to Your Child

Our children tell us what's important to them and how they feel about their lives—whether they communicate in words, through their tears or smiles, or some other way—but sometimes we don't listen. In a perfect world, *everyone* who touches our children's lives would listen to them, and that's a goal we can work toward. But as parents, we, of all people, *must* take the time and make every effort to hear and respond to our children.

If *we* are not on our children's side against forces that might cause harm, who do they have? If they do not learn that the world is sometimes a scary place, but trust and safety can always be found at home, how can we expect them to feel confident and make their way in the world? If our children grow up feeling their own parents don't *hear and understand* their needs, do they not learn *their feelings and their lives* are unimportant? If so, how do we expect them to become successful when they're adults? How do you become a Somebody if you've grown up being a Nobody?

We need to listen well to *all* that our children communicate, but especially about therapy and other Services. *Whose life is it anyway?*

Have you ever *asked your child* if he wants to receive the therapies and interventions that have been imposed on his life? Many parents bristle at this—"ludicrous" say some; "ridiculous" say others. "It doesn't make any sense to allow a child to make such a decision," say others. "We don't let *children* make *important* decisions..." Yes and no.

Parents *do* make many important decisions for the well-being of *all* their children. We may decide our children cannot play in the street, drive the car after dark, drink and drive, and more. But many of us *do* let children make decisions about issues *that are important to them*—issues which are not safety-related and which have no impact *on our lives*, like what recreational activities they'd like to try, what band instrument to play, and so forth.

In other circumstances, we make decisions based on our belief about "what's in the best interest" of the child, like taking her to the doctor when she's sick, getting orthodontic braces so she'll have a nicer smile and her teeth will be easier to keep clean, and so forth. But these, and many other routine situations, *do not have the potential to send repetitive negative messages to the child, nor do they have an impact on the child's life for years: today, tomorrow, and maybe forever.* In other words, these routine situations don't have the capacity to scar the child for life, the way years of Traditional Therapy and other Services might.

As important as Traditional Therapy is in a child's life—important in the sense that it consumes many hours, days, weeks, months, or years of a child's life and important in the unintended negative consequences—shouldn't we *ask our children how they feel about therapy?* Shouldn't we explain what the therapy is for; ask the child if the therapy goals are *relevant and meaningful* to her; ask what *she* would like therapy to accomplish; share, to the best of our knowledge, how the therapy will affect the child and the rest of the family; offer alternatives; and then seek the child's opinion?

If you're influenced by the PRESUMED INCOMPETENCE, NOT-OK, or NOT-READY mentalities, you might not think your child *has* an opinion (but I assure you, she does), or you might not think her opinion is important. But I hope you'll feel differently after you finish this chapter.

Perhaps *we* would be wise to follow the advice of Roy Gerstenberger (from Chapter 4) and give full disclosure to our children about therapy and other Services we want them to have. We might say something like one of these two examples (you could substitute any disability), and the third example could be tacked on to one of the first two:

> Honey, you have autism: you don't make eye contact, have few social skills, can't communicate very well, have trouble learning, and spend lots of your time rocking, moaning, and perseverating. But we've heard that Applied Behavior Analysis (ABA) therapy can help with all your problems, so it will start on Monday. Several different people will come into the house five days a week, for eight hours a day. This might take weeks or months, we just don't know right now—and the therapists will be in your face most of the time—but it will really help.

-or-

> Sweetie, you have cerebral palsy, and because you can't walk, sit up, feed yourself, hold a pencil, or talk, we're going to get you all the help you need so you can do these things. A physical therapist will work on your legs, feet, and whole body movements, and will also provide water therapy and hippo-therapy; an occupational therapist will work on your arms, hands, sitting up skills, eye-hand coordination, and a little oral motor control; and the speech therapist will also work on oral motor control and talking. We'll take you to the therapy clinic, the therapists will also come to our home, and when they're not working on you, I'll do home programs. This will take at least twenty hours per week, not counting drive time.

And in either case, we could add:

> These therapies might make you feel bad about yourself—like you're NOT-OK, but most of the time you'll have fun with the therapists, so it will all turn out all right. We think you're *sort of* OK, but you'll be *more* OK after these therapies help you achieve the goals we have for you. You won't have

Shouldn't we care how our children *feel* about therapy?

much of a life during all this (and, frankly, neither will we, but we'll suffer through it)—you won't have as much time to play or be a child, but you *will* get lots of attention from grown-ups, and it will all be worth it in the long run. We'll have to make sure the therapies are done whether you like it or not, whether you're crying or are scared, and regardless of the effect is has on us, your parents, or your older brother. The therapies will cost thousands of dollars in insurance benefits and our own personal income, but, again, it will all be worth it. Sometimes the therapy might physically hurt or be emotionally painful, and sometimes you might wish you were doing something else, but remember: this is all for your own good and, once again, it will all be worth it in the long run. We hope you'll appreciate all we're doing for you—it might be hard to understand when you're small, but certainly when you're an adult you'll appreciate all we did for you and be eternally grateful. Even though it's going to be very difficult, you must know that this is for your own good and we hope this proves how very much we love you.

If we presented one of these or a similar scenario (you can make up your own) to a child and then gave him the choice or whether or not to receive therapy, what do you think he'd say?

If you're still not convinced of the value of your child's opinion or of our need to be honest with our children, you might be thinking something like, "I doubt if the parents of a child with cancer or leukemia describe the difficult treatments the child will have to go through and then give the child a choice..." But think again, *and* consider the important differences between this scenario and the ones facing our children:

- Autism, cerebral palsy, and the majority of other conditions we call developmental disabilities are not life-threatening illnesses like cancer, leukemia, and other diagnoses.

- In the case of children with serious, life-threatening illnesses, parents and health care providers generally *are* far more open and honest about the treatments the child will receive, including sharing the negative consequences of the treatments.

- Many children with life-threatening illnesses frequently *are* given some choices if different types of treatment are available, and they're expected to be active participants in the treatments they've chosen.

Let's look at one more comparison. A child with cancer might be told: "For the next year, we can give you these treatments that might be painful and very difficult for you to endure, but we hope they will kill the cancer so you can live a long life. *Or,* we could give you no treatments, and you will probably die soon. Which do you prefer?"

A child with a disability might be told: "For the next ten years or more, you can have Traditional Therapy which may be painful or otherwise uncomfortable, prevent you from doing other things that are important to you, and/or make you feel bad about who you are as a human being, but we hope these therapies will help you walk, talk, feed yourself, behave, or achieve some other functional

> FOR YOUR OWN GOOD. WHAT A GHASTLY PHRASE THAT WAS. IT COVERED THE MOST BARBAROUS AND INHUMAN CRUELTIES EVER INFLICTED.
> *Margaret Millar*

ability. *Or*, you could have no Traditional Therapy, and instead, we'll find ways to help you do what's important to you within typical activities in our home or in the community, and we'll provide you with the assistive technology devices, accommodations, modifications, and supports to enable you to do what you'd like to do. Which do you prefer?"

If you decide to honor and value your child by asking him if he wants to have a particular therapy or intervention, the *way* you ask can have a powerful influence on his reply and/or whether he answers you honestly.

For example, *you* might feel therapy is the only way to go, and you want proof that you're making the right decision for your child, so you ask, "Do you want to keep going to therapy and have fun with Miss Julie?" But you've loaded the question by including "...have fun with Miss Julie," and your body language and tone of voice might telegraph the answer you're hoping for—"yes." If your child wants to please you (and if he thinks you're not happy with him because he can't walk, talk, or whatever, he'll probably do anything to make you happy), he'll read your body language and tone of voice, and will give you the answer *he hopes will make you happy* (which may or may not be a truthful answer).

On the other hand, if you give him choices, and remain *neutral* in your body language and tone of voice, he will most likely be honest. For example, you could ask something like, "Would you like to keep going to therapy with Miss Julie to work on [whatever] or would you like to do some other things—you could take karate lessons, or all of us could go swimming together or we could play some fun games at home so we could all get some exercise?"

We can choose to listen to our children, expect them to make decisions that affect their lives, and help them learn how to do so, all of which will set them on a path of self-direction. Or we can continue to ignore their feelings, make decisions for them, and send them down the road to learned helplessness. Or we might find a mediocre solution somewhere in the middle. Which will it be for your child?

Child-Directed Natural Assistance

Does all that I've described so far mean there is no need for therapists and/or no need to help a child or provide assistance? Not at all. It *does* mean:

- The help provided to a child is driven by the *child's* interests, wishes, needs, wants, hopes, and dreams, and is *relevant and meaningful to the child.*
- Therapists move from being "hands-on" providers to *consultants* who provide assistance to the child, the family, and others in the child's life, on an "as-needed" basis.
- Assistance is provided in natural environments, within the context of ordinary, age-appropriate experiences.
- Tools for success (assistive technology, modifications, accommodations, and supports) are provided to the child so he can enjoy, participate in, and benefit from typical, age-appropriate experiences, in inclusive settings.

ASK YOUR CHILD!

After hearing me speak about therapies during a conference, Anne told me her son, Kurt, had received therapy for 10 of his 11 years, and added that she had never looked at therapy from a child's point of view.

A few days later, I received an Email from Anne. After arriving home from the conference, she asked her son how he felt about therapy. "It hurts," he said. When she asked if he wanted to continue, the answer was "no." Kurt resigned from his therapy career, and he and his mom began looking into golf lessons and soccer for exercise and fun.

In her Email, Anne noted the irony that, in the past, she had prevented Kurt from playing in inclusive sports activities *because they interfered with the therapy schedule!* Now that Anne is listening to Kurt, he's living a REAL LIFE!

Traditional Therapy seldom takes the *child's* wishes, interests, needs, hopes, and dreams into account. What's done *to* a child is often based on (1) achieving an "able-bodied" standard, (2) what the therapist or other provider thinks is important, or (3) what the parents think is important.

Within the new therapeutic landscape, and in alternatives to therapy, the child tells us *what's important to him,* and his wishes direct the actions of the adults (therapists, other providers, parents, etc.). If the child is very young and/or is not able to effectively communicate, the parents share what they believe *the child would say* with therapists or other providers, based on the child's preferences and interests. (But even very young babies can communicate quite well!)

This means parents will need to cede some power to their children. I hope you're willing to let your child begin the important step of being in charge of his own life. It also means we have to talk to a child about what's really important to him, and we have to listen—really listen—and respect our child's wishes and support his dreams!

For these efforts to bear fruit, we have to begin doing things differently. First, we're not going to think or talk using "therapeutic jargon," and ask a child, for example, "Do you want your hamstrings stretched?" We will, instead, ask about all the things she wants to do: play with friends, dress herself or *help* dress herself, get from point A to point B without help, have a job when she grows up, and more. We'll ask her about the smallest to the largest hopes that are age-appropriate (per her CHRONOLOGICAL, AGE, not the silly DEVELOPMENTAL AGE), which are *relevant and meaningful* to her. In other words, we're going to ask questions related to the child participating in ordinary age-appropriate activities, so she can lead a REAL LIFE. Then the parents, and therapists or other providers, if necessary, along with help from the child, figure out what it takes to achieve the child's wishes. The help she needs will be provided in these typical, ordinary environments—at home, at dance class, in school settings, or wherever!

Second, we need to *trust children* more than we usually do! Our children are *very smart,* so let's give them credit for that, even if their wisdom isn't always overtly apparent through their words or actions. If, however, we begin listening more closely, we'll see the wisdom that's always been there.

When my son said he wanted to stop going to therapy, I supported his decision, but added that there were still some things he needed help with, and he agreed. At age six, Benjamin didn't know exactly what his body needed, but he knew, for example, that when his shoulders stayed in a forward-sloping position, it was hard for him to hold his head up and see the TV, computer screen, or anything else. So I told him we would need to "stretch" his shoulders back to help this, and he agreed. (This only took a few minutes a day, and we did it 365 days a year, twice each day—when we dressed and undressed him. Better than once a week by a therapist, wouldn't you say?)

If your child indicates she wants to achieve such-and-such, you can talk with her about what it will take to accomplish that hope. She may agree that she's willing to do what it takes to make the hope a reality, and she'll work diligently and happily to achieve the goal. If, however, she balks at some point, you can

> WE WORRY ABOUT WHAT A CHILD WILL BE TOMORROW, YET WE FORGET THAT HE IS SOMEONE TODAY.
> *Stacia Tauscher*

(1) take a break for a day, a week, or longer (our children are not robots!), (2) try to find another way to accomplish the same thing, (3) remind her this is part of what's necessary for her to achieve her stated goal, and/or (4) have another discussion about the goal, listen to her ideas, and respect her wishes *if she decides she no longer wants to achieve that goal.*

What might child-directed assistance, in natural environments, with or without the assistance of a therapist as a consultant, look like? There are infinite possibilities, depending on the child and our creativity, but I'll share a few scenarios.

Instead of taking your child to therapy and/or therapists coming into your home to provide direct services, you, your child, and other family members could meet with a therapist to discuss your child's interests and needs, and ways to incorporate beneficial "therapeutic-like" activities into your child's day which can meet those needs. (This does not simply represent an expansion of parents doing home programs—as I'll detail in a moment, this is a whole new "therapeutic landscape.")

The therapist can also meet with others who interact with a baby or young child on a regular basis, such as typical preschool/daycare providers, extended family members, etc. If the child is preschool-aged or above, the therapist can work with the child's teachers on ways to incorporate beneficial activities throughout the school day ("school therapy" for children five and above is covered in more detail in Chapter 9).

Simultaneously, parents can—with or without the help of therapists or other providers—replace hours of weekly therapies with fun activities in our communities (karate lessons, dance/ballet class, T-ball, swimming, art lessons, etc.). In doing so, our children can get the exercise or activities they need, make new friends, and be included—all at the same time!

See Your <u>Real</u> Needs

This new approach requires us to *see* our children differently and to think about their *needs* differently. Specifically, we'll need to see a child's *real* needs, using plain language—not therapeutic or medical deficit-based jargon.

Traditionally, a child's needs have been seen as the mirror-image of his perceived deficits. For example, a parent, therapist, physician, or someone else may decide: "The child cannot walk/talk/feed himself/whatever; therefore, *his needs* are to walk/talk/feed himself/whatever." These are then turned into goals for the child, and therapies and other interventions attempt to ensure the child meets these goals.

Looking at your child's needs differently involves rejecting the "able-bodied" standard and embracing *what's really important to your child.* This can be very difficult for some parents—it truly requires us to *let go* of some hopes and dreams *we've* had, such as the hope a child will walk or talk or behave like other children or look like other children or whatever. The process of letting go can be easier if we *think like our children* and consider what's really important to *them.* For example, is it more important:

WHAT'S REALLY IMPORTANT!

The decision to get Benjamin a power wheelchair came not from a therapist, but from my friend, Tom, a successful man who had CP and used a power wheelchair.

When Benjamin was eight, Tom bugged me about getting Benj a power chair, and even though I had come a long way in my thinking, I was still embracing some CONVENTIONAL WISDOM: I thought it would be better for Benj to "work harder" to push himself, and this would keep his arms "strong." Sounds good doesn't it? It makes sense from a MEDICAL MODEL perspective, but not from a REAL LIFE perspective.

Tom's reply was this: "Kathie, pretty soon Benj is gonna' be in middle school. How's he gonna' get a girlfriend—you think he can meet some chick and say, 'Will you please push me?' He needs a power chair so he can say, 'Come sit in my lap, baby, and we'll ride off into the sunset.'"

I got the point, Benj got his power chair, and just as important, I finally got the *Big Picture* about what's *really* important!

• To get from point A to point B by walking, or in the most effective way (like using a walker or wheelchair)?

• To speak, or to communicate using whatever method works best?

• To hold a fork and eat the "right way," or to feed yourself any way you can and/or learn to ask someone to help you at mealtime?

• To achieve an arbitrary measure of "appropriate behavior," or to be supported and understood so you can be who you are? In the big scheme of things, how important is something like "making eye contact"?

• To read a book like other children your age, or to have the opportunity to learn by using books-on-tape, computer games, and/or hands-on activities?

These are just a few examples—go ask your son or daughter what's really important to him or her (but finish reading this chapter, first). Ask other family members, too—this *is* a family affair, and as you'll see in a moment, many of the ways to meet your child's needs are also fun activities for the whole family!

When you think and talk in ways that reflect your child's real needs and interests, you'll get a better handle on what's really important and you'll move away from deficit-based solutions. For example, if you think, "My child needs to walk [a functional skill]," this will lead you down the path to Traditional Therapy. But if you think: "My child needs to get from point A to point B in the most effective means possible," this will probably lead to you an assistive technology device (walker or wheelchair).

If you think, "My child needs to learn to make eye contact and have better social skills," you'll probably seek professional interventions. But if you think, "My child needs to learn how to play with other children," this can take you in the direction of the natural learning environments of typical youth activities (Scouts, karate class, etc.).

If you believe, "My child needs to talk," you might focus on oral communication and therapy, and ignore other options. But if you think, "My child needs to be able to communicate his wants and needs," this could lead you to explore a communication device, communication cards, signing, and/or facilitated communication; as well as singing, playing word games, and/or other typical activities that encourage oral communication.

Let's look at some examples of alternatives to Traditional Therapy, with or without the assistance of a therapist as a consultant:

• If a therapist has been working on range-of-motion or stretching activities, ask the therapist—or figure it out on your own—how to incorporate these into fun "exercises" all your children/family can do together, in time to music or while everyone sings or chants an exercise ditty. (Benj often asks me to "pull on his legs"—a hamstring and/or heel cord stretch—while he's watching *Jeopardy!* and *Wheel of Fortune.*) Alternatively, your child and/or other family members can "get in shape" with the help of an exercise video—and there are several made for people who use wheelchairs!

• If deep-muscle rubs are part of your child's therapy routine, you or another family member can do this as part of your child's waking up or bedtime routine, or whenever is the best time for everyone. (After our son's recent scoliosis surgery, a physical therapist showed us how to worm our hand underneath Benjamin's scapula bone in his upper back to loosen it, and we do this every night before he goes to sleep.)

- With or without the help of a therapist, figure out how routine activities around the house can be turned into beneficial exercise activities. Washing dishes or grasping silverware to set the table might be helpful to encourage a child to use her hands. Carrying the laundry basket, folding clothes, and similar activities could allow a child to use both arms at the same time.

- Spend some time looking at all the games on the market—board games, as well as the new-fangled fun games on DVD/video—that the whole family, or all the kids, can play together. These could meet your child's physical, oral, and/or social needs, and everyone can have fun at the same time!

- Instead of a "social skills" therapeutic class (with other children who also have "behavior issues"—how goofy is that?), enroll your child in a Scout troop, karate class, or other community activity. We learn by doing!

- If "making eye contact" is really important to the child (and it might *not* be, or he'd be doing it), but he struggles with it, role-play social interactions or have a staring contest (remember those from when you were a kid?).

- Instead of horseback-riding therapy, just go horseback riding. Make it a family affair or enroll your child in a riding class of children who don't have disabilities. If your child really enjoys riding a horse, but you don't feel he'd be safe on a horse by himself (without being surrounded by numerous adults like at hippo-therapy), the child and a parent (or an older child) can ride double on a horse. He'll still get the benefits of feeling the horse's "weight shift" and "reciprocal motion."

- Instead of water therapy, go swimming or get in a hot tub (with family and/ or friends). Play games in the water that work on the muscles/body parts that need exercise. Ditto other types of therapy: instead of music therapy, just let your child enjoy music, and so forth. As necessary, get help from a therapist on how your child can achieve her goals within such an activity.

- Physical exercise, social skills, and other needs can be met at the neighborhood gym, in a class at the YMCA, a park and rec activity, and in many other typical, inclusive environments.

- You and/or your child's therapist/provider can spend time with grandparents, the teachers at your child's school or preschool, the leader of a Scout troop, the karate class instructor, and/or anyone else who interacts with your child, to help them learn beneficial, natural strategies which would be helpful to your child.

In thinking about your child's real needs, move beyond the "able-bodied" standard, so your child can participate in age-appropriate activities regardless of the disability. We often get tunnel-vision, focusing all our energies on "disability-related" needs, while ignoring typical childhood needs that are important to a child's growth and development.

For example, a common need of children is to express themselves artistically—through coloring and drawing. And some children want or need to do this more than others. What does your child need to be able to do this? A table-top easel, with the paper taped down, and extra-large markers? If he has difficulty holding a marker, maybe he could finger-paint with his fist, or he could make a pretty picture for Mommy with blow-pens. Alternatively, he could "color" on the computer with one of the many fun drawing programs available today.

As another example, having the ability to compose written communication is an important skill for life—in school, and as an adult. If handwriting doesn't come easily to your child, move on to the computer (and the earlier the better). Why torture a child for years trying to force his fingers, hands, wrists, arms, and/or brain to do something he may not ever do (or if he *can* do it, it's laborious and time-intensive)? If a typical computer keyboard doesn't work, investigate all the great modified keyboards, touch screens, and other adapted devices that can open the door to your child's success!

There are many strategies we can use to move beyond Traditional Therapy, meet our children's interests and needs, and ensure they live REAL LIVES. Listen to your child, brainstorm, listen to your heart, get input from other members of your family (you're all experts!), and, as necessary, seek the consultation of a therapist or other professional.

Changing the Therapist's Role

If your child's therapist is currently a "hands on" practitioner, how can you make the switch to the therapist becoming a consultant? In some cases, this might be simple; in others, you might need to find a different therapist!

First, sit down and talk to her about what you want to do. Should you tell her *why* you want to make the change? It depends on the therapist and your relationship with her. I don't believe we need to justify all our actions to others, as regards our children. They're *our* children—they don't belong to therapists, educators, or anyone else. In some instances, trying to explain *why* you want to do something or *why* you feel the way you do can set up an argument, which can lead to a fracture in the relationship.

On the other hand, if your child has received therapy for many years from the same therapist, and you've been pleased with how and what she's done up to this point, she'll certainly wonder what's going on when you propose a different way of doing things. So a friendly comment like, "We'd like to do things more naturally, and we'd like your help figuring out how to assist Susanna throughout the day..." or "Evan wants to take karate lessons, instead of doing more PT, and we'd like you to help us, Evan, and the karate teacher figure out how to make this work best for Evan."

If your child's therapist is unwilling to become a consultant, begin looking for a new therapist! On the upside, some therapists will be more than willing—and maybe even excited—about your ideas. Others, however, may be unable to make this change because of constraints they have no control over—like billing. Some therapists have told me they'd love to move into more of a consultant role, but because of insurance regulations, guidelines for state services, or some other barrier, consultation isn't a "billable" service.

Every situation is different, and we certainly don't want a therapist lying about how she's spending time with your child at the risk of losing her license! But sometimes a compromise can be worked out. For example, perhaps she could "do therapy" in the form of showing you and your child how to do things more naturally at home. What she does during that hour could be very different than "hands-on" therapy, but maybe it could still be classified as therapy for billing purposes. Alternatively, and if your budget allows, you could pay the therapist for occasional consult hours out of your own pocket.

How much help will you and your child need from a consultant therapist? There's no set answer. It's not like Traditional Therapy: two times a week until further notice! You might want to meet with her on a regular basis for the first month or so, maybe you'll need her less, and/or you might want her help on a sporadic basis, like when your child/your family decides to do something new and you're not sure how to make a new activity work best for your child.

On the other hand, you might realize you don't need help from a therapist anymore, and if so, that's fine! Thank her for all the help she's given you and move on. You can always call her for help later on, if necessary.

Therapists Share Their Wisdom

I began sharing alternatives to traditional therapy with audiences at conferences and seminars in the mid-1990s, after our son decided to resign from his therapy career and we began helping him in more natural ways—and I included this information in the first edition of this book (published in 2001). While I wrote the book for parents and anyone else who cared about children with disabilities, I was delightfully surprised when we began receiving orders from several different universities who were using it as a college text. One of these was the University of Oklahoma Health Sciences Center, where my book was used for a Master's Level PT/OT course taught by Beth DeGrace (Occupational Therapist, Ph.D., and Assistant Professor), Rene Daman (Physical Therapist, M.S., and Adjunct Professor), and Lorrie Sylvester (Physical Therapist, M.S., and Adjunct Professor). They have many years of experience in a wide variety of arenas: institutions, hospitals, therapy clinics, private and public schools, and NICUs; they've provided Early Intervention services, consultations to state agencies, and employment assistance; and they now focus on "doing things differently" to ensure people with disabilities and their families live their dreams in inclusive environments.

In this class, Beth, Rene, and Lorrie, along with Dee Blose, a Family Faculty Adjunct Professor and the mother of child with autism—educate therapists about new ways of thinking and new ways of assisting children and adults with disabilities and their families. In the process, the students—some who have been practicing for 20 years and are now earning their Master's degree—learn about the importance of typical opportunities in natural environments, and strategies to help children and adults do what's important to them without making them go to therapy! Beth and her colleagues were already on this track when they discovered my book; they chose to use it since it offered a parent's perspective on therapy.

> THE MEANING OF GOOD AND BAD, OF BETTER AND WORSE, IS SIMPLY HELPING OR HURTING.
> *Ralph Waldo Emerson*

I was intrigued by their work and requested an interview, which I turned into an handout article I distribute at many presentations. I think their insight will be helpful to readers of this second edition. Following are selected excerpts from that interview.

ON HOW THEY CHANGED, AFTER FIRST PRACTICING TRADITIONAL THERAPY—

BETH: I kept going back to school—and ended up with three degrees—because I felt like I must have missed something! As an OT, I was trained to believe that my job was to help people occupy their time doing what they wanted to do, and that when this happens, a person is in good shape. But in practice—in a therapy clinic—it made me sick to pull kids away from their parents, put them on scooter boards, and charge money for this!

I wondered, "How is what I'm doing having a positive impact on kids' lives? Maybe I'm not doing the right stuff, maybe I didn't learn it right, maybe I missed something." I went back for my Ph.D. so I could do research on how to do things better.

I also worked in a school for kids with autism and I interviewed the families. I learned that their worlds revolved around the condition of autism. They had very difficult days and nights, and they couldn't enjoy vacations or even family dinners! I thought, "Shame on me!" I had been doing things *to* kids, but had done nothing to help the family as a whole! I realized I needed to focus on doing things so a child and his family could have good days and nights, good family vacations, good dinners, or anything else!

> "I thought, 'Shame on me!' I had been doing things *to* kids, but had done nothing to help the family as a whole! I realized I needed to focus on doing things so a child and his family could have good days and nights, good family vacations, good dinners, or anything else!"

RENE: My experience is somewhat similar. I came back for my Master's, and am now working on my Ph.D., so I could learn more and do better. Before coming back for my Master's, I worked in a therapy clinic with therapists who had more experience. I felt they were the experts—they were NDT certified and it seemed what they were doing must be the "right" thing to do. But as I mentioned before, I was uncomfortable with many therapeutic practices and I wanted to learn more.

As a PT, your goal is to help a child learn to access the environment. But over and over again, when I suggested that parents might want to consider getting a wheelchair for a child so he could have independent mobility, parents would say, "But if we get him a wheelchair, he'll never learn to walk." I needed to understand all this better: the resistance, fear, grief, guilt, or whatever. So for my Master's thesis, I interviewed nine families whose children used wheelchairs to better understand the process parents go through in accepting their child's disability as it relates to equipment and supports. This was the first time I had really *listened and talked* to families—letting them take the lead and tell me their stories. We were taught to "interview" families to gather treatment-focused information. But this really helped me learn to value the family and acquire new ways of thinking.

LORRIE: My change came from having a friend with cerebral palsy who had lived in an institution for many years. She finally got out and moved into her own apartment. I went to visit her one day and we talked about how things were going—with cooking, laundry, and so forth. Things were going fine, but she told me she was still having to go to PT and OT in town. When I asked why, she said the therapists were worried about her range of motion. Well, she had better range of motion than I did! Yet the therapists weren't helping her learn to do what she needed to do in her new home. She wasn't getting support for the things that were really important to her.

On changes in therapeutic practices—

BETH: I think many universities *are* changing the way they teach today, but there is often a very big discrepancy between what PT and OT students are taught and what's actually happening in therapy settings. We still see kids crying during therapy, parents being told to sit in the waiting room, therapy in meaningless environments, and other ineffective practices.

RENE: There are new theories on how people learn to move or accomplish a task, and some therapists *are* modifying how they practice. But I'm amazed that many of the therapists I meet don't know about these newer theories, such as motor learning and motor control. It's as if some therapists stop learning once they're out of school.

BETH: We begin by talking about children without disabilities and the importance of every child having opportunities to participate in typical environments and activities. We also talk about ways of looking at children differently—as children, first—instead of diagnoses, and the importance of focusing on children's interests and abilities, what they want to do, need to do, and are expected to do. Then problem-solving the supports they need to do these things emerges. Students soon realize that the only way to learn these things is by *talking* to the child and the family! And when this occurs, we see very positive outcomes for the child and family. We want our students to first learn what's important to the child.

LORRIE: The class also helps students learn about assistive technology (AT)—something most therapists, including us, were not taught. They learn about high-tech and low-tech devices that can enable a child to do what she wants: have mobility, communication, or whatever!

BETH: The class we're teaching challenges the developmental model. We look at outcomes in terms of participation: "Is the person able to do what he wants to do? Can he participate in the activities he enjoys and those he is expected to do?" For example, an outcome shouldn't be that a child will crawl, but that he can participate in what he wants to do! It shouldn't be that a child can hold a spoon, but that she can spend mealtimes with her family. When a therapist can help a child and her family spend time doing what's important to them, developmental milestones are practically irrelevant.

We decided to use your book because it put words and stories and examples to ideas I had been thinking about for years, relative to a therapist's goal of supporting and assisting families to be successful. It's an awesome tool and a powerful agent of change.

RENE: Some of us were already moving in that new direction—looking at people as people, first. And a parent's words and experiences—like your book—are more powerful than anything we (as teachers) can ever say. We wanted our students to think differently and your book helps them do that. It teaches them to look at children in terms of strengths and competencies, and the importance of being a part of every day situations.

> "...an outcome shouldn't be that a child will crawl, but that he can participate in what he wants to do! It shouldn't be that a child can hold a spoon, but that she can spend mealtimes with her family. When a therapist can help a child and her family spend time doing what's important to them, developmental milestones are practically irrelevant."

LORRIE: Your book also helps our students understand that having a developmental disability is a natural part of life. Our students are learning that a child with a label is a child, first—he's not sick. And our job is to help discover the supports he'll need to be successful and happy in life.

BETH: Recently, Lorrie and I presented at our state's OT conference on the new ways we are doing things. A therapist came up to me afterwards and said, "You're asking me to change my identity!" All therapists have the ability to help people live the lives they want, but many may need to shift their thinking.

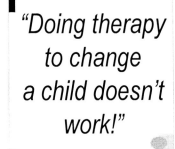

"Doing therapy to change a child doesn't work!"

LORRIE: *Doing therapy to change a child doesn't work!* I do some work in employment now—helping adults with disabilities be successful in real jobs, included in their communities. The kids I treated years ago have now grown up, and some are coming back to me. They still have CP or whatever! Therapy didn't make the condition go away. As kids, they all had dreams—none of which were addressed during typical therapies—and now they want to work. It makes me want to cry that I didn't listen to their dreams when they were children. If I had spent more time listening to their dreams and helping them do what was important to them, maybe they would have gone on to college or done other things to be successful as adults. I'm doing my best to help them be successful now, but things could have been so different!

RENE: I agree. The most important thing we can do, as therapists, is to help a child have the best quality of life, *as defined by the child and the family!* And we have to question whether making a child go to therapy two or three times a week really contributes to a child's quality of life, like you write about in your book. When kids are going to therapy all the time, they're missing out on ballet or karate, playing, and so many other typical opportunities. It's so sad that we've believed therapy was more valuable than listening to what a child thought was important.

> "And I remember, just as clearly as if it happened yesterday, that I was always scared to death of being taken away from my mom by the therapist—even when I was a 10-year-old!"

LORRIE: When I was a child, I had three knee surgeries, and was taken to PT all the time. My mom had to drag all four kids to therapy or else find a babysitter. It was hard on the whole family. I missed out on doing lots of things that were important to me. And I remember, just as clearly as if it happened yesterday, that I was always scared to death of being taken away from my mom by the therapist—even when I was a 10-year-old! And much of the therapy really hurt—I remember that very clearly, too. I cried a lot, and the therapist just ignored my tears and pain. Well, my dad was a bricklayer—he was very handy and very creative. He figured out how to help me do the exercises at home so I wouldn't have to go to therapy. I have a lot of empathy for what many children go through with traditional therapies.

RENE: I never felt right about trying to treat a child when he's crying. And once I read an article by an adult who received lots of therapy, and he wrote about feeling violated by the therapist's hands...I remember treating a 14-year-old boy on a mat to stretch his hamstrings. I realized how boring it was for me, and I assumed it was even more boring for him (and probably painful). I thought, "What am I accomplishing? This doesn't help him do what he wants to do!" I realized there were other ways to help him do what was important to him, instead of doing what was important per the "therapy plan."

ON THE IMPORTANCE OF ACCESSING TYPICAL COMMUNITY ACTIVITIES—

LORRIE: Yes, we need to ask, "What is this accomplishing?" A lot of what we do could be done better in different locations—like the YMCA or a gym—places in the real world. It's lots more fun and more meaningful to the person.

RENE: Sadly, therapists can often have a very negative influence on parents, by sending the message that a therapeutic activity—like stacking donut rings—is so important! We need to focus on what's really important in someone's daily life.

LORRIE: That can be very important. First, therapists can be instrumental in helping families learn what's available in their communities. Second, we can work with families and the staffs of community activities on ways to ensure people with disabilities/families can use or enjoy those activities in the same ways other people do.

ON THE PARENT'S ROLE WITHIN THE NEW THERAPEUTIC LANDSCAPE:

LORRIE: [Parents need to talk to] their kids about their hopes and dreams, and do whatever it takes so a child does *not* go to therapy! Parents need to help their kids pursue their dreams, and going to therapy can clutter those dreams. Therapy, goals, and all that stuff makes us lose sight of dreams. We're reduced to thinking about some therapy goal instead of what's really important...I hope parents and people with disabilities can learn to use therapists on an "as needed" basis. There shouldn't be this lifelong relationship of "provider/recipient." That creates intimidation and dependence—not a good relationship.

> "[Parents need to talk to] their kids about their hopes and dreams, and do whatever it takes so a child does *not* go to therapy! Parents need to help their kids pursue their dreams, and going to therapy can clutter those dreams."

RENE: People with disabilities and families need to feel they can call us anytime they need us, and they don't need us *all the time.* A therapist should be someone who comes in and out of your life, not someone who is a permanent fixture!

BETH: Parents also need to focus on a child's strengths and interests. If families share this information with therapists—along with their hopes and dreams—that would help therapists be "opportunity focused" instead of "technique focused." This would also enable us to be more effective helpers, and meet the real needs of people.

Parents should ask a therapist what her role is. Not, "Are you an NDT therapist?" but what the *real* role is. Is the therapist there to "fix the child" or to help the child and the family live a life of participation, opportunities, and more? Next, parents need to realize that *there is no evidence to support the notion that therapy "fixes" people with developmental disabilities.* Therapy is not a cure! If it was, there would be no adults with developmental disabilities!

Before a therapist touches a child, parents should ask, "Can you show me the evidence that what you want to do is effective?" And once a therapist has started working on a particular thing, if there isn't change within a reasonable amount of time, the therapist needs to stop wasting time and money!

RENE: Therapists need to discriminate between "evidence" and "promotion." An article in a magazine or newspaper is not evidence! In addition, when someone comes up with a new therapy or intervention, they do their own studies. This is passed off as "research" when it's actually the creator promoting the product. Therapists, as well as parents, need to be aware of the difference!

On the big picture—

BETH: ...we don't see health and well-being in the traditional medical sense. Like quality of life, health and well-being are defined by the person! And in this context of promoting a healthy life, a therapist could be thought of as a "life" coach, someone there to help when a person needs assistance in orchestrating her life so she can enjoy typical, everyday activities. Traditionally, we've focused on a hands-on approach to get a person "doing." But we feel it's more helpful to use a person's hopes and dreams and focus on a person "being" and "becoming." What could be more important than that?

> "Traditionally, we've focused on a hands-on approach to get a person 'doing.'
>
> "But we feel it's more helpful to use a person's hopes and dreams and focus on a person 'being' and 'becoming.'
>
> "What could be more important than that?"

What indeed?

I have such admiration for these three extraordinary therapists, and I wish I had known them when my son was very young. It's apparent that *their* hearts are truly in the right place—*because they care deeply about the hearts and minds of the children and adults they work with.* Beth, Rene, and Lorrie effectively put themselves in the shoes of the children and adults they work with to see what it was like from the other side (and Lorrie also had personal experience while being on the receiving end of therapy).

We can do the same. Throughout various chapters in this book, I've asked you to "think like a child," and to wonder, "how would this feel..." If we ask these questions regarding our children's experiences with Traditional Therapy, and if we listen to our children and learn from the wisdom of Beth, Rene, and Lorrie, we'll find solutions to ensure our children can achieve their hopes and dreams, while experiencing the joys of inclusion and leading a REAL LIFE.

Traditional Therapy also impacts children's lives in school settings. In Chapter 9, Beth, Rene, and Lorrie share their thoughts about that issue.

Tools for Success

In the REAL WORLD, all of us—from the tiniest kiddo to the oldest granny—use TOOLS every day. In this, and later chapters, I'm using the word TOOLS to mean assistive technology (AT) devices, accommodations, modifications, and/or supports of any kind.

Computers, cell phones, appliances, and electronics are examples of high-tech AT devices that are common in homes and offices across the country. Low-tech devices include a hammer, a fork, or a stick of glue. There's no mystery to AT devices: they're anything that makes life better—objects that enable us to do what we want, easier, faster, or more effectively.

Similarly, everyone *needs and uses* accommodations, modifications, and supports. The offer of "paper or plastic" is one way your neighborhood grocery store accommodates the different needs of its customers. Inserting a piece of plywood under your side of the mattress to provide more support is a modification. And your best friend being there for you when you're stressed out is a support.

When our children have the TOOLS they need, wondrous, amazing, and awesome outcomes are possible! In addition, when a child with a disability is provided with the right TOOLS, on-going Traditional Therapy may no longer be needed. For example, if a child has been receiving physical therapy to learn to walk, and he's provided with a power wheelchair so he can go where he wants, when he wants, physical therapy is no longer needed. Instead, he may only need occasional help from a therapist or a seating specialist as he grows, when a new seating system is needed, and so forth.

Once again, changes in the way we *think and talk* will help us understand the value of Tools for our children. Like many other parents, *my* thinking had been corrupted by Conventional Wisdom when my son was young. For many years I believed what he *really needed* was years and years of therapy to make sure he would be able to sit up, walk, feed himself, yadda, yadda, yadda. From a Medical Model deficit-based perspective, that made sense. But from a Real Life perspective, it didn't. Hours of therapy each week didn't allow Benjamin to enjoy a Real Life *at that time.* The years of therapy were actually an attempt to help him achieve an "able-bodied standard" *at some point in the distant future.*

I look back at those years in amazed dismay, realizing that therapists spent only a small percentage of time helping Benjamin learn to do things he could use in his life *right then*. Few of the therapists, for example, helped him learn to do things in the way his body *could* do them. Instead, they tried to get his body to do things the "right way."

When I regained my common sense, I realized what Benjamin *really needed* was independent mobility (a power wheelchair) and other Tools so he could do what he would be doing if he didn't have a disability—living a Real Life.

So—major changes in our thinking are very important. We may need to "unlearn" what we've been taught—give our brains a good scrubbing until we find the common sense that's been covered up by the layers and layers of Disability World paradigms. And this can be very difficult. Been there, done that. I have been a very slow learner, I didn't always listen to my son, and I buried new information if it made me uncomfortable! I hope this book makes it easier for you (and I wish I had such a book when my son was younger—the only ones available then focused on "fixing" a child's "problems").

While you're scrubbing away the old ways of thinking, make sure to get rid of the Not-OK, Not Ready, Developmental Age, and Presumption of Incompetence paradigms. Continuing to embrace these may prevent you from seeing the value of Tools. For example, your three-year-old child could be "living the good life" by attending a typical neighborhood preschool if he had a communication device. But if you think he's Not-Ready for a neighborhood preschool, the idea of a communication device won't even enter your noggin!

Similarly, your 10-year-old could be having the time of her life in a karate class—earning belts and making new friends—if she had a power wheelchair, instead of the manual chair which someone has to push. But if the Presumption of Incompetence clouds your mind—if you think she doesn't have the cognitive or physical abilities to drive a power chair—you won't even consider the value of this important Tool.

When our children have the Tools they need, wondrous, amazing, and awesome outcomes are possible!

Your child with autism (or other condition) could be happily and successfully included in a Regular Ed class at the neighborhood school. But if you think she doesn't have effective oral communication, the emotional maturity, social skills, and/or the ability to "attend" in such an environment, you won't even consider the importance of a communication device, natural supports from classmates, or other TOOLS. See how our attitudes really get in the way?

Recipe for Success: Your Child + TOOLS = REAL LIFE

Use the same recipe I described in the section in the "Child-Directed Natural Assistance" section. Ask yourself: what age-appropriate activities would your child be doing in natural environments if she didn't have a disability? Now consider what TOOLS would enable her to participate in those activities. If you have older children, think about what they did at the age your child with a disability is now. If your child with a disability is the oldest child or the only child, look at children without disabilities who are your child's age to see what they're doing—not what their *bodies* can do, but what *activities* are typical.

Alternatively, if your child is under five, ask a physician, a therapist, or educator for a "developmental milestones" chart for your child's age, or find one in a book at the library or a bookstore. It will be used in a very different way than how it might have been used in past. Instead of using it to see where your child is "behind" or "deficient," look at it to see what *activities* are typical for children of your child's age. Here are some examples:

- Eighteen-month-old children (and some even younger) are roaming in their environments and learning every step of the way; so an eighteen-month-old (or older) child who cannot walk needs independent mobility so he can roam and learn in the same way.

- Two-year-old children are mastering their environments through language. Being a "terrible two" and saying "no" many times a day are hallmarks of typical development we value (even though this is a difficult time for parents!). So a two-year-old (or older) child who doesn't speak needs an effective method of communication so he can master his environment.

- Many four- and five-year-old children are drawing, painting, and beginning to write letters, numbers, and their own names. So a four- or five-year-old child who has difficulty putting pencil-to-paper may need to have the paper taped to the table or a table-top easel, and larger crayons or a device to hold the crayon which he can grasp with his whole hand. Alternatively, the child might need a computer, with or without an adapted keyboard and other accommodations, so he can draw or color with a computer program, learn to write his name on the keyboard, and more.

- Ten-year-old children participate in park and rec activities or take classes in the community (art, drama, etc.). Their parents drop them off and pick them up—what freedom! A child with autism or another condition that involves communication and/or behavior may need an effective communication method and behavior supports to enable him to participate in such activities. Such behavior supports might include peer support from another 10-year-old or from the adult instructor, modifications of the "rules"

IF A MAN DOES NOT KEEP PACE WITH HIS COMPANIONS, PERHAPS IT IS BECAUSE HE HEARS A DIFFERENT DRUMMER.

LET HIM STEP TO THE MUSIC WHICH HE HEARS, HOWEVER MEASURED OR FAR AWAY.

Henry David Thoreau

of the activity, or any other accommodation (and more about these types of Tools later in this chapter).

- Sixteen-year-olds are working part-time, hanging out with their friends, learning to drive, and/or thinking about college. What AT devices, modifications, accommodations, or supports are needed to ensure a 16-year-old with a disability can participate in and learn from these activities?

AT—A Great First Choice, Not a Last Resort

In the Real World, AT is almost always viewed as a great first choice, not a last resort. Few people balance their checkbooks without the assistance of a calculator—doing it with pencil and paper would take too long and be less accurate. Few choose a "push" lawn mower over a power mower. Most of us want—no, *demand*—whatever gadgets and gizmos will make life better; we want them sooner rather than later; and we do whatever it takes to get them, at just about any cost! The same is not true in Disability World, where a widespread bias exists against providing children and adults with the AT devices they need. The Disability Double Standard is once again at work: AT devices are often seen as a last resort, instead of a first choice, based on a variety of different attitudes.

"If we get him a _____, he'll never_____."

This is the rationale used by many parents and/or professionals when they refuse to consider a wheelchair or a communication device—the two "biggies"—or even "smaller" devices.

The reality is that none of us have any way of knowing if a child will walk or talk or master other functional skills. We can, however, look reality in the face and recognize that a child needs independent mobility and effective communication in order to learn and grow, feel wonderful about themselves, and lead a Real Life as a child, so he can lead a Real Life as an adult!

When my son, Benjamin, was very young, physical therapists *discouraged* us when we wanted our son to have mobility devices. The physical therapist (PT) warned that if we got him a pediatric three-wheeled scooter (so he could have fun with his friends during recess at school), he would "never learn to walk." By this time, I had learned from adults with disabilities that Benjamin *didn't need to walk* to have a good life; he did, however, need independent mobility so he could go where he wanted, when he wanted. This PT was obviously influenced by the Medical Model and the Quality of Life paradigms: in her mind, his legs "didn't work," so they needed to be "fixed;" he wouldn't have a good life if he didn't walk; and his use of a scooter would prevent him from walking. But I held a different perspective: having independent mobility would enable Benj to have a *great* Quality of Life, at school, so he could play with his friends; at home so he could be a more active member of the family; and in every other environment!

Why do we still see children and adults with disabilities struggling in walkers or being pushed in wheelchairs—like they're babies in strollers? *What would you want if it were you?*

Similar attitudes swirl around the idea of providing a child with a communication device, communication cards, sign language training, or other forms of alternate communication. Many professionals are adamant that if a child with autism, for example, is given a communication device he'll "never learn to talk." They might be partially right—the child may never master oral communication, *but that doesn't mean she isn't in desperate need of effective communication—right this minute!*

Too many children, and their parents, have first-hand experience with the negative outcomes when children don't have a means to effectively communicate: the child communicates with his behavior *(but we don't* see *the behavior as communication)*, his behavior is then seen as "inappropriate," so he is assigned another label ("behavior problems"), a behavior plan is written which usually results in greater exclusion and segregation, and if the behavior plan doesn't work, we medicate the child into compliance. It's a downhill spiral—and what chance does this child have for a REAL LIFE under these circumstances?

Dylan, my best friend's son, had *some* oral communication as a young child, but it was hard to understand his speech pattern. So his parents taught him sign language *and* they also got him a communication device. Between the three, he communicated very effectively. As he grew, his vocabulary increased and his speech was easier to understand, so he discarded signing and then later, the communication device. Today he uses neither. Did signing or a device prevent him from wanting to talk? *No!*

When my son was very young, and I was heavily invested in the MEDICAL MODEL paradigm, I pestered professionals about when my son would walk. I stopped asking after one doctor shared this wise counsel:

> I don't know, Kathie—I don't know if Benjamin will ever walk. I've seen some kids that I think *should* be able to walk one day, and they never do. And I've seen other kids who I don't think will *ever* walk, and they do. It's really up to Benjamin—not us.

I value this doctor's insight: if a child is going to walk or talk or master some other functional skill, he will, *if his body can*—not because of what *we* do to or for him. I believe that being able to walk, talk, feed yourself, interact socially, or perform other functional skills is not a *choice*. It's not as if a child or adult with a disability thinks to himself, "Hmmm—I can't decide if I should talk or not." I feel these skills are as natural to us as breathing. If a child *can* walk or talk or feed himself or whatever, he will. If he cannot, we need to provide him with the TOOLS to help him achieve *the same or similar end result.*

I believe that we (parents, professionals, therapists, etc.) have an overinflated perception of our power to change a child's body or brain, and we show little or no respect for a child's inherent humanity. We sometimes treat a child like blob of clay that can be molded into the shape of our choice. In the process, it seems we ignore the fact that each child came into this world already perfectly formed. And it makes me sadder than sad to think about the physical, emotional, and spiritual pain we inflict on children in our efforts to change them.

"...I don't know if Benjamin will ever walk. I've seen some kids that I think *should* be able to walk one day, and they never do. And I've seen other kids who I don't think will *ever* walk, and they do. It's really up to Benjamin—not us."

We do not need to change our children—so they can master a functional skill. Instead, we need to give them whatever TOOLS they need so they can do what's important to them—so they can lead REAL LIVES.

THE DEATH OF A DREAM

Some parents view getting their child a wheelchair or a communication device as a "defeat," a "loss," or the "death of a dream." When parents invest years of time, energy, and money in their child's therapy, they don't want to believe that their efforts (their child's efforts, actually) have been "wasted"—that's too bitter a pill to swallow. So some never give up: their children receive therapy until they're grown. At that time, many of these young adult children are still PRESUMED INCOMPETENT—they "can't" work or care for themselves (because they don't have independent mobility or effective communication), so their parents turn them over to the Adult Service System, where most will continue to be deprived of the AT devices they need.

Other parents swallow the bitter pill—reluctantly. They don't embrace a wheelchair or communication system with joy—they don't see it as a great TOOL for their children. It's perceived, instead, as a hated symbol of failure. So instead of getting their child the best and/or experimenting with different devices until they find the one that's just right, they accept the minimum offered by professionals in the System and/or their insurance coverage.

To a large degree, the attitudes and ensuing actions of such parents may be a direct result of DISABILITY WORLD language and perceptions. If they *believe* their child will be "mute" or "non-verbal" or "confined to a wheelchair" or "wheelchair bound," I can see why they would resist. These are descriptors that represent "a tragedy" and/or "pitiful life." If, however, they changed their own attitudes and language, they would see things differently. I've never "confined" Benjamin to his chair (only to his room sometimes, when he was younger—Tee-Hee), and he's also not "bound" to his chair. He *uses* his chair to go where he wants, when he wants, and his chair gives him *freedom, power, and self-sufficiency.*

I have great empathy for parents struggling with this decision—we struggled, but just a bit (see box). I have even greater empathy, however, *for the children*—because the denial of effective communication and independent mobility is also the denial of opportunities to lead a REAL LIFE. We all have dreams for our children, but at some point, *their dreams* must take precedence over ours—and the sooner, the better. And I believe, with all my heart, that their dreams include power wheelchairs, methods to communicate, and/or other TOOLS, so they can have friends; play; do what they want, how they want, where they want, when they want; be competent and be seen as competent; learn and grow; and so much more!

"BUT HE DOESN'T REALLY NEED IT..."

Ten-year-old "Joshua" is pushed in a manual wheelchair and has two big "buttons" for communication. When asked why he doesn't have a power wheelchair and a more effective communication system, his mother says, "There's always someone to push him, and he can say 'yes' or 'no' with his buttons."

"LOOK AT THE BABY"

We only struggled a little with the decision to get Benj a manual wheelchair at age four—the actions of children provoked me!

While pushing Benj in the fancy orthopedic stroller at the mall, children who were *younger* than him pointed and said things like, "Look at the cute baby!" Benj has always been tall; he only looked "like a baby" because he was in a stroller! I realized it was terrible for Benj to hear other kids say those things—I didn't want *him* thinking he was a baby!

That was basically all it took to make the decision, and I'm glad the words of those little kids helped me see what was important. When children or adults are pushed, regardless of age, they're perceived as "babies" and/or "unable."

But what does *Joshua* want? He cannot push himself in his manual chair; does he like being pushed around like he's a baby in a stroller? Does he like having to wait for others to push him *at their convenience?* With his simple two-button communication system, he can only *respond*—he cannot *initiate* conversations. When told, "Touch the red button if you want vanilla ice cream or the yellow button for strawberry," what does Joshua do if he wants chocolate, instead?

It's bad enough that Joshua isn't able to be in control of his life—by having independent mobility and effective communication *as a 10-year-old.* But how in the world do we expect him to lead a REAL LIFE as an adult when he has to be pushed and can only respond? How will he get a job? Sadly, his mother doesn't have Big Dreams for him. She's already decided he'll "never have a job," so he'll go into a group home when he turns 18, and he'll probably spend the rest of his life being pushed like a baby and responding to "yes/no" questions. *Is this what Joshua wants?*

"Chloe" has *some* oral communication, but only her immediate family can understand her. The six-year-old also communicates through grunts, pulling on her mom's clothes, and other behaviors. Her mother says Chloe doesn't need a communication device because, "We can understand her just fine—and besides, we know what she needs even if she can't tell us." The attitude and actions of Chloe's mom are setting Chloe up for big problems, now and in the future.

First, many children with speech delays or difficulties are automatically placed in Special Ed classrooms. (In the minds of many, lack of speech automatically triggers the PRESUMPTION OF INCOMPETENCE.) But if Chloe had an effective communication system, she could be successful in a Regular Ed classroom, make friends, and do so many other activities that constitute a REAL LIFE!

Second, children who communicate through their behavior are at great risk of acquiring "behavior labels," as I described earlier in this chapter. Many children are able to communicate certain things through their behavior and/or body movements. They can indicate that they're hungry or want a certain toy, for example. But trying to communicate *feelings* through behavior is a risky proposition. When a child screams at the top of his lungs, *"I'm really mad at you,"* we see this as "appropriate behavior"—the child is using words instead of fists to communicate his feelings. But how can Chloe communicate these same feelings? Her words aren't understandable (and she knows it), so her only alternatives are to scratch, bite, hit, push, screech, or run—all of which would be considered "inappropriate behaviors."

Chloe's mother is unintentionally setting her daughter up for failure. *It's not enough* that *family members* can understand Chloe and anticipate her needs. Chloe needs to be able to communicate effectively with anyone and everyone, in any setting!

There's a second issue to consider in the "He doesn't really need it..." philosophy. Some professionals or parents insist that a child doesn't need *power* mobility—that it's "healthier" for the child to use a walker to continue building leg strength or a manual chair to build arm strength. And

---

REAL LIFE!

At a conference, "Rosie" proudly shared that her 10-year-old son had recently started using a power wheelchair—but added they weren't letting him drive it! Rosie and/or the aide at school controlled the joystick. Why? They were afraid Zak would run into a wall or hurt himself.

I assured her that he *would* run into some walls—but letting Zak drive himself was the only way he would learn! She sighed—and said that was probably right, but added she was afraid he could tip the chair over. I agreed—he probably *would* tip it, my son has!

Rosie was still fearful, so I asked what was the worst that could happen. "He could tip it over on the side and break his arm," she said. "Yep, he could," I replied, "and then he could wear a cast and all the kids could sign it! Kids who walk fall down. Kids who drive power chairs run into walls and tip them over—that's REAL LIFE!" Rosie agreed to manage her own fears so Zak could have the freedom he needed.

here's my response to such a statement: "Yes, and it would be healthier for *you* to walk everywhere—better for your heart, lungs, and overall health—so let's take your car away from you!"

Similar responses can address other silly statements. If Someone doesn't think a child needs a communication device, let's seal Someone's mouth with tape to see how well he could communicate. If handwriting is a difficult, laborious process for a child, and Someone says this child doesn't need a computer, let's take Someone's computer away and see if he can still do his work well. If Someone refuses to provide a child with a calculator so he can learn math in the way that's best for him, we can take Someone's calculator away and see how well he can keep his checkbook balanced.

In all these situations, the DISABILITY DOUBLE STANDARD is being applied: those who would impose certain standards on others aren't willing to live by those same standards. How can we live with ourselves when we don't do everything possible to provide our children with the TOOLS they need?

"BUT SHE ISN'T ABLE TO OPERATE IT..."

One of the biggest barriers to children having the AT devices they need is the PRESUMED INCOMPETENCE mentality: a parent or professional believes the child could not benefit from a device because he is incompetent to use it. And in most cases, this *is* just a presumption—a guess, an opinion—*for the child has never even been given the opportunity to try!*

The bicycle analogy may help put things in perspective. When your parents bought your first bicycle, did you know how to ride it? For most of us, the answer is probably "no." *But your parents bought it for you anyway!* Why? Because they *presumed* you could learn how to ride it if you were given lots of opportunities to try (with or without training wheels!). *And you did.*

We need to apply the same positive attitude. Let's presume our children "can," instead of "can't." And let's give them as many opportunities to try, for as long as they need, with as many different pieces of equipment, if necessary. Some of *us* needed our *bicycle training wheels* on longer than others, but in the end, so what?

"But my child couldn't drive a power wheelchair because she can't use her hands," you might be thinking. Two responses are relevant (and you can apply these examples to other scenarios). First, when given the opportunity to succeed, children are highly motivated—and the girl who isn't able to "use her hands" might decide she *can* use one hand or even one finger to push the joystick on a power chair. Second, this same girl can drive a power chair using whatever part of her body she has the most control over. A joystick can be located by her feet and she can use her big toe, it can be mounted by her shoulder and she can use her head to push it, she can use a puff-and-sip method, etc.

"But my child is blind/has low vision—how could he drive a power wheelchair," you ask. Well, that's like asking how a person who's blind/has low vision can walk! With aids or supports, of course—like using a cane or holding his hands out to feel where things are. Similar accommodations can be made so the

Some parents, sadly, may not provide their children with AT devices because they don't want their children to "look" like they have a disability, or "more of" a disability. They hope their child can "pass" as a child without a disability. These parents are ashamed of the child and/or don't want to be embarrassed. I can only say such parents *should be ashamed*—of themselves!

child can drive a power chair. A device that emits an audible directional signal can be attached to the chair, wire springs can be attached so the child knows when he's close to a wall. Or the child could also use a guide dog, in the same way "walkers" use guide dogs.

Creative thinking can be applied when considering a communication device, computer, or other high-tech equipment. When I harp on this during presentations, some parents tell me, "You don't understand—we spent *years* trying different devices for my child, and nothing worked. Not *everyone* can benefit from an AT device." Let's not be hasty! Technology is changing faster than we can keep up with it. Even if your child has experimented with different devices in the past, go back and try again—there are gazillions of new products on the market, and more arrive every day!

If we PRESUME COMPETENCE, "remember the bicycle," think creatively, and maintain a steadfast determination to find the solution, our children's lives will be enriched beyond imagination! They'll be living REAL LIVES now, and they'll be on the road to success as adults. Isn't this the fulfillment of their dreams *and* ours?

"WE DON'T HAVE THE FUNDS..."

Many parents and professionals see AT devices as an "extra" that will be provided "if there's money." This way of thinking represents the DISABILITY DOUBLE STANDARD in spades! As I mentioned earlier, all of *us* use AT devices every minute of the day—cell phones, computers, cars, microwave ovens, and zillions of other pieces of equipment. And when we need a new gizmo or gadget, we *find a way* to pay for it! Shouldn't we do the same for our children?

Under Special Ed law, school districts are required to purchase the AT devices a child needs to be successful in school (as determined by the IEP Team). If your child is attending a wonderful school, you may have no problem getting the school to fulfill its obligations. However, the majority of parents have to fight tooth and nail to get the school to pay for such items, and the process may take months or even years. *But our children don't have that long to wait!* Some schools agree to buy an item, but then they're stinkers about letting the child take the device home every night, on weekends, or over the summer! (The item is legally the property of the school, but educators are supposed to allow the child to use it wherever—at school or at home.) And there are other less-than-desirable outcomes when schools are involved in the purchase of AT devices (see box on next page).

Here's the bottom line: if the school is not helpful and supportive, don't even go that route. Instead, get the AT device on your own—*any way you can*—per the suggestions below. Our children's lives are too precious to put them at the mercy of bureaucratic hoopla—we cannot make them wait even one more day for what they need, and *we must not let them go without.*

If the AT device is a high-dollar item (like a manual or power wheelchair or a communication device), get a prescription from a physician, and try to get it paid for by your health care plan. Some parents have learned, to their

---

LOOK EVERYWHERE!

Turn over every rock to find AT! As I write this, we're preparing to install a SureHands transfer system for Benj. This is, as far as I can tell, the only self-transfer (meaning Benj can do it by himself) system available. It will enable him to get out of bed and will carry him into the bathroom! A new system is around $10-12,000, which insurance might have paid for, with a fight. But we kept our eyes peeled on Internet sites and disability newsletters and found a used one for $1,000!

Need a wheelchair accessible vehicle? Check your state government's annual auction of vehicles! A mom in Nevada bought one for about $2,000!

great dismay, that they don't have the backing of a physician, therapist, or other professional whose "stamp of approval" is needed before insurance will pay for an AT device. In this situation, it's time to get a new doctor, therapist, or whatever! Years ago, we dropped all the pediatric specialists my son had in favor of a family practice physician. Some of the pedi-specialists didn't support the ideas we had for AT devices for Benj—one "didn't like" the power chair I had in mind. He had never seen one, mind you, but he thought it looked "too big" in the product literature. When we switched to a family doctor, he readily admitted he didn't know anything about cerebral palsy and power wheelchairs, so he depended on me to tell him what Benj needed! *Yippee!*

If insurance/Medicaid won't pay, don't despair. Find the dough anywhere you can. If it's something that can be charged on your credit card, do it. Pay it out over time. Yes, you might have to go without some other things for awhile, but won't it be worth it? And wouldn't you do this for yourself or your other children if the item was really important?

Alternatively, don't be shy about asking others for help. This is no time for our pride to get in the way—*a child's future is at stake!* Go to your extended family and ask for a loan or a gift—ask everyone to pitch in what they can. Wouldn't you do the same for them, if they needed your help?

Go to your community: to Kiwanis, Lions, Rotary, and other clubs. Ask each to contribute a portion of the total needed for a power wheelchair, communication device, laptop computer, or other high-dollar device. Your child is a citizen of your community and these groups work to make their communities better. Propose that if they can help you in this important endeavor, you'll promote it in the local news so they'll get the credit they deserve. Then you and your child can go to the organizations' meetings, do a presentation, and show off how great your child's life is now! (And make sure any news coverage is positive and upbeat, not a "pity" story!) Some or all of these groups might also help you sponsor a fundraising event—a dance, pancake breakfast, etc.

You can also look for community support from local/state foundations (research them at your public library). And don't forget to check out disability-related organizations. Most don't have any extra money to put in your hot little hands, but some have equipment banks. Each organization works differently, but some actually donate the equipment to a child who needs it, some ask for payment for used equipment, and some simply let the child borrow it (for however long he needs it).

There's one more alternative to consider: your school's PTA/PTO or other parent group. When I was involved in the PTA at my children's elementary school, we were always fundraising for one thing or another (that's what these organizations do!). Why couldn't the parent group at your child's school raise funds for something your child needs? If, for example, your child needs a computer, could the PTA donate the $50.00/month payments to Dell, Apple, or some other computer company?

Let's get creative—and stay creative—so our kiddos will have what they need to succeed! We can do this!

SHARING IS NOT ALWAYS CARING!

I helped "Jenny" with some strategies to get the school to purchase a comunication device for her six-year-old daughter, "Alicia." Sadly, Alicia was still in a segregated classroom, with 7-8 other students, and most of them were not talking, either. Jenny was working hard to get Alicia moved to a Regular Ed classroom.

After a long wait, the communication device arrived and Alicia was finally able to express her wants and needs. But the Special Ed department wouldn't let her bring it home every day.

Jenny discovered even worse news when she dropped in on Alicia's class one day. The Special Ed teachers decided it wasn't "fair" that only Alicia had a device, so it was being "shared" by the other students. When Jenny protested, they said, "You don't have a say in this; the device doesn't *really belong to Alicia*—it belongs to *us,* and we can use it any way we want!"

Be aware of this mentality if the school agrees to buy your child an AT device.

NOT REAL LIFE!

When we finally got Benjamin his power chair at age nine, we were ecstatic over his new freedom—it was awesome! But there were some unexpected hitches. For example, we had never taught Benj to *look both ways before crossing the street!* Why? Because *we* had always looked when pushing him in his manual chair!

This is just one example—but there are many more—of the dangers of not getting children the TOOLS they need, at the age-appropriate time so they can learn to be safe and successful and live a Real Life!

What has *your child* not yet learned, because he hasn't had the TOOLS he needs at the right time?

Timing is Everything!

The "when" is a critically important consideration when thinking about AT devices. Our children need these devices at the age-appropriate (chronological, not developmental) time. (The same is true when thinking about accommodations, modifications, and supports, which will be covered later in this chapter.)

If I had to do it over again, my son would have had a power wheelchair by the time he was two, instead of when he was nine. Benj had a power scooter at age six and this was a great TOOL that allowed him to play with friends during school recess and come and go on his own. But he couldn't sit in the scooter at his desk at school or the dinner table at home, so there was still a lot of transferring and Benj didn't have the self-sufficiency he craved.

Unintentionally, my husband and I "retarded" Benjamin's growth and development by not giving him the independent mobility he needed to explore and master his environment. During those early years, I was aware of the importance of a child exploring his environment—but not as aware as I should have been—and I made conscious efforts to move him to different rooms in the house and sit him in different places (on the floor, on the couch, at the table, etc.) so he could see things differently and have different experiences. In hindsight, my efforts were minuscule as compared to what he could have been doing *on his own in a power wheelchair.* Our initial inability to recognize the value of independent mobility prevented our son from enjoying the typical, ordinary, every day experiences that are crucially important to a child's social, emotional, and cognitive development and his overall success.

The lack of effective mobility or effective communication at the age-appropriate time (in other words, when a child would naturally be doing it if she didn't have a disability) has global repercussions on the child's whole life. In addition to diminished opportunities for learning, this leads to *learned helplessness*—a condition that may be a bigger barrier to a child's success than the actual disability. A child without effective mobility or communication is made dependent on others; he can exert little or no control over his environment; and he has little or no personal power—he remains more like an infant. As a result, he doesn't learn to make decisions or be responsible for himself, so as an adult, he has been "prepared" only for a life dependent on others—in a group home, sheltered workshops, etc. (And those who were responsible for not providing him with the TOOLS he needed as a child share the responsibility for the unsuccessful status of his adult life.)

If you still have doubts about the importance of AT devices for mobility, communication, or other needs, consider these examples. Would you rather have your two-year-old say, "I love you, Mommy," with a communication device or *not at all?* Would you rather have your two-year-old "run up to you" in his power wheelchair when he needs a hug, or do you want to always have to *go to him?* Think of some examples in your own child's life.

Finding the Right AT Device

There are many, many AT devices (including specialized products as well as ordinary items) that might be of value to your child. Some are high-tech/high-dollar, some are low-tech/low dollar, and some are no-tech and free (you can make them yourself)!

Finding the "just-right" AT device may take time and experimentation, but our children's are lives worth it! If we have the will, we'll find a way to ensure our children have the TOOLS they need. It once again goes back to our attitudes!

When thinking about AT devices in general, start with the stores in your neighborhood—Target, Wal-Mart, Radio Shack, and many others—in order to buy "off-the-shelf" for the lowest prices. If you can't find what your child needs there, search the Internet, look at catalogs, visit durable medical equipment dealers, and talk to others who may use the same or similar devices.

When considering high-tech devices, like wheelchairs, communication devices, laptop computers, etc., how do you know what's best for your child? Go look in the mirror and see the face of an Expert. You may know diddly-squat about fancy equipment right now, but you know your child better than anyone. And it's not hard to learn about AT devices, especially if you have access to the Internet. Every state has an AT agency, many disability organizations have AT departments, most school districts have AT teams who are responsible for assessing a child within the AT arena, and some physical and occupational therapists have expertise in AT devices.

Some parents have had excellent help from these different sources, while others experienced nothing but frustration and wasted time. Like anything else, some folks are really good at what they do, others are not. At state-funded AT agencies and AT departments at disability organizations, the AT experts may only recommend what they're personally familiar with and they may or may not have experience with the items your child might need. On the other hand, some folks at these organizations provide excellent information, advice, and recommendations. And some have loaner equipment your child can experiment with. So give these organizations a try, but if you don't find the help you need in a relatively short period of time, move on.

In public schools, some AT teams are very good, others are dismal. Our small school district had access to a regional AT team that served the rural school districts in our area. The principal at my son's school was a parent's best friend, so my son and other children with disabilities at this school received whatever they needed. But the same was not true at a nearby school. I learned that when an AT assessment was scheduled for a child, the principal was notified—as part of the usual paperwork distribution. But he routinely called the AT team leader ahead of time, told her his school had no "extra" money, so he did not want the team to recommend any AT devices! This horrible (and illegal) practice was allowed to continue because the AT team members (who were all educators) were afraid they would lose their jobs if they reported this principal.

More and more PTs and OTs are gaining expertise in AT devices; some are becoming specialists and are very good. Others have little or no knowledge or

D-I-Y

If you're not yet a *Do-It-Yourselfer,* this might be the time to become one! After a therapist made a standing frame for Benj out of PVC pipe and lawn chair webbing, my husband and I were inspired! We made Benj a bath chair out of PVC pipe and lawn chair fabric, and learned to make other things, as well. Mark and I remodeled our house to make it accessible—and learned plumbing and electricity in the process!

experience. We need to be wise consumers and ask lots of questions to determine which sources—if any—can provide the expertise we need. Go back to the mirror to see the face of an Expert again.

When we decided to get Benjamin a power chair, I researched them on the Internet, called the manufacturers for brochures, asked others who used wheelchairs, and window-shopped at durable medical equipment dealers. When we found the one we thought would be best, I called the company headquarters, and was directed to the regional representative. It only took one phone call to him and within a week or so, he delivered a "demo" chair for Benjamin to try out at home for a couple of weeks. Bingo—that was the chair for Benj!

You can do the same. The process will almost always go faster if *you* do the legwork instead of waiting on an AT expert. They have many people to serve and you child is one of those "many." You only have one customer: your child! Again, ask other parents; search the Internet; check out any equipment banks nearby; and contact manufacturers, distributors, and durable medical equipment dealers. Ask for a loaner or a demo, and allow your child to try out as many different pieces of equipment, for as long as possible, before deciding which is best. This is an exciting time! I'll never forget the ear-to-ear grin on Benjamin's face when we picked up his power chair and he raced around, bouncing off a few walls in the process!

AT Examples

Below you'll find a list of AT devices that might be helpful to your child. This is a partial list—by the time this book gets into your hands, there will be newer products available! Remember how to think about AT devices: they can enable your child to participate in and benefit from typical, age-appropriate activities in inclusive environments (e.g., lead a REAL LIFE); they can make life better; and they can also reduce and/or eliminate the need for therapeutic interventions. These examples reflect a child being at home, school, or in other environments. Keep these ideas in mind, for later chapters will focus on your child at home and in school, and AT devices are important in all areas of a child's life!

- Power wheelchair, manual wheelchair, walker, service dog.

- Communication device or communication cards.

- Laptop computer—with "voice output" software, can be used as communication device or can be used in FC; can also be used in lieu of paper/pencil for writing; with voice-recognition software, child can dictate instead of using keyboard; with appropriate software, can be used for drawing, coloring, doing math, learning geography, history, and every other subject under the sun (at home and at school).

- Calculator, talking calculator, abacus, other math helpers.

- Adapted eating utensils, plates, bowls, and other kitchen goodies to enable children to feed themselves, learn to cook, help in the kitchen.

- Kitchen appliances, TVs, radios, clocks, etc., that work for the child and everyone else in the home.

MORE D-I-Y

When Benjamin was first learning to use the computer, he had difficulty seeing the keyboard. Before searching for a high-tech/high-dollar accommodation, I tried to come up with a solution on my own— and I did! I bought a card of "colored dots" from an office supply store. I placed yellow dots over the letters of Benjamin's name. Then I put red dots on the top row, green on the next, and so on. As I placed the dots, I wrote each key's symbol in big letters, then trimmed the dots to fit each key. When Benj sat at the computer, I told him to look at the yellow keys to spell his name. When he wanted to spell another word, I helped him by saying, "Look on the red row..." and so forth. Within a short time, he learned the keyboard and didn't need the dots anymore.

- Table top easel, adapted writing/painting instruments, to allow a child to draw, paint, learn to write.
- Positioning chairs to allow very young children to sit up and interact with the world from an upright—not lying down—position.
- Bath chairs, shower chairs, adapted toilet seats, "bidet" systems (to clean bottoms), to enable more self-sufficiency in the bathroom.
- Hospital-type beds (head and feet raise/lower), trapeze systems, grab bars, and transfer systems, to enable a child to get in and out of bed.
- Wheelchair-accessible desks for school and home.
- Adapted play equipment (swing-sets, rocking horses, etc.).
- Touch-lamps; voice-activated systems for turning appliances off/on; environmental control units (ECUs); automatic door openers; keyless locks; and other devices to enable a child to control the physical environment.
- Non-slip fabric, to keep a bottom from sliding out of a seat; to hold toys, plates, and anything else in place.
- Digital clocks and watches (including talking devices) to allow a child to "tell time" his way.
- Books on tape, large print books, books on computer, "pen readers," Braille materials, to help children with reading and learning.
- Captions on the TV, for children with hearing impairments, and for those without—a great way to help children learn to read! (We leave ours on all the time.) FM system for child to use at school to hear the teacher better.

Accommodations, Modifications, and Supports

In addition to AT devices, making changes to the environment or providing supports can have a powerful impact on a child's ability to lead a REAL LIFE, and may also reduce or eliminate the need for therapeutic interventions. Here are some examples to consider:

- Install a rope/net swing in your home, or provide a rocking chair, rocking horse, or other "moving" device so a child who "needs to move/rock" has a safe, fun place to do his thing.
- If a child is considered a "runner," help him do it safely, by setting up a "running track" in your home or in the fenced yard. Put tape on the floor to indicate where he can run in the house or set up traffic cones in the back yard, and give your child the power to run when he wants, in safe places you've agreed on. (More details about behavior and emotional needs are covered in the next section.)
- If your child needs less or more sensory stimulation around the house, change the house instead of trying to change your child. Before your child was born, you and your spouse furnished your house in ways that met your needs. When your first child was born, you "baby-proofed" your home so your baby wouldn't hurt himself or your things. So why wouldn't we do the same for our children, regardless of age or condition? We should always attempt to change the environment, when necessary, instead of the child. And we won't be able to change every environment, but certainly a

---

MOBILITY DEVICES

Here's my take on walkers and wheelchairs: unless a child has great balance, coordination, and leg strength, *and* can transfer independently, walking—with or without a walker—is probably not going to be the most efficient form of independent mobility.

Similarly, if a child cannot push himself in a manual wheelchair, *the vast majority of the time, and over uneven terrain,* a manual wheelchair is probably not the best form of independent mobility.

When thinking about mobility, think REAL LIFE: can the child play with friends, help with chores around the house, get himself to/from classes at school on time, etc. If a walker or manual wheelchair won't enable a child to do these typical activities, go with a power wheelchair and watch your child succeed!

Also, make sure you have the right seating and positioning system! A custom-made seat cushion changed my son's posture dramatically, enabling him to hold his head upright, use his arms and hands, and more. And a child should not have to be "tied" into a chair with straps across his torso. Instead, he needs a better positioning system, including a reclining seat back so he's not always fighting gravity.

MORE D-I-Y:
COMMUNICATION
CARDS!

Ready-made communication cards can be purchased, but the best are the ones you make yourself! Use your digital camera to take photos of your child eating breakfast, lunch, and dinner; drinking juice; swinging; and/or doing other activities. Your child can use these to tell you, and others, what he needs.

Most importantly, though, take pictures of your child when he's happy, angry, sad—and expressing any other emotions. These are almost more important than "activity" cards so your child can more effectively communicate his feelings.

Before printing the cards, type what the card represents: "I want juice," "Breakfast time," "I feel angry," etc.—this will help your child with reading skills!

child's home (and especially his own spaces in the home) should be warm, welcoming, and "user-friendly." So change the lighting, move the furniture, and/or do whatever is necessary to meet the needs of everyone in the family.

• If the child is over the age of two and still sleeping in a crib, replace it with a bed, along with protective bed rails if needed, so the child is treated per his CHRONOLOGICAL AGE, and not like a baby. At the same time, if no one at your house gets much sleep because the child with a disability has difficulty sleeping alone, let him sleep with you or another family member! Benj slept in the bed with Mark and me until he was five. Then he and his sister slept in the same room, each in their own trundle beds, for the next couple of years. Do whatever you need to do so everyone gets a good night's sleep!

• Replace traditional dressers (and those hard-to-open drawers) with counter tops, shelves, and/or containers for clothes, toys, and other goodies, so the child can do more for himself.

• Remove doors from the closet and replace with a cloth "door" hung on a rod (cloth shower curtains work great for this); rearrange the closet interior to allow the child to pick out his own clothes.

• Place step stools around the house to allow the child to reach things.

• Lower/raise counter tops in kitchen or bath to accommodate a child using wheelchair or for child with short stature.

• Replace kitchen and bath faucets and/or sinks so the child can be more self-sufficient.

• Rearrange kitchen items (in pantry, cupboards, drawers, and in refrigerator) and/or remodel so the child can learn to help in kitchen, get her own food, help clean up, etc.

• Rearrange furniture, replace some, and/or get rid of some to ensure child with mobility device has ease of movement throughout home (in some cases, you might need a different house altogether).

Behavioral-Emotional Supports

As I've mentioned previously, "inappropriate behaviors" are often the direct result of children not having effective communication. So the first solution to try when there are behavioral or emotional concerns is a communication device, communication cards, facilitated communication, signing, or some other method of effective communication.

Beyond finding a communication solution, however, some children still need other types of behavioral or emotional supports. The traditional solution has been to write "positive behavior plans" for use at home, school, and/or other environments. Unfortunately, however, many of these plans are built around rewards and punishments, which may work in the short-term, but are often ineffective in the long-term, because they're usually based on external motivation, instead of internal motivation. If and when the child "fails" in meeting the goals of plan, more restrictions are usually put in place, including more punishments and a more restrictive environment, and medication might be prescribed to force compliance. We can do better for our children.

In my opinion, there are only a handful of professionals in the field of behavior who truly value and respect the people with disabilities they work with. Joe Schiappacasse was in this group. He was my friend and a fellow Colorado resident. Sadly, Joe unexpectedly passed away in 2002, but his work lives on.

Joe had a brother with a disability and a child with a disability, and he had been a behavior specialist for over fifteen years. For the twelve years before his death, he was involved in a federally-funded project involving several universities across the nation that specialized in understanding behavior supports. It was a network of over 20 state projects which, along with universities, conducted research, developed training materials, and tried to capture and expand examples of best practices in positive behavior support for public dissemination and application. He was also a member of the Community Circle, a Denver-based consortium of mental health professionals that focused on under-appreciated populations, providing education, consultation, and behavior pharmacology clinics. In 2001, Joe generously shared his wisdom in an interview with me, and I'll share some of Joe's thoughts with you here.

Joe noted that people with disabilities need the same behavior supports that people without disabilities take for granted:

> I'm talking about the *unconscious supports* that are so common, most of us don't even think about them—those things that are the "positive natural consequences" of living in a community. Being part of a family, having at least one unpaid person in your life who is a friend, easy access to one's community, healthy sexuality, frequent social opportunities to belong, and a wide array of other typical activities that provide natural behavior supports. The ability to call in sick when you're not really sick is a natural behavior support! But these things are missing from the lives of many people who have been labeled. They don't have the same level of power, choice, and control of their lives that most of us take for granted.

> Think about all the self-help things we do on a daily basis to manage our own mental health and behavior: we exercise, use relaxation techniques, go shopping, take medication, go out to dinner, eat chocolate, and do so many other things for ourselves! We use a wide, wide array of self-help strategies.

> Then there are the *active* strategies we consciously use to manage our behavior, such as counseling and other mental health assistance. But even these are often denied to people with disabilities. Let's take the example of someone who is thought to have a "low IQ." Many mental health professionals don't believe the person has the insight to benefit from counseling. It's easier and safer to assume this, rather than taking the time and making the effort to figure out *how* to make it work.

> We've all heard the recommendation to "count to ten" when we're upset or angry. How many of us really do it? Yet this is one of the most common strategies offered to people with disabilities! Why? Because it's a simple activity we can easily get our arms around and it meets *our*—the support giver's—immediate needs. Many of us simply don't want to take the time or spend the effort trying to figure out what's really right for a person.

"[People with disabilities] don't have the same level of power, choice, and control of their lives that most of us take for granted."

What we do with *our* behavior is based on our *capacities;* what's done to people with disabilities is usually based on a person's *perceived deficits.* "Behavior reduction plans" are the logical outgrowth of this type of focus.

Our behavior supports are usually in alignment with what internally motivates us. People who are labeled are frequently limited to *external* motivation strategies. The methods we use on ourselves are based on pleasurable activities, while methods used on people with disabilities are often based on pain and restriction.

There are awesome discrepancies between the quality and characteristics of behavior supports available to people with disabilities as compared to people who haven't been labeled. Ultimately, the way a person is *valued* dictates what opportunities are available to him.

Joe believed misunderstanding and misdiagnosis are the greatest issues facing people who have been labeled with "behavior problems:"

> "Over 85 percent of the people we see in our traveling clinics actually have an undiagnosed or untreated medical or neurological condition that is causing or contributing to the 'problem behavior'."

Many serious, ongoing behavior issues are actually the result of undiagnosed and untreated pain. By not looking at the whole person, we fail to identify all the contributing biological, neurological, medical, and contextual conditions. For example, many people have undiagnosed or misunderstood seizure disorders. Some seizures can look like a sudden outburst or aggression which we see as "problem behavior." But because the person doesn't foam at the mouth or fall to the floor when a seizure occurs, the condition is misdiagnosed.

Our behavior pharmacology clinic is geared to understanding folks with complex behavior issues. Over 85 percent of the people we see in our traveling clinics actually have an undiagnosed or untreated medical or neurological condition that is causing or contributing to the "problem behavior." We've been programmed to see a person's "problem behavior" as a *willful act of choice,* instead of as a *symptom* of a person's whole being—current biology included.

We've seen many people who have been misdiagnosed with autism, because assessments were focused on perceived deficits rather than actual capacities. For example, a family member of a person labeled with autism will describe the person as the most loving and intuitive person in the family, as someone who enjoys physical closeness, who enjoys change, and so forth—all of which are in opposition to some of the classic characteristics of autism. But because the person has a certain type of communication pattern or behaviors we see as "self-stimulation," he has been labeled with autism. In some cases, an individual may have been the recipient of certain types of behavior strategies for years, or been in a particular environment, and these strategies or environments have imposed limitations on what he can do. Thus, the *symptoms* of autism have become entrenched and the *autism label is erroneously validated.*

We've seen many people in our clinics who have been labeled with autism when they actually have Tourette syndrome or a type of movement difference. Here's what happens: as a child, the person exhibited certain characteristics which led to his being labeled with autism. Then he's put in environments with others who share the same or similar label. Many people with Tourette syndrome have echopraxia—which means they have a tendency to imitate the behaviors of others. If this person has received treatment for autism, and has been put in "autism environments," he'll *learn* to mimic symptoms of autism. No one questions the diagnosis, since his "autism symptoms" not only continue, but expand the more he is isolated with persons with autism! Based on national averages, we should be seeing four times the number of people with Tourette syndrome compared to the number of people with autism, but the reverse is occurring.

The solution to people being undiagnosed and misdiagnosed rests in providing a "whole person" evaluation, which includes current medical, neurological, and biological—as well behavioral, contextual, cultural, and spiritual—assessments. A person's full life history is a critical component in the "whole person" evaluation.

Here's what Joe had to say about Applied Behavior Analysis:

Applied Behavior Analysis (ABA) is the attempt to understand a person's behavior and use that information to support a better life. However, it has been misinterpreted by many as a way of *managing* a person's behavior. ABA can be a good source of information when it's viewed as just *one of many ways* to learn more about a person. It can be a valuable tool to help us understand the conditions under which certain behaviors do and don't occur. But serious miscalculations occur when people expect it to provide all the answers—the whole solution.

Unfortunately, we often use ABA to *reinforce* the perceptions we already have about a person! ABA should never be seen as the whole solution, but it should also never be totally disregarded. ABA is a tool that can help us better understand by providing useful information. But it must be combined with medical, neurological, biological, contextual, spiritual, and cultural assessments. And through these processes, our goals must always include a plan to discover, *from the individual being assessed,* "Who do you want to be?" and to learn what intrinsic (internal) motivators and reinforcers he prefers.

Unfortunately, there is a center on the East Coast that still uses electric shock, noxious stimuli, and other forms of diabolical punishment to manage or control a person's behavior. What other population is subjected to these strategies? It's *against the law* to use these methods on the most heinous criminals in our prison system. Yet they're used on people with developmental disabilities, without the choice or consent of the individual! We must get better at offering the right supports—*in our communities*—to individuals and their families.

Some people with autism (especially young children) are frequently subjected to highly-mechanized, intensive 40-hour- a-week therapies. But we have to ask ourselves: how does the *person receiving this treatment* feel about it? Shouldn't we care? And, second, is the person really benefiting from the treatment? Often, no benefit is seen, but we keep doing it, thinking if we do it long enough or with enough intensity, we'll eventually see

> "[ABA] has been misinterpreted by many as a way of *managing* a person's behavior."

> "Some people with autism (especially young children) are frequently subjected to highly-mechanized, intensive 40-hour-a-week therapies. But we have to ask ourselves: how does the *person receiving this treatment* feel about it? Shouldn't we care?"

results. In the meantime, we could have been using other strategies that work—strategies that are important and relevant to the individual.

Many parents may have learned what Joe learned: that "help" for a child's "behavior problems" was often based on the perceived deficits. Joe saw solutions that are different from many in the behavior field:

> The real—and long-lasting—solutions to a person's "problems" will come from understanding his strengths, the things he's good at, his personal goals, and what he enjoys in life. So we need to use more assessments that examine a person's strengths, capacities, dreams, and gifts.

> Many people still rely on assessments and analyses focused primarily on core "problem behavior." But that's just one small part of a functional analysis. We must also analyze *what works* in people's lives. We need to ask questions about positive behavior: "When does the 'problem behavior' *not* occur? In what settings? With whom? Under what circumstances?" and so forth. Then, not only can we *add* more of those things to people's lives, we can also—and perhaps more importantly—do in-depth analysis of *why* those things work. This information will tell us more and help us better understand a person's successes, and it will give us direction for expansion and growth.

> Here's an example. If the main place you *don't* act up is at church, Kathie, we could say, "OK, Kathie could benefit from spending more time at church." But that's probably not a practical solution, day in and day out. So we'd ask, "What are the *characteristics* of church that make the difference? Where else can we find similar qualities in other environments? What's the intrinsic motivation for positive behavior and participation in the church environment?" This is probably at the core of what we need to better understand behavior issues.

> Traditionally, a person with a disability is on the receiving end of punishment, aversive behavior management, and extrinsic/external reinforcers that someone else dishes out, as methods of control. But if I use these strategies to control you, Kathie, not only do I remove the balance of equity in our relationship, but I'm also making you dependent on me, and we know this is not good. Your dependence on me (or anyone else in a similar position) will not lead to long-lasting change or success for you and, in fact, it sets you up for greater victimization. I'm not saying all extrinsic reinforcers are bad, but they should *not* be the main form of teaching and encouragement.

Joe also believed parents were their children's best teachers, but he recognized that because we're so close to the situation, we often "can't see the forest for the trees," so the opinions of others might be helpful:

> Parents and children develop invisible patterns of behavior and systems of interactions over the years, and it can be very difficult for parents to step back and analyze what's really happening...Parents can get a clearer picture when they ask family and friends for help. Ask, "What do you see going on here?" Others will often have valuable perspectives because they're not so close to the situation. In the realm of professional help, moms and dads

"...many forms of behavior—especially what's called 'problem behavior'— is a *symptom* of something not working right in a person's life."

should make sure their children receive a "whole person" evaluation which includes medical, biological, neurological, contextual, cultural, and spiritual assessments...and parents need to get references...[from] real families and individuals...before deciding if this is the right professional...

According to Joe, educators and parents both have critical roles to play in supporting children's behavioral and emotional growth:

Educators and parents both need to be really clear about what the goals are for the child. And the goals should be growth-oriented, leading to the child's greater self-control and self-management.

In many cases, one of the first behavioral actions of a teacher at the beginning of the school year is listing the classroom rules on the blackboard, basically saying: "You must do/not do this or you can't be in my classroom." But this creates a situation in which children are responding to a teacher's rules—which are temporary, during the time the child is in the class—instead of a child's own rules which will last a lifetime. We end up focusing on obedience and compliance instead of creativity and internal motivation.

When we allow children to generate their own rules, they create rules that are usually more stringent than the rules adults set for them! And kids will help each other honor their *own* rules more than they'll honor the rules of others. When children are *internally* motivated, they are much more likely to experience long-term success in inclusive, natural environments—in other words, in the real world of community. In addition, at school, home, and in other settings, we must give people real reasons for why they're expected to behave and participate, rather than just obedience for the sake of obedience. And then we must ask ourselves hard questions. *Why* should he do such-and-such? Is it *important* to him? Is it *relevant?* Is it *right* for the person? What supports does he need to be successful in this activity or environment?

For many years, I had heard (and believed) the concept that "behavior is communication," and Joe explained it better than anyone:

Yes, behavior *is* communication. In some instances, it's not necessarily a direct attempt at communication, but an attempt to address what's important to a person at the time. And we can move even further and recognize that many forms of behavior—especially what's called "problem behavior"—is a *symptom* of something not working right in a person's life. All behavior meets a need or serves a purpose. One behavior may meet multiple needs, while the very same behavior can mean two or more *different* things.

Not only is behavior communication, but it is frequently *more valid* than typical communication. It takes much more effort to lie with your behavior than to lie with your words. My older brother, who has been labeled with a variety of disabilities, taught me, "The truth is in what you do, not what you say."

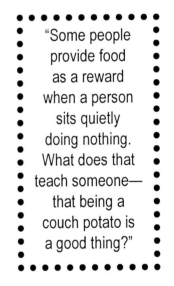

"Some people provide food as a reward when a person sits quietly doing nothing. What does that teach someone—that being a couch potato is a good thing?"

Finally, Joe went beyond "positive behavior supports" to "enviable behavior supports," which he defined this way:

It's a concept I use in an attempt to get at the core of what positive behavior supports really are. The concept of positive behavior supports has been twisted into so many different things. Some people define positive behavior supports as "not using aversives." Well, that's a nice start, but it's only a fraction of what positive support requires. While I appreciate the concept of not using aversive treatments, people with disabilities *can still be hurt* under the auspices of what some people call positive behavior supports. Not taking a long-term, whole-person perspective; building in artificial supports without a plan to fade them to natural and community supports; indiscriminately reinforcing certain system/staff behavior; or predominately using extrinsic forms of reinforcement are just some of the ways that well-intended support can create greater problems for the individual.

For example, food is often used as an extrinsic reinforcer. Some people provide food as a reward when a person sits quietly doing nothing. What does that teach someone—that being a couch potato is a good thing? Positive behavior support is a good process, but it's often misconstrued. Part of this comes from its name: we assume we're doing a good job if we provide positive reinforcers, instead of negative ones. But, again, these can do more harm than good.

It's time to up the ante and focus on *enviable* behavior supports. We'll know supports are "enviable" when a person looks at the supports and approaches being used in another person's life and says, "Hey, that looks good to me! Can you do the same thing with me? Those are the things I need in my life."

Consider the flip side: how many of *us* have ever read the behavior plan written for a person with a disability and said, "Gee, I'd like this to happen in *my* life."?

Providing enviable behavior supports is really a common sense approach that's right for all human beings. We've got to move beyond offering supports from an "us vs. them" orientation.

It's time to recognize first and foremost that people with disability labels have *abilities!* The solution to behavioral complexities will come not from focusing solely on a person's perceived deficits, but from identifying and understanding a person's abilities, gifts, and desires. Looking at the whole person is the key. And the ultimate test of whether we're providing healthy behavioral supports is really quite simple: do the supports sustain and increase an individual's belonging, autonomy, and competence?

> "...the ultimate test of whether we're providing healthy behavioral supports is really quite simple: do the supports sustain and increase an individual's belonging, autonomy, and competence?"

What I've learned from Joe and a few select others goes way beyond what most so-called experts preach about "positive behavior supports." And this wisdom has helped me, with my own behavior and the interactions I have with my family members and many others. Joe's words don't apply only to children and adults with disabilities! I hope his expertise is meaningful to you in a variety of ways.

Each child is different and each family is different. And a child who needs behavior supports may be in many different environments besides his home. Thus, he may need different types of behavior supports depending on where he is, who else is there, and so forth. So it's important to be both creative and flexible when thinking about and implementing enviable behavior supports.

The principal at my children's inclusive elementary school was not a noted behavior expert, but he had great love for children and a great understanding of their needs. He learned that when a child feels secure and is engaged in something he's interested in, most "inappropriate behaviors" disappear. There's no way to recommend the specific supports your child might need, but if you combine your own wisdom with the opinions of others who know your child well, and blend in Joe's recommendations and the principal's observations, I have no doubt you'll find solutions. Here, however, are some ideas to whet your creative whistle for use at home (strategies for school are in Chapter 9):

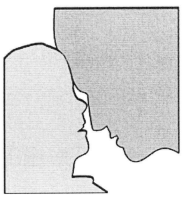

- If a child needs a "lovey" to feel secure, let him have it, regardless of his age. We often strip children of their "security blanket" (in whatever form it really is) when they're two or three, even though they may still need it! Adults use "loveys" as behavior supports all the time, although we call them tobacco, liquor, chocolates, sports, shopping, or something else.

- If a child needs a safe place to retreat to when he's upset, we can give him that place *and* the power to go there on his own: under his bed, in a snug corner of his closet, or wherever. We do this for ourselves (and so do our other children) when we go for a ride alone in the car, spend some time in our bedrooms alone, and so forth—and we've learned to do this before we go ballistic and before someone has to "send us to our rooms." We can give our children the power to be in control of their needs and behavior.

- We can relax our list of "inappropriate behaviors" and recognize that much of what *we* do could be considered "inappropriate," too—maybe we just don't get caught as often, or perhaps others *who do the same behaviors* don't see *our* behavior as inappropriate. If what the child is doing isn't hurtful to himself or others, what's the big deal? If it's just annoying to you or others, get over it! There's a lot of annoying behavior that goes on within families and out in public, too. It's best just to ignore it. (Ladies: how many of our husbands' annoying behaviors have we learned to ignore and/or tolerate. Ditto, men and your wives.) And have we ever considered that trying to stop a child from flapping or doing something similar just makes the child want to do it more? If *you're* afraid someone has the power to take something from you, you'll probably hold on to it even tighter!

- In settings outside the home—like a typical, recreational activity—a child might get just the right kind of support from a peer who can help him stay on track, stay engaged, not get distracted, etc. Alternatively, in an art class, drama group, etc. a child might be more successful with older children or even adults who can be more "forgiving," "tolerant" of differences, and/or provide better support.

Just as our children should not be denied AT devices, modifications, or accommodations, they should not be denied enviable behavior supports.

—WISDOM—

Giving your child the power and authority to make decisions about therapy, Services, and TOOLS will contribute to his self-determination (being in charge of his life).

When I present at Partners in Policymaking programs, I'm often on the agenda with an adult with a cognitive disability, who is presenting about the Self-Advocacy Movement. During one of these trainings, the presenter was Joe Meadours, a leader in the Self-Advocacy Movement. Joe also talked about the importance of children learning self-determination. A parent asked, "At what age should that start?" Joe didn't need to think about his answer. He immediately and vehemently replied, "At birth!"

The Big Questions

Whether you're ecstatically happy with the Traditional Therapy (PT, OT, speech, ABA, hippo-therapy, etc.) your child is receiving, if you're mired in misery, or fall somewhere in between, it's important to look very closely at your family's present and future. Put a magnifying glass on today's life, use a telescope to gain some foresight, and circle your answers to the following questions:

- Is your *child's life* better *today* than it was before he began receiving Traditional Therapy?   YES   NO   NOT SURE/MAYBE

- Is your *family's life* better *today* than it was before your child began receiving Traditional Therapy?   YES   NO   NOT SURE/MAYBE

- Will your *child's life* be better *in the future* because of the Traditional Therapy he's receiving today?   YES   NO   NOT SURE/MAYBE

- Will your *family's life* be better *in the future* because of the Traditional Therapy your child is receiving today? YES   NO   NOT SURE/MAYBE

Based on today's CONVENTIONAL WISDOM—that Services improve the QUALITY OF LIFE of a person with a disability—the "automatic" response to all these questions would be "yes." But some of us instinctively know a different answer to these questions, and others might arrive at a different answer if we're thoughtful and introspective.

You might, for example, instantly respond that your *child's life* is better because he can do such-and-such as a result of physical therapy, but at the same time, the therapy *has not made your family's life better.* If so, your family's emotional health is being compromised by your child's therapy sessions.

Moreover, you might want to consider whether the achievement of a functional skill (walking, talking, etc.) has actually had a profoundly positive impact on your child's life. I say this with the experience of years: if my 18-year-old son could jump out of his wheelchair and walk today, it would have a pretty insignificant effect on his life. With his power wheelchair and other AT devices and accommodations, he's been able to do pretty much whatever he's wanted to do.

Back to the four questions above. If your response to any of the questions is "no" or "not sure," it's time to ask yourself some serious questions about continuing on the path you're on, and to consider the alternatives detailed in this chapter or those you come up with on your own.

If your reply to all four questions was "yes," I hope you'll give these issues more thought. While doing hundreds of presentations, I've often asked the audience of parents, "In thinking about any difficulties you're facing right now, would you say the majority of these difficulties stem from having a child with a disability or from problems dealing with Services?" And every time, the unanimous response was, "Services."

In my own life (and other parents have reported the same), it was very difficult to even *begin* to acknowledge that the Traditional Therapies and other Services I embraced might not be all they were cracked up to be. I resisted even looking at the issue for a long time. The brainwashing we receive—some of which we've done to ourselves—was very thorough! And once a sliver of doubt crept in, I *still* resisted seeing the reality because it made me feel foolish and angry, and I didn't want to deal with those, so it was easier to bury them.

But when my six-year-old son said, "Going to therapy doesn't make me feel like a *regular person*," I no longer needed to wrangle with *my own* internal demons—I just needed to listen to *him.* It was that simple. It can be that simple for you, too: just listen to your child.

Making a change in our children's therapy services can be scary. We've been programmed to believe our children are in dire need of therapies or other interventions for a certain number of hours each week. But when my son stopped going to therapy at age six, the sky didn't fall and his life wasn't ruined. On the contrary, his life and our entire family's life, improved greatly—immediately! For some of us, therapy has become a familiar routine that we do without thinking—a habit—and changing habits can be very difficult. We may also be afraid of what professionals will say or do. But shouldn't we be more concerned about the feelings and lives of *our children and families*, instead of what others think?

After reading this chapter, I hope you'll feel confident about making some changes. Some parents are able to simply begin saying "no" to all Traditional Therapy, knowing they're competent to meet their child's needs and interests in more natural ways. Some readily embrace the ideas for providing their children with whatever Tools they need for success, like a power wheelchair or communication device—after which the child no longer needs to go to therapy for help with walking or talking. Other parents begin using a therapist as a consultant. And still others take a more gradual approach: they begin by cutting back on the number of therapy sessions, then a month or two later, cut back some more, and so forth. Another option is to "take a vacation" from therapies/interventions: take two weeks off and see how it goes. If everything seems good and right, take another two weeks off, and so on.

No change is permanent. If you make changes and find that—for whatever reason—your child is not happier, you can always go back to the way things were before. And I do hope your *child's* wishes—not yours—are the primary force driving your actions.

Regardless of the age of your child and regardless of the past, know that you can make significant, positive, long-lasting changes in the life of your child. I've met parents of five-year-olds and 25-year-olds (and all ages in between) who moaned, "I wish I knew all this when my child was younger. It's too late, now." And I lovingly hold them by the shoulders, put my face up to theirs, and say, "It's not too late—*it's never too late!*"

> THE WORLD HATES CHANGE; YET, IT IS THE ONLY THING THAT BRINGS PROGRESS.
> *Charles F. Kettering*

> THE REASONABLE MAN ADAPTS HIMSELF TO THE WORD, BUT THE UNREASONABLE MAN TRIES TO ADAPT THE WORLD TO HIMSELF—THEREFORE, ALL PROGRESS DEPENDS UPON THE UNREASONABLE MAN.
> *Samuel Butler*

We don't need to panic, but I do hope a sense of urgency and determination gets us off our behinds. Our children's lives are passing before our eyes. Can we afford to let them wait one more day to lead a REAL LIFE and have what they need for success? It was only yesterday that my son was three and now he's a young adult. Where did the time go?

What's Next?

This chapter has, in many ways, laid the foundation for the next three chapters, which focus on: (1) ensuring your child lives a REAL LIFE at home and in the community, (2) alternatives to the traditional practices for young children (birth to five), and (3) Inclusive Education for children aged five and above. Recommendations in each of these chapters are based on the philosophies in this chapter, such as child-directed assistance, therapists as consultants, alternate ways of providing children with the help they need, and the importance of providing TOOLS for success.

Chapter 7 is focused on the importance of children with disabilities being fully-participating, responsible members of their homes and communities. And, as you'll see, many community activities can be used to meet your child's needs in place of traditional therapies. When you embrace these strategies, your child will be able to accomplish what's important to him, make new friends, and be included in the community!

If your child is age five or older, you might be tempted to skip Chapter 8, about the lives of very young children. I hope you won't, for two reasons. First, this chapter can provide insight into what has occurred in your older child's life, as a result of the Services she received as a young child. Second, I hope you'll share the ideas in Chapter 8 with friends who have young children.

Conversely, if your child is *under* the age of five, you might think you should skip Chapter 9, on Inclusive Education, since your child is not yet in public school. But your son or daughter *will be* before you know it, so now's the time to be thinking ahead.

Adopting some of the strategies in this chapter regarding therapeutic interventions and ensuring your child has the Tools he needs for success will pave the way for your child to live a REAL LIFE in any environment: home, school, and community. I feel relatively sure that *your child* wants to lead a REAL LIFE, and I hope you want that for your child and your family, too!

Real Lives at Home and In the Community

7

Your child is a member of your family, your neighborhood, your community, your city or town, your state, and our nation. I hope you feel it's important for her to take her place as a *fully-participating member,* included in all areas of life!

Your attitude—not your child's disability condition—is the most important factor in whether or not your child lives a REAL LIFE. This can be verified by the lives of many of today's *adults* with developmental disabilities. While meeting these good people in my travels as a presenter, their stories tell the tale. With anger, sadness, despair, and/or confusion, many relate that their parents did not *expect* them to be active members of their families, with responsibilities within the home, like their brothers and sisters. They were not *expected* to be active members of their communities, nor were they *expected* to become successfully employed as adults. These self-fulfilling prophecies sadly came true. Am I blaming everything on parents? Of course not! Parents of that generation may have faced more prejudice and discrimination than we do today, and they didn't have some of the laws we have today. There were, however, some parents who rose above the prevailing societal attitudes and did whatever was needed to ensure their children lived REAL LIVES—these pioneering souls rejected CONVENTIONAL WISDOM.

Over and over again, adults with developmental disabilities who attend my presentations approach me afterward and say things like, "I wish my parents had believed in me, the way you believe in your son. I wish they had expected me to do more, and had helped me learn what I needed to learn..." Many of these adults are doing their best to break free of the chains that have caused them to lead separate and unnatural lives—and many are making it! Others are still under the influence of today's CONVENTIONAL WISDOM, and Service Providers have taken the place of their parents.

I know you're aware that your child's life is in your hands—and that's a huge responsibility. If today's CONVENTIONAL WISDOM has caused you to believe this responsibility means you should try to make your child "normal," through therapies, interventions, etc., I hope you're ready to toss that belief in the garbage can where it belongs. I hope you'll feel that your true responsibility is to believe in your child, dream with her, and provide opportunities for her to live the life of her dreams—which is the same for parents everywhere! I also hope that the previous chapter helped you see that changes in the therapies and interventions your child receives can have a profoundly positive influence in helping her lead a REAL LIFE today!

> **THE REVOLUTION BEGINS AT HOME.**
> *Cherrie Moraga and Gloria Anzaldua*

The primary message of this chapter could be summarized as: Treat your child like she doesn't have a disability! This *doesn't mean* you're not going to meet your child's needs; it *does mean* you no longer have to allow your child's disability label and/or Services to run your child's and your family's lives. It's time for your child to be a child, first and foremost.

It all starts in the home, so that's where we'll start. Your home is a microcosm of the bigger world: if your child is successful there, he'll have a strong foundation for success in other environments.

Your child's *history* is not his *destiny!*

Community activities are covered next. In the previous chapter, alternatives to Traditional Therapy—using more natural methods at home and the community—were described. I'll expand on that, and describe the importance of typical community activities for our children with disabilities. Many of these suggestions will apply primarily to children aged five and above, since most community activities are for children in that age bracket. However, if your child is under five, this information—especially the proactive strategies for ensuring your child is included—will still be helpful, now and in the future. Chapter 8 builds on what you'll learn here, as I detail alternatives to traditional services for young children (birth to five).

When children enjoy success and inclusion at home and in the community, they're more competent—and are *perceived* as such. This, in turn, can lead to greater inclusion in educational settings—including typical preschools, as described in Chapter 8, and in K-12 classrooms, as covered in Chapter 9.

Whether your child is a baby, a young adult, or somewhere in between, these strategies can work. And as I mentioned in the previous chapter, it's never too late to make changes that can have a positive influence. You can't undo the past, but you can change the future. And regardless of the age of your child, *his history is not his destiny!*

Our Families, Our Homes

In many families, the child with the disability takes center stage. This might be the result of the Services for the child running the whole family's life. It might also be a consequence of family members (parents, brothers, sisters, and others) "babying" the child, or the parents may spend much more time and energy on the child with the diagnosis, and little time with the other children. Regardless of how or why this happens, it's not beneficial for anyone in the family. The child with the disability may learn to be helpless; the other children may learn to resent the brother or sister with a disability and feel anger toward the parents, as well; and parents feel worn out, torn, frustrated; and much more.

When one member of a family has a disability, it *can* affect every other member of the family. But the presence of a disability doesn't have to be a negative influence. When we change the way we do things, it can be a very positive one!

As you read the suggestions about making changes at home, you might want to make immediate changes. You may also be concerned that there could be some resistance to change—change can be hard, and not everyone eagerly welcomes change. So I suggest that before doing anything, finish reading this chapter, do some careful thinking about what changes you'd like to put in place, then sit down with your family to share what you're learning. Express your enthusiasm and excitement, but also ask for and listen to the ideas of everyone in your family. Changes within a family are always easier if everyone buys in to the new ways of doing things. So respect and value the opinions of others, while you lead your family with a brave heart!

And remember: treat your child like he doesn't have a disability. As you read this chapter, ask yourself, "What would my child be doing—what would we expect him to do within the family and the community—if he didn't have a disability?" Then think about what needs to change (your attitude, how your family does things, providing Tools for your child, etc.), so your child *can do* what he'd be doing if he didn't have a disability.

All Our Children are Wonderful

Make sure *all* the children in your family know they are equally wonderful: no more of that silly "special needs child" business! *Gag!* The child with the disability does not want to be "special," and the other children want to feel as loved and as important as the child with a disability. The information presented in Chapter 5 can help you create positive change in your family's language and attitudes, and the remainder of the suggestions in this chapter will also help remove the "special" stigma within your family.

"Age-Appropriate" Starts at Home

As I mentioned earlier, many children with disabilities are "babied" by their parents and even their brothers/sisters. Several of the suggestions throughout this chapter will—as a side-effect—help to eliminate this particular situation. But there are also some very specific actions we can take to make sure the child with a disability is treated as his Chronological Age.

First, eliminate "baby-talk" unless the child is really a baby! Second, and as described in Chapter 6, get your child whatever assistive technology devices he needs to "be his age." If he's two and he's not talking, he needs some form of effective communication (a device, cards, etc.). If he's two and not walking, he needs independent mobility. Children above the age of two who do not have effective communication or independent mobility are likely to be thought of—and treated like—babies. This is a horrible thing to do to a child!

Third, eliminate other baby-like accoutrements for children over the age of two. If he wears a bib because he drools, substitute a neck bandana. If he wears a bib because he's a messy eater, substitute a chef's apron. If your child is still in diapers past the age of three or four, and you think he has the ability to be "potty-trained," get to work on that. It might take a few years, but that's OK. If your child will always need to wear diapers, ensure the method used to change her diapers is not "baby-like." Give her the responsibility of telling you she needs to be changed and/or get her to help in whatever way she can, and make sure others who might help with this receive your new instructions.

Fourth, make sure your child "looks" her age. I once met "Kim" and "Kay," 15-year-old identical twins. Kim had a disability and used a wheelchair, Kay did not. Kay dressed herself, of course, and looked like a 15-year-old: pierced ears, highlighted hair, jeans and a Gap T-shirt. Kim was dressed by her mother, and looked like a 10-year-old: her pigtails were fancied up with bows and she wore "little girl" clothes. Kay—and others—*treated* Kim like a 10-year-old.

Fifth, if you have one or more children who are younger than your child with a disability, make sure all your children know the "hierarchy." In some families, for example, a seven-year-old child might "pass up" a 10-year-old child with a disability in physical or cognitive skills, and the younger child might begin thinking, *and acting like,* she's "older." The actions of parents or other family members might contribute to this situation. This is very harmful to both children, and can create a self-fulfilling prophecy for the child with a disability: she will always be the "baby" of the family, regardless of her actual birth order. Do what it takes to change this situation! Some of the suggestions in this chapter can help, but you might need to take other actions, as well.

If your children are younger than the scenario above, you can prevent this from occurring in the first place. For example, if you have a four-year-old child with a disability and a two-year-old, say and do things to let both children know that the four-year-old is the "big brother." When you take a shower, tell the four-year-old big brother to "watch over" his little sister. In practice, the four-year-old might not be able to physically "take care" of his little sister while you're in the shower, but you can set things up so he could at least give a holler if something's going on. And, yes, the younger child might, at some point, "pass" the older child in walking or some other functional skill. But for the sake of both children (and the family), it's critically important that everyone treats the child with a disability as his Chronological Age.

If your children are older than the scenario above, you might need to do some damage control, in order to help the child with a disability reassert his place within the family structure. You can talk to everyone in the family about it, and then change your language and your actions (including the steps below).

Everyone Helps Everyone

Everyone in the family needs help and everyone in the family should provide help to one another. You—the mother or father—are not your child's personal maid or butler! Everyone needs to pitch in and help whoever needs help. Parents help children, children help each other, and children help parents.

In Chapter 1, I described how, at the age of four, Benjamin must have thought the umbilical cord was still attached: he called out to me for help even though he was sitting on the sofa next to his dad! We then made the rule that Benjamin had to ask for help from whoever was closest to him—his sister, dad, a playmate at home, a classmate at school, and so forth. Learning this skill—*how to ask for help*—has made an incredible difference in his life. It's enabled him to move from the social isolation that often accompanies dependence on one or two "caretakers," to interdependence and inclusion in any environment.

No one is truly *independent;* we're all *interdependent.* We all need help at different times. So throw out the notion that you want your child to be independent; work to ensure he's interdependent and think in terms of his *self-reliance.* He doesn't have to be able to *do* everything for himself; he does need to know *how* to ask for the help he needs.

In Benjamin's case, learning *how* to ask for help has helped him feel confident about going off on his own during family shopping days at Big Box stores: he asks for help from store clerks and other shoppers if he can't get something off a shelf or needs other assistance. One day, when he couldn't find me in the store, he wheeled up to a check-out counter and had *me* paged!

When Benjamin was a young teenager, he took several drama classes at a local museum/art center. During his first year, my husband, Mark, stayed close by. He knew it wasn't appropriate for him to sit next to Benj during the classes—*how uncool*—none of the other kids' parents did that! So he lurked outside the room, ready to step in if Benjamin needed something. When Benjamin took classes the next year, he announced, "Dad, this time, I want you to take me to class and then leave—really leave—and then come back and pick me up." Mark nervously agreed, and after dropping Benjamin off, he called me to report this development. He and I both hoped all would be well. I might be an author and a public speaker, but I can be a nervous mom like anyone else!

When Mark and Benj arrived home, I asked how everything went. "Fine," was the one word answer from Benj. I pressed for details, wanting a blow-by-blow report! Benj shared that the drama instructor asked all the students to fill out a questionnaire. I held my breath, wondering what happened next since Benjamin doesn't write with a pencil. If his dad had been with him, Mark could have filled out Benj's form. With bated breath, I asked Benjamin, "How did you handle that?" "Well," he answered, "I just looked around the room and saw a cute girl and asked her to help me." It wasn't a big deal to Benj; and *his* confidence breathed relief into me!

Your child can also learn to ask for help from whoever is closest. If she doesn't currently have effective speaking abilities, you'll need to make sure she has a method (a communication device/cards or whatever—as described in the previous chapter) that will enable her to ask for help, now and in the future.

In addition to having a "voice" to ask for help, your child may also need practice in knowing *how* to ask for what he needs. Our son taught my husband and me a valuable lesson in this regard.

For years, I dressed and undressed Benjamin every morning and night. Mark left for work early in the morning before the kids were up, so I handled this responsibility. When Benj was about eight, he announced, "I want Daddy to get me dressed on Saturday and Sunday." Yippee—I was delighted with Benj's decision! When that first Saturday rolled around, I was enjoying my "free time" in the kitchen, and I heard what sounded like World War III coming from Benjamin's room. He was screaming and crying and Mark was yelling back!

I ran into the room to see what in the world was going on. Mark said, "He's upset because he said I wasn't doing it right, but I don't see what difference it

---

SELF-RELIANCE

Your child doesn't have to be able to *do* everything for herself; she does need to know how to *ask* for the help she needs. Teaching your child how to ask for this help—from whoever is closest, at home, school, in a store, or in any other setting—is one of the most important things you can do to help your child be successful, now and for the rest of her life!

makes!" I told my husband it *did* matter—that he needed to help Benjamin get dressed *in the way that felt right to Benj.* Then I turned to Benjamin and said, "Instead of screaming at your dad, why didn't you just tell him how to help you get dressed?" At that, Benjamin started wailing all over again and said, through tears, "Because I didn't know *how!*"

Wow! What a lesson this was. I realized Benjamin was right. He and I had a "dressing routine"—many different small steps, done in the same way every time, for many years—and *we never talked about it.* Sort of like when you brush your teeth: you don't think about which hand to hold the toothbrush in, how you pick up the tube of toothpaste, which hand does the squeezing, etc. You do all this without thinking (or talking) about it!

Right then, I taught Benjamin how to tell his dad (or any one else) how to help him get out of his pajamas and into his clothes for the day. And I was amazed! Something that seemed so simple *to do* had many different small steps to describe—and in a certain order: the pajama top came off first, and the right arm was done before the left arm, and then the sweatshirt was pulled on while he was perched on the edge of the bed, but then I transferred him to his wheelchair to do the pants, and...Whew! It was a lot of detail, but Benj needed to know how to ask for this help if someone other than me was going to help him *in the way he needed it done.*

Benjamin—and maybe your child, too—will need help with certain things all his life. Mark and I aren't going to be around forever (and neither will you), so our children need to know *how* to tell others *how* to help them. Think about your child, and the ways you (or others) currently help him. Then begin teaching him *how* to ask for the help he needs. This skill will have a profoundly positive affect on your child, now and for the rest of his life.

Now let's put the rule of "asking for help from whoever is closest" into practice. When your child asks for help from a family member who is closest, that person needs to provide the help—in the *way* the child needs the help—because that's what families do: love, support, and help one another, whether or not it's always convenient! So if your child with a disability asks his brother for help, brother needs to help. When possible, the help should be provided immediately. I've come to realize that children and adults with disabilities are the most patient people in the world: we make them wait and wait and wait, for lots of different things. At the same time, your child with a disability needs to know that help might not *always* come immediately. For example, "Suzanne's" sister is on her way to the washing machine with a load of clothes, and Suzanne asks for help as Sister passes close by. Sister can tell Suzanne she'll be right back, as soon as she dumps the clothes by the washing machine.

This might be a learning experience for everyone in the family—and there might be some tension as your family learns new ways of doing things—but it will pay off in the long run, for everyone. The world is a better place when cooperation and kindness are the norm. If these characteristics become part of *all* your children's lives now, they'll enjoy better relationships for the rest of their lives, in school, at work, and when they're married and have children!

> WHEN PARENTS DO TOO MUCH FOR THEIR CHILDREN, THE CHILDREN WILL NOT DO MUCH FOR THEMSELVES.
>
> *Elbert Hubbard*

As your child learns to ask for help from family members, extend this rule to other environments: at school and in community activities. Children help each other all the time at school: in their classrooms, the lunch room, on the playground, and in other locations at school. Why shouldn't the same apply to children with disabilities? (This will reduce the need for an adult aide being assigned to your child in school—more about this in Chapter 9.)

When your child becomes involved in community activities (church, recreation, etc.), his ability to ask for help can help ensure his inclusion. In some instances, children with disabilities have been turned away from typical activities because Someone-in-Charge thinks the child would need a one-on-one assistant and there are no funds to provide one. Alternatively, some parents have been reluctant for their children to participate in such activities if such help isn't available. But when you know your child can ask for help from anyone who's close, *you'll* feel more confident about his participation in typical activities. And when you and your child share this information with Sunday School teachers, park and rec coaches, or anyone else, those folks will see that your child is very competent and they'll be more likely to welcome him!

Your child, however, cannot always be on the *receiving end* of help. Being "needy" *without also being "needed"* feels awful! Your child needs to provide help to others: at home, in school, and in other environments. We might need to be very creative in figuring this out, but we can do this—and the best experts are our children. Making this happen at home is covered next, and you can apply the strategies for home to other environments.

Equal Opportunities: Benefits and Responsibilities

All the children in your family need to be treated equally, in terms of benefits and responsibilities. If the other children in the family receive an allowance, get to take turns deciding which DVD to rent, or enjoy any other benefits, so should the child with a disability. By the same token, if the other children in the family have chores to do and are responsible for picking up after themselves, maintaining their bedrooms, and so forth, the child with a disability should be expected to do the same.

When we don't give our children with disabilities the same benefits and responsibilities, we're sending them an unspoken PRESUMED INCOMPETENT message. In addition, children may learn to be helpless; many will stay helpless, which will land them in the Adult Service System and segregation. In order to enjoy these benefits or assume these responsibilities, your child might need certain TOOLS (assistive technology, accommodations, modifications, or supports) as described in the previous chapter. If so, do what it takes to put these in place as soon as possible. Similarly, you might need to make physical changes to your home, your child's room, your family schedule or way of doing things, in order for your child to become a fully-participating, valued member of your family. Whatever changes you make, at whatever cost in time, effort, and money will be returned to you many times over in the form of your child's growth and development. You're investing in his future, and the return on your investment would make Wall Street brokers green with envy!

TOO MUCH HELP

Here's a rule you can make for yourself: do not help your child unless he asks for it! In our efforts to be kind, loving parents, many of us routinely anticipate what our children want and need and we do "for" them without waiting for them to ask for help. This might *seem* kind and loving, but it's really teaching a child learned helplessness—he will learn to do little for himself. In addition, what will your child do when you're not around and others can't or won't anticipate his needs?

Here's a "trick" I used when my son was younger: when Benj asked for my help with something I knew he could do or I hoped he could for himself, I replied, "I'm busy right now—I'll be there in minute." He didn't want to wait, so he would do it himself!

In thinking about benefits, you might feel your child won't understand and/or appreciate the benefits which your other children enjoy. If so, there's no better time to start teaching her! How will she learn to make big choices when she's an adult, if she doesn't have the opportunity to make little choices as a child—like choosing which DVD to rent or deciding how to spend her allowance. In the area of money, some children might have difficulty—physically or cognitively—handling cash. If so, deposit her allowance into a bank account and get her a debit card.

When Benjamin was younger, his Dad or I helped him at the check-out counter when he bought something with his allowance or birthday money. He had some difficulty with the "math" of money, as well as physically handling bills and coins. So we were delighted when debit cards became available!

To help your child keep track of the funds in her account, you can help her learn how to handle a check register (and use a calculator), or you could set up a database/spreadsheet on the computer, and she can enter her deposits and money spent, the computer can do the calculations, and she'll always know how much money she has!

Giving your child the same benefits as your other children is simply the right thing do to. And when you add in all the great outcomes of these experiences, benefits pile on top of benefits!

On the responsibility side, you may also think your child with a disability is physically or cognitively unable to do chores, but she can do *something* to help. When my son was preschool age, he spent lots of time playing on the floor: lying on his tummy playing with his Thomas the Tank Engine toys, pushing a ball and then dragging himself over to it, and so forth. We kept these small toys in a rectangular plastic bin, which I placed on the floor next to Benjamin so he could reach the toys he wanted. When it was time to stop playing, there were train engines and toys all over the floor, and it was Benjamin's responsibility to put them back in the bin. He dragged himself across the room, picked up one item, dragged himself back to the bin and dropped the toy in it, and continued until they were all back in the bin. Sometimes, depending on the circumstances, someone else in the family helped by moving the bin around the floor so Benj didn't have to drag himself so far to get each toy. But picking up after himself was his responsibility.

We can modify the environment (like the simple step of putting Benj's toys in a plastic bin) so that a child with a disability can do more for himself. Do not put any of this off until you think your child is READY; she may never achieve whatever READINESS standard you're using, and she will have missed out on many opportunities for growth and development. We don't need to change the child to enable her to be more responsible; we need to change the environment.

When Benjamin was about seven or eight, he spent most of his time on the computer, reading, or playing with action figures. To make his bedroom more accessible, we got rid of dressers with drawers he had difficulty manipulating, and installed kitchen counter tops along two walls, placed at the right height for his wheelchair. His books and action figures were placed in bins which lined the counter tops.

At this time, Emily, (who was nine or ten) had a couple of guinea pigs, and it was a constant battle to get her to keep the cage clean (so the smell didn't infect the whole house), and the rest of her room was a mess, too. So one day I had enough, and my nagging turned into a yell: "Go clean your room and don't come out until it's done!" She stomped off to do her work, and Benjamin wheeled up to me and said, "Mom, do you want me to go clean my room, too, and not come out until it's done?" *Whoa*—this brought me up short!

My husband and I had done a good job of making sure Benj picked up after himself when he was younger, but we had slacked off over time. With the bins of stuff on the counters in his room, it really didn't get very messy, but when it did, his dad or I *put things away without thinking.*

So on the day Benj asked if he should go clean up his room, too, I realized *we hadn't been treating him like his sister:* we weren't expecting him to be in charge of keeping his room clean! So with a firm voice, I said, "Yes, Benjamin, get in there right now and get your room clean, too!" With a pleased look on his face, he wheeled off. A few minutes later, he called to me, crying, "Mom, I don't know what to do!" And he didn't. As I said, his dad and I had been putting his stuff away for him! This was an important wake-up call for us. We realized we needed to expect more from Benjamin, and we needed to stop doing so much for him. We're no different from many other parents: sometimes it's easier and faster to do things *for* our children, instead of helping them *learn how to do things for themselves.* And that's certainly not good for our children in the long run—this is how learned helplessness begins.

There are lots of ways to begin ensuring *all* the children in your family take responsibility for their own lives. Parents can make a list of all the things that need to be done on a daily, weekly, and/or monthly basis—include *everything* (vacuuming, dusting, changing the oil in the car, balancing the checkbook, shopping, cooking, cleaning, washing clothes, etc.). Then call a family meeting to discuss who can do what. Our children may be unaware of just how much *does* need to be done, especially all the things that can only be done by adults (balancing the checkbook, changing the oil, etc.). During the family meeting, parents can share the list with the children, note which things they (the parents) are responsible for, then the children and the parents can divide up the remainder of the chores. If desired, the assignments can change from week to week, or whatever is agreed upon by the family.

During this process, it's important to figure out which chores the child with a disability can do. In some instances, it might be helpful to share a chore. For example, older sister "Susan" might be the dishwasher loader/unloader—a chore which might be impossible for "Julie" to do from her wheelchair. But Julie might be able to bring the dishes from the table to Susan.

Everyone, it seems to me, ought to pitch in and help with the family meal—the preparation and the clean up. "If you don't help, you don't eat,"

> THE PROVERB WARNS THAT, "YOU SHOULD NOT BITE THE HAND THAT FEEDS YOU." BUT MAYBE YOU SHOULD, IF IT PREVENTS YOU FROM FEEDING YOURSELF.
> *Thomas Szasz*

might be a good motto to adopt. All of our children need to learn self-sufficiency and responsibility, and it starts at home.

If we don't give our children the opportunity to be responsible as children, when and how do we expect them to learn this? There's no way we can expect the child to be a responsible adult at age 21 if he hasn't been learning to be responsible as a child. How can we rob a child of the *privilege of being responsible?*

Self-Determination in Action

When you allow your child to enjoy the benefits and responsibilities of being a fully-participating member of your family, you're helping her acquire self-determination. What is self-determination (SD)? Being in control of your own life: making decisions, learning autonomy, becoming more self-reliant, and more. Children *without* disabilities learn SD automatically: when a baby chooses which toy to play with, when a two-year-old asserts his independence with "No," when a four-year-old picks out what to wear, and much more.

Many children with disabilities do not learn to be self-determined (also known as self-directed), because they're "taken care" of by others—and are given no opportunities to make decisions or be responsible. As adults, many are judged to be incompetent—so they're *still* not allowed to make even the simplest decisions. Some of these adults are now enrolled in self-determination classes to learn how to make decisions. I'm glad this effort is being made, but I hope today's generation of children with disabilities learn self-determination naturally, the way other children do! Don't *we* have a responsibility to help *our children* learn responsibility?

Making the Changes

Any efforts to create changes in your home routine need to done carefully, using the most positive, upbeat manner. Share what you're learning from this book with your family, then discuss how you'd like things to be different and better for every member of the family. Again, be very positive! If we're heavy-handed or demanding, we'll get zero cooperation! I've always had good luck simply telling my family, "I need your help—I can't do it all alone." Some of us portray ourselves as Super Moms, but on the inside, we may feel overwhelmed by the responsibilities facing us. We don't need to do this anymore! It's OK to be human and ask for help from every member of the family, including the child with the disability. It's good for our children to feel needed, and it's good for them to learn that *we're* not perfect, *and they don't have to be perfect, either!*

Typical Activities in Natural Environments

Many—far too many—children with disabilities have lived abnormal lives in DISABILITY WORLD, socially isolated and physically segregated from the REAL WORLD. While every family is different, a couple of factors may contribute to this situation. First, many parents rely on traditional Services (therapies, interventions, etc.) to meet their children's needs. The schedule of Services may leave little time or energy for anything else—for the child or family. Second,

---

Self-Determination Projects

In recent years, and in a variety of states, "Self-Determination Projects" have sprung up for adults with disabilities who receive SSI and other government assistance. These are worthy efforts, and include a focus on people being in control of their benefits.

The "self-determination" I'm referring to is being in control of your life—which most children and adults *without* disabilities acquire naturally as they grow. Be careful not to confuse "true" self-determination with Self-Determination Projects.

parents may not believe their children are able to participate in typical activities; they may be afraid to try, fearing rejection; and/or they may not recognize the importance or value of these experiences.

In the previous chapter, I provided suggestions on how to replace Traditional Therapies with typical activities in the community. When this occurs, some wonderful outcomes are possible! Our children will be included in these activities, and they'll meet new friends, have new experiences, and enjoy enhanced opportunities for growth and development. They'll see themselves in a new light, and others will, too. In this section, I'll expand on this topic, by sharing some strategies to match your child's *interests* with his *needs*.

It seems easy to overlook the value of these experiences. When we think about our other children (or our own early years), common childhood activities seem just that: common and ordinary. We may not give these too much thought—we *expect* children to join a Scout troop, play on a Park and Rec sports team, take ballet or karate classes, and/or participate in a variety of other activities. And while we may not give these much thought, most of us *do* recognize their value. If nothing else, they're valuable simply because our children enjoy doing them! But a little deeper thinking on the subject reveals many more valuable benefits: children may feel better about themselves because of the accomplishments gained in such activities, they meet new people and learn how to get along with others, they learn new things, and much more. Aren't these benefits important for children with disabilities, too?

I believe these activities are *even more important* for our children who have disabilities—for a variety of reasons. First, children in segregated Special Ed classrooms are surrounded by other children with disabilities. In these settings, they may not make friends; educators may have low expectations for them, so they're undereducated; and many students may acquire a very skewed view of the world. But if they participate in typical community activities, they can make new friends, learn new things, and see how the world really is!

Second, children with disabilities who receive many Services may spend years on the receiving end of Not-OK, Not-Ready, or Presumed Incompetent messages. How can they feel good about themselves? But these messages can be erased when children participate in typical activities. Their *accomplishments*, not their perceived deficits, will be what's most important. And this might be the first time—ever—a child really feels good about who he is!

Third—and this is especially important for teenagers—meeting new people in new activities can lead to other new people and activities, which leads to the ability to network. When it's time for a part-time job as a teen, or full-time employment as a young adult, this network can be invaluable! It will be far easier for a young person with a disability to get a job if he knows a variety of people in the community and if he has a history of involvement in the community.

Fourth, when children—with or without disabilities—are involved in community activities, their *families* are more involved in the community. As a result, parents meet other parents: new people who can provide friendship, support, and more. Imagine having other parents who can babysit your kids, and you

> CHILDREN ARE NOT BORN KNOWING THE MANY OPPORTUNITIES THAT ARE THEIRS FOR THE TAKING. SOMEONE WHO DOES KNOW MUST TELL THEM.
>
> *Ruth Hill Viguers*

can reciprocate. In addition, these parents can become great allies during the IEP process (more about this in Chapter 9).

These are just some of the more easily-recognizable benefits, from my perspective; there are many more which may be unique to your child and family. Doing what it takes to enable your child to participate in typical community activities can provide many benefits, now and over the long-term.

There is, however, one more benefit that may impact our *society*, which I mentioned in earlier chapters. When your child participates in community activities, his presence will teach others more than you or I could ever do. When my son expertly played the title role in a children's theater production of the Wizard of Oz, his presence on stage—decked out in a metallic green costume, wheeling around the stage to bestow the awards on the Tin Man, the Scarecrow, and the Cowardly Lion—taught his fellow actors and everyone in the audience about the capacities of people with disabilities, inclusion, and much more. His presence smashed prejudicial stereotypes—and your child's presence can do the same. This will open more doors to inclusion: when my son's drama teacher learned he could easily include my son, he also learned he could do the same with other children and adults with disabilities.

Inclusion is a State of Mind

As I mentioned earlier in this chapter, *your attitude* is a critical factor in your child's ability to lead a REAL LIFE. When thinking about your child's inclusion in the community, know this: inclusion is—first and foremost—*a state of mind*. If you *believe* your child can and should be included—if you "take for granted" that your child will be included, just as your other children are—your *actions* will reflect this belief. You won't feel or act like a "beggar"—pleading your child's case—or getting angry and wanting to sue! Nor will you feel that others shouldn't be "burdened" by your child. Your attitude and actions will indicate that your child can and should be included in community activities because he's a member of the community!

Generic Services and Natural Supports

As I described in Chapter 1, our family joyfully jumped out of DISABILITY WORLD and rejoined the REAL WORLD when my son resigned from his therapy career. No longer was our daily scheduled built around physical and occupational therapy appointments, we were free to be spontaneous, do what was really important to us, and enjoy a more relaxed life. The conversation at the evening meal no longer focused on Benjamin's body, what happened in therapy, or whether "progress" was being made. And for Benjamin, personally—*wow!* A six-year—*lifelong*—regimen that defined his daily existence was over, and he then had the freedom to define his life in his own way, *and* to get the help he needed in more natural ways.

Many of us have been led to believe there's only "one way" for our children to get the help they may need, and that way is via professional Services. But there are many ways—more natural ways via the generic services and natural supports in our communities.

Generic services are the same services used by others. These may not be commonly known as "services," but that's what they are, such as:

- dance, exercise, and sports programs, from Park and Rec, YMCA, Scouts, martial arts schools, dance studios, health clubs, and more;

- art, drama, music, photography, and other activities and classes offered by libraries, museums, community colleges, and other entities;

- hobby and interest groups, such as computer, book, cooking, scrapbooking clubs, etc.;

- volunteer opportunities through hospitals, senior centers, food banks, and other non-profits;

- fellowship opportunities through churches and synagogues, service clubs, and community organizations.

Natural supports are the everyday people in our communities: friends, neighbors, church members, PTA members, and others we may have associations with in typical activities. In some cases, there can be overlap between generic services and natural supports. For example, you might enroll your child in a church's Vacation Bible School (generic service) and you and your child will make new friends (natural supports).

If you treat your child like he doesn't have a disability, your eyes will be opened to new ways of meeting your child's needs through the generic services and natural supports in your community. And the outcome? Your child will be included and will live a REAL LIFE.

While presenting in South Dakota several years ago, the wisdom of an adult with a developmental disability helped educate everyone in the audience. I was speaking about the issues I'm sharing with you here, and Travis, a vibrant, handsome man who happens to have spina bifida and uses a wheelchair, raised his hand. "You know, Kathie, when people *without* disabilities want to get their bodies in shape, they join a health club, buy exercise equipment to use at home, or find an exercise partner. But when people *with* disabilities want to get in shape, they're supposed to go to therapy! Why shouldn't people with disabilities do the same things as those without disabilities?"

We can and should! In the following sections, I'll provide suggestions on how to match your child's interests to a generic service or natural support that can meet your child's needs—from disability-related needs to the typical needs of all children, such as friendships, having fun in the community, and more. It's very important to recognize that our children probably have more *typical* needs than *disability-related* needs. Because of the influence of today's CONVENTIONAL WISDOM, physicians, therapists, educators, and/or other professionals recommend treatments and interventions for our children's bodies and brains, yet few (including many parents) seem to consider what's important for their hearts and minds. Few professionals see the whole child and, in many ways, that's understandable: they're specialists, focused on a narrow aspect of our children. It's up to us, as caring moms and dads, to see our sons and daughters as whole children who have a wide range of needs. And regardless of disability, *their greatest need is to experience a wonderful childhood!*

> "You know, Kathie, when people without disabilities want to get their bodies in shape, they join a health club, buy exercise equipment to use at home, or find an exercise partner. But when people with disabilities want to get in shape, they're supposed to go to therapy! Why shouldn't people with disabilities do the same things as those without disabilities?"

The Basic Formula

In the REAL WORLD, children and adults *without* disabilities create connections to others based on their strengths, interests, and dreams. In DISABILITY WORLD, connections to others are based on a person's perceived deficits or problems. So if our children are going to lead REAL LIVES, included in their communities, our focus needs to be on their strengths, interests, and dreams.

Like Travis said, when people *without* disabilities feel the need to improve their bodies, they exercise in natural environments, but people with disabilities are supposed to go to therapy. So if our children are going to lead REAL LIVES, we need to find the *natural environments* where our children's needs can be met.

In order to do this, however, we need to think and talk using REAL WORLD—not DISABILITY WORLD—language, as I described in Chapter 6. Let's compare two ways of thinking. In the REAL WORLD, a concerned parent might say, "My son needs to learn how to get along with other kids better—maybe a Scout troop would be a good solution." In DISABILITY WORLD, a concerned parent might say, "My child needs to improve his social skills, so we're enrolling him in a Social Skills class for kids with autism, which is taught by a psychiatrist." The REAL WORLD mother thinks and speaks in plain language; the DISABILITY WORLD mother speaks and thinks in jargon.

Here's another example. A parent in the REAL WORLD might say, "There aren't very many kids in the neighborhood for Thomas to play with, so we're going to check out Park and Rec sports—that way he'll also get some exercise." A parent in DISABILITY WORLD might say, "Ellie doesn't have any friends—maybe she could meet some kids like her in a Special Sports program." Ellie doesn't have any friends because she's in a segregated Special Ed classroom, so the *last thing* she needs is to be in a segregated sports program!

The best place for a child to learn how to be successful—successful meaning being able to get along in the world with others—is in typical activities in natural environments. A Social Skills class or Special Sports represent the NOT-OK, NOT READY, and PRESUMED INCOMPETENT mentalities.

Identify Your Child's Strengths

What are your child's interests? What does he choose to do in his free time? What is he good at? What would he like to do? What are his hopes and dreams? You've done some of this work, already, in earlier chapters.

The answers to these questions represent your child's strengths! One of my son's strengths is his great auditory memory: he can hear movie dialogue, the words to a song, a conversation between me and my husband, and more, and memorize these instantly. He has a memory like an elephant! We build on this strength—we use it—to help him be successful in many ways. It led to his taking drama classes (actors have to be able to memorize their lines). He loves to talk (and is good at it), and words are very important to him—more strengths. These contributed to his success with drama classes. Benjamin loves movies—and the dialogue (using his great auditory skills) is always more relevant to him than the moving pictures on the screen. All of these experiences and strengths have

> THE NAME WE GIVE TO SOMETHING SHAPES OUR ATTITUDE TOWARD IT.
>
> *Katherine Paterson*

combined to influence his career choice: as I mentioned before, he wants to be a movie critic (the next Roger Ebert) when he grows up.

When you identify your child's interests, abilities, hopes, and dreams, you'll begin to create a picture of the REAL CHILD. And from this image will spring forth all kinds of wonderful possibilities! As you think about your child, don't focus on functional abilities, per se. For example, if I listed my own strengths, I would *not* include: can walk, can talk, can feed self, etc. Instead, I would include things like: likes to talk (words are important to me); can sew by hand and with a sewing machine; like to travel—by car, train, plane, and would like to travel overseas; like to listen and sing along to classic rock, Tina Turner, and Cher; enjoy camping; and so forth. These (1) tell you something about me; (2) can be used to help me be more successful; (3) help me make connections with others who share my interests/strengths; and more. And I hope you noticed that these are not extraordinary characteristics, they're very ordinary!

I'm going to ask you to make a list of your child's strengths, but first, I want you to keep reading a couple of more sections so you see the whole process, along with some examples I'll share. When you make your list, be specific, as I was in the paragraph above. If your child loves music, what kind of music—country, rock, or ??? Does he listen on the radio or on CDs? And does he like to listen, sing the songs himself, or both? Be very specific!

Identify Your Child's Real Needs

What are your child's *real* needs? Some of these may disability-related—like exercise (*don't say therapy*). If so, what kind—to strengthen arms or what? The ability to talk better—if so, how? Other needs are typical needs, like having friends and/or opportunities to do more of what he loves, like painting, learning to use a computer, play basketball, or ??? Does your child need an AT device that's financially out of reach—what kind—how much does it cost? Does he need to learn math or other subjects? (Inclusive education is covered in Chapter 9, but there's no reason we shouldn't be helping our children learn academics, at home or in other environments!)

When you list your child's needs a little later, phrase them in plain language, not disability, medical, or therapeutic jargon. And, again, be very specific!

Map Your Community

What's in your community? There's much more than you know, and it's exciting to mine the gold that's in your own backyard, so to speak! You're probably very familiar with what's on the routes you travel daily. You probably know the businesses and buildings between your home and your office, your child's school, and your church. And you may be familiar with other places in your community that have store fronts and/or signs: library, swimming pool, mall, museum, and many more. But you may not have thought about those places in terms of how helpful they could be to your child and/or your family.

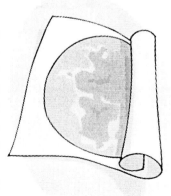

Also, you may not be aware of other potentially valuable gems in your community that *do not* have store fronts, like hobby or interest clubs that meet in churches, private homes, or other locations. How do you find these? Begin reading your local newspaper every day and start a scrapbook of the "community calendar" column; call your Chamber of Commerce; peruse the Yellow Pages; and ask others. If, for example, you're looking for a scrapbooking club, call or visit fabric or hobby stores.

The Big Picture

Now I'll share some examples to give you the Big Picture! "Serena" is a 12-year-old girl who has Down syndrome. One of her *strengths* is that she wants to wear make-up. This is an ordinary characteristic of many 12-year-old girls, and that's what makes it a strength: it tells us that Serena is more like 12-year-olds than different (regardless of what silliness the school believes about her DEVELOPMENTAL AGE—*Gag!*).

One of Serena's *needs* is to have friends. She's in segregated Special Ed classrooms where she hasn't made any friends, but she *is* "allowed" to go to Regular Ed art, PE, and music classes. Her mom, "Janie," knows Serena likes a few girls in those Regular Ed classrooms. So here's Janie's plan: she's going to throw a "make-up party" for Serena on a Friday night, and she'll help her daughter invite several of the girls from the Regular Ed classes. Janie can let the girls take all of her make-up in to Serena's bedroom; she and Serena can go buy some new make-up for the party; or she can really "wow 'em" by having a Mary Kay or Avon lady at the party to give all the girls facials and make-overs! She'll have pizza and DVDs for the girls to enjoy, too. This party doesn't guarantee friendships, of course, but it's a beginning.

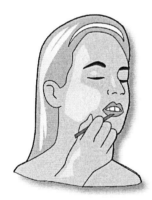

Many parents have expressed concern that their children have made initial friendships, but they're one-sided: the child with a disability doesn't get invited to the new friend's home. My response is to not sweat the small stuff, and to not presume that this is related to the child having a disability.

When my daughter was in elementary school, her best friend was always over here, and Emily was seldom invited to "Melanie's" house. Emily didn't know why, but *I* figured it out on one of the few times Emily *did* get invited to play at Melanie's. When I went to pick her up, she and Melanie were in Melanie's bedroom playing—and the rest of the house was immaculate. I made a comment to Melanie's mom about what a beautiful, organized home she had, and she responded that the only way she kept it that way was by keeping her children out of every room, except their bedrooms. She didn't *like* to have kids in her house—even her *own* kids, it seemed—which is why she seldom allowed her children to invite their friends over. Our house, on the other hand, looked like a tornado hit it most of the time (still does)—our children played everywhere—isn't it *their* home, too? If we make our homes *magnets* for children—if we're welcoming, have fun stuff for them to do, etc.—our children will have greater success with friendships.

In my son's case, few of the homes in our mountain town are wheelchair-accessible, so when he was little, his friends were always here—and it wasn't a big deal. Benj was more comfortable here, anyway. So don't get too hung up on whether things are "even-Steven" in this regard.

And here's one more suggestion about friendships. When Benjamin was five or six, we learned that when friendships *were first being formed,* it was better to have only one friend over at a time. Boys had to play with Benj the way *he* played—he couldn't do everything they could do, so they had to adjust and make accommodation. If *two* boys came over at the same time, they would play with Benj for awhile, but then would go off by themselves and leave Benj alone. But if only *one* boy came, he and Benj had a good time together. So use your best judgment about this, and know that you and your child will learn valuable lessons from any and all experiences.

Now let's look at other examples. The example with Serena was imaginary, but the following two are true stories.

"Randy" is 16 and he has autism. His older brothers have moved off on their own, so he's the only child left at home. His mom and dad ("Marie" and "Jerry") are afraid to let Randy stay home alone—they still get a babysitter for him when they go out for the evening, and Randy can't stand this! He's very angry about it, saying he's too old for a babysitter (and he's right).

Jerry shared this information during a presentation I was doing on this subject. I ask for volunteers to do a practice exercise, so folks can learn how to do this in their own families. Jerry volunteered the information above, and said their family's need was to find a way for he and his wife to go out to dinner twice a month, and for Randy to be safe during this time, without making their son feel incompetent by having a babysitter!

I asked Jerry to share some of Randy's strengths; one was that Randy loved country *and* rock music, and he hoped to one day learn to play the guitar and drums. Next, I asked Jerry if there were any restaurants or clubs that featured live bands. Yep—the "Two Sisters" restaurant. Weeknights, the Two Sisters was only a restaurant. But on Friday and Saturday nights, live entertainment began at 9:00 PM. I suggested that Jerry, Marie, and Randy start going to Two Sisters on Friday nights, on a regular basis, in the hope that Randy would get to know the band members—and to see what might develop. This is called "hanging out with intent." (Remember this and use it yourself.) I gave Jerry a few more ideas; he was doubtful anything good would come from these suggestions, but he agreed to keep an open mind.

A few weeks later, Jerry sent me an Email and proudly shared his good news! They did, indeed, hang out with intent. On the first Friday night, Jerry and Randy approached the band during the break and introduced themselves. Randy doesn't talk a great deal, so Jerry did most of the talking—telling the band members how much they liked the music, how Randy *really* loved being there, and so forth. The second Friday night, they again talked to the band members—they were becoming friends. The third Friday night, during the band's break, Randy (with a little coaching by Jerry), asked one of the band members if he could hold his guitar, and the band member went out of his way to be nice and helpful to Randy. At the end of the evening, Jerry offered to buy the band members a "round" (a couple of them were over 21, and were married; the others were 18-19—they drank sodas). By the fourth Friday night, the band members, according to Jerry, had put two and two together. They didn't know Randy had autism—that was irrelevant—they just knew something was a little different about him, and they also realized most 16-year-old boys don't spend every Friday night with their parents! At any rate, on that night, after Randy and his family had finished their meal, one of the band members told Jerry and Marie, "We'd like Randy to sit by the bandstand with us—you could leave and come back to pick him up when we're through playing." They did—Randy became the band's helper; a couple of them began giving him informal lessons (they came to Randy's house); and on future Friday nights, Marie and Jerry dropped Randy off at the restaurant, where he was safe and happy with the new friends who cared about him; and they had their own night out.

It can be more beneficial for some children with disabilities to be with others who are a little older. In this case, Randy might not have been very successful with other 16-year-old boys—many are pretty egocentric and "status" is everything. The band members, however, were a little older—the two who were married were pretty "settled" and mature. Their status wasn't threatened by Randy—and they remembered what it felt like to be a "geeky" 16-year-old. They had good hearts and saw Randy for the neat kid that he was!

The next true story was shared with me many years ago, by "Hugh," one of many people I've learned from. Hugh was a professional in the human services industry who was trying to get people out of institutions and into their communities. While this story isn't about a child with a disability, it illustrates the importance of reframing a person's perceived deficits into strengths (as I described in Chapter 5).

"Tony" was a man in his 40s who had grown up in an institution; he had been abandoned by his family. Tony had a cognitive disability and didn't have a lot of speech, and he had learned some pretty unusual behaviors during his lifetime in the institution (and most of us would learn those same behaviors if we were in such an environment).

The staff at the institution told Hugh that Tony could *never* be successful outside the institution. They thought Hugh was chasing a pipe dream, and seemed to be waiting for Hugh's effort to fail—they gave him no help.

According to the staff, one of Tony's "obsessions" (a deficit) was a deck of cards. Tony *loved* cards—they were like a security blanket. In fact, if Tony misbehaved in the institution, staff routinely took his cards away from him as punishment. Tony didn't know how to *play* cards—he didn't really understand what cards were for. But he loved handling them; "counting them" (he didn't really count, but he went through the motions that looked like counting); and he didn't know how to shuffle them, but he'd "thumb" them to make noise.

Hugh saw Tony's love of cards as a strength, not as an "obsessive deficit," and he thought about how this could be a connection to the community. Who plays cards in the community, and who could help Tony with the transition back into the community? Can you guess what Hugh came up with? A bridge club! Tony needed a little "mothering," he needed to learn how to have good manners and get along with others, and he needed people who would be patient with him. Who better to fill this role than some nice old ladies!

Hugh got in contact with a bridge club, and told the ladies about the hopes and dreams for Tony. They were a little nervous, but agreed to give it a try. Tony began attending the bridge club parties. He didn't play cards, but they taught him how to shuffle and deal. They also taught him how to drink hot tea and eat cookies, wipe his mouth with a napkin, engage in conversation, say please and thank you, and a whole host of other skills he needed to be successful in the community. They accomplished all this not through formal lessons where he was graded (or reprimanded), *but through the experience of doing it*—with patience and love.

After several weeks, the businessmen husbands of these women got into the act: they got Tony a REAL JOB, which enabled him to get his own place. He was part of the community, and was living the life of his dreams—finally. This is what can happen when people make friends and connections!

Here are a few more brief examples to inspire your creativity! Seven-year-old "Gloria" is struggling with reading. An emerging reader needs lots of practice reading, with someone who can sit with her, help her when she needs it, and be very patient. Gloria's mom is a good helper, but between her job and the other children, she can't give Gloria as much help as she needs. But who can? Who's got lots of time and would be helpful and patient? How about an older person at a nursing home/senior center? What does a person in that situation need? Companionship! Gloria can provide needed companionship, and "Grandma" can give Gloria the time, help, and patience she needs to learn to read! Community is all about *reciprocity:* each person gives, each person receives!

"Shane" is nine and, for the last eight years, he's received Traditional Therapy at the clinic to strengthen the right side of his body. And he's sick of therapy! His mom's solution? The family is joining the neighborhood gym, and Shane will work out on the exercise machine with his Dad and older brother.

Seven-year-old "Michael" needs a communication device, but his parents aren't having any luck getting insurance to pay for it. They're going to look to their community for help. His mom, "Lisa," knows exactly which device he needs and the cost, and she's prepared a plan (similar to what I described in the previous chapter): she's going to contact every service club in her community (Lions, Rotary, Elks, etc.) and ask them to pitch in to purchase Michael's device. These clubs exist to provide community service, and *Michael is a member of the community!* After he gets the device, Michael will do a presentation at a meeting of each club, and Lisa will contact the local media to make sure these groups are recognized for their good work.

Thirteen-year-old "Jodey" has had difficulty making friends because of his unusual behaviors. But Jodey has many strengths, including great outdoor skills—his family camps out on a regular basis. His mom is going to enroll him in a Scout or Campfire troop, and share Jodey's strength with the group leader. She feels confident that the group leader can use Jodey's strength as a bridge to

smooth over any concerns about Jodey's behavior. And once Jodey is with other pre-teenage boys—instead of only being with other students with autism in the Special Ed room at school—he can learn typical behaviors.

Now it's time to make your lists! One to identify your child's strengths, one to identify needs (typical needs, disability-related, and/or the family's needs), and a third to "map your community." Each of these will take some time; each needs your deliberate and careful thinking. You might want to start each list, then post them on the refrigerator and add to them over several days—it can be difficult to think of everything in one sitting. In addition, get help from others! Ask your child with a disability, and others who know and love your child (including other children), to contribute to the lists of your child's strengths and needs. The community map may also take some time, require the input of others, and/or a little research.

When you're ready, begin putting two and two together: where can your child's needs be met in a natural, inclusive environment? And how can your child's strengths contribute to his inclusion? How can your child's strengths be used to show the world what a wonderful child he is?

Strategies to Ensure Inclusion

Many parents have said, "Kathie, I *tried* to get my child included in the community, but no one will accept my child—it just won't work!" "Tell me how you tried," I ask. "Well, I called the such-and-such place and asked if they took children with disabilities and they said no."

The best of intentions can blow up in our faces because of the methods we use. The biggest offender? Asking for "permission."

Would a parent call and ask, "Do you take Methodist children," or "Do you take Asian children"? Of course not! So why do *we?* I can't say why any one particular parent might do this, but in general, I think some parents ask permission because (1) they want to make sure "it's OK" with the The-Person-in-Charge (being dependent on the System has turned many of us into "pleasers"); (2) they feel their child might be "difficult" for someone to handle, and they don't want to "burden" anyone unless the person is willing; (3) they don't *really* believe their child "belongs" in such a place, so they're looking for the approval of some authority; and/or (4) any other cockamamie reason!

In the end, it doesn't matter *why* we ask, the negative outcome is still the same. So the first strategy is: *never ask permission!*

When you identify a typical community activity for your child, do what any other parent would do (or what you'd do if your child didn't have a disability): ask lots of questions, check it out in person (when appropriate), then sign your child up! But there's a little more to it, as I'll describe. The following strategies can be applied to typical preschools (which I recommend for young children with disabilities, as described in Chapter 8); Park and Rec sports; dance/karate classes; and/or anything else. I'll use "activity" as a generic descriptor.

If the activity is one you're not familiar with, learn as much as you can about it: talk to other parents, ask lots of questions of the Person-in-Charge, and/or make a personal visit to observe. If it's not feasible for you to make a personal visit, the questions you ask over the phone are even more important. For example, it wasn't feasible for me to visit the drama class we enrolled Benjamin in—the class wouldn't start for six weeks! So I had to do the best I could by asking questions, but I *could* drive to the arts center where the class would be held and snoop around to get the lay of the land.

If you're not able to personally observe the activity, the questions you ask (over the phone or in person) are vitally important. When does the activity meet? For how long? How many children are in the activity? What ages? How many adults are present? What's the location like? If appropriate, ask the person to describe the activity. Ask whatever you'll need in order to get the Big Picture!

During this process, do not mention that your child has a disability, and do not take your child with you on the personal visit. While you're observing, picture your child in the activity and consider what he'll need to be successful. Think positive! Don't think, "Oh, my child could never do this." Instead, consider *how* he could be involved. Will he need accommodations, modifications, supports, or assistive technology (AT)? You might provide some of these, and the activity might provide some. For example, when my son took the drama class, he needed the scripts in large print. We offered to do this—the teacher could give us the scripts on a disc or via Email, and we could enlarge it. She appreciated our offer of help, but said she could easily do it. She would be printing out scripts for all the students, and it didn't take much to make the font size larger. Offering to help, in any way you can, will foster a positive relationship and build goodwill.

If you're looking into a Park and Rec sports team, a Scout troop, or something similar that needs parent volunteers, consider volunteering. Your job is not to be your child's "aide," but simply to help *all* the children—like any other volunteer. But your expertise will come in handy.

Back to picturing your child in the activity, and considering accommodations, supports, modifications, and AT. If your child might need the support of another person to successfully participate, don't think in terms of an adult helper (or yourself) for this role. Instead, plan on other children providing the help your child needs—this will enhance your child's inclusion. An adult helper will just get in the way and socially isolate your child (more about this issue regarding paraprofessionals at school in Chapter 9).

In general, you would be responsible for providing AT devices, unless they're something low-tech. For example, in an art class, your child might need larger brushes, which the art school could probably provide. And there might be other things you could send from home that would help.

During this process talk to your child to get his opinion. As an example, when Benj played T-ball in kindergarten, the coach talked to me on the phone about how Benj would get around the bases after he hit the ball. Benj could wheel his chair for short distances, but not very fast—he would be put "out" every time! The coach offered to assign a "pinch-runner"—another child would run the bases for Benjamin. But we had talked to Benj about this, and he didn't want that, so I suggested that my husband, myself, or another adult volunteer could push Benj as fast as possible (he liked going fast)—and that's what happened! (If Benj had played baseball when he was older, another child could have pushed him, but a five-year-old couldn't.)

Have your older children been involved in community activities? Would these be appropriate for your child with a disability? If so, you'll already have some familiarity with the activity and with the people involved.

Whatever activities you're considering, make sure you think "age-appropriate"—CHRONOLOGICAL, not DEVELOPMENTAL, AGE. This is especially important if your child is in an ungraded segregated Special Ed classroom and/or if he's not in an age-appropriate class at school (if he's 10, but in the third grade, for example). If these situations exist, a community activity with similar-aged peers may be his *only* opportunity to learn "how to be a 10-year-old."

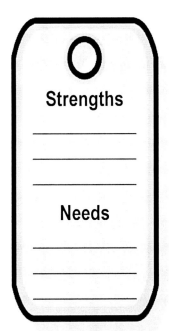

After you've checked out one or more activities that you believe your child will be interested in, share the information you've learned, along with your excitement, and let your child make the decision. Once you and your child decide to go forward, sign him up, and pay the tuition (if there is one). Then, use your best judgment about *when and what* to tell the Person-in-Charge regarding your child. In general, I recommend that you share information about your child's *strengths*—let him shine—and *needs* (supports, accommodations, etc.) without disclosing the actual disability diagnosis. This is not a case of hiding anything. Remember, a diagnosis is *private information.* If you signed one of your other children up for an activity, would you reveal private information? I hope not.

If you share the diagnosis, the Person-in-Charge might react in a negative way, especially if he's fearful of liability issues, if he's had a previous negative experience with someone with the same diagnosis, or if he's ignorant or prejudiced. And remember, the diagnosis doesn't really tell him anything important about your child! But sharing your child's *strengths and needs* provides very relevant and helpful information.

It's possible, however, that after you've mentioned the needs, the Person-in-Charge might ask you something like, "What's wrong with him?" or "Why does he need this?" With grace and tact, you can reply, "There's nothing wrong with him, he simply needs some extra assistance because [he learns differently or whatever]." If you've indicated that your child will be using a wheelchair (or something else), and if the Person has some experience with people with disabilities, he might ask something like, "Is he paralyzed or something?" At some point, you might need to share the diagnosis in order not to lie.

As appropriate, you and your child demonstrate any AT devices your child needs, and discuss any supports or accommodations. And let the Person know that your child is competent and can ask others for help, as needed (remember the "ask for help from whoever is closest" rule). Demonstrate your enthusiasm and confidence! If the Person is a little apprehensive, your attitude, tone of voice, and words can make all the difference in the world!

On the other hand, if your child won't need any significant modifications, accommodations, etc., you might not need to say anything. (And, in general, the less said, the better.) Just take your child to the activity, along with your enthusiasm. Proudly introduce your child to the Person-in-Charge, and, if necessary, you and your child share any information that may be helpful. Let your child shine! Her wonderful personality and bright smile can change a person's heart!

I'll share some examples of my son's experiences in typical activities. When we signed Benj up for T-ball when he was in kindergarten, I hadn't planned on saying anything to the coach until just before the first practice. The sign-up time was several weeks before the first practice, and the sign-up sheet indicated the children would be assigned to a coach, and the coach would call a week or so before the first practice to provide details about the schedule. I anticipated Someone-in-Charge at the Park and Rec Department might tell me my son wouldn't be allowed to play, so I was prepared with my Americans with Disabilities Act speech about non-discrimination on the basis of disability. But living in a small town, word got out that my son had signed up, and the coach called me almost immediately! I don't know if it was Divine Intervention or my common sense kicking in, but I came up a different response than my ADA speech!

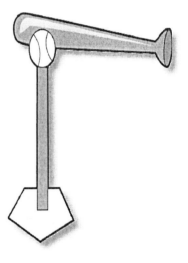

> *Coach:* I see you've signed your son up for T-ball—he's scheduled to be on my team.
>
> *Kathie:* Oh, that's great! *[I'm really nervous, but trying not to show it, anticipating the hammer falling.]*
>
> *Coach:* He uses a wheelchair, doesn't he?
>
> *Kathie:* Yes, he does.
>
> *Coach:* Well, um—er—well, um [clears throat], well, you know we've never done anything like this before. *[This is where I planned to give my ADA speech, but—thankfully—other words came out of my mouth.]*
>
> *Kathie:* We never have either, so we can learn together!

That's what happened, and it was a great experience for everyone! Benj made friends and had a great time, and the other players, their parents, and the coaches learned his disability wasn't a big deal. The coach turned out to be a big teddy bear, and *he made accommodations without being asked.* During practice, we agreed Benj should be in a shortstop position. There was no way for him to catch a ball that was hit, pick it up off the ground, or chase after it. But a player in the outfield could toss the ball to Benj on occasion, and he could throw it to one of the players in the infield. This could happen, of course, only when the players (Benjamin *and* others in the outfield) weren't picking their noses, watching cars go by, or otherwise ignoring what has happening on the field!

The coach also made accommodations in the hitting department. During practice, it was quickly apparent that Benj had difficulty making contact with the ball, which rested on the T (a pole on a stand). We had provided Benj with a very short, fat plastic bat, since he couldn't wield the typical T-ball bats. Even so, it took several tries before Benj made contact with the ball, and when he did, it just dribbled off the T. In order to be a "good hit," the ball is supposed to cross a line that's about eight feet from the T.

I wasn't sure what would happen when the first game rolled around. I didn't know if Benj would be at bat all day or if they'd give him a "walk." Imagine my delight when the following happened: the coach stood next to Benj when it was his turn at bat (just like he did with all the players), clapping and providing encouragement. When Benj made contact with the ball and it dribbled off the T, the coach casually gave it a kick to get it past the "good hit line," and yelled, "Good hit, Benjamin—go on to first!" Was the coach "breaking the rules" for Benj? Yes, but rules were broken for other players, too! For this coach and others, a player's *effort and determination* were more important than skill, and Benj put a great deal of effort into getting his fat blue bat to touch that little white ball!

A couple of years later, when Benj took a karate class, we didn't do *anything* ahead of time; we simply took him to the first class extra early so we could have a chat with the instructor—with Benj present and Benj speaking for himself, as much as possible—before the other students arrived. We didn't mention his diagnosis, and the instructor never asked. We usually had a friendly chat with the sensei before and after each class to answer any questions he had, give him suggestions on how to modify the moves for Benj, if necessary, and so forth.

When we signed Benj up for drama class (six weeks ahead of the first class), we didn't call to ask the teacher about the large print scripts until a week before the first class; the teacher didn't ask "why," and I didn't mention anything about Benjamin having cerebral palsy. When my husband took him to the class, he simply brought our seven-foot portable ramp so Benj could get on stage!

Now, back to the process of ensuring your child is included. If, for whatever reason, any difficulties arise—like resistance to your child participating—stay positive. Many people are simply fearful, and you can calm their fears and reassure them.

If necessary, negotiate—using the "what will it take" strategy. You could ask something like, "What will it take to make you more comfortable?" When *we're* willing to work with others, they're more willing to work with us. (More details about this strategy are in Chapter 9.)

In some instances—and for your child's benefit—it might be important to present information to the other participants about your child. If, for instance, other children in the activity are going to be gawking at your child until they understand more about him, it's better to answer their questions from the get-go so everyone is more comfortable! But instead of presenting "disability awareness" information, present *"similarity* awareness." People are all too aware of differences—that's what has perpetuated prejudice and discrimination! We need to point out the similarities that our children share with other children, so everyone will know our children are more *like* others than different. Here are some guidelines to consider:

- Keep your child's dignity and privacy in mind at all times.
- For an activity that includes children ages 5-7, the parent (or other adult) can facilitate a "presentation," by asking questions of the group. For example, "Who likes to go to McDonald's? Who likes Burger King?" and so forth. Within each question, the child with a disability answers, too, and the parent points this out ("He's just like you!"). But then point out that some like BK better than McD, so that means some are different from others. A series of questions like this can be asked, until you get to something like, "Who uses a wheelchair?" Only the child with a disability—so he's different in that respect, but he's similar in many other respects. To the greatest degree possible, the child with a disability needs to participate in this exercise so all the children can see that he's competent! Toward the end, the facilitator or the child can demonstrate any AT devices the child uses, explain about seizures, or whatever, to "take the mystery" out of everything and make it familiar.
- If the child is 8 or above, she should be in charge of this to the greatest degree possible. If the child uses a communication device, she can program a short "speech" to provide answers to questions other children might have.
- In all cases, use People First Language, and "reframing" as described in Chapter 5 (use "need" instead of "problem" and so forth).

> **Similarity Awareness**
> **Instead of**
> **Disability Awareness**
> Children with disabilities are more like children without disabilities than different! Always focus on the similarities first—*maximize* those—before sharing differences (and *minimize* those).

Again, consider doing this *only* if you anticipate the reactions of others might create discomfort for your child. In many cases, the less said the better, and children will "learn as they go."

Once your child is participating in the activity, it's important for you to stay involved one way or another. Volunteer, if that's feasible. When you drop your child off or pick him up, take the time to chat with the Person-in-Charge to see how things are going. Let the Person know you're always available to answer questions or provide advice (but also let him know he can talk to your child, too). Try to anticipate issues and resolve them before they become problems. Offer to provide training to the Person and/or others. Hopefully, they'll welcome your expertise. Don't be pushy, be gentle and enthusiastic.

If, for whatever reason, things don't work out, cut your losses and move on. Learn from the experience and find another activity for your child. Recognize that things don't always work out for children who *don't* have disabilities—keep things in perspective! Not everything is a "disability issue"!

Your child's participation in one activity will open the door to other activities—his "resume of success" can be shared with others when it's time to enroll in the next activity. And as I mentioned earlier, your child's success will open the door to other children and adults with disabilities!

If your child is a pre-teen or a teenager—and depending on the circumstances—encourage him to take a more active role in exploring potential activities, checking them out, asking questions, etc. Instead of you doing the initial legwork, your child can; help him learn, if he's not sure what to do. This experience will help him later on when he looks for a job, an apartment, and so on. And the next section looks at that part of a child's life!

Opportunities for Teens: Work and More

It's never too early to start thinking about your child's future as an adult. Chapter 9 details education, which is *supposed* to help prepare all children for post-secondary education and/or employment, but the strategies in this chapter can also help our children move toward success after their school years.

Some teens with disabilities receive employment help through the school district's Special Ed department and/or the state's Vocational Rehabilitation agency. In general, however, this isn't the best we can do for our children.

While planning for a presentation for the Special Ed department of a large school district, I had many questions for the Director of Special Ed. During one conversation about teens with disabilities and employment, I almost dropped the phone when he said, "Well, we're slowly learning how to do things better. Last year, for the first time, we allowed students to resign from jobs if they weren't happy in them." What?!? I couldn't believe my ears, so I asked, "Do you mean that before that time, if the Special Ed department got a student a job, and the student didn't like the job, he was forced to work where he didn't want to work?" The Special Ed director replied, "I'm afraid so—we made the job part of his IEP, and wrote goals, and he had to attend the job, just like he had to attend school—whether he liked it or not." He reluctantly admitted that they labeled many children as failures because they did poorly in such jobs. And we really shouldn't call these jobs—the students were not paid! The DISABILITY DOUBLE STANDARD rears its ugly head again: teenagers who *do not* have disabilities are not slave-laborers, chained to jobs they don't like, but somehow this is OK for teens with disabilities!

Unless the Special Ed department and Voc-Rehab agency in your area are extraordinarily wonderful, I hope you won't leave your child to their mercy when it comes to employment. Instead, help your child learn to get a job on his own—in the same way teenagers without disabilities get jobs!

Dylan, the son of my best friend, got his first job last summer: dispensing sodas at the Park and Rec refreshment stand during softball season. His older brother, Matt, had a similar job for several years, and Dylan and his parents used this valuable connection. In the REAL WORLD, many people get jobs through connections and networking—our children can do the same thing. If you're friends with business owners, and if your child is interested in a job they have to offer, go there first!

HANGING OUT WITH INTENT is another beneficial strategy. If a typical teenage job in a fast food restaurant is something your child would enjoy, go to that restaurant on a regular basis for awhile and get to know the people who work there. It's much easier to apply for a job if your child already knows the staff. Ditto the grocery store or other potential job sites.

While a permanent slave-labor job (working for free) is not desirable, a short, unpaid internship might pave the way to a paid position. "Christine" and her 18-year-old son, "David," had zero faith and zero luck with DISABILITY WORLD employment help (Special Ed and Voc-Rehab). David didn't know exactly what type of job he wanted, he just knew he wanted to drive a van or a pick-up truck and he wanted to wear a uniform. Being a resourceful mom, Christine went to work. Using the Yellow Pages as one guide, and keeping their eyes open when out and about in town, she and David began compiling a list of companies who employed "drivers of vans or pick-up trucks who wore uniforms."

Then they got on the phone and also made personal visits. In short, they approached potential employers this way: David doesn't have experience, but he's bursting with enthusiasm. Would you give him a chance by allowing him to intern for free, for a few weeks, and if it works out, hire him? (And they did *not* talk about David's disability!) A few employers practically hung up on them, others listened patiently and said no, but one said yes—and all it takes is one. David was paired with an experienced employee, he began learning a new trade, and the internship was successful. David's enthusiasm and determination paid off, and he was hired. He loved wearing his uniform and was the proud driver of a cool-looking van with a bug on top—he was now an exterminator!

Can one of your child's interests be turned into a job? When "Jose" was young, he loved to follow his dad around: when he mowed the lawn, edged the driveway, trimmed the hedges, blew the leaves, and so forth. And Jose was intrigued by the engines of this equipment. His dad encouraged this interest and let Jose help him. Over time, Jose's interest and proficiency grew. His dad began buying "broken-down" lawn mowers that Jose could repair. Soon, Jose started mowing lawns to earn money. Sometimes he used one of his mowers, other times he used the equipment of the homeowner—and he offered to repair any of the homeowner's equipment that wasn't up to par. Jose's business is growing—what started out as an interesting hobby will most likely turn into Jose owning his own small business. His parents help Jose with bookkeeping and other details which are difficult for Jose to handle. And this is no different than other business owners who hire people to do the work they're unable or unwilling to do!

Volunteer work—real volunteer work, not just working for free—can also pave the way to employment. Volunteer experience is a valuable addition to a person's resume! If your child loves animals, check out volunteer opportunities at a zoo, farm/ranch operation, humane society, vet's office etc. Museums, libraries, food banks, hospitals, senior facilities, schools, and other entities all need volunteers. What if your whole family volunteered at a food bank every weekend? Then everyone in the family gets to meet new people and contribute to the betterment of your community!

If your child is interested in doing something like this, but no volunteer position exists, create one! For example, if your teenage daughter dreams of working in a childcare center (or owning one later on—think big!), but there are no paid or volunteer positions available, your daughter can offer to volunteer anyway. This may or may not lead to employment at that particular childcare facility. The owner of the facility might figure, "Why pay her when she'll work for free?" However, this volunteer experience could open the door to a paid position at a *different* childcare facility.

Look into other long-term volunteer opportunities like AmeriCorps (www. americorps.org). They specifically recruit people with disabilities! Volunteers sign on for a certain length of time, receive a stipend for living expenses, and, in some cases, also receive funds that can be applied to college tuition.

And what about college? Think your child isn't college material? Think again! "Barbara" always had high expectations for her son, "Andrew," who has Down syndrome. When he finished high school, Andrew enrolled in college—he audited all courses, instead of taking them for credit. He would not earn a degree, but that wasn't the goal. His family thought it was important that Andrew have "college experience." They wanted him to meet new friends, learn from his peers, and benefit from the social and emotional growth that comes with college. They also knew that even though he might not master academics, he would still learn a lot from his classes. He moved into a dorm, became the assistant equipment manager for the hockey team, and traveled around the country with the team, hanging out with all the burly hockey-jocks!

My son plans to enroll in community college next semester, taking credit courses, and he'll need assistance from the disability student services office. It might take him several years to complete his degree—but the same is true for young people (and old) who *don't* have disabilities, right?

I hope the dreams for your child include college or trade school. Whether she audits the classes or takes them for credit, the experience will enhance her personal growth and her opportunities for future employment!

Driving

Is driving a car in your child's future? I hope you haven't written off your child's potential before giving him a chance! Far too often, we PRESUME INCOMPETENCE in this area, and our children lose, big-time.

On the whole, public transportation in our country is dismal. In a few big cities, people can get to and from work and other places without cars. But in most cities and towns, a personal car is a must. If your child is not able to drive himself, his opportunities for employment may be diminished.

There are many driving aids available today—that were not available when you and I first began driving—which can enable people with disabilities to be safe drivers. Hand controls, oversize rear-view mirrors, and GPS systems are the tip of the iceberg. While searching the Internet for driving aids, I learned a person can drive a car with a joystick—just like the joysticks on power wheelchairs! This is something my son might need. We're beginning the process now, and Benjamin might learn to be a safe driver in a short time, with a few modifications, or it might take several years of trying different driving aids. If that's what it takes, that's what we'll do!

I hope you'll give your child *the opportunity to learn to drive* before deciding he can't. He may only be a part-time driver, and if so, that's OK. Benjamin has already said he may not want to drive at night—it's too hard to see in the dark. We'll help him master driving during daylight hours, then see what happens at night.

If it's determined that your child will *not* be able to drive, I hope you'll do some serious thinking about alternatives. If you live in a small town where no public transportation exists, you'll need to begin thinking about natural supports for your child's transportation. Will he be able to get a job and join a carpool? You might consider moving to a bigger city where better public transportation is available. Alternatively, it might be important for your young adult child to move to such a city when he's ready to leave the nest. If your child is very young right now, this might be the furthest thing in your mind—you're worried about what's going to happen tomorrow, not 15 years from now. But I hope you *will* begin thinking about it now—and begin making plans so your child will be able to live the life of his dreams.

Adult Services

By now, you know I'm not a fan of today's traditional Adult Services. Other parents may not be happy with them either, but many still lead their children into the confining arms of Adult Services, believing there are no other alternatives—but there are.

It would take another book to adequately detail the current state of affairs of Adult Services, and such a book would be out of date before it left the printer. But here's the Big Picture in a nutshell: because of budget cuts in many states, things are getting worse, not better!

Adult Services vary from state-to-state, but as I'm using the term here, they include SSI (Supplemental Security Income), Medicaid, group homes ("habilitation services"), employment assistance (provided by Voc-Rehab and other agencies), and day programs (what many *people with disabilities* call "adult babysitting").

It is my fervent hope that you will consider Adult Services for your child only as the last, last, last resort, not the first choice. In more than a decade of meeting adults with developmental disabilities across the country, I have not met one who is receiving Adult Services who is happy with how his life is going!

Many are living in group homes where their every move is programmed, they're treated like children, and/or they have no privacy or autonomy. In some group homes, people with disabilities have been emotionally, physically, and/or sexually abused; in some, people's possessions are routinely "borrowed" by others and/or their possessions mysteriously disappear; and in some, the "residents" are given a small weekly allowance. Are some group homes better than others? Of course, but even the best group home, run by "good" staff who *support* instead of *manage* the people in their care, cannot replicate living in the home of one's choice, with the supports of one's choice.

While their nights are spent in the congregate setting of a group home, their days are usually spent in congregate settings of sheltered workshops (where they're paid sub-minimum wage, working in jobs they may hate); in enclave settings (a group of people with disabilities are all transported to the same work site, where they're supervised by an agency staffer and paid sub-minimum wages); or in day programs (where, according to many people with disabilities,

No Freedom; Few Choices

Many—far too many—adults with disabilities who are in group homes (or other congregate settings) don't have the freedom, nor the power, to lead the lives of their choice. For example, many cannot be spontaneous and take a walk around the block, go to a movie with friends, or do other typical adult activities.

In some instances, this is the result of transportation not being available. But in other cases, it's the result of people with disabilities not being allowed any "alone time"! They are supervised by someone at all times. Their "free time" is programmed: they go to the mall as a group (called an "outing" in Service System vernacular).

I can't imagine living a life like this, can you? Yet it's the norm for thousands of adults with developmental disabilities. Many of their situations seem closer to "prison life" than life "in the community," yet all the rules and regs of government policies and provider agencies are being followed perfectly!

People in these situations have no freedom and few choices. Is this what you want for your child? Is this what your child wants for himself?

they're supposedly being trained in life-skills, but where they actually learn little or nothing—and this is after some have spent years in Special Ed Life Skills classrooms in the public school!!!). When you have some free time, take a tour of a group home or sheltered workshop in your area—visualize your child there as an adult, and see if this matches the dreams you have for him.

In some states, baby-steps of progress are being made that may affect a very small number of adults with disabilities: "two-bed" apartment living is offered to some people (depending on their "qualifications"), while others enter supported employment—a REAL JOB in the community, with help from a job coach.

Here's a typical scenario of today's Adult Services. In general, 18-year-olds with disabilities are eligible for SSI. Once a person receives SSI (in most states), he's also eligible for Medicaid insurance, as well as other Services. In other words, SSI becomes the ticket for Adult Services. In some instances, a person is not entitled to some Services unless he *is* a SSI recipient. In other instances—like Voc-Rehab Services, for example—this is not the case, but those who *are* SSI recipients are considered "more needy," so they go to the top of the list.

Let's take a fictional person, "Catherine," and look at what happens. (While Catherine may be fictional, the scenario I'll describe is based on the real life experiences of adults with developmental disabilities.)

When she turned 18, Catherine's parents took her to the Social Security office to sign her up for SSI benefits. (When a child with a disability turns 18, *her income*—not her parents'—determines eligibility.) And what is the criteria for receiving SSI as an adult? In essence, poverty and/or being "unemployable." Catherine—who has a cognitive disability—*had to state that she is unemployable in order to qualify for SSI.*

In the state where Catherine lives, she was also eligible for "habilitation services." Catherine's parents decided it was time for their daughter to move out, so into a group home—"Hope House"—she went. Hope House is licensed as a provider, and Catherine's care (room, board, and supervision) will be paid for by her $500 (in round figures) monthly SSI check. (Other state and/or Federal funds may also supplement the cost of Catherine's "care" at Hope House). Thus, the agency who runs Hope House becomes the "payee" of Catherine's monthly check. An IHP (Individualized Habilitation Plan) was written for Catherine, complete with goals about personal grooming, self-help skills, "adult behavior" (like getting up on time), and more. And because Catherine's parents don't trust her to know how to take care of herself, they went to court to "get guardianship," and they put their two-cents' worth into the IHP. (But don't you have to wonder why they didn't teach Catherine how to take care of herself???) Her parents' contribution to the IHP is that Catherine must be supervised by someone at all times.

Catherine is "placed" in a part-time job by an employment provider ("Jobs Unlimited"). She works three mornings a week, from 9 AM to noon, at "Fabric Warehouse," cleaning and stocking shelves, under the supervision of a job coach who is employed by Jobs Unlimited. After a year of employment, the job coach is still deemed "necessary"—and why not, Catherine is a cash cow!

Catherine is paid $3.00/hour. But her wages don't actually come from Fabric Warehouse—she's paid by Jobs Unlimited. This agency has contracts with different businesses around town for "job placement." In essence, Fabric Warehouse (and similar "contractees") pays Jobs Unlimited a small percentage of Catherine's wages. "Vera," Catherine's job coach, is paid $12.00/hour by Jobs Unlimited. When she's not "shadowing" Catherine three mornings a week, Vera does the same for other "clients" at other job sites.

Jobs Unlimited has overhead costs for Catherine's job—staff at the office who have to process paperwork, supervise, etc. So on top of Catherine's paltry $3.00/hour wages, and Vera's $12.00/hour wages, the agency has $15.00/hour overhead costs (for office staff, managers, etc.) which means Catherine's job *costs* $30.00/hour.

Now let's do the math. Catherine works 468 hours/year (9 hours/week x 52 weeks), so she *earns* $1,404.00/year. But her job *generates* a total of $14,040.00/year (468 x $30.00).

Keep in mind that Catherine is only one of 50 people with disabilities "employed" by Jobs Unlimited. For sake of discussion, let's assume their situations are similar to Catherine's. This means their jobs cost $702,000.00/year. Where does this nearly three-quarters of a million dollars come from? Taxpayer dollars, for the most part. Jobs Unlimited generates very little income—the funds collected from Fabric Warehouse and other contractees is a pittance of the whole budget. And you thought snake oil salesmen ran a racket! (Am I saying people who work in Adult Services are crooks or terrible people? Some may be; others are wonderful. It's the Service System itself—how it's operated, what it does to people, and more—that's terrible.)

To add insult to injury, half of Catherine's $117.00 monthly wages are handed over to Hope House, since her SSI check only partially covers the cost of her care. So Catherine has a net income of $58.50/month from her job; and Hope House gives her a $10.00/week allowance. Is this the future you want for your child?

I mentioned earlier that things are getting worse. And after reading Catherine's story (which is very typical), you might wonder *how* things could get worse. But they can—and are—when a state cuts Services to remedy the budget crisis. Waiting lists for Adult Services are long, and getting longer.

In addition, there are many "disincentives to work" once a person is receiving SSI. If, for example, Catherine quit her job with Jobs Unlimited and got a Real Job, she probably couldn't work full-time, at minimum wage, without losing some of her benefits. SSI would deduct money from her check, depending on how much she earned in her new job. She would also be in jeopardy of losing her Medicaid, and she might even get kicked out of Hope House. (But she might not be "allowed" to quit her job without permission from the IHP Team!)

Society—and our Federal and state governments—*say* they want people with disabilities to be employed, but you wouldn't know it by the disincentives within the system. To remedy this, waiver plans and some changes in legislation have taken place—and more are promised. And while these are good, they've only made a small dent in the problem. These *can* make a difference for some adults with disabilities, but don't count on significant changes in the near future.

Here's another scenario. This one is also based on compilations of real people's lives, and it's in sharp contrast to Catherine's story.

"Bobby" has a significant physical disability, and he uses a power wheelchair, a communication device, and a service dog. His parents had Big Dreams for Bobby, and those dreams have become a reality. Bobby went to college, and earned a Master's degree. It took longer than average, but he persevered. He lived at home with his parents during the college years; and even though he was eligible for SSI and other Adult Services, he said "no" to all of them. That wasn't the path that would take Bobby to the world of his dreams.

During the 8-9 years he was in college, Bobby held a variety of part-time jobs. Once he was no longer covered by his father's group health insurance policy, Bobby purchased an individual health insurance policy (with financial help from his parents) through his state's "uninsurable" agency (every state has one).

Upon graduation from college, Bobby got a job with the Federal government (which is estimated to be one of the largest employers of people with disabilities). He earned good pay, had great health insurance, and enjoyed job security—it's almost impossible to get fired when you work for the government!

When he moved into his own apartment, Bobby did not want paid personal assistant services (for help with things he can't do for himself). Instead, he wanted to use natural supports and generic services. When he looked at apartment complexes, he searched for one that had the physical access he needed, but he also looked for one that had a sense of community—where tenants knew each other, were friendly, and so forth.

He found one, and life was good. A self-transfer lift was installed so he could get in and out of bed, to/from the shower, etc. with little or no human assistance. (When he occasionally needed help in this area, he called on close family, friends, or neighbors—not a paid personal assistant). Bobby shopped online for most of what he needed, including groceries: the big chain grocery store a few blocks away delivered. And he used the help of many of his neighbors—who he got to know and trusted enough to give duplicate keys to his apartment. The grocery store delivered during the day when Bobby was at work, so neighbor "Mary" accepted the deliveries of Bobby's groceries, and then put them inside Bobby's apartment (and placed the milk in the refrigerator). Another neighbor picked up Bobby's mail and slit the envelopes open (since this was very hard for Bobby to do), and placed the mail on Bobby's kitchen table. Other neighbors helped; none was given a huge job—most were willing to help in small ways.

In return, Bobby helped his neighbors in various ways. He fed pets and watered plants when his neighbors took trips, baby-sat some of the neighbors' children in his apartment on many Friday nights, and did other helpful things to reciprocate. Bobby, with the help of others (and we all live by the help of others), is living a typical, ordinary, fulfilled live, included in his community. Is this the kind of life you want for your child?

What would we do if there *was* no Service System? Would we let our children go without, or would we become very creative in finding ways to meet their needs from other sources?

This is the kind of life I want for my son—and it's the life he wants for himself. If you haven't already—and depending on the age of your child—paint some scenarios for your child to consider. I've talked with my son, sharing the REAL LIFE stories of a variety of people with disabilities, like Catherine and Bobby, and Benjamin is vehement about the type of life he wants. He's already said he does not want paid personal assistants to help him with things that are difficult, "I want my family and friends and neighbors to help me, Mom."

We're doing what we can to ensure Benjamin's life will turn out the way he wants. As of this writing, we're having a self-transfer system ("Sure Hands") installed, so Benj can get in and out of bed, to/from the bathroom, etc., by himself. As I mentioned in a previous chapter, we found a used one for $1,000.00, instead of fighting with the insurance to pay the usual $12,000-$15,000 cost. Installation is costing another $2,500.00, which is going on our credit card. When he moves away from home, this transfer system will go with him.

Benjamin has had his service dog for almost two years. With her help, Benjamin is able to be more self-sufficient (needing less "human" help). At the present time, Benjamin plans on living at home and attending community college for two years. Then he wants to transfer to a four-year school to finish his degree, and he plans on living in the dorm. Instead of paid personal assistance, he'll look to roommates for help. Benj will always need a wheelchair accessible van at his disposable (whether he drives himself or someone drives him). We figure we can "trade-out" help for Benjamin when he moves to a dorm: if his roommate will help with dressing and undressing (and other things that are difficult), he can share Benj's van. Will it work out perfectly all the time? Probably not—that's life. But we'll try to anticipate issues and solve them before they become problems!

When Benj turned 18 a few months ago, he could have applied for (and probably received) SSI—along with Medicaid and eligibility for other Adult Services. My husband and I talked with Benjamin about all this, giving him the pros and cons. The thought of a $500-something check each month was initially appealing—what 18-year-old wouldn't want to get a few hundred bucks a month for doing nothing? But is that really the case? No, in order to get his hands on that money, he would have to give up much, in my opinion. He would have to state that he is unemployable, and would also have to abide by government rules, and lose some dignity, autonomy, and self-direction.

Well-meaning family members and friends have encouraged us to try to change Benj's mind: "You and Mark have been paying into the tax base for years—why shouldn't Benjamin get what he's entitled to?" But it's not that simple to me. And since we believe in our son, and have told him all his life that he can grow up to do whatever he wants, the idea of stating that he's "unemployable" is abhorrent to all of us. Worse, do I want my son to become dependent on the System, and then—at some point in the future—he'll be caught, like so many others, between trying to get a REAL JOB and losing his "benefits"?

Later in his life, Benjamin might change his mind about applying for SSI. If so, it will be probably be a decision of last resort, and we'll support his decision.

What Would *You* Want?

If you acquired a disability tomorrow, which scenario would you choose for yourself?

1. Stay in your own home, and get the help you need from family, friends, and neighbors, along with whatever AT devices and accommodations you need so you can go back to your old job and live the same life as before you acquired the disability.

2. Collect Disability Welfare, and move to smaller, cheaper place; get some in-home help from paid providers; work part-time so you don't lose your benefits.

3. Collect Disability Welfare, move into a group home with others you don't know, and have Staff write a Plan for your life.

Which would you choose for yourself?

Which would your child choose for himself when he's an adult?

But we will have also done everything in our power to ensure Benjamin doesn't become dependent on the government and its Services.

Living a REAL LIFE cannot be achieved through the "benevolence" of government handouts and the artificial environments of the Service System. It can come only from living the same type of life Americans *without* disabilities live: working hard to get and keep a job; being as self-reliant as possible, while simultaneously getting help from the natural supports of family, friends, and neighbors; being involved in one's community; and enjoying both the opportunities and responsibilities of being a contributing member of society.

Some parents feel they already have enough on their plates, and the suggestion of "doing even more" to ensure their children lead REAL LIVES is enough to push some over the edge. But be aware that when you cut back and/or eliminate traditional Services, your family's schedule will change—you'll take your family's life back—and you'll have *more time* in which to enjoy natural activities within your own home or in the community. And you don't have to be a social butterfly to make this happen. When Benjamin stopped going to therapy, we did not automatically replace the hours spent in therapy with an equal or greater number of hours spent "doing therapeutic activities" at home or in the community. We were selective in our choices of activities, and had more time to be a family. The serenity we felt was unbelievable—we *all* had our lives back!

I hope you feel a tinge of excitement and hopeful anticipation that your child's needs can be met in typical inclusive activities. If you make the switch, your family will once again have the autonomy, privacy, and self-direction you once had, and you'll no longer live under the yoke of today's CONVENTIONAL WISDOM and/or the directives of others. I believe you'll also feel more confident about your child's future. As he lives a REAL LIFE as a child, you'll know he's on the path to a REAL LIFE as an adult. And this means you can dream Big Dreams for your child—the same dreams you had before D-Day (the day of diagnosis). Dream with and for your child, so he can dream for himself—and do whatever it takes to turn those dreams into reality!

So far, you've learned about new attitudes and actions; a new therapeutic landscape and tools for success that can make a difference in your child's life; and strategies to ensure his needs can be met in inclusive community activities. But there's one more area of our children's lives that needs a closer look: education. In the last two chapters, I'll describe alternatives to today's traditional services for young children (birth to five) and for school-aged children. We can do better than following today's CONVENTIONAL WISDOM when it comes to our children's educational experiences.

> THE ULTIMATE CONSEQUENCES OF INACTION COULD BE GREATER THAN THE CONSEQUENCES OF ACTION.
>
> *Dean Koontz*

Babies, Toddlers, and Preschoolers

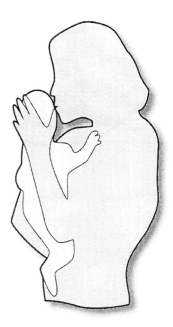

8

"Sarah" was the proud mother of a beautiful eight-month-old baby, "Alex," and two older children. Luckily for Alex, Sarah had never bought into the MEDICAL MODEL of disability, and she continuously rejected the negative prognoses about her son's future as well as the routine assessments that showed how "delayed" he was because he has a diagnosis of Down syndrome. Sarah maintained an assertive stance with professionals in defense of her son's humanity, strengths, and individuality.

But Sarah struggled with a sister-in-law—Missy—whose first baby was about the same age as Alex. At family get-togethers, Missy positively glowed as she described every new feat little Becca accomplished—rolling over, sitting up, and many other typical developmental milestones. After each description of Becca's new abilities, Missy turned to Sarah and asked if Alex was doing the same things. As Sarah fought back tears, she told me she was sick of the comparisons, tired of being hurt by Missy's questions in front of a roomful of in-laws, and was thinking of cutting off contact with her husband's family.

Sadly, Sarah's story is all too common. We may be surrounded by people who love us, but we're also surrounded by negative attitudes and perceptions about our children that pierce our hearts again and again and again. So one solution I shared with Sarah was to toughen up a little—after all, she *does* need to role model for her son how to handle insensitive clods, since he'll have to deal with similar people the rest of his life. And one way Sarah could toughen up was through her own words and actions. I suggested she do two things the next time Missy proudly shared her daughter's accomplishments. First, she should "ooohh" and "aaahh" over whatever baby Becca was doing, remembering the pride she felt when *her* first baby achieved those same milestones. She could express her happiness for Becca and Missy without it taking anything away from Alex. Neither Sarah nor I could know if Missy was intentionally gloating or if she was just an ecstatic new mom who was oblivious to everything but her own feelings and her own child, so it wouldn't do to assume the worst about her.

Next, I suggested for Sarah to share wonderful stories about Alex—his marvelous, easy-going personality, a new toy he had fallen in love with, a developmental milestone (even if he achieved it at a different time than Becca), or how he sleeps through the night. And I encouraged Sarah to use the same positive stance she maintained with professionals: show her pride in everything about Alex and reject any negative comments. She stood a little straighter, dried her tears, and said she could do this—then added that she wished she didn't *have* to do it with family. I know what she means, and perhaps you do, too.

The early years are precious and all too fleeting, and every day of a child's young life is unique as it brings the first smile, the first laugh, and many other "firsts." You want to enjoy these firsts with as much joy as other parents, but CONVENTIONAL WISDOM may get in the way—in the form of negative attitudes and perceptions, or the Services that are intended to help our children. And, unfortunately, there are some less-than-joyous firsts that many babies and young children with disabilities routinely experience: the first time they're assessed and found to be "deficient," the first day of Traditional Therapy to "fix" the "deficiencies," the first day of segregation in a Special Ed Preschool, and more.

These and other differences between the lives of babies and young children with and without disabilities occur primarily because of the *impact of Services,* not because of a child's disability, in and of itself. In addition, the funding streams of Services create an artificial "transition" process that can wreak havoc in the lives of a child and his parents.

Most of the DISABILITY WORLD paradigms described in Chapter 4 are present in Early Intervention (EI) and Special Ed Preschool Services, and there are other issues of concern that are *specific* to Services for young children:

- the assumption that young children and their families need and/or benefit from professional assistance of government-funded programs;

- when Early Intervention becomes more like Early Interference;

- the tendency for parents to become dependent on the System;

- the artificial "transition" process;

- the segregation of young children in Special Ed Preschools;

- the myth that a Special Ed Preschool is the ticket to an inclusive Regular Ed kindergarten class.

Before going further, it's important to add this reminder about my criticisms: they are not to be construed as personal attacks on any who provide Services for young children. I have personal friends who are, or have been, Service Providers, and I have presented at many conferences for Service Providers. Most are wonderful people who care deeply for the children and families they serve, and they do their jobs very well. My criticisms are of the Service System itself: the rationale for its existence and the manner in which Services are provided, which can lead to unintended, harmful consequences for very young children and their families.

Many people within the Service System have recognized some of these consequences and are making positive changes. I salute them! Others know changes need to be made, but they may be stuck in a System that reveres the status quo. Some inventive and determined souls "break the rules" in order to do what's best for a child and the family, often at the risk of their careers. I salute them, too.

Are there benefits to interventions and educational Services for young children with disabilities and their families? Certainly. In my own personal experience, I learned some information and strategies that were beneficial to my then-young son; a number of parents have shared similar stories about their

---

HOW MUCH HAVE THINGS REALLY CHANGED?

In the 20th century, parents were thought to be incompetent to raise their children with disabilities, so physicians and others told parents to put their children in institutions. Have things changed so very much since then? The *environment* has changed—from Services in an institution to Services at home, a Special Ed Preschool, or other setting, but the mentality seems similar: parents need professional help in order to raise children with disabilities. When will our society reject the prejudices, stereotypes, and misinformation that perpetuate the myth that some parents are inherently incompetent on the basis of disability or income? *When will we, as parents, reject this myth about ourselves?*

experiences. But do all families and children *really need* government-mandated Early Intervention and Special Ed Preschool Services, and are these the *only way* parents and children can get whatever help they might need? I'll discuss this further. Because very young children with disabilities are said to be "at risk," extraordinary efforts are directed their way. But the very Services which are intended to help may sometimes be the source of greater, and different, risks. We can all do better for children with disabilities, but change will come only if we're willing to lift the veil and see what lurks behind the benevolent facade of Services for young children.

Unspoken Assumptions and Broken Promises

IDEA, Part C (which covers children birth to age three) states,

> Congress finds that there is an urgent and substantial need—
> (1) to enhance the development of infants and toddlers with disabilities, to minimize their potential for developmental delay, and to recognize the significant brain development that occurs during a child's first three years of life;
>
> (2) to reduce the educational costs to our society, including our Nation's schools, by minimizing the need for special education and related services after infants and toddlers with disabilities reach school age;
>
> (3) to maximize the potential for individuals with disabilities to live independently in society;
>
> (4) to enhance the capacity of families to meet the special needs of their infants and toddlers with disabilities...

Let's look at each of these declarations. I hope you'll do your own thinking about these important issues, too.

(1) To enhance the development of infants and toddlers with disabilities, to minimize their potential for developmental delay, and to recognize the significant brain development that occurs during a child's first three years of life.

The first two parts of this goal are somewhat dependent on the third, so we'll start there, first. For about the past 25 years or so—and especially during the past 10 years—"new brain science" has promoted the idea that the first three years of life are the most critical. This theory obviously influenced the U.S. Congress, as evidenced by the declaration above, as well as advocates of Early Intervention Services. It's also influenced society, as evidenced by parenting books, magazine articles, and news reports that routinely beat the drum about the "critical" importance of the FIRST THREE YEARS of life. Because many babies and young children with disabilities are *already* thought to be delayed or at-risk of having delays, the FIRST THREE YEARS are considered even more important for this population. Furthermore, it appears that professionals, advocates, and others have *generalized* the NEW BRAIN SCIENCE (with no evidence) to *all* early childhood development—physical, social, intellectual, and everything else.

> ONE OF THE LUCKIEST THINGS THAT CAN HAPPEN TO YOU IN LIFE IS TO HAVE A HAPPY CHILDHOOD.
> *Agatha Christie*

I first became skeptical of the FIRST THREE YEARS mentality when a physical therapist (PT) warned me, "If children with cerebral palsy don't sit up by the age of two, they never will." This was meant to scare me, and it did—I believed it for a short time. But my natural skepticism kicked in, I wondered how she knew this, and I asked myself questions like, "Would this be true for *all* children with cerebral palsy? Has someone *studied* children with cerebral palsy to prove this? What if my son is different? What if Benjamin can't sit up by the age of two, because he can't get his muscles or coordination going right, but then at age three, his muscles and coordination are working better—so is the PT saying it would be *impossible* for Benj to sit up at three if that's when his body has learned to do it?" The PT's "fact" didn't make sense, and I realized it was a bit of nonsense, a theory, or a generalization. Did she learn it in college, had she figured it out on her own, or heard it from someone else? I don't know, but she presented it to me as truth with a capital T—and it makes me cringe to think of how many other "facts" have been reported to parents which have no evidence to back them up.

I'm no expert on the brain, just a mother who tries to use her common sense. There are, however, experts who use more than common sense to effectively challenge and debunk the FIRST THREE YEARS theory (several books of interest on this and similar topics are included in the Bibliography).

In *The Myth of the First Three Years*, author John T Bruer, Ph.D., explains how the MYTH was born—through a little research, a lot of assumptions and generalizations, and mass promotion—and then he thoroughly debunks it. In short, *there is no "new brain science"* to support the belief that the FIRST THREE YEARS represent a crucially-important "window of opportunity." After reading Bruer's book, parents can take a deep breath and relax, knowing their babies will do just fine, thank you, without "extra" help!

Bruer describes several studies of different Early Intervention programs—non-disability related, disability-related, and Head Start—which indicate that the IQ scores of children in those programs *do* rise a few points in the early years of public school, but by eighth grade (in one study) or by age 15 (in another study), *this increase disappears.* Another study of children who were born prematurely showed similar long-term results—that is, the Early Intervention programs had no effect on a child's intelligence.

What *did* have a long-term effect on children's development? *Mothers!* Bruer writes, "...the mother's IQ was a more powerful factor in explaining a child's performance...Maternal characteristics, either genetic or *as provided in home environments,* had a larger impact [by the time the child reached age] 12 than did the Early Intervention program." (Italics added.) *Go, Moms!!!!*

Bruer is not against early childhood education, per se. He does, however, express concern about government policies that create Early Intervention programs, costing billions of taxpayer dollars, which are based on the MYTH instead of *credible evidence*, and which do not actually generate the outcomes such programs advertise. In addition, accepting the MYTH, "...can weaken our willingness and resolve to aid older citizens...If we take the MYTH to heart, it

---

FROM *MISEDUCATION:*
PRESCHOOLERS AT RISK
BY DAVID ELKIND

"...the choice of the term 'Head Start' for [programs designed for disadvantaged young children] was an unfortunate one, inasmuch as...it suggests that education is a race... Education is not a race A child who learns to read at age three has in no way 'won' over a child who learns to read at age six or seven...There are no finish lines...Learning and education are lifelong processes that come to an end only when we do.

"...e d u c a t i o n a l programs intended for school-aged children are being appropriated for the education of young children...[which ignore] how young children learn and how best to teach them."

seems to follow that if we can't help children by age 3, then we can't help them at all...[this] weakens the policy case for supporting programs and interventions to assist older children and citizens." The evidence throughout his book shows that all of us continue to learn throughout our lifetimes, and there are many older children and adults who could benefit from more opportunities to enhance their learning.

Bruer has this advice for parents: "There is no research on how different kinds of day care or preschool affect a child's brain...The first years do not last forever in the strong, formal sense of a critical period... Parents should realize that children thrive in a wide variety of physical and cultural environments and learn and benefit from experiences throughout their lives. *Being highly critical and skeptical of any claims to the contrary* is one of the best things parents could do for their children." (Italics added.)

One of my concerns about Early Intervention Services is the unspoken assumption that parents are somehow not competent to raise their children without professional assistance. In EI Services, the child's diagnosis triggers this *assumption:* the parents don't "know" about developmental disabilities, their children are *already* considered to be at-risk, and they'll be at even greater risk if professional intervention is not started *immediately* (as the "babies can't wait" slogan reminds us). In Head Start programs, a family's income is the trigger: "poor children" are already considered to be at-risk, and their "poor parents" don't have the smarts to raise them properly, so professional intervention is necessary to prevent these children from being at greater risk.

This mindset is abhorrent to me—it's patronizing and arrogant. Who has the right to judge parents who happen to have a child with a disability and/or who happen to be poor? Aren't there plenty of parents of children *without* disabilities and parents who are in the middle-income and even the high-income groups who are terrible, neglectful, and ignorant when it comes to raising their children? Don't we all know people who probably should have never had children? Yet no one presumes these parents are incompetent; no one tells *them* they should effectively relinquish control of their children to experts furnished by the state! And whether we like to admit it or not, that's essentially what happens within government-funded programs. No, the state doesn't literally remove our children from our homes and take physical control of them, but it does exert great influence over children and families—in the form of Service Coordinators and other providers—not to mention "watching" what goes on in our lives and recording the information in its files. I am greatly concerned about the level of government influence and interference in our private lives. And there's the rub, of course: if we accept government help, we also must accept the lack of privacy and self-direction that are by-products of government Services.

So I appreciate Bruer's thoughts on this subject: "Rather than focusing on changing children's brains, we should think more about changing parents' brains and improving their and their children's lives through job training, adult literacy programs, and appropriate continuing adult education. We might do better by transforming our culture into one that recognizes that anyone, at

NATURAL SOURCES OF HELP

Instead of going to professionals in the Service System, we can find the help we need from the natural supports in our communities. The best source may be other parents of children *who have similar values and beliefs as yours: children with disabilities are children, first, and they need to lead Real Lives.* Other sources include disability advocacy groups (including those populated by adults); general parenting resources; church groups; and others, including our own family members.

If your mother, your husband, or others close to you have been saying, "Relax, everything will be fine," listen to them—they're right!

any age, can benefit from education than by transforming our culture into one based on the notion that children belong to the community or the state, and not to the parents."

Some could say that Head Start and Services for young children with disabilities are doing what Bruer recommends since they include a "parent training" component. And, yes, parents may receive instruction, information, and more. But this occurs *only as a result of* their children receiving Services. It would be nice if parents could simply receive adult education specific to their needs. But that's obviously not enough: the government must also get its hands on the *children* of certain parents, and the sooner the better!

All parents—not just those who are poor or have children with disabilities—could benefit from adult education to meet their specific needs, to enable them to better parent their children. The better parent I am, the better my children's lives will be.

The FIRST THREE YEARS mentality can trigger great stress in families. How can parents *not* feel pressure when the "babies can't wait" theme is everywhere? And now some agencies are using a "families can't wait" mantra. Babies *can* wait! And so can families! Each family needs the time, privacy, and autonomy to be a REAL FAMILY. When the focus is to "hurry-up" lest we miss the *theoretical* "window of opportunity," the stress and tension are almost unbearable. While parents are busy getting all the Interventions and Services offered to their children, they're missing out on precious family experiences.

Now, back to declaration #1. Do Early Intervention Services fulfill the intent of the law to "enhance the development of infants and toddlers with disabilities" and "minimize their potential for developmental delay"? I don't know if we have the answers to these questions. As I previously mentioned, many parents and children probably *do* receive some benefits from EI Services, which may "enhance" a child's development, but EI Services are not the only source of that help. And it's debatable whether EI Services minimize a child's "potential for developmental delay." In general—based on the stories of parents and the philosophy of the Service System ("once in the System, always in the System" in most instances), the vast majority of children who receive EI Services continue to have developmental delays (as judged by professionals) and thus, continue to "need" Services, so toddlers "graduate" to Special Ed Preschool Services.

(2) To reduce the educational costs to our society, including our Nation's schools, by minimizing the need for special education and related services after infants and toddlers with disabilities reach school age.

Did you know your baby or toddler with a disability is seen as a potential financial burden on our society? But if EI Services can "fix" your child quickly enough, maybe he won't need Special Education Services when it's time for public school, and then he won't cost the schools and our society so much money. What do you think of that? The very first time I read this part of the law I was appalled that my son and millions of other babies with disabilities were perceived this way. But the more I learned, I realized this is a pervasive attitude in

> "The FIRST THREE YEARS mentality can trigger great stress in families. How can parents *not* feel pressure when the 'babies can't wait' theme is everywhere? And now some agencies are using a 'families can't wait' mantra. Babies *can* wait! And so can families! Each family needs the time, privacy, and autonomy to be a REAL FAMILY."

the Service System. Children and adults with disabilities "use" taxpayer dollars, and so are seen as financial burdens. Simultaneously, hundreds of thousands of people who provide Services are dependent on our children and others with disabilities for their jobs. The "disability business" is quite an industry!

But do Early Intervention Services "reduce the educational costs to our society, including our Nation's schools"? The answer is "probably not," since the majority of children who receive EI Services are said to be in need of Special Ed Services when they reach school age.

(3) To maximize the potential for individuals with disabilities to live independently in society.

The estimated 70 percent unemployment rate of adults with disabilities in our country seems to indicate EI Services have had no effect on this hoped-for outcome. If one is unemployed, it's hard to live "independently"!

In all fairness, Federally-mandated EI Services have been provided nationwide only since 1986, so the first group of children who received these Services would now be 18 to 21 years of age, and data for this group is not available (but a dab of info is available; see box). Some states, however, *did* begin providing EI Services before the Federal mandate in 1986. Nevertheless, according to the 2000 U.S. Census, the unemployment rate of people with disabilities has not changed since at least 1990 (some employment experts say it hasn't changed for 30 years)—and this is despite (1) the passage of the Americans with Disabilities Act (in 1990) which prohibits discrimination based on disability in employment and other areas, and (2) the addition of transition services to IDEA for high school students with disabilities (also in 1990). Many factors contribute to the static unemployment rate. But in the opinion of many (including me), it demonstrates that the Services provided to individuals with disabilities aren't working.

(4) To enhance the capacity of families to meet the special needs of their infants and toddlers with disabilities.

As previously mentioned, EI Services probably *do* have some positive effects on parents' abilities to meet the needs of their children with disabilities. But, again, EI Services are not the only source of such help. Moreover, this rationale assumes—again—that parents aren't capable on their own: it's assumed professional intervention is needed by parents.

It seems the four goals of IDEA for EI Services are not being met. Yes, many children and families are being served and receive some benefits. But is that enough to call EI Services a "success"? If this were a company that didn't come close to meeting its goals, it would be out of business. Not so, however, with government programs. What's new?

What might happen if, at the very first meeting between parents and an EI Service Coordinator, the Coordinator whipped out a paper that included the four IDEA goals for EI Services, and the Coordinator reviewed each with the parents, saying something like:

A few years ago, I met a graduate student who was in the early stages of a research project to determine the long-term effectiveness of EI Services. Her mission: to track young adults who had received EI Services. At the time of our conversation, she had contacted about half of the people on her list. She was dismayed to learn that the vast majority of these young adults were still living at home, had not attended college or trade school, and had not held a job. Most had aged-out of high school Special Ed Services and were sitting home, doing nothing. Did EI Services have a positive long-term effect on their lives?

We need to provide you with EI Services because with *our* help, your baby's development will be *greatly enhanced* and the potential for developmental delay will be minimized. And because of our help—hopefully—your child won't need Special Ed Services later on, which would cost lots of money to our society and our Nation's schools. We also anticipate that, because of our help, your child will be able to live independently when he's an adult. We're not really sure *how* to influence his life that far into the future since he's just a baby right now, but we all know how very critical these first three years are, right? Finally, our help will also *enhance*—yes, *enhance* (we really like that word)—your family's capacity to meet your child's needs! Now, in all fairness, we can't prove that we've achieved any of these goals with other children, and we don't know, for sure, if we'll achieve *any* of these goals for your child, but you and your child will get *some* benefits—so why not give it a go? Sign right here, please, and we'll get started!

Full disclosure is required by the seller when we buy a house, a car, and other products. Even sweepstakes companies who *give away* prizes must disclose all the rules, regulations, and odds of winning to entrants. Shouldn't people who may have a profound influence on our families' lives also provide full disclosure—the "whole story"—to the best of their knowledge?

Early Interference?

"Vicky's" precious daughter, "Alana" was born with several conditions, any one of which qualified her and her family for EI Services. Like many others (including me, at one time), Vicky jumped into Services with both feet. Because Alana had three different labels, she received about three times the amount of Services to meet her very unique needs. Alana had, in the vernacular, specialists out the wazoo! And Vicky was delighted—at first.

> MORE CHILDREN SUFFER FROM INTERFERENCE THAN FROM NON-INTERFERENCE.
> *Agatha Christie*

When Alana was two, Vicky read the first edition of this book, then sent me an Email that brought tears to my eyes. "I'm just now realizing that I never really bonded with my baby. There was too much going on her life; too many people providing Services—in our home, the therapy clinic, at doctor's offices, the genetics clinic, and more. It seemed we got all the help we could possibly get for her, *but I feel like I don't know my daughter.* Thanks to your book, we're cutting back on Services and I'm going to spend time with my two-year-old, like I should have done when she was a tiny baby."

It's estimated that each letter sent to a U.S. Senator or Representative represents the opinions of at least 30 other constituents. I don't know if this same rule of thumb can be applied to the letters I receive from people who have bought my book, visited my web site, or attended one of my presentations. But if so, it is heartbreaking to consider how many other parents don't feel they had the time and the opportunities to bond with their precious sons or daughters because Services interfered with this very important time in a family's life.

As I've described previously, the schedule of Services—Traditional Therapies, interventions, etc.—can disrupt a family's schedule, affecting everyone in the family, not just the child with a disability and the parents. I'm sure EI Service Coordinators and Service Providers don't intend for this to happen, but it happens anyway. In many cases, parents may be hesitant to speak up about this. Some are fearful they'll be perceived as "ungrateful," while others are afraid to challenge those in authority, lest they be "written up" or their child's name gets dropped to the "bottom of the list."

In Chapter 4, I described the FOLLOW THE LAW mentality, which affects many parents whose children receive EI Services. Some are hesitant to talk to EI professionals about reducing and/or changing the Service Schedule: they believe they have to take "all or nothing." But the law is very clear on this. Section 639 (a) (3) of IDEA states that parents have the right to "determine whether they, their infant or toddler, or other family members will accept or decline any early intervention service...without jeopardizing other early intervention services."

However, the *intent* of the law and the *reality of its implementation* are two different things. Many parents have shared their personal experiences about trying to reduce and/or change Services, only to be warned that doing so might cause their children to lose their "slots." In other cases, the response wasn't quite as definitive: no direct warnings were given, but parents felt the EI professional "disapproved" of the parents' desires.

Parents are the only ones who can judge if Early Intervention becomes Early Interference. Each family is unique, and what seems the "right" amount or type of Services for one family may be very "wrong" for another family.

Birth of Dependence and Loss of Community Connections

Whether or not we're aware of it at the time, many parents become dependent on EI professionals and in the process, mothers (primarily) and fathers may also cut themselves off from the natural supports they have in their communities. Fortunately, some EI Service Provider agencies have recognized this unintended negative outcome and have taken steps to reverse the situation and/or prevent it from happening in the first place. Let's look at what's involved in this birth of dependence and loss of community connections.

First, parents may quickly begin to feel more comfortable around EI professionals and/or therapists than their extended families, friends, neighbors, or others who provide natural support. Parents feel the EI folks "understand" what they're going through, while others (they think) don't. Also, parents learn therapeutic jargon, and the ability to converse fluently with EI professionals in this new language provides a certain level of comfort—they feel they "belong" in the group of people who provide EI Services, while they may feel like "outsiders" within their extended families and/or circle of friends.

Many parents are not aware that *their* actions may be at the root of this dilemma. I know; been there, done that. When my son was receiving EI Services, there were times I was really uncomfortable with all the Services and the focus on my son's perceived "deficits." But simultaneously, I often felt more

BETTER EI SERVICES:

Parents lead, EI providers follow.

EI Providers ask, parents tell.

And EI Providers
—maximize attention on a child's strengths, and minimize attention on a child's perceived deficits;
—share info on assistive technology and other TOOLS for success;
—reinforce the importance of inclusion and the use of generic services and natural supports;
—ensure all Services are provided in natural environments;
—ensure they don't create parental dependence;
—support, not supplant, parent's autonomy and self-direction; and
—help parents see the long-term view of their child's life, along with alternatives to the System across the lifespan.

In the best-case scenario, EI Providers would be almost invisible, and parents would always feel competent.

comfortable in the presence of my son's Service Providers because we "spoke the same language." I didn't realize at the time that any feelings of "distance" from my own family and friends were the result of *my actions,* such as not sharing information with them and giving them opportunities to learn. I felt cut-off from those who were closest to our family, but I was actually the one who was shutting them out of our lives.

In many families, the dependence begins to grow as parents look to EI professionals, therapists, and others in the System for more and more guidance. Some parents no longer trust their own instincts, while others don't want the responsibility for making decisions about their child—and there are many scenarios in between. In any case, the outcome is usually the same: parents cede a certain level of responsibility for their children to others and they look only to the Service System—instead of the natural supports in their communities—for assistance.

In 2002, a friend who lives in another city in Colorado and who works in EI Services called to ask a question: "Kathie, I'm seeing some things here in Colorado that I'm concerned about, and I'm wondering if it's just happening here or if you see it in other states, too. More and more parents of young children seem to care more about getting Services than about ensuring their child and their families are included in their communities." I had to admit that this seemed to be happening in many areas of the country—it still is, and I'm not sure why. Is it because parents of young children want as many Services as possible in the hopes their children will be "fixed"? Is it because they don't understand the value of inclusion in the community for their children's long-term success? If so, does this occur because EI professionals and/or others promote the importance of Services over inclusion in the community? I don't know.

> **SEGREGATION BEGETS SEGREGATION;**
>
> **INCLUSION BEGETS INCLUSION.**
>
> A child who is included is more likely to stay included; a child who is segregated is more likely to remain segregated.

But like my friend, I'm also concerned about this, for dependence on the Service System seems to go hand-in-hand with isolation in one's own community; and the greater dependence, the greater isolation. If, however, we use the natural supports in our community to meet our children's and families' needs (which are described later in this chapter and in Chapters 6 and 7), our children will be included from the beginning. As many parents have learned, segregation begets segregation, and inclusion begets inclusion. Put another way, children who are included tend to stay included, while children who are isolated and/or segregated tend to stay that way, too. You might not have ever thought about it this way, but inclusion is the default position. When children with disabilities are born, they're born included. They become excluded, segregated, and/or isolated when parents follow today's CONVENTIONAL WISDOM and use the Service System's special, segregated programs.

Stressful Goals

As part of the Individualized Family Service Plan (IFSP), goals are written for babies and toddlers with disabilities and/or their families. Goals for the child often represent the acquisition of skills and/or developmental milestones. These goals serve as the guide for Traditional Therapies as well as for home programs provided by a Service Coordinator and/or the parent. This is supposed to be helpful, but it can actually cause great stress.

For example, a typically-developing one-year-old can do this-or-that. The IFSP that's written for four-month-old "Tanisha" reflects several of these goals—which everyone hopes she'll achieve by the time she's 12-18 months of age. When Tanisha's parents and the other members of the IFSP team write these goals, they seem to make sense, and Tanisha's parents are eagerly anticipating their daughter's achievement of these goals.

Once these goals were written, however, they effectively took over Tanisha's life. While her parents want to be able to enjoy her, spend time with her, let her be a baby, and rejoice in any and all new things she's doing, the IFSP goals are always a looming pressure. Tanisha's mom is often torn between focusing on doing what needs to be done to ensure Tanisha achieves the goals and doing what Tanisha and her family would rather be doing.

In the best-case scenario, these two would be blended, so Tanisha and her family could do the things that are important to them, while incorporating strategies to achieve the goals. But far too many parents continue to report this isn't the case. Hours of traditional therapy and other interventions take over the child's life and the family's life.

So Tanisha's mother often feels a great deal of (1) pressure when she's not doing the home programs like she's supposed to, (2) guilt if her lack of attention to the home programs results in Tanisha's not achieving the goals, (3) stress, as she's torn between enjoying happy times with her daughter and her other children vs. attending to the therapies and interventions, and (4) fear—what happens if Tanisha doesn't achieve the goals?

On the surface, it appears that IFSP goals are for the sole benefit of our children and families. However, it's important for us to remember that they are, in effect, a medium of exchange with which the EI provider "buys" the EI Service dollars from Federal and state governments. In other words, in order to comply with state and Federal laws—*and receive the money to pay for the Services provided to your child and family*—an EI provider has to file the paperwork which shows the IFSP goals written for your child and family. (The same is true for any other government-funded Services provided to children and adults with disabilities, at any age.) And these goals need to "look good" (on paper, anyway) and represent traditional achievements and/or functional skills (the "able-bodied" standard) *which require the assistance of EI Service Providers.*

What if Tanisha's family wanted an IFSP goal like, "Tanisha will be a happy baby," or "Tanisha and her family will enjoy quality time together and enjoy natural, typical lives." Aren't these the things most of us want? In general, these would not be "appropriate" IFSP goals. First, they don't represent functional skills. Second, Tanisha's family wouldn't need the help of EI Services to achieve these goals. And wouldn't it be wonderful if the EI Service Coordinator said to Tanisha's parents, "You don't need us for these goals—you're competent to achieve them on your own." In the best-case scenario, this would happen. In the worst-case, Tanisha's parents would be told to come up with "real" goals.

Under Federal law, states are mandated to provide—as a minimum—a Service Coordinator to help parents write and implement the IFSP. Some states, however, do more than the Federal minimum; they also provide therapies, family support, and other Services. Often, there's a correlation between the amount of Services and the dependence of parents: the more Services, the greater the dependence. So "more" help may not really be all that helpful!

SHORT-TERM THINKING

No one in the Service System looks at your child with a Whole Life perspective, so it's up to *you* to keep the Big Picture in mind! EI Services are only concerned about your child's life to age three; Special Ed Preschools handle the next couple of years; Special Ed takes over for the next 12 years or so; Adult Services are next. The result? Short-term thinking. In general, no one in EI warns parents to not become dependent on the system, nor do they tell us to stay away from segregated Special Ed preschools: that's "not their job." No one in a segregated Special Ed Preschool warns parents that their children might be segregated for the rest of their school years; that's "not their job," and so on and so on and so on! Before accepting and/or continuing with any given Service, ask yourself if it will lead to your child's success as an adult.

Of *all* the Services provided to children and adults with disabilities, EI Services could be considered the *most progressive* in that they're supposed to be family-driven, culturally competent, performed in natural environments, and more. In practice, some EI providers *are* way out in front of others, and are doing a wonderful job in supporting families' hopes, dreams, and desires to lead REAL LIVES. Others, however, set families up for dependence, operate from a deficit-model paradigm, and provide more interference than intervention.

Before moving on, do you even *like* that word—*intervention?* Do we really want people "intervening" in our family's life? Think about it for awhile.

An Artificial Transition

Federal Special Education law (IDEA) covers children from birth to age 22. Part C of IDEA is specific to children birth to age three (EI Services); while preschool-aged children are covered by those parts of the law that apply to children ages 6-21. (That seems odd, doesn't it? Preschoolers are very different than high-schoolers, but the same legal provisions apply.)

In many states, Services for preschoolers with disabilities are handled by the state's department of education (in the form of your local school district), while Early Intervention Services are often under the direction of a state's health, developmental disabilities, or other human services agency. And this "division of Services" can create dilemmas for children and their families.

Let's say the "Martinez" family has been receiving EI Services on behalf of "Claudia," who is two-and-a-half. The parents know the EI Service Coordinator well, and while things haven't always been perfect, they've been able to work through most issues to their satisfaction. The Martinez parents have become comfortable in their abilities to advocate for what Claudia needs—they know how the EI Service System works.

When Claudia turns three, however, and the Martinez parents are "handed off" to the next level of Services (Special Ed Preschool), it's like they ran headlong into a brick wall! In most states, it's a totally different System, with different rules, different people, different expectations, and more. Most parents have shared stories similar to the fictional Martinez family. EI Services, in many cases, can feel like a snuggly warm blanket. For many families, what should be a joyous occasion—a child's third birthday—turns into a chilling new experience as the warm blanket is ripped away and parents and children are thrust into the cold, bureaucratic maze of the public school system. Of course, this change doesn't always occur on a child's actual third birthday—it generally occurs adjacent to the beginning of the school year during the year the child turns three, when he's eligible for Special Ed Preschool Services.

What makes this all so ridiculous is that the day *before* a child is three and the day *after* (or a week or a month), *he is the same child*—but the funding streams of Services result in him being treated like he's almost a different person!

So I have great concerns about the consequences of this artificial transition. We *could* consider it a "real" transition in that a child is "transitioning" from one set of Services to another. But it's *artificial* because there is no similar "transition" for children who do *not* have disabilities. In general, *their* lives change little when they turn three. If they stay home with mom or dad, there might be absolutely no change in their lives. Others, however, might begin attending a neighborhood preschool two or three half-days a week, for the social experience. For children in daycare there is, again, probably no change in their lives when they turn three: they're not treated differently and they're not put into a different environment just because they had a birthday!

And how *about* the birthday situation? Children who *don't* have disabilities have a *birthday party* when they turn three. Children *with* disabilities have a *Transition Meeting and/or an IEP Meeting!* But there's more. This artificial transition can create greater dilemmas, described next.

How Can Segregation Be Helpful?

At age three, many children with disabilities are "placed" in segregated Special Ed Preschool classes, where they're surrounded by other children who have disabilities. I've already discussed how ridiculous it is to put a child who is not yet talking with other children who are also not talking. If we want a child to learn to talk, shouldn't he be surrounded by others who talk? If children who have unusual behaviors are surrounded by others with unusual behaviors, what do they learn? And the examples could go on and on.

In addition, we put very young children with disabilities—children who may be very vulnerable if they don't yet have effective communication or independent mobility—on school buses for a long ride across town. Yet the majority of parents whose children do *not* have disabilities wouldn't dream of putting their little kiddos in the same position!

Some parents argue that their children *are* in inclusive environments: a blended Head Start/Special Ed Preschool classroom. And this does, on the surface, seem to be better than a Special Ed Preschool class *only* for children with disabilities. But remember that *all* children in Head Start have a label of some kind (poverty, primarily) and are considered "needy" or NOT-READY in one way or another! So a Head Start class is still not a typical, inclusive environment.

Other parents claim their children's classrooms are not segregated because (1) there are a few typical peer role models and/or (2) kindergartners or first-graders who do not have disabilities are brought in to the Special Ed Preschool class on a regular basis for "visits." And still other parents report that their preschoolers with disabilities attend two different schools: a segregated Special Ed class for half the day, and a typical preschool or a Pre-K/kindergarten class in the public school for the other half. These efforts reflect good intentions on the part of educators: to ensure children with disabilities are around "typically-developing" children. But this also seems to *prove* that these educators are aware of the dangers of isolating young children with disabilities!

The inclusion of school-aged children with disabilities is covered in detail in the next chapter, but I'll share what IDEA says about least restrictive

> **NATURAL ENVIRONMENTS**
>
> IDEA Part C defines Natural Environments as the home and community settings in which children *without* disabilities participate. It's estimated that 10 percent of children in our country have disabilities (this is called the Natural Proportion). Thus, a Natural Environment is one that includes no more than 10 percent children with disabilities.

environment—and remember that these provisions also apply to preschoolers who are being served by the public school system:

Section 612 (a) (5) Least Restrictive Environment—To the maximum extent appropriate, children with disabilities, including children in public or private institutions or other care facilities, are educated with children who are not disabled, and special classes, separate schooling, or other *removal* of children with disabilities from the regular educational environment occurs only when the nature or severity of the disability of a child is such that education in regular classes with the use of supplementary aids and services cannot be achieved satisfactorily. [Italics added.]

The intent of the law is that children with disabilities *start out* in the Regular Ed environment. But many schools start children out in the *most restrictive setting* (segregated classrooms).

This is, unfortunately, where most Special Ed Preschool *Services* are delivered: in a segregated Special Ed classroom. There is—to me and many others—a severe disconnect in the law when it comes to preschoolers with disabilities. First, the law does *not* instruct school districts to set up "programs"—it says schools are to "provide services." Second, the law says children are supposed to be included in the "regular educational environment," but *there is no such thing* in the public school system because the majority of schools in our society do not have "regular educational environments" for three- and four-year-olds—children this age *don't go to public school!*

Yes, some states are now offering optional pre-kindergarten for four-year-olds, but this is not a nationwide practice (and I hope it doesn't become one!). Are Head Start classrooms considered the "regular educational environment"? No, they're not "open to the public"—admission is "by label" only.

So what *is* the "regular educational environment" for three-year-olds (and four-year-olds in most states) with disabilities? From a common sense perspective—not a legal one—it's actually their homes, a daycare center, or a neighborhood (inclusive) preschool. And some parents have elected to keep their preschool-aged children with disabilities in these natural environments. A few don't even mess with the public school system until they must, knowing *that* time will come soon enough (I was one of those).

Others, however, do "enroll" their children for Special Ed Preschool *Services,* and their children have IEPs, but they do not attend the segregated Special Ed Preschool. Instead, the children are at home or in a neighborhood preschool/daycare setting, and itinerant therapists, teachers, and others take the Services to the child in these natural environments. And this same scenario occurs in some school districts that—for a variety of reasons—*never set up Special Ed Preschool classrooms.* In these districts, young children stay in their natural environments and Services are brought to them.

In general, most school districts make preschoolers with disabilities "go to where the Services are"—and that means segregated Special Ed Preschool classrooms, which are usually similar to a district's kindergarten model. There may be no overt *intent* to segregate children, but this *is* the outcome. In some states, preschoolers with disabilities are expected to attend school for the full

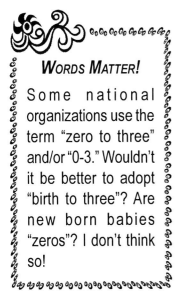

WORDS MATTER!

Some national organizations use the term "zero to three" and/or "0-3." Wouldn't it be better to adopt "birth to three"? Are new born babies "zeros"? I don't think so!

day, five days a week. In other states, the schedule may be half-days, for two or three days a week.

As I'll detail further in Chapter 9, the 1954 *Brown v. Board of Education* Supreme Court ruling outlawed "separate but equal" education. In writing the decision, Chief Justice Earl Warren wrote, in part: "segregation...generates a feeling of inferiority as to [the children's] status in the community that *may affect their hearts and minds in a way unlikely ever to be undone...*"

How can we risk this harm to our children's hearts and minds? Segregating children of color was wrong. *How can segregating children with disabilities be right?*

The Special Ed Preschool Myth

Many parents are led to believe that their child's attendance in a Special Ed Preschool is an automatic ticket to an inclusive kindergarten class. No one actually *tells* us that—we just make that assumption, based on our belief that the purpose of Special Ed Preschool is to help children with disabilities GET-READY for kindergarten. But *unless*—and it's a big unless—the neighborhood elementary school is *already* an inclusive school, very few "graduates" of Special Ed Preschools move into a Regular Ed kindergarten class.

Here's what generally happens: a kindergarten teacher and/or Someone-in-Authority presumes your child is incompetent to be in a Regular Ed classroom because of your child's "history." The kindergarten teacher thinks, "This child has been in that 'special' class where there are only ten children and four or five adults [teachers, therapists, etc.], but I've got 25 students and it's just me!" The presumption is that your child was in the Special Ed Preschool class because he was so "needy" or "special" or "deficient," and *he probably still is.* Therefore, he could not possibly be successful in a Regular Ed kindergarten class.

The decision about where your child will spend his kindergarten year may be made by someone *who has never met your child* and this decision may be made *prior* to the IEP meeting—a violation of the law (placement is supposed to be decided by the IEP Team *at* the IEP meeting and parents are members of the IEP Team). Also, placement is supposed to be based on your child's *individual needs,* not on his "history."

Many, many parents come away from the kindergarten IEP meeting disappointed and shocked because their children are being "placed" in an ungraded, segregated Special Ed classroom. For most parents, never in their wildest dreams did they think this was even a *remote possibility.* And, unless the school is (or becomes) inclusive, they'll be fighting for their children to be in Regular Ed classroom for the next twelve years.

On the other hand, a child who does *not* attend a Special Ed Preschool has a better shot at being in a Regular Ed classroom because the school has no "history" on the child. If, for example, your child stays home with you or attends a neighborhood preschool (and you and your child have no contact with the public school system during this time), your child will not be "known" by

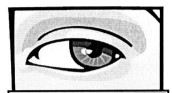

BEWARE OF "OBSERVATION"

Are you aware that when your child is in a Special Ed preschool he may be observed by the school psychologist and others? Before my son's kindergarten IEP meeting, I learned that the school district psychologist (Dr. K) would be in attendance. I didn't see any need for him to be there—he didn't even know my son! I called Dr. K to let him know we had no concerns about Benjamin in Dr. K's "area of expertise," and politely said he didn't need to attend the IEP meeting. He said, "Well, since your son didn't attend the Special Ed Preschool, I wasn't able to observe him on a regular basis like I do the other kids, so I have a couple of questions." I later found out that he did, in fact, routinely visit the class without talking to parents *before or after,* and his observations went into the children's permanent files! Do you know if this has happened to *your* child?

the school. He will not have a *history that will be held against him.* Instead, his history of inclusion in the community (while staying home with mom or dad and just being a "real kid") and/or in a typical neighborhood preschool/daycare setting will be an *asset.* The presumption: if he was successful in these typical environments, he can be successful in a Regular Ed kindergarten classroom.

How Does a Child <u>Fail</u> Preschool?

The segregation of young children in Special Ed Preschool classrooms and the resulting "promotion" to a segregated Special Ed elementary classroom are bad enough. But equally harmful is the practice of retaining children with disabilities in the Special Ed Preschool for another year! How does a child *fail* preschool? Children *without* disabilities do not fail preschool. But of course, we don't call it that. We say things like, "He's *not ready* for kindergarten."

Keeping in mind what I detailed in the previous section, how likely is it that a young child with a disability who has failed Special Ed Preschool will be included in a kindergarten class? The original two years (at ages three and four) have already put a black mark next to his name; spending a *third year* there may doom his future chances for being in an inclusive classroom, as far as Regular Ed teachers are concerned.

The practice of holding children back isn't limited to children with disabilities. Some children *without* disabilities are held back. But we have to question this practice for *any* child. First, let's examine the rationale for retaining a child (with or without a disability) because we believe he's not socially or emotionally ready for the next grade. Let's think about this carefully, using the following scenario: "Thomas" turned five in May, and he's been in the Special Ed Preschool for two years. Based on his age, he should start kindergarten when the new school year begins. But his parents and/or educators have decided he doesn't have the social or emotional skills to move on, so they've decided to hold him back in the Special Ed Preschool. Hmmmm—we want Thomas to "mature," so we're going to keep him in a classroom where he'll be surrounded by children who are one and two years *younger* than him. How, pray tell, will being around younger children help him mature? Isn't it possible that his behavior will stay the same—or even "regress"—since he'll be with children who probably have even *less* maturity? If we really want Thomas to have the social/emotional level of a five-year old, who should he be with? Bingo! Other five-year-olds!

Let's paint another scenario. Five-year-old "Zoe" is in a similar position, but in her case, she's being held back in the Special Ed Preschool because her parents and/or educators believe she hasn't "mastered the curriculum." When this is the justification, we're essentially "blaming" Zoe for not succeeding. But there's another perspective to consider. If the teacher didn't help Zoe master the curriculum last year, what makes us think the teacher is going to do *a better job next year?* It takes two to tango; in this case, a student and a teacher. Why do we always blame the student instead of looking at what the teacher did or did not do?

THE HEARTS OF SMALL CHILDREN ARE DELICATE ORGANS. A CRUEL BEGINNING IN THIS WORLD CAN TWIST THEM INTO CURIOUS SHAPES.

Carson McCullers

And there's one more issue to consider—one that can last a lifetime. How does retention make the child feel about himself? "Janet" is the parent of five-year-old "Ryan," who has a diagnosis of Down syndrome. When I met Janet at a conference, she said she was planning on holding Ryan back in the Special Ed Preschool for another year. She also said this Special Ed Preschool classroom was located in the neighborhood school—*an inclusive school*—so it was a virtual certainty that Ryan would go into a Regular Ed kindergarten classroom. When Janet told me her plans to hold Ryan back, I shared the information described above, and the conversation continued:

Kathie: How will you explain this to Ryan? Will you tell him he failed preschool and that's why he has to do it again?

Janet: Well, no—I wouldn't want him to feel bad about himself. Hmmm—I haven't thought about this. [She wrinkled her brow and thought for a moment.] I guess I'd tell him that since he loves his teacher so much, we thought he'd like to spend another year with her.

Kathie: That might work for now. But what will happen a few years down the road when he realizes that's a lie—that children are held back because they failed. How will he feel about your lying to him?

Janet: I never thought about that, either. I guess it wouldn't be very good.

Kathie: What would *Ryan* want to do if you let him make the decision?

Janet: Oh, he'd want to go on to kindergarten with his classmates.

Kathie: I think so, too. So—how do you think he'll feel about *himself* if you hold him back?

Janet: Hmmm—you're asking me hard questions I've never thought about. [She wrinkled her brow again, sighed several times, and then held back tears.] He probably wouldn't feel very good about himself, would he?

We talked awhile longer (and she did a lot of wondering why educators hadn't brought these issues up), and she decided to talk this over with her husband *and* with Ryan. About a week later, my phone rang, and Janet was on the phone, in tears. She had just come from a meeting with her son's teachers and the school principal, informing them that she wanted Ryan to go on to kindergarten. The teachers and the principal disagreed, informing Janet that Ryan was NOT-READY for the kindergarten curriculum. Janet held firm; she had learned that Special Ed law requires schools to provide curriculum modifications to enable a student with a disability to participate and progress in an age-appropriate Regular Ed classroom.

A tension-filled discussion followed, and Janet finally said, "I believe it's really important to Ryan's social and emotional development for him to move up to kindergarten with his classmates." The principal responded, "Janet—come on! He has Down syndrome—*he won't know the difference!*"

Barely able to contain her hurt and anger while relating this story to me on the phone, Janet said, "How can they think he *wouldn't know*, Kathie? *He's not stupid!* What kind of people are they, that they could think that way?"

> A CHILD WITH AN INTENSE CAPACITY FOR FEELING CAN SUFFER TO A DEGREE THAT IS BEYOND ANY DEGREE OF ADULT SUFFERING, BECAUSE IMAGINATION, IGNORANCE, AND THE CONVICTION OF UTTER HELPLESSNESS ARE UNTEMPERED EITHER BY REASON OR BY EXPERIENCE.
>
> *E.M. Delafield*

They're people who look at children with disabilities and *PRESUME INCOMPETENCE*—and worse. And, sadly, sadly, sadly, in my travels across the country, I learn that attitudes like this principal's are all too common.

I'm sorry to say I don't have an ending for this story. Janet wasn't giving up on this, and we planned some general strategies (which are included in Chapter 9). Later, a mutual friend let me know Janet was making progress, but I don't know what the final outcome was.

Retaining children in school can have very harmful effects on the child, which may last a lifetime. My best friend's husband—they're both teachers—was held back during the elementary years. He once told me that it wasn't until he graduated from college that he stopped feeling he was stupid.

Mike Galvin, the principal at my children's inclusive school, studied the research on retention—which confirmed his beliefs about the harm it can cause—and decided no students would be held back at his school. Chapter 9 includes excerpts from an interview I did with Mike, including more information about retention. If you decide to do some research on retention yourself, you'll probably come across a study or two "proving" that retention is *beneficial*. But consider whose perspective is represented by such a study: educators or students?

Now let's move on to different ways of thinking about the lives of young children with disabilities.

The Big Picture

Dream, dream, dream for your child and his future! Dream the same dreams you had before your child was diagnosed with a disability! Your dreams for your child will lay the foundation for his success. If you have Big Dreams, you will automatically put in place whatever is needed to turn the dreams into realities. To help you think long-term, let's jump ahead in your child's life and work backward.

Do you want your child to become a successful, self-supporting adult? If so, he'll need an academic education in Regular Ed classes so he can enter the workforce after high school and/or go on to college or vocational school (as described in Chapter 9).

In high school, he'll need to be taking the classes that will get him into college or into the workforce. He'll also need to work part-time to earn money, hang out with friends, and do all the other things high-schoolers do to prepare for adulthood.

To be successful in high school, he'll need a successful middle school experience. To be successful in middle school, he'll need a successful elementary school experience. To be successful in elementary school, he'll need a successful early childhood experience.

In addition to success in the public school arena, your child needs to have opportunities to live a REAL LIFE at home and in the community, as described in the previous chapter. And for your child to be successful in any and all environments, he may need a variety of TOOLS (assistive technology devices, modifications, accommodations, and supports) as described in Chapter 6.

What I've just described is the path to a successful adult life. Do you see that this is the same path taken by children who *do not* have disabilities?

As I hope you've figured out by now, if you follow the path of CONVENTIONAL WISDOM as described in Chapter 4, your child and your family will stay in the Special Programs of DISABILITY WORLD, and you can expect your child to be unemployed as an adult, living and working in sheltered, segregated environments, while collecting disability welfare. This, too, could be considered a dream—*a nightmare!*

Let's go back to dreams for a moment. Regardless of what physicians or other "experts" have told you about your child and/or your child's future—*you must dream Big Dreams for your child!* Dream that he'll have playmates and go to birthday parties as a preschooler; dream that he'll have a wonderful time throughout his childhood—learning at school, making friends, and enjoying typical experiences; dream that he'll be able to lead a successful life as an adult. And, yes, he may need lots of support, but so does everyone else!

On a regular basis, while talking with parents after doing a presentation at a conference, a parent has told me something like, "But my child has _____, and there's no way he could ever go to college..." and I no longer try to persuade them. Instead, my reply is, "You're right. *If you don't believe* your child could go to college or trade school, and/or become successfully employed, *it will probably never happen.*" Your dreams are more powerful than any prognosis by a doctor, educator, or anyone else!

Consider this: *our* parents didn't know what *we* might accomplish, but hopefully they dreamed for us so we could dream for ourselves. If you do *not* dream for your child—if you don't let him know what you think is possible for him—*he will not know <u>what's possible</u> and he will not be able to dream for himself.*

But dreaming alone is not enough. You need to ensure your child has opportunities and experiences for success, and these will take place when you follow the REAL LIFE path, which means you'll *treat your child like he doesn't have a disability!* This does not mean you're "in denial" or you pretend he doesn't have a disability. It *does* mean you want him to have the typical experiences as other children his age, so you provide those opportunities for him in inclusive settings at school and in the community; you have high expectations for him; you believe in him (just as you believe in your children who do not have disabilities) and his future; and you give him the TOOLS he needs to succeed, now and in the future (as described in Chapter 6).

If your child leads a REAL LIFE when he's very young, he'll most likely continue to lead a REAL LIFE. If he's included when he's very young, he'll most likely continue to be included. The path to success begins early, with—

> SEE YOUR SONS AND DAUGHTERS; THEY ARE YOUR FUTURE.
> *Proverb of the Oneida Tribe*

Natural Lives for Young Children

While traditional Services for young children with disabilities generally impose an artificial transition around the time a child turns three, *I will not* when describing alternatives to Early Intervention and Special Ed Preschool Services. And I hope you'll recognize the absurdity of treating a child differently just because she's had her third birthday! This time of her life should include a joyous birthday party, not an *upheaval* known as "transition."

In a moment I'll share alternatives to the traditional Services for young children with disabilities—and they're not anything earthshaking. They are, in essence, the same ordinary things parents do with and for their children who do not have disabilities. On the other hand, they're like manna from heaven because they'll enable your child to lead a REAL LIFE! Some people, however, *do* consider these to be earthshaking—they can't imagine a young child with a disability being anywhere but in Special Programs!

First, however, I'm giving you a homework assignment: find out what's happening in the elementary school you hope your child will attend when she turns five. While you're helping your baby, toddler, or preschooler lead a REAL LIFE—a more natural life—you also need to be thinking about kindergarten and beyond.

What's Happening at the Neighborhood School?

If you don't know what's happening at the neighborhood school, begin investigating now. If you have older children at that school, ask them if children with disabilities are in their Regular Ed classrooms; ask other parents; begin volunteering at the school so you can see for yourself; and/or do whatever it takes to find out the status of students with disabilities in that school. Are they in Regular Classrooms all the time? Are they in Resource/Special Ed classrooms? Are there different "levels" of Resource/Special Ed classrooms? (Unbelievably, some schools have segregated *and even more segregated* classrooms, and some districts ship their students with disabilities to other school districts!) Has the school district set up "programs" for children with autism, physical disabilities, etc.? If so, these are most likely segregated Special Ed classrooms, which may *not* be in the neighborhood school.

Find out *where* children with disabilities spend the day. In the worst-case scenario, you might have to call the school district and ask. If this is necessary, do not identify yourself as the parent of a baby or toddler with a disability. They might take your name, open a file on you (whether you know it or not), and then tell you over the phone—without even meeting you or your child—where your child will attend school when he turns five (see box)! This is a clear violation of the law—a child's placement is to be decided by the IEP Team (which includes you). Still, school districts all across the country routinely decide placement based on a child's *diagnosis*—not on his individual needs as determined by the IEP Team. So if you have to call the school to find out, call from a friend's house or a pay phone (the school might have Caller ID), pretend to be a parent moving to the district from another area, and give a fake name!

"PLACEMENT" BY PHONE!

When Benjamin was two, and before I knew anything about Special Ed law, we were thinking about moving from our two-story house into a one-story home in a new suburban neighborhood. A friend lived in this area and her six-year-old son with CP was included in Regular Ed classes. I wanted to learn where the "dividing line" was—to make sure we bought a house in the neighborhood that was served by the school my friend's son attended.

I called the school district to ask about the "boundary lines" because I wanted my kids to go to "ABC" school, and then described my two children. I was shuttled to several different people before being connected to the school district diagnostician. She informed me that my daughter would go to "ABC" school, but my son would go to "DEF" school since he had a disability.

(continued on next page)

If, however, your child is in a Special Ed Preschool in the district, ask the Special Ed Preschool teachers where kiddos in the Special Ed Preschools typically move to: a Regular Ed kindergarten class; an ungraded, segregated Special Ed class; or where? In some school districts, the Special Ed Preschool teachers are considered part of the bigger "team" of teachers in a school, and they might know a lot. In others, they're seen as "outsiders"—not really a part of the "real" school, and they might know very little about kindergarten and above.

If your child is receiving EI Services, ask the EI Service Coordinator and/or Service Providers what they know about the neighborhood elementary school. Under IDEA, EI Services are *supposed* to help a child and his family with the "transition" to Special Ed Preschool and they *should* have information to share with you. But they might not—it depends on whether or not EI Services are provided by the school system or a different agency. There are, unfortunately, turf issues and/or rivalries between different agencies, schools, etc., and parents and children may bear the brunt of their lack of cooperation with one another.

Regardless of what a Special Ed Preschool teacher or an EI Service Coordinator tells you, *make sure to find out for yourself and keep abreast of what's happening at the school until your child turns five!* If you don't, the turf issues mentioned above and/or other issues you're unaware of may end up biting you in the behind. For example, the EI Service Coordinator may assure you that your child *will* be included in the kindergarten classroom when your child turns five. So you take her word for it, and relax until then. But all kinds of things can happen that cause a reversal. On the other hand, the EI Service Coordinator may be unaware that only "these kids" are included, while children who have "this condition" are not. Or, the school might be inclusive today, but the principal retires next year, and the new principal does not want an inclusive school. So do whatever it takes to find out about the school you hope your child will attend, and stay on top of things.

If the neighborhood school is already inclusive, you're probably home-free, as long as it *stays* inclusive! If it's *not* an inclusive school, you'll need to get to work—to influence educators to move toward inclusion. You can begin networking with other parents, and strategies detailed in Chapter 9 will be helpful in this effort.

Whether or not you have older children at that school, begin making yourself known to the school in a very positive way, through volunteering, serving on committees, etc. Details of how this can be accomplished are included in the next chapter, and the strategies are the same, whether your child is school-aged or younger.

Living and Learning in Natural Environments

Where is your young child spending most of her time today? And what is she learning *in* and *from* these environments?

Are young children with disabilities learning in segregated environments such as Special Ed Preschools, Early Head Start, Head Start, and/or similar settings? Yes, they may learn their colors, numbers, pre-reading skills, and

(cont. from previous page)

I protested slightly, telling her about my friend's son. She blew that off, telling me she could only talk to me about my children. Again, I knew nothing about Special Ed law, but it didn't seem right that my children couldn't attend the same school, so I pressed some more, asking if there was any recourse. "Could I go to the School Board to get permission for my son to attend the same school as his sister," I asked. "No," she replied and added that these were "school rules" and there was nothing I could do about it!

I didn't learn about Special Ed law until a year later (Benj's EI Service Coordinator never told me anything about it). And when I *did* learn the facts, I realized this diagnostician was breaking the law by telling me where Benj would go to school. She—not the IEP Team—was deciding placement. And never once during the phone call with her did she ever mention anything about the law, the IEP process, or anything else!

more. But many may also learn unusual behaviors from other children with disabilities; they may not be exposed to children without disabilities who are walking, talking, and doing other typical age-appropriate things; they may get a skewed view of the world; they may be with educators who have low expectations for them; and participation in these Special, segregated environments can effectively "brand" them in the eyes of future educators.

Children with disabilities can learn just as much or *more*—and they will *not* be subjected to the risks described above—in the natural environments of their own homes, at grandma's house, and/or in typical preschool/daycare settings. *You are your child's first and best teacher,* and you can also teach others, as needed, such as the teachers at a neighborhood preschool/daycare center. If and when additional help is needed, you can call on specialists (therapists, EI/Special Ed Preschool personnel) for consultation. The other great benefit of a child remaining in natural environments, as I've mentioned previously, is that the child's "history" of inclusion will be an asset when it's time for him to go to public school.

If you're ready for your child and family to move out of DISABILITY WORLD and take your rightful places in the REAL WORLD, you'll need to carefully consider changes to the Services your child currently receives. The last section of this chapter details how to go about making these changes.

> THE MOTHER'S
> HEART
> IS THE
> CHILD'S
> SCHOOLROOM.
> *Henry Ward Beecher*

Now I want to take a moment and share my very personal bias. If you're not already a stay-at-home mom, I hope you'll do whatever it takes to become one! I believe, with all my heart, that young children (with and without disabilities) need to be at home with mom or dad—and *we* need that, too! I realize studies have shown that children who attend daycare during the early years "turn out fine"—and they probably do. But when children are put in full-time daycare, we miss out on so much of their childhoods!

When my husband and I got married, we were in agreement that when we had children, I would quit work and stay home with them until they began kindergarten. To ensure this would happen, we made the decision to live on his salary alone—mine was put in savings—so that when I *did* quit work, we would already be accustomed to living on one salary.

When our children were born, I *was* able to be a stay-at-home mom, and I treasured every moment! Yes, there were times when I got tired of changing diapers on two bottoms and times when we wished we had more money. But any and all tensions were routinely eclipsed by the smiles and laughter of my children; the hugs and kisses given and received; the pleasures of helping them learn new things; the joy of watching them master some new feat; the comfort of napping with my babies; and so much more.

In addition, *we* wanted to be the primary influence on our children's lives. When children are in daycare, they're shaped by the values, attitudes, and language of others. If parents only see their children for a few minutes in the morning, and a few hours in the evening before bedtime, how *can* they be the primary influence on their children's young lives?

If you're a single parent, not working probably isn't a choice. But you might be able to change your work schedule or change jobs in order to spend more time at home with your young child. Perhaps you could work from home, one way or another—or start a small home business.

If you're a two-parent family and both are working, what would it take for one of you to stay home with your child/children? My husband and I have had many financial ups-and-downs—I know what it's like to be poor and I know what it's like to be middle-class. (I doubt if I'll ever know what it's like to be rich, but that's OK—our family is rich in far more important things than money!) We've "gone without" many times, so I could be home with our children. What are you willing to give up, in exchange for time with your children? Can you change jobs? Get different work schedules? Can one of you quit work to stay home? This might mean moving to smaller house or getting rid of two expensive cars or....?

In some families, both parents may work so they, and their children, will "have more." In my experience, your children would rather have more of you, than more "stuff." And, frankly, some of *our* lean years were the best years for all of us: when we had no money for movies or "extras," we got our children involved in brainstorming what we could do for free and how we could shop smarter for groceries and other things. Those were wonderful times that helped us grow even closer—and our children learned life-lessons that have served them well.

With both of my children young adults today, I look back on their early years and am eternally grateful that I didn't miss the precious moments that came only once. If at all possible, I don't want *you* to miss those moments in your child's life! And now, I'll step off this particular soap box.

Learning at Home

If your young child from birth to age five can stay home and learn with you (or your spouse or other stay-at-home family member) *rejoice!* Enjoy this precious time and celebrate the opportunities you'll both have for learning. *You* will learn more about your child than you knew before and your child will learn from you—his colors, numbers, and the alphabet, and valuable life lessons *only you can teach!*

Read to your child, sing to him, play with him, and follow his lead. Use the television as a supplement, not as an electronic baby-sitter. If you need inspiration on activities to do with your child, visit your local library, search the Internet, access parent resources in your community (including Park and Rec, a school PTA, etc.), and/or talk with other parents.

Your child—like all children—is a natural-born learner. A trip to the grocery store is rich with learning opportunities about colors, shapes, numbers, money, and so much more. Ditto involving your child in cleaning the house, doing chores, taking care of a pet, and other ordinary activities that are part of our household routines. Your child will also learn so much from brothers and sisters—children are the best teachers of other children!

> Treat your child like he doesn't have a disability! Do what it takes to ensure he has a wonderful, typical childhood! *And Dream Big!*

When your child is about four—and if she's interested—get her involved in community activities, and throughout her childhood, make sure she's a fully participating and contributing member of your family (as described in Chapter 7). These experiences will contribute to her overall growth, development, and success. If your child has learned how to get along with others, how to be responsible, how to ask for the help she needs, and how to be self-directed, she'll have a strong foundation for success in kindergarten and beyond.

If you're a stay-at-home mom or dad, does your child *need* to go to preschool? I say no. My daughter, Emily, did not go to preschool (although I did use Mom's Day Out as the babysitter for her on the days I took her little brother to therapy). My son, Benjamin, went to preschool for social reasons—so he could be in natural environments with children who *did not* have disabilities, since he was in the unnatural environments of therapy clinics during all the years of his "therapy career." And Benj's preschool experiences were very typical: as a three-year-old, he went Tuesday and Thursday mornings; as a four-year-old, he went on Monday, Wednesday, and (sometimes) Friday mornings. And if he didn't want to go on a particular day, I didn't make him go!

Your child can learn just as much from you, at home and in the community, as he would at preschool. If you want him to go for social reasons and/or so that you'll have a break, go for it—*but do not let anyone pressure you* into enrolling your child in any preschool. Follow your heart; listen to your child, and check out the suggestions for typical preschool/daycare settings in the next section.

If you need the support of other parents, identify other stay-at-home moms or dads and their children who live nearby, or join (or start) a neighborhood play group that meets on a regular basis. Your child will benefit from being around typical children, and parent-to-parent friendship and support will be helpful to you.

If you're already friends with other parents of children with disabilities, maintain and nurture those friendships, but *do not* start a play group only for children with disabilities! This would be no different than the segregation practiced by the System, right?

Learning at a Typical Preschool/Daycare

You, as the expert parent, can teach the preschool/daycare staff what they need to know about your child and you can also instruct them to *listen to your child and learn from her,* as well.

It's critically important that your child be in the age-appropriate class: if she's three, she needs to be in the three-year-old class, whether or not she's exactly like other three-year-olds. Some parents are told a preschooler who is still in diapers cannot be in a preschool class—this issue is covered later in this chapter.

When talking with the staff about your child, remember to focus on her strengths, and reframe "problems" into "needs," as described in Chapter 5. If you want a preschool/daycare to welcome and respect your child, present her as the wonderful child she is, not as a "bundle of problems." Do not share information that will create negative perceptions about your child—like the yucky Developmental Age garbage, assessment results, or similar information. Educate the staff about any AT devices your child uses, as well as the supports, modifications, or accommodations she needs to successfully interact with other children and teachers, and to participate in and make progress in activities.

Just as I'll describe in the next chapter about school-aged children, the teacher in a neighborhood preschool/daycare needs to see your child as a typical child who is three (or whatever his actual age is), and who is competent, expected to participate and succeed, and more. This is crucially important, for your child's peers in that environment will model the teacher's behavior. For example, if the teacher treats your four-year-old child like a baby, if she excuses your child from participating in activities, and so forth, the other children will not see your child as an equal peer and will not become friends with him.

Make a point to meet other parents, by Hanging Out with Intent when you take or pick up your child. Begin inviting your child's classmates over to play, and make the time to establish friendships with their parents. They'll be excellent allies and supports when it's time for your child to go to kindergarten, especially if the neighborhood elementary school isn't already inclusive. These parents, as well as the preschool/daycare staff, can provide "testimony" to educators at the public school regarding your child's success in an inclusive setting. In addition, some of your child's peers in the typical preschool/daycare may be in your child's kindergarten classroom when he turns five, and this can be an awesome contribution to your child's success. These friends will know how to help your child naturally, because they learned how in preschool/daycare, and they can literally teach the kindergarten teacher helpful strategies to ensure your child's success!

Blending Special Ed and Typical Preschool/Daycare

Alternatively, and as described previously in this chapter, some parents enroll their children in typical preschools/daycare centers (and pay the tuition themselves), then have Special Ed Preschool *Services* provided to their children at the typical preschool. An itinerant therapist and/or Special Ed Preschool teacher, for example, visits the typical preschool/daycare on a regular basis, as determined by the IEP Team, to provide consult services to the preschool/daycare staff.

If you go this route, make sure the Services provided to your child promote his inclusion. For example, instead of the itinerant therapist pulling your child out of class and/or taking him to the back of the room to "do therapy," she could work with a small group of children (which includes your child), doing exercises or activities that are beneficial to your child, and which are enjoyable and relevant to *all* the children. (Chapter 9 has additional information about this issue.)

If you go this route, keep in mind that, even though your child is not in the segregated Special Ed classroom, because he's receiving Special Ed *Services,* he'll be "known" by the school district and will have a "history." This history will be "good" in the sense that it will show your child was successfully included in a typical preschool/daycare, but it will also include Special Ed "stuff" that

NO ONE-ON-ONE

Your child will not need a one-on-one aide in a typical preschool/daycare.

Teach your child how to ask for help from whoever is closest, the way we did with Benjamin, so he can receive help from his peers. Also, you can educate the staff on how to help your child. Yes, your child might need more help than other children, but this can be accomplished without a "personal aide." There are many dangers of this practice, which I describe in the next chapter.

Some preschoolers with disabilities are riding school buses several times a day to get from daycare to the Special Ed Preschool, and then back to daycare. We wouldn't expect most *ten-year-olds* to be able to handle such a daily schedule, but somehow we expect three- and four-year-old children with disabilities to be able to do this!

has the potential to be a negative influence on his inclusion in a Regular Ed kindergarten classroom. If you learn what's going on in the neighborhood elementary school, you'll probably be able to figure out what strategies will be most helpful to ensuring your child is included in kindergarten.

Some young children with disabilities attend a segregated Special Ed Preschool class *and* typical preschool/daycare. This might seem like a great idea, but the positive influences of the natural environment don't always outweigh the negative consequences of the segregated environment.

"Ellen" enrolled her son, "Phillip," in daycare when he was two, and things were going fine. When he was three, Ellen followed CONVENTIONAL WISDOM and enrolled her son in the Special Ed Preschool. Monday through Friday, she took Phillip to the daycare center early in the morning. Four days a week, the Special Ed Preschool bus picked Phillip up after lunch and returned him to the daycare center in the late afternoon.

I asked Ellen *why* she chose to enroll Phillip in the segregated Special Ed Preschool. At first, she didn't know what to say—no one had ever asked her this question. In a round-about way, she eventually explained that she thought she *had* to send him ("I have to follow the law."). She was shocked when I told her she did not—it was her choice. This "news" opened the floodgates, and Ellen began describing several negative outcomes of her son's attendance at the segregated Special Ed Preschool. (Like many other parents, Ellen felt she should never criticize any Services—she thought she should always feel "grateful." She felt relieved that I had "opened the door" for her to express her honest feelings.)

Ellen noticed that Phillip was picking up unusual behaviors from other children with disabilities. Also, the daycare teacher reported that Phillip became tense at lunch, in anticipation of the Special Ed bus coming for him, and he was usually agitated and "out-of-control" when the bus brought him back in the afternoons.

Ellen described other concerns, and asked, "Why am I doing this? Phillip does great at daycare—they love him and he's learning and he has friends—so what good is the Special Ed Preschool doing him?" She answered her own question and pulled Phillip out of the Special Ed Preschool.

If a child is already enrolled in a typical preschool/daycare, there's no reason for him to also attend the Special Ed Preschool. Remember: it's your choice! Do not let anyone pressure you into using Special Ed Preschool Services!

But It's Free!

Many parents say they'd like their children to attend an inclusive typical preschool/daycare instead of a segregated Special Ed Preschool, and then add, "But I'd have to *pay* for it and the Special Ed Preschool is *free!*" My usual replies include, "You get what you pay for," and "What would you do if your child *didn't* have a disability? Wouldn't you be paying for his preschool/daycare? Did you do it for your other children?" Most usually answer in the affirmative, but they're reluctant to give up this "freebie."

This is when we know our dependence on the Service System is firmly entrenched, *and this should be seen as a very important wake-up call.* We have been seduced. Are we willing to forego wonderful opportunities for our children to lead REAL LIVES *and* risk all the unintended negative consequences detailed in this chapter, in order to get something that's free? Isn't your child's life—now and in the future—worth more than that?

Would you even *consider* doing the same thing to one of your other children? If, for example, karate lessons were important to your 10-year-old, would you enroll him in *free* karate lessons, if the teacher, the other students, the environment, and/or other aspects of the class might be harmful to him? Or would you (1) make some financial sacrifices in order to pay the tuition of a good karate class, (2) look into options for tuition assistance or tuition reduction, or (3) find a substitute for karate which you could afford, which your son would enjoy, and which would not put him at risk?

We can and should do the same things for our children with disabilities when it comes to figuring out how to afford a quality, inclusive preschool/daycare. Be creative! Ask the preschool/daycare provider about scholarship funds and/or other options to reduce the tuition. Some parents receive a reduction in tuition in exchange for volunteering at the facility. Cut back on other expenses so you can afford the tuition, if necessary.

Finding the Right Preschool/Daycare

Some parents have enrolled their children in Special Ed Preschools only because they could not *find* a typical preschool/daycare that would accept children with disabilities. Others started their children out in typical community settings, but their children were "kicked out." Still other parents have never looked very hard, but they don't think any typical preschool/daycare will accept their child because of the nature or severity of their child's condition. In some cases, this can be a difficult task to achieve, but there are strategies that can work.

In general, follow the steps outlined in "Strategies to Ensure Inclusion" in the previous chapter. I'll reinforce these strategies and add a few ideas that apply specifically to preschool/daycare settings:

- Unless you know for sure that the preschool/daycare routinely includes children with disabilities, *never, ever call and ask,* "Do you take children with disabilities?"

- Investigate/research potential preschools/daycare centers: look in the Yellow Pages; ask other parents where their kids go; drive around and look at places from the outside and get a feel for them; call the Director of the center and ask general questions (make a list and have it in front of you while you're on the phone); and inquire about when you could drop in for a tour. If the answer is "anytime," that's a good sign. If, however, the Director schedules an appointment time, this could be a sign that they'll "get the place ready" for a visitor (not good). On the other hand, this could mean nothing sinister, it may simply represent the Director's desire not to have specific activities interrupted. If you're given an appointment time, use your intuition and decide if you should just "drop by" at a time different than your appointment. Drop-in visits can be very enlightening.

- While you're talking with the Director, she'll probably ask *you* questions—about your child and family. Give basic information, and do not indicate that your child has a disability at this time. When you visit the facility, do not take your child with you. (If the Director asks why you didn't bring your child, make up a plausible excuse: "His grandma took him to the zoo..." or whatever works for you.) Tour the facility, ask more questions, and, again, do not mention your child's disability *at this time.*

- While you're at the facility, look with a critical eye. Are the children happy and having a good time? Are the *teachers* happy and having a good time? Are they kind to the children? Next, imagine your child there—in the age-appropriate class/section. Will the building work for him if he has a physical disability and/or uses mobility equipment? Will the atmosphere work for him, based on his individual needs? What about the outdoor areas? The daily routine? The number of children? The size of the place? Think, "How could my child participate in these typical activities? What will he need in the way of supports, accommodations, modifications, or assistive technology?" Think *that* way, instead of, "My child could never do this."

Once you've found the right place for your child, use your own intuition and best judgment to consider which of the following strategies to use:

- Return for a second visit, sign your child up, and pay the tuition fees. Then show the Director the cutest photo you have of your child, and describe his unique needs and how they can be met successfully at this facility, indicating you'll provide all the help and training the director and teachers will need. If you think the actual diagnosis will frighten the director, don't mention it. Just talk about your child in terms of his strengths (paint a wonderful picture) and needs (as detailed in Chapter 5), answer any questions the director might have and reassure her in whatever ways are necessary.

- Return for a second visit *with your child*, and follow the other ideas above (making sure to speak respectfully in front of your child, include him in the conversation, and let him speak for himself as much as possible). Our children's sweet faces and charming personalities can often negate any fear or discomfort generated by their disabilities. Reassure the director that you'll help the staff learn how to best help your child, sign your child up, and pay the tuition.

- Make no second visit, simply sign your child up, and pay the tuition. On his first day, arrive early so you'll have time to speak to the director and/or your child's teacher about his needs.

If, at any point, the Director says, "You didn't tell me your child has a disability," use your own good sense in coming up with a reply. Remember: your child's diagnosis is private information. If *you* feel you're being sneaky or underhanded, this will "come out" in your body language, your words, or your attitude and, in turn, the director will feel she's been lied to or manipulated, and this is not a good beginning. Your response should be friendly and casual, and should indicate that your child's disability is "not a big deal," and his strengths and abilities are what's most important about him. We can sometimes be caught off-guard by questions, and we don't always handle the situation in the best fashion. So as you're meeting preschool/daycare directors during your "investigation," practice how you could respond to this question—if necessary, role play with a family member or friend so you'll feel confident.

It's very important that *you* believe (1) your child has the right to a REAL LIFE; (2) his medical diagnosis is private business; and (3) the information you *are* disclosing—about his strengths and needs—is the same information a preschool/daycare staff needs to know about *other children* in their care. Your attitude, demeanor, words, and body language can have a very powerful influence (positive or negative) on others. Again, if necessary, role-play with a spouse or friend so you'll feel comfortable talking with a preschool/daycare Director.

Once your child is enrolled and attending, do not leave things to chance! You might need to stay with your child for awhile to make sure he's comfortable. If your child is very tearful or scared, this is doubly important. I think it's terribly harmful, not to mention cruel, when we allow children to feel they've been abandoned. Do whatever it takes for your child to feel safe, comfortable, and happy in his new preschool/daycare.

Stay in close touch with the preschool/daycare staff about how things are going. Talk to your child to get his perspective. Stay close to the parents of your child's peers for their wisdom, insight, and support. Anticipate dilemmas that might arise and solve little issues before they become big ones.

The strategies I've described are examples to consider. You might come up with even better strategies, on your own, or with the help of friends, family members, or others who know you, your child, and/or your community. Keep these two things in mind: *expect inclusion* and present your child as the wonderful, precious child he is. Inclusion, in any area of life, is first and foremost *a state of mind.* If you expect your child *can and will be successfully included,* and if you're also sensitive to other people's potential fears about including your child, your friendly, supportive, confident, can-do attitude and your child's shining personality can diminish any opposition.

Child Care Facilities and Non-Discrimination Laws

Now let's look at some legal issues regarding the Americans with Disabilities Act (ADA), Section 504 of the Rehab Act, and child care facilities. Title II of the ADA prohibits discrimination on the basis of disability within programs of state and local governments. So, for example, a child care facility run by a city Parks and Recreation falls within this category. Title III of the ADA prohibits discrimination on the basis of disability within public accommodations (businesses that serve the public). So typical preschools/day care facilities fall under this category. Section 504 prohibits disability discrimination within facilities that receive Federal funds. Most colleges, universities, and medical facilities receive federal funds, so Section 504 would apply to a preschool/daycare located in one of those settings.

A MOTHER SPEAKS

"Kate" knew she didn't want a segregated Special Ed Preschool for four-year-old "Max," who has autism. But at the urging of professionals and other parents of children with autism, she checked out *a private school* for children with autism where ABA and other "autism strategies" were part of the "treatment." Being a wise mother, Kate visited the school and realized it was not the place for her son: "There was no joy or happiness there! The kids weren't laughing or smiling and neither were the teachers! Max has a great sense of humor—he's so funny! I don't want this ABA'd out of him!"

The ADA *does not* apply to religious entities. A preschool/daycare *located within and operated by* a church/synagogue is exempt from these laws. However, some child care facilities are located *on/within* church property, but they are *operated* by a non-church entity, which simply leases/rents the space. These facilities *do* have to comply with the ADA.

In general, a preschool/daycare facility cannot refuse to enroll your child simply because he has a disability. In theory, you could sue such a facility if they discriminated against your child. In practice, however, I wouldn't send my child to a place where he was unwanted, or where the people in charge hated my guts because I sued them! A legal decision might force them to accept my child, but I would worry about my child's safety, wouldn't you?

Under the ADA, a business is not obligated to provide "extra" services. Thus, a preschool can legally refuse to enroll a three-year-old (or older) child who is still in diapers *if* the preschool does not provide this service *to other children.* But here's the important thing to know: if the preschool/daycare center changes the diapers of *any* child (babies, for example), they cannot refuse your three-year-old child just because he's still wearing diapers. So if your toddler/preschooler is still in diapers, look for a preschool/daycare that includes younger children, since they'll have "diaper-changing facilities" and state child care/health licensing for this service, as well.

Making Changes

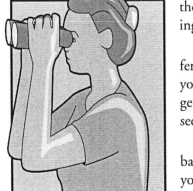

How do you go about making changes to the Services your child is currently receiving, so he and the rest of your family can live a REAL LIFE? Talk things over with your spouse or others you respect, including other parents who may be traveling this new path. Talk to your child. If he's not yet talking, think about how *does* communicate his feelings about the Services he receives. A number of parents have painfully admitted that their children cry when the EI Service Coordinator or therapist arrives, and/or when the parent drives into the parking lot where Services take place. So even children who aren't yet talking, communicate very well. Are we listening?

Think about how you want your child's life and your family's life to be different, and think about what changes will make that happen. Picture the life you want—don't let "what is" or "what has been" get in the way. We can really get stuck in habits of thinking and habits of actions, making it impossible to see *what really is possible!*

Look far into the future and see your child as a successful adult, then go backwards to see what needs to happen now. Your child will be an adult before you know it. It might not seem that way right now, especially if you're in the midst of dirty diapers, bushels of dirty clothes, a house you can't keep clean, and a schedule that's impossible to maintain—but I assure you it's true. And here's something else to consider. If you get the Big Picture in mind (your child being a successful adult) and hold it there from now on, you will automatically begin taking the steps necessary to ensure his success. If, however, you're "sweating the small stuff" (will he walk, talk, make eye contact, read a book, etc.) you'll stay sidetracked, focused on these "problems," and you won't be able to even *see* the Big Picture!

Once you've decided on the changes you want to make (big or little), talk to Service providers about how you want things to change regarding home visits, home programs, the time spent on Services, how and where Services are provided, and other issues. Switching from direct, hands-on Services to a consult or coaching method is an option (as described in Chapter 6). You may decide to cut back on some Services, while keeping others intact for now. Some parents have taken a leap of faith and decided they no longer need *any* Traditional Therapies, EI Services, and/or Special Ed Preschool for their children.

We have inherent wisdom about our children, and we've also learned many valuable strategies from professionals. Our children's needs *can* be met, in our homes and in natural, inclusive activities in our communities, with little or no direct help from experts. If/when help is needed, we can find it in lots of different places. We can call on professionals on an as-needed basis; we can get help from other parents, friends, and family members; we can use the generic services in our community; and more!

Whether you simply make changes or reduce or eliminate Services, put on protective armor and be prepared for an onslaught of criticism. Some Service providers and even family members and friends might think your decision will cause the sky to fall! They might assume a reduction or elimination of Services means your child's needs will not be met. CONVENTIONAL WISDOM has so infected our minds that we believe a person's needs can only be met by the Service System, but you and I know this isn't so.

Making any changes may require courage, determination, and steadfastness. It can be scary to "go without" something we're accustomed to. Being questioned and/or criticized by others can sap our confidence. It's especially difficult if those who you thought were "on your side" (family members and friends) don't support your decision. In my own life, I've learned to state my intentions and if the response is criticism, I end that part of the conversation by changing the subject, and if that doesn't work, I say good-bye for now.

Many parents aren't sure how to "legally" make changes to EI Services or Special Ed Preschool Services. If so, this is a sure sign that Service Providers haven't done a thorough job: they haven't made it explicitly clear that Services are an option, they haven't informed parents how they can initiate changes in the IFSP or the IEP, and/or they may work on the assumption that a child will remain in EI Services or the Special Ed Preschool until the child "transitions" into the next level of Services.

If *changes* in Services are desired, notify the EI Service Coordinator or Special Ed Preschool Coordinator/Teacher that you need to schedule an IFSP/IEP meeting to make these changes. If you're ready to *eliminate* Services, a meeting may not be necessary—instead, write a letter to the EI Service Coordinator or the Special Ed Preschool department, stating your wish to terminate Services, and give the effective date (immediately, the first of the month, or whatever). It's possible the Person-in-Charge may insist that an official meeting be convened. If so, the Team members might try to talk you out of your decision, so take your spouse, a friend, and/or a family member with you for moral support.

Finally, some Service Providers are avid believers of the PRESUMED INCOMPETENT mentality; they believe parents are not capable of raising their children without professional intervention. Thus, when parents decline Services, these Providers believe the parents may be "guilty of neglect." *In a very small percentage of cases,* this can result in Service Providers making a call to Child Protective Services! This is a horrendous situation—and it's a terrible consequence of Big Brother's "interference" in our lives. This probably won't happen to you, but I wanted you to be aware that it *has* happened on rare occasions.

Forewarned is forearmed—so as you're preparing to make changes to Services and/or decline them altogether, talk to other parents about their experiences and think about the Service Providers who are currently in your family's life. Do they seem "the type" to be heavy-handed? Have you, up to this point, felt you could trust them? Do you recall any conversations about other parents making changes and what the Service Provider's response was? Be prepared!

As Mark Twain once said, "It's easier to stay out than to get out." You and your child entered DISABILITY WORLD without knowing it; getting out is a little harder than getting in. But you can do it—you can make whatever changes need to be made in Services so you can take your family's life back. Be strong; be hopeful; listen to the Little Voice in your head; as well as the little voice of your precious child.

I am appreciative of the hard work done by many professionals who provide Services for young children with disabilities and their families. They have the best of intentions and, for the most part, they follow the rules and regulations of EI Services and Special Ed Preschools. But I have also seen the chaos that even some of the best Services can unintentionally generate. I've listened to too many parents painfully share their frustrations about Services taking over the lives of their children and families. I've seen too many tears flow as mothers describe how they want to enjoy their children and believe in their future, but the ongoing assessments that measure their child's "deficiencies" pound another stake in their hearts and their hope. I've heard the anger expressed by parents after hearing one of my presentations on these topics, when they ask, "Why didn't the EI Service Coordinator explain what a segregated Special Ed Preschool was really like?" or "Why didn't the Special Ed Preschool teacher tell me my child's participation in the segregated class would lead to a segregated placement in kindergarten?"

I've also joyously witnessed the metamorphosis of parents as they learn new ways of thinking; realize their children are perfect just the way they are; regain their common sense and feelings of competence; and shed the cocoon of dependence on the Service System for the wings of interdependence and inclusion in the community.

School-aged children—your child will be there soon—will be on the path to success when they learn and grow in inclusive Regular Ed classrooms. That's next.

> THERE CAN BE NO HAPPINESS IF THE THINGS WE BELIEVE IN ARE DIFFERENT FROM THE THINGS WE DO.
> *Freya Stark*

Inclusive Education and Beyond

9

What's so special about Special Education? According to the National Center for Education Statistics (www.nces.ed.gov), the graduation rate for students with disabilities who receive Special Education services is *half* that of students without disabilities. Perhaps the opposite of Regular Education isn't *Special* Education—it's *Irregular* Education. And this must be considered a contributing factor to the estimated 70 percent unemployment rate (and the dependence on government assistance) of adults with developmental disabilities in our country. With all this in mind, I think we can accurately say that for the majority of students with disabilities, Special Education—as it's practiced today—isn't working.

I could find no statistics that would enlighten us as to *why* the graduation rate of students with disabilities is so low, nor statistics that would reveal *how* a student's education (or lack of) contributes directly to the shameful unemployment rate. There are, however, statistics which document where students with disabilities spend most of their time in school, and this may be a contributing factor to the low graduation rate and the high unemployment rate. First, however, let's look at what the Individuals with Disabilities Education Act (IDEA) says about where students are *supposed* to spend their time:

> Section 612 (a) (5) Least Restrictive Environment—To the maximum extent appropriate, children with disabilities, including children in public or private institutions or other care facilities, are educated with children who are not disabled, and special classes, separate schooling, or other *removal* of children with disabilities from the regular educational environment occurs only when the nature or severity of the disability of a child is such that education in regular classes with the use of supplementary aids and services cannot be achieved satisfactorily. [Italics added.]

Did you notice the word "removal"? The intent of the law is that children with disabilities *start out* in Regular Ed classes, with the use of supplementary aids and services. But as millions of parents could testify, many students with disabilities *never* start out in the Regular Ed environment, with supplementary aids and services. Instead, they start out in the *most restrictive settings* (segregated Special Ed classrooms), and are forced to "earn" their way out to a Regular Ed classroom—and most never do.

In traveling across the country, I've heard Special Ed classrooms called by a variety of names: Resource Room, Life Skills Class, Autistic Class, EMR (Educable Mentally Retarded) Class, TMR (Trainable Mentally Retarded)

> THE SCHOOLS OF THIS COUNTRY ARE ITS FUTURE IN MINIATURE.
> *Tehyi Hsieh*

Class, SLIC (Severely Limited Intellectual Capacity) Class, EBD (Emotional-Behavioral Disturbance) Class, and many others. Some of these are classrooms where students with disabilities spend all or most of their day, while others are places students go in and out of during the day.

As I mentioned in Chapter 4, only 46.5 percent of students with disabilities spent 79 percent or more of the day in a Regular Education class. Let's look at some more statistics (for the 2000-2001 school year, from www.nces.ed.gov, Table 53). Of all students ages 6-21 "served in federally supported programs for children with disabilities," 29.8 percent spent 21-60 percent *outside* a Regular Class; 19.5 percent spent more than 60 percent *outside* a Regular Class; and 4.2 percent were in a separate facility. "Outside a Regular Class" is not defined, so we can only assume it means some sort of separate, segregated Special Ed classroom. Interestingly, however, the "History of IDEA" section of the U.S. Department of Education web site (www.ed.gov) proudly states, "The majority of children with disabilities are now being educated in their neighborhood schools in regular classrooms with their non-disabled peers." This statement is purposely vague—for obvious reasons. It does not factually represent the Department's own statistics included here!

Now let's see how the numbers break out by disability category, for the *less-than-half* of students with disabilities who spent 79 percent or more of the school day in a Regular Class:

- Speech/language impairments: 85.6 percent
- Visual impairments: 50.5 percent
- Orthopedic impairments: 46.4 percent
- Developmental delay: 46.4 percent
- Other health impairments: 45.1 percent
- Specific learning disabilities: 44.3 percent
- Hearing impairments: 42.3 percent
- Traumatic brain injury: 32.3 percent
- Emotional disturbance: 26.8 percent
- Autism: 24.3 percent
- Deaf-blindness: 18.1 percent
- Mental retardation: 13.2 percent
- Multiple disabilities: 12.1 percent

> WITH THE RISE OF INDUSTRIALISM, WORDS LIKE "NORMAL" AND "DEFECTIVE" THAT HAD ONCE ONLY BEEN USED TO REFER TO THINGS, BEGAN TO BE USED TO REFER TO PEOPLE...IN THE INDUSTRIAL AGE, A NEW DEGREE OF UNIFORMITY WAS EXPECTED OF PEOPLE.
>
> *Anne Finger*

Let's look from the other direction, at a few categories of students who spent *the most time* (60 percent or more) *outside* a Regular Class. The largest category was mental retardation (51.7 percent), followed by autism (46.4 percent) and multiple disabilities (45.5 percent).

If your child is currently school-aged, which statistical classification is he in? If he's not in the "higher" or the "lower'" end of time spent outside a Regular Class, he might be in the middle: students with disabilities who spend 21-60 percent of the school day *outside* of a Regular Class. Are you happy with where your child is spending his time at school? Are you happy with what he's learning and how he's progressing? If your child is younger than five or six, jump ahead a few years. Based on the disability category he would be in, where would he be spending most of his time at school: in or out of a Regular Class? Is this what you've been looking forward to?

How do the statistics I've shared translate into the reality of a child's school day? Some students are in segregated Special Ed classrooms all day. Some attend a Regular Ed homeroom, but as soon as attendance and other morning routines are completed, they're herded to a Special Ed class for the rest of the day. For others, a Special Ed room *is* their homeroom and where they spend most of the day, but they're "allowed" to go to Regular Ed classrooms for art, PE, and music. And there are many scenarios in between.

Students in any of these situations may also eat lunch together, seated at specific tables in the school cafeteria, under the watchful eyes of their teacher or other adult. During recess in elementary schools, they may also be restricted to a certain area of the playground and/or go to recess at a separate time from other children. So not only are they prevented from having typical social and educational experiences within a Regular Ed classroom, they're socially isolated from other students during lunch and playtime. Finally, students who spend the most time in a Regular Ed classroom are often pulled out for therapies and/or specialized help.

IDEA is specific about *where* students with disabilities are to be educated: in Regular Ed classrooms. Still, many educators (and some parents) use "to the maximum extent appropriate" phrase to justify more restrictive settings. The placement of students in segregated Special Ed classrooms is usually *not* based on the individual needs of a student (and this is contrary to the law), and in many cases, the decision is made *before* the IEP meeting is even held (contrary to the law since placement is to be determined at the IEP meeting by the IEP Team and parents are on this team). Instead, the decision is based on a student's diagnosis—many children with disabilities are placed into a "program."

> IF WE FIND THE FOUNDATIONS OF OUR EDUCATIONAL STRUCTURE UNSATISFACTORY, WE FIND IT EASIER TO ADD A NEW STORY OR COURSE OR KIND OF SCHOOL THAN TO REORGANIZE EXISTING CONDITIONS SO AS TO MEET THE NEED.
>
> *John Dewey*

The law requires IEP Teams to write *Individualized* Education Programs for children; it does *not* instruct schools to set up programs, but they do. For example, a program for children with physical disabilities may be located in the most (or only) physically accessible school building in a district. In some districts, a program for children with autism may be set up in one particular school. It's easier to make students go where the Services are, instead of allowing students to attend Regular Ed classrooms in their neighborhood schools and take Services to them.

In addition, many educators continue to embrace the MEDICAL MODEL of disability, believing students within the same disability category have the same needs, learn the same way, and so forth, which justifies (in their minds) the creation of such special programs. Yet, the intent of Congress in mandating that each student have an Individualized Education Program was to *move away* from the MEDICAL MODEL paradigm of disability, which had dictated the treatment—and the segregation—of people with disabilities in institutions and other segregated settings for decades. Over and over again in the law, the word is "services" not "place." But many schools *have,* in general, made Special Ed into a "place."

There are, however, schools where the law *is* followed, and where children with disabilities are successfully educated and included in Regular Ed classrooms. How do educators in these inclusive schools differ from the rest? In their attitudes. As you'll see later this chapter, inclusive education has nothing to do with the disabilities of the students, and everything to do with the attitudes of educators!

Before moving on to inclusive education, it's important to examine the practices of segregated Special Education a little further.

Negative Consequences of Segregated Special Education

In 1896, the United States Supreme Court decision in the *Plessy v. Ferguson* case allowed "separate but equal" to become the law of the land. For decades, this decision mandated the segregation and second-class citizenship of people of color. But in 1954, the landmark *Brown v. Board of Education of Topeka* Supreme Court decision struck down the *Plessy* ruling. You probably remember this case from your high school civics class, right? The Brown family tried to enroll their daughter in the neighborhood school in Topeka, Kansas, but they were told their daughter would have to go to the "colored" school. The parents sued and their case, along with several others, made it to the Supreme Court.

Seventeen years later, parents of children with disabilities were fighting a similar battle: schools would not educate *their* children. Like parents before them, they fought this discrimination in state courts across the country—and won. In one of these cases (*PARC v. the Commonwealth of Pennsylvania*) the attorney for the parents, Thomas Gilhool, used the *Brown v. Board of Education* decision in his argument. These right-to-education cases paved the way for the eventual passage of Federal Special Ed law (P.L. 94-142) in 1975.

> SEPARATE EDUCATIONAL FACILITIES ARE INHERENTLY UNEQUAL.
>
> *Chief Justice Earl Warren*

In the *Brown* decision, Chief Justice Earl Warren wrote (I've modified some of the language to eliminate antiquated descriptors and added italics for emphasis):

> To separate (children) from others of similar age and qualifications... generates a feeling of inferiority as to their status in the community that *may affect their hearts and minds in a way unlikely ever to be undone...* Segregation...has a detrimental effect upon the (segregated) children...(as it's) usually interpreted as denoting the inferiority of the (segregated) group. A sense of inferiority *affects the motivation of a child to learn.* Segregation...has a tendency to *retard the educational and mental development of (the segregated) children* and to deprive them of...benefits they would receive in an...integrated school system... We conclude that...the doctrine of "separate but equal" has no place. Separate educational facilities are inherently unequal.

There is no doubt in *my* mind that the segregation of children with disabilities *does* "affect their hearts and minds in a way unlikely ever to be undone." I believe we hurt children deeply when we segregate them—in ways we may never even understand. How could we? Most of us have never been segregated. But we can learn from those who have been, can't we?

Over the past decade, hundreds of adults with developmental disabilities have told me about their experiences in the public school system. The majority feel they were not educated and did not have the academic knowledge (much less high school credits) to go on to college. Most were also judged incompetent to go into the workforce, so into a sheltered workshop or adult day program they went. Additionally, most also revealed the personal pain caused by segregation. They didn't have friends, did not participate in any typical school activities, were made to feel stupid, were ashamed of being members of "the retard room," and worse. No one, they felt, believed in them; not their parents and not their teachers. How could they believe in themselves? How could they have hope for the future?

I am routinely amazed that many of these wonderful men and women haven't given up on the world. Most are unemployed, living in group homes, and getting by on "disability welfare," but there's still a spark of hope that a job, their own home, and a REAL LIFE will come one day. Those with the most hope seem to keep going because they also have a spark of anger: anger over the injustice of wasted years of public education and a society that continues to devalue them because of their differences.

In general, we've made segregation a *legal* issue, as well it should be. But compliance with IDEA is skirted through interpretation or outright violation, and segregation continues. We need laws, but until we take segregation—and its mirror image inclusion—beyond the law, little will change. What's beyond the law? Morals and ethics. And I believe it's *morally and ethically wrong* to segregate children with disabilities (or anyone else, based on a characteristic).

How can we, in good conscience, segregate children *for any reason*—educational convenience, school policy, or misguided notions—and risk life-long harm to their hearts and minds?

There are other specific negative consequences to Special Education in segregated settings. Some of these, I believe, contribute directly to harming children's hearts and minds, and some result in other negative consequences.

Ungraded Classrooms

Many segregated Special Ed classrooms are ungraded. At some elementary schools, students of all ages may be in the same classroom. I once met a 16-year-old girl who was still being educated in a segregated classroom at an *elementary* school. We certainly have to question not only the appropriateness of this practice, but also the validity of it. For example, students with emotional disabilities ages 6-12 may be placed in the same segregated Special Ed classroom, based on educators' assumption that this is where their needs can be met. But how in the world could the needs of six-year-old be similar to that of a 12-year-old? For one thing, they have very different academic needs, don't they? And what about their social needs? Aren't six-year-olds very different from 12-year-olds, even if they do share the same diagnosis?

> IT IS ALWAYS EASIER TO MANIPULATE THE CHILD TO FIT THE THEORY, THAN TO ADJUST THE THEORY TO SUIT THE CHILD, PROVIDED OF COURSE, ONE IS VERY CAREFUL NOT TO LOOK AT THE CHILD.
>
> *Judith Groch*

In these settings, few children make friends, they have no social identity (it's hard to know what grade you're in if the class is ungraded), and they are not exposed to their same-aged peers who do not have disabilities. All of these effectively prevent children from "being" their CHRONOLOGICAL AGES. How can an eight-year-old, for example, know what it means to "be" an eight-year-old if he's not with other eight-year-olds?

Equally important, most of us would consider it extremely inappropriate, and maybe even dangerous, to group children of such a wide age range in the same classroom. But somehow this is acceptable if the children have disabilities. Several years ago, while presenting at a conference in Michigan, I learned this state's Special Ed law went further than Federal Special Ed law: Michigan schools serve students with disabilities to age 25, not 22. One mother was horrified to learn her three-year-old daughter with a disability would be in a classroom that included "students" with disabilities who were in their early twenties!

Low Expectations

Low expectations are the norm in most segregated Special Ed classrooms, especially those that are disability-specific ("the autism class," "the MR class," etc.). Many teachers in such classes *do* expect their students to learn, but expectations are often referenced against "others like them." The attitudes of teachers may prevent children from ever escaping the stigma of their diagnoses. Additionally, such an educational placement may permanently "brand" a student in the minds of many educators and parents. During a break at a conference where I was presenting, an administrator readily admitted that, "Children who have been in Life Skills classes could never be successful in Regular Ed classrooms." And many *parents* believe their children could never be successful in a Regular Ed classroom, since they've always been in segregated Special Ed rooms.

The structure and atmosphere of many segregated Special Ed classrooms prevent students from learning typical, age-appropriate behaviors. Again, low expectations and disability bias rear their ugly heads, as educators assume children with a particular disability cannot learn typical behavior, so "unacceptable" behaviors are accepted as the norm. And these same behaviors may later become barriers to employment and/or inclusion in typical community activities.

No General Ed Curriculum

Children who spend all or much of the day in segregated Special Ed classrooms may not be given access to the general ed curriculum (contrary to IDEA), which means they will not receive the academic education that can pave the way to college, trade school, or employment. Low expectations are again involved. It's heartbreaking to realize five- and six-year-old children (and those who are older) are put into Life Skills classes, based on the *assumption* that they can not learn, nor benefit from, an academic education. We *demand* that children *without* disabilities learn academics, while children with disabilities are robbed of this same opportunity. How can some educators (who are supposed to love helping children learn) and even some parents (who are supposed to love and believe in their own children) so easily write off a child and his potential?

> CHILDREN WHO ARE TREATED AS IF THEY ARE UNEDUCABLE ALMOST INVARIABLY BECOME UNEDUCABLE.
>
> *Kenneth B. Clark*

Pull-Out

Students who are in Regular Classrooms for much of the day, but who are pulled out for therapies and/or specialized assistance are not immune from negative consequences. If they're pulled out for PT, OT, or speech therapy, what are they missing in the Regular Ed classroom? How do they stay caught up with social studies or other subjects if they're routinely pulled out of the Regular Ed class? And do the therapies they're receiving actually contribute to their academic education? In general, pull-out therapies tend to focus on the acquisition of functional skills, which may have no relevance to a child's academic progress. In the big scheme of things and as one example, which is more important: staying balanced on a scooter board or reading, writing, and arithmetic? Moreover, Traditional Therapy in a public school setting can send the same NOT-OK message as described in Chapter 4, as well as a "you don't belong in this classroom" message.

> THE WORLD OF EDUCATION IS LIKE AN ISLAND WHERE PEOPLE, CUT OFF FROM THE WORLD, ARE PREPARED FOR LIFE BY EXCLUSION FROM IT.
>
> *Maria Montessori*

Both of these messages are also sent when children are pulled out for specialized help in reading, math, or other subjects—with terrible consequences for the student. He may feel like a dummy, and this is made worse if, as commonly happens, the Special Ed room is known as "the retard room." How can a child feel good about himself, and be motivated to learn, under these circumstances? In some classrooms, all the students know *why* a student is pulled out and they know *where* he goes. In other situations, they don't—they can only wonder where he goes and why. Is he a "bad" kid, and is the pull-out some form of punishment? If so, other children might have second thoughts about being friends with *him*.

What the Law Says

The scenarios described above, and many others, are all too common in schools across the country, and they certainly don't represent the best we can do, nor do they represent the intent of IDEA. Special Education is not supposed to be a "place"—a place where students are socially isolated, physically segregated, and undereducated. Nothing in the law mandates schools to set up segregated Special Education classrooms or programs.

What *does* the law say? As you read the following excerpts, note the concerns of Congress and think about your own child's experiences.

The purpose of the law (from IDEA 2004, Part A, Section 601 (d)) is "to ensure that all children with disabilities have available...a free appropriate public education that emphasizes special education and related services designed to meet their unique needs and prepare them for further education, employment, and independent living..."

IDEA 2004 Section 602-Definitions (29) defines Special Education as: "*Specially designed instruction,* at no cost to parents, to meet the unique needs of a child with a disability..." [Italics added.] And included in the law are a variety of components or techniques which might be necessary for the successful delivery of such "specially designed instruction," such as assistive technology, curriculum modifications, accommodations, and/or supports.

IDEA 2004 Part A, Section 601 (c) Findings, states: [Italics added]:

(1) Disability is a natural part of the human experience and in no way diminishes the right of individuals to participate in or contribute to society. Improving educational results for children with disabilities is an essential element of our national policy of ensuring equality of opportunity, full participation, independent living, and economic self-sufficiency for individuals with disabilities.

(4)...the implementation of this title has been *impeded by low expectations,* and an insufficient focus on applying replicable research on proven methods of teaching and learning for children with disabilities.

(5) Almost 30 years of research and experience has demonstrated that the education of children with disabilities can be made more effective by—

(A) Having high expectations for such children and ensuring their access to the *general education curriculum in the regular classroom,* to the maximum extent possible, in order to meet developmental goals and the challenging expectations that have been established for all children; and be prepared to lead productive and independent adult lives, to the maximum extent possible...
(C) Coordinating this title with other...school improvement efforts... in order to ensure that...*special education can become a service for such children rather than a place where such children are sent;*
(D) Providing appropriate special education and related services, and aids and supports in *the regular classroom,* to such children, whenever appropriate...
(H) Supporting the development and use of technology, including assistive technology devices and assistive technology services, to maximize accessibility for children with disabilities...

Is your child's school following the law?

Now onto another question. Are you wondering how educators are able to "break the law"? Because there are no "IDEA police" running around issuing tickets or arrest warrants! The Federal Department of Education is in charge of compliance, but its oversight is sorely lacking.

Parents must often take charge of compliance, in the form of invoking their legal right for a due process hearing (filing a lawsuit). In theory, this legal maneuver would seem a sensible solution. In practice, however, it's a different story. Generally, if the parents "win" the due process complaint, the school is ordered to change its ways, but parents may still have to be vigilant to make sure the school really does mend its ways. And as many can attest, the rocky relationship between parents and educators is further deteriorated by legal action (whether the parents prevail or not). From a purely practical standpoint, if someone sued you, how kindly would you feel toward them? How likely is it that you'd want to have *any* kind of relationship with them, much less a friendly, helpful, positive relationship? Between the loss of trust and the anger on both sides, it is often the child who pays the price.

Parents, as too many already know, are caught between the proverbial rock and a hard place. However, the suggestions provided later in this chapter can make a positive difference in our relationship with educators and the education of our children!

Is Our Nation Serious About Educating Students with Disabilities?

There's one more important concern I hope you'll think about. As parents of children with disabilities, we have essentially used Special Ed law as "permission" for our children to attend school.

The responsibility of providing a public education is a "state's right"—not the right of the Federal government. The Feds have been involved in public education only in the last several decades, by offering Federal funds to improve education which states can *choose* to accept or not. Here's how it works: the Feds say to the states, "We think you should be doing such-and-such in education [or transportation, utilities, or other areas]. So we'll provide funds to make this happen *if* you follow our rules and regulations."

In essence, states don't have to follow IDEA, and many other Federal regulations, unless they want Federal funds. Most states *do* want the Federal dollars, so they comply with these Federal mandates.

I'm glad we have IDEA, but just how serious *is* our nation about educating students with disabilities? The answer can be found if we look at other laws. (The following discussion is based on an article I wrote in 2004).

Congress passed the Civil Rights Act in 1964, because some states refused to guarantee civil rights to people who were labeled Black. At the time, there were furious outcries: many said the Feds had no right to interfere in states' rights. But Federal law prevailed, and was enforced by the National Guard, when necessary.

Section 504 of the Rehab Act of 1973 prohibits discrimination by any entity *that receives Federal funds.* Thus, for more than 30 years, hospitals, universities, local and state governments (which includes public schools), and a whole host of other entities have been prohibited from discriminating against people with disabilities.

The ADA (Americans with Disabilities Act) is similar to 504, but Federal funding is not a criteria. The ADA prohibits discrimination based on disability by any business, public services (including local and state governments), and in the telecommunications industry, *irrespective of Federal funds.* With 504 and the ADA, there were a few outcries about states' rights, but the Civil Rights Act of 1964 set the precedent that the Feds could (and would) "interfere" in *states'* rights in order to protect the rights of *individuals.*

With the Civil Rights Act and the ADA, the Feds said, "Follow these laws, period." With Section 504, the Feds said to hospitals, universities, and local/state governments, etc., "*Because* we fund some of your activities or research, we will not allow you to discriminate based on disability." But with IDEA, the Feds basically said, "*If* you do what we say, we'll give you some dough." Do you see the difference?

What's going on here? Are students with disabilities just a commodity (States: "We'll educate those kids only if you pay us.")? Or is the Federal

WANT INCLUSIVE SCHOOLS?

Because many schools routinely follow school policy instead of IDEA, perhaps it's time to make inclusion part of a school district's policies! And the way to do that is for parents and others who believe in inclusion to join their local school boards! If you're ready to consider moving into this leadership role, do not run for office as a "special ed" or "inclusion" candidate—this will limit your appeal to voters. Instead, run as a "parent" who is concerned about all issues. Once elected, develop allies, "pay your dues," and *then* begin educating other board members about IDEA, why inclusion is important, and more. If the school board is not your cup of tea, volunteer on school district committees, and follow the suggestions above. Finally, there's strength in numbers! Spearhead a group of parents of children *with* and *without* disabilities to meet with the school board and/or administrators to inform them about inclusive education, and urge the adoption of inclusive practices.

government afraid (and unwilling) to be heavy-handed with the states because the educational rights of children with disabilities aren't as valuable or important as the rights of others?

In enacting Special Ed law, Congress had the best of intentions: to ensure that children were not excluded from public school based on disability. But Congress didn't simply say to states, "You cannot discriminate on the basis of disability, *period,* and you must provide students with disabilities with accommodations, curriculum modifications, assistive technology, etc. to ensure they benefit from education just like students without disabilities."

Instead, Congress wrote a whole new set of rules—a "separate set of rules." And because of the way state departments of education, school districts, and in some cases, the courts, have interpreted these rules, there are many loopholes. Furthermore, some school district lawyers and other "anti-Special Ed advocates" spend an enormous amount of time researching and/or counseling schools on ways to "get around" IDEA.

More importantly, however, this separate set of rules has, in many ways, *contributed* to the separate education of children with disabilities. There is no other *group* of children who, because they share one common characteristic, have a separate set of rules which, intentionally or not, leads to segregation and substandard educational outcomes.

Now let's go back to the beginning of this discussion and the idea that (1) many of us have used IDEA as "permission" for our children to be educated and (2) education is a state's right. Do the "general" education laws in your state use language like "children without disabilities"? No, they say "children" or "students." In other words, don't laws regarding publicly-supported education apply to children with disabilities? Yes, they do. So what if instead of using Federal Special Ed law as *permission,* we begin seeing our children as children, first, and use our state laws, just as other parents do? And if necessary, we could use the ADA and/or Section 504 to ensure our children were not discriminated against based on disability.

After the passage of Federal Special Ed law in 1975, most *states* enacted Special Ed laws that are similar to the Federal law. We can look into using these, too, instead of only Federal law.

If we chose this route, our children might not receive some of the Services that are particular to IDEA—such as school therapies and others. But this might not be such a great loss, as I'll detail later. It would also mean we would need to work closer with our children's teachers, and this would be a very good thing.

All this might sound like heresy to some; others may think I must be from Mars. But I present it as food for thought. I'm not suggesting that every parent abandon the value of IDEA. I do hope, however, that we learn to see beyond IDEA, to see our children as children, first, who have the same rights to an education as other children, within our *state* educational laws.

Now we'll look at inclusive education. And you'll see that in schools where all children are valued, Special Ed law can become irrelevant: educators teach and include all children *because it's the right thing to do.*

I THINK IT WOULD BE SHORTSIGHTED OF A SOCIETY TO PRODUCE, BY ITS NEGLECT, A GROUP OF FUTURE CITIZENS VERY LIKELY TO BE UNPRODUCTIVE AND CHARACTERIZED BY BITTERNESS AND ALIENATION.

John W. Gardner

What is Inclusion?

Inclusion has been defined in many ways by many different people. (Some principals have said students with disabilities are included if they're in the *same building* as the majority of students!) In general, however, parents and educators who have experience with inclusive practices agree on the following definition:

> Inclusion is children with disabilities being educated in the schools they would attend if they didn't have disabilities, in age-appropriate Regular Education classrooms, where services and supports are provided to both the students and their teachers, and students with disabilities are fully participating members of their school communities in academic and extra-curricular activities.

Inclusion is *not:*

- children with disabilities spending the majority of the school day in a Special Ed room, and being "included" in Regular Ed art, PE, and/or music—this is visitation;
- children with disabilities attending Regular Ed classes, but being pulled out throughout the day—this is part-time mainstreaming;
- children with disabilities being in Regular Ed classes, but sitting in the back of the room with full-time aides—this is physical integration;
- children *without* disabilities ("peer role models") visiting children with disabilities in Special Ed classrooms—this is reverse mainstreaming.

In 2002, I interviewed Mike Galvin, the principal of Columbine Elementary, the inclusive neighborhood school which my children attended. I turned the interview into a handout that I share with participants when I present inclusive education seminars. I've included parts of that interview in different sections of this chapter, and his "principal's" perspective is very enlightening. In this first excerpt, I asked Mike for his definition of an inclusive school:

> An inclusive school is one in which educators create a natural school environment for all children. Services for kids with disabilities are as transparent as possible. The help provided to any child is based on what he or she needs, and it's provided in the natural environment. You take a child where he is and give him what he needs in the most natural and informal ways possible. An inclusive school provides all kids with whatever they need to master the regular ed curriculum, which may include curriculum modifications, supports, assistive technology, or other assistance. And in my opinion, you don't call a student an "inclusion student" or have "inclusion classrooms."

What about Special Ed rooms that are only for students with disabilities?

I've heard some people say "special ed is not a place" and that's true. At Columbine, we saw no reason to segregate students with disabilities in a special classroom! A more natural way of providing services to all children is in the regular classroom. Now, there may be particular places in a school—like a reading lab, for example—where children with and without disabilities receive specialized help.

SPECIAL ED ADVISORY GROUPS

In my district, we realized the school board ignored the concerns of our Special Ed group because they saw us as a "special interest" group that represented only a small number of students.

So we disbanded our group in favor of a different strategy: we all joined other committees that were more valued by the school board. We did *not* join as Special Ed "representatives," but as concerned parents/teachers; we made allies and then introduced Special Ed issues to the committee's business. A Curriculum Committee, for instance, could address curriculum issues as they affected students with disabilities.

There are many ways to influence what happens in our schools, and it's important to widen our efforts and our perspective, and make inclusion a school and societal issue, not just an issue about students who have disabilities!

Inclusion doesn't mean that every single thing happens in the classroom. Overall, however, the natural organization of a school is groupings of similar/same-age students, and that's true for kids with and without IEPs.

Tell me more about the "age-appropriate" issue.

It's really critical in a lot of ways. We need to look carefully at the research on retention. There's not much evidence to support its use, and there's a lot to suggest it's actively harmful. Research [Holmes and Matthews, 1984; Meisels and Liaw, 1993] demonstrated that (1) retention has a negative impact on "social adjustment, behavior, self-competence, and attitudes toward school" and (2) retention does *not* remediate academic difficulties. Children who are retained are at greater risk for dropping out of school. A study by Grissom and Shepard [1989] showed that children who have been retained just one year are five times less likely to graduate! This increases to almost 100 percent if a child has been retained two or more times. In one study [Yamamoto, 1980], students were asked to describe the greatest stresses they face. Being retained was in the top three; the other two were "going blind" or "losing a parent." The fear of retention puts extreme pressure on children. Some people recognize how emotionally harmful retention can be to older kids, but they don't think it's a big deal to hold kids back in kindergarten. Well, we may not see an immediate impact when retention is done early, but the negative outcomes may show up later.

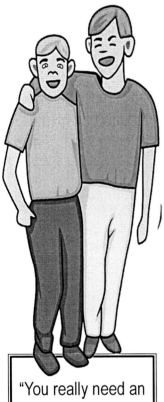

"You really need an ethic or a core belief that relationships are at the heart of learning and what a school is all about."

I believe kids need to be with similar-age peers for social needs. At Columbine, we were very concerned about the relationships kids have with others. First, being able to develop friendships and acquiring other social skills is important for every child. These are difficult to learn if you're not with other kids your same age. Second, kids often learn as much from peers academically as they do from their teachers! Educators can learn to adapt the curriculum to the learning needs of a child. It may be more *convenient* for a school or a teacher to maintain the same curriculum for all kids and insist that a child must fit into the curriculum. But adapting the curriculum, when necessary, is in the best interest of the child. We didn't hold kids back at Columbine. There were times we knew a child wasn't at "grade-level," but moving him up with his peers was the right thing to do, and that's what we did. Then we adapted the curriculum and modified instructional strategies to meet his needs.

What does it take to create an inclusive school?

You really need an ethic or a core belief that relationships are at the heart of learning and what a school is all about. That's a necessary first step. The relationship between the principal and teachers and the relationships among teachers are models for the way students relate to each other.

We created an atmosphere which we called "pervasive caring." We believed it was very important to care about how kids feel and how they fit in with their peer groups. Under this operating procedure, the first priority is supporting kids' emotional needs. The way you provide academics and deal with the technicalities of following the law are influenced by a core belief of caring. Inclusion is the result. It's really about focusing on what it means to be a good human being. As adults, we try to do this within our families; as educators, we can do this in our professional lives at school, too.

Our mission was to help children maximize their own learning within this pervasive atmosphere of caring. Under these circumstances, it's hard *not* to have an inclusive school!

Why is inclusion in public schools important?

Because the potential of every person needs to be recognized! And this is what happens in an inclusive school. Each and every student is encouraged and allowed to contribute and be part of something; no one is discounted or negated as a human being. Inclusion helps all students make the most of themselves.

When I was growing up, kids with disabilities were warehoused in one of those "special" rooms. I even remember where it was: in the basement next to the furnace room! The way I see it, schools can be the first place that *limits* a person's potential. In our society, we have put so many limitations on people in terms of gender, ethnicity, disability, or some other characteristic. Society has set up these barriers, and thankfully, many have fallen by the wayside. With inclusive schools, limitations based on disability can fall by the wayside, too. Inclusive education is one way to eliminate the societal limitations imposed on people's potential. What's worse than putting limits on a child's potential? We just can't do this anymore!

Inclusive schools give us a new and different—and positive—way of looking at people. Educators are in this profession because they want to help children learn, but we need to carefully consider how our traditional special ed system may *limit* the potential of kids with disabilities.

School is where we open children's minds, bodies, and spirits to their potential in life. At Columbine, the efforts to ensure all kids learned in an inclusive environment were driven by the hope that when children with disabilities left the educational system, they would have the same opportunities as kids without disabilities: employment, emotionally healthy adult relationships, successful families, self-fulfillment, and the ability to accept personal responsibility and be contributing citizens.

How did you get interested in inclusion?

I was profoundly influenced and disturbed by the research about what happens when children with disabilities leave the traditional special ed system. The special ed system didn't seem to do very much to encourage self-reliance and independence; in fact, it seemed to *discourage* the development of these important traits! For example, developing an understanding of yourself—building on the strengths you have and understanding your limitations—is an important piece of any person's whole development. The traditional special ed system doesn't focus on strengths. I remember hearing research about people with disabilities who are still living at home at the age of 24, with no prospects for living on their own, having jobs, or doing any other "real-life" adult things, even though they went through many years and many programs designed to educate them. These programs seem to actually encourage dependence, instead of promoting interdependence!

What did it take to become an inclusive school?

What got us started was a discussion of how classroom teachers could more meaningfully collaborate with specialists. For example, how could a third grade teacher have meaningful and effective relationships with a variety of professionals—

therapists, teacher assistants, and others—who come into her classroom to support students with diverse needs? As a teacher, myself, I always had a problem with people pulling kids out of my class all day. I didn't know how to catch kids up with what they had missed when they were pulled out for therapy or other specialized assistance. This was very frustrating for me, as a teacher, and in my opinion, it was harmful to the children.

When I first became a principal, I once spent an entire day in a first grade classroom. I watched carefully when kids returned from their pull-out programs. They had missed learning opportunities and instructions from the teacher, and their classmates had moved on to other things. The kids who had been pulled out were just lost. I thought, "What's the point? Why not have the pull-out teacher come *into* the classroom?" Pull-out just didn't make any sense. Here we were pulling kids out to give them additional help, but they were actually falling further behind! Our collective experiences led us to look at alternatives to the pull-out method.

You'll hear more from Mike later in this chapter, when he shares more strategies to ensure all children belong and all children learn, together.

Does the Law Mandate Inclusion?

While you won't find the word "inclusion" in IDEA, the law is very prescriptive about placement. The law, as reauthorized in 2004, lists the general provisions. At the time of this writing (May 2005), the actual *rules and regulations*—the specifics of implementation—have not been published, and according to the Department of Education, the 2004 IDEA revisions will not take effect until July 1, 2005. While some changes were made in the 2004 reauthorization, as far as I can tell, the following rules and regs from IDEA '97 will continue unchanged (italics and underling added):

- Each public agency shall ensure (1) that to the maximum extent appropriate, children with disabilities, including children in public or private institutions or other care facilities, are educated with children who are nondisabled; and (2) that *special classes, separate schooling or other <u>removal</u>* of children with disabilities from the regular educational environment occurs only if the nature or severity of the disability is such that education in regular classes with the use of supplementary aids and services cannot be achieved satisfactorily. [Section 300.550, General LRE Requirements]

- Each public agency shall ensure that the child's placement:
(1) is determined at least annually; (2) is based on the child's IEP; and
(3) is as close as possible to the child's home;

  Unless the IEP of a child with a disability requires some other arrangement, the child is educated *in the school that he or she would attend if nondisabled;* in selecting the least restrictive environment, consideration is given to any harmful effect on the child or on the quality of services that he or she needs and a child is *not removed from education in age-appropriate regular classrooms solely because of needed modifications in the general curriculum.* [Section 300.522, Placements]

- In providing or arranging for the provision of nonacademic and extracurricular services and activities, including meals, recess periods, and the services and activities set forth in Section 300.306, each public agency shall ensure that each child with a disability participates with nondisabled children in those services and activities to the maximum extent appropriate to the needs of that child. [Section 300.553, Nonacademic settings]

If you compare these provisions of IDEA with the definition of inclusion I provided earlier, you'll see that the concepts are the same.

It's All About Attitude

The most significant difference between an inclusive school and one that practices segregation is *the attitude of educators.* The overall attitude at an inclusive school represents a belief that all children are competent learners and belong together, and all educators are competent teachers.

At Columbine, the attitudes and actions of educators resulted in the elimination of Special Ed classrooms. And I've learned, over the years, that the absence of a Special Ed classroom (or whatever name it might go by) *is* the mark of a truly inclusive school.

When all students with disabilities are in Regular Ed classrooms, there is *no need* for a Special Ed classroom. Under this circumstance, and to meet the needs of students and classroom teachers, Special Ed teachers provide services and assistance in the Regular Ed environment. This is the practical reality at an inclusive school. But there's a philosophical component, too: as long as there *is* a Special Ed classroom, *there will be a separate place to put children with disabilities.* Conversely, if there is no Special Ed room, all children will be included—*there is no other place for them to be except in Regular Ed classrooms.*

> *"...as long as there is a Special Ed classroom, there will be a separate place to put children with disabilities."*

Columbine's Journey to Inclusion

As you heard from Principal Mike earlier, and as I just mentioned, an attitudinal change is the first step in moving toward inclusion. Once the change was made, the school staff, parents, and students learned that inclusion is a *process* of trial and error; it's not a *product.* There is no one-size-fits-all recipe. Every child, every teacher, and every classroom is different. Mistakes will be made and patience is needed, but if the commitment to inclusion is firmly embraced, the goal will be achieved. After the attitudinal shift, what's next? Here's more from the interview with Mike.

What did it take to actually implement an inclusive model of education?

One of our first steps was to end special ed pull-out and make sure all students with disabilities were served in the regular ed classroom. It seemed to work okay for the students and the specialists who went into the classroom. But as it turned out, this wasn't an effective practice for the classroom teachers! They felt there were too many different people coming into the classrooms, and they were frustrated that they didn't always know what a specialist was doing with a student, how to continue the support once the specialist left the room, and so forth. From a practical standpoint, it really wasn't possible to have effective collaboration between so many adults.

So as a staff, we spent a lot of time talking and thinking, and came up with the concept of the specialists forming a resource team for the next school year. The team included special ed teachers, a gifted/talented teacher, a speech therapist, and a Title I teacher. With the permission of the rest of the faculty, we gave it a try.

These specialists essentially cross-trained each other. Each member of the team was assigned one grade level. For example, "Mary" was assigned to third grade. She worked with all the third grade teachers to plan instruction, develop curriculum modifications, create different instructional strategies, identify how to meet the needs of specific students, and so forth. This allowed us to be very proactive—educators weren't always playing catch-up, trying to help a student who had fallen behind. We *anticipated* who needed help and provided it.

Members of the resource team met every Friday morning to brainstorm, learn from each other, and have meaningful conversations about students and their work. And, of course, they met informally at other times as well. Throughout the year, as children grow and learn, their needs change, and the dynamics in each classroom change as the months pass. So these regular meetings helped the resource team stay on top of things.

Inclusion can be messy in practice. We had places where we fell down, places we learned from—we're imperfect humans! To succeed, we had to have an atmosphere where it was okay to fail! We learned so much from our mistakes. Parents need to give teachers permission to fail. Parents of typical kids give teachers a certain amount of trust; the parents of kids with disabilities in our school tended to do the same thing.

Why does the idea of inclusive education seem to strike fear in the hearts of many educators?

I don't think regular ed teachers are afraid of inclusion, per se, or of kids with disabilities. I think they're afraid of not being able to do the job. Almost every teacher I've ever known is really committed to teaching and helping kids learn. But if classroom teachers think they're not going to be successful, they probably won't support inclusion. I feel it's basically a fear of the unknown. Many are afraid they'll be expected to do things they don't know how to do. For example, some teachers feel they haven't been trained in curriculum adaptation. To address those fears, teachers need to be assured they'll be provided with the support they need.

Special ed teachers often have different fears. Many are afraid that if they work in a regular classroom their role will be marginalized. Nothing could be further from the truth! Their skills are extremely important in inclusive classrooms. They're needed, and they're extremely valuable, in all areas—from the planning process through the actual teaching in the classroom.

Educators who have been trained in special ed and who work in the traditional resource room/pull-out model do very different work than classroom teachers. And it can be hard to address all their fears ahead of time. It's almost as if you just have to do it and learn as you go along. Inclusion helped our resource teachers experience great job satisfaction. Rather than trying to remediate a child's disability, they

---

"Permission to Fail"

I gave my son's teachers "permission to fail." I am not a perfect parent—I make lots of mistakes, but I keep trying. Shouldn't I allow teachers the same? So I told my son's teachers, "I don't expect you to be perfect. I trust you enough to put my son in your care every school day. I hope you trust *me* enough to be able to say, 'Today was awful...' and then tell me what happened, so I can help figure out how to make things better. I can handle it if you make mistakes. What I *can't* handle is anyone giving up on my son, so I hope you'll try new things—again and again—if that's what it takes."

Giving teachers "permission to fail" also gives them the support and trust they need to succeed! It works—try it!

successfully helped a child master the general curriculum. And they were truly a part of a team, working with classroom teachers and parents in a meaningful way, toward a set of shared goals, based on real student needs.

You know, *special ed isn't a subject!* It's supposed to be a method of helping a child become successful in the same world the rest of us are in. And we can do this by using assistive technology, curriculum modifications, and different types of instructional methods, as well as finding other ways to help a child learn. Our teachers enjoyed great job satisfaction using unique skills in the general ed environment.

We had high expectations of success and achievement for teachers and students at Columbine, and these could only be met by providing massive doses of emotional and technical support. To be successful, we all need support from people around us. When we set up our inclusive model, the explicit agreement was this: as the classroom teacher, you're responsible for the learning of all your students; in exchange, we'll provide the support you need to be successful. We can't expect teachers to experience success unless they're provided with the support they need. And supporting teachers is no different from the process used with kids: create an atmosphere of pervasive caring.

Many educators say they can't "do inclusion" because it costs too much. What about that, Mike?

Columbine was the only elementary school in our district that was inclusive, yet we didn't have any more money than the other schools. Colorado is in the middle of the pack when it comes to funding—in the neighborhood of $5,500 per student. It was important to use our resources wisely. Special ed rooms are staffed at a really high level: a 5 to 1 student/teacher ratio. We didn't have anything like that, so that saved a great deal of money.

In addition, we were very careful about not hiring a para unless it was absolutely necessary. And when we *did* hire a para, that person worked in three or four different classrooms. For example, one child needed behavior support during recess, so "Kay" was on the playground at that time. Another student needed support during the literacy block and another needed help with math. Through careful planning and scheduling, Kay could help all these students with their unique needs in inclusive settings. Thoughtful planning and a wise use of resources were very important.

Also, the atmosphere of pervasive caring included the belief that children with disabilities can reach higher levels of achievement. This flies in the face of the notion that kids with disabilities are limited in their learning because of "lower-intellectual functioning" or physical limitations or whatever. In other words, we didn't put limits on kids' potential. We set high expectations and then did everything we could to help children meet them. To ensure higher levels of achievement, we needed to create a whole menu of instructional strategies. So we used staff development funds to help teachers learn different strategies to meet children's learning styles.

At Columbine, we saw it this way: what society calls a "disability" often simply represents differences—sometimes extreme differences—in learning styles. We know that everyone has different ways of learning, and the belief that *every child is a lifelong learner* permeated the culture at our school.

When an administrator believes the school is responsible for helping every child learn in the regular environment, and when an administrator equips all teachers

> "You know, *special ed isn't a subject!* It's supposed to be a method of helping a child become successful in the same world the rest of us are in."

with the tools they need to do this, the payoff is more "real learning" and less remediation. Part of the inclusion model at Columbine involved the staff—with the help of parents—working hard to predict which children might have difficulty learning, and then coming up with strategies to help kids learn right from the start. If you identify and meet a child's learning needs from the beginning, you spend less time on remedial instruction. Being thoughtful about instructional practices, having the willingness to try new things, and embracing the "whatever it takes" philosophy ensures more real learning and less remediation.

What about the belief that educators can't do inclusion until the staff is "ready." How can an administrator address this issue?

Before we moved toward inclusion, we spent a lot of time on a "Best Hopes/ Worst Fears" exercise. We talked about the best things that could happen if we became an inclusive school, and then we shared our worst fears. We listed all these on chart paper, taped them to the walls in the teachers' lounge, and left them there for two weeks. This gave us time to think about things.

After the two weeks, we talked about what we needed to do to make sure the Worst Fears wouldn't happen and the Best Hopes would! It's always helpful when administrators give teachers the opportunity and the freedom to express their feelings—you can't deal with fears until they're out in the open. So I feel it's really important to go through this exercise.

Attending an inclusive education conference was something else we did to learn more, and it had mixed results. There was a lot of teacher bashing by some militant parents. This actually created more fears! Some of our teachers felt they would become targets of angry parents if they didn't know how to do inclusion "right." When we analyzed this, it seemed these parents were angry for two main reasons: they felt they weren't being listened to and they felt their children's needs weren't being met.

We believed we *did* know how to listen to parents and that we *could* meet children's needs. So we thought, "We can do inclusion." We knew we didn't know everything, but we believed we could figure it out. You learn as you go along. Every child is different; every classroom is different. Children change and grow; teachers change and grow. Inclusion is a dynamic, evolutionary process. It requires that we put meeting a child's needs—learning needs and other needs—first.

Inclusion also requires educators to embrace an atmosphere of risk-taking. When we didn't get things right the first time, we had to take risks and try something new. And we always hoped parents would give us the space to learn. We discovered that if we listened to parents, if we were on the same page, and if our interests were the same, parents allowed us the freedom to experiment with new ways of doing things to help their children learn.

Snapshots

A few descriptive snapshots will give you a better idea of what inclusion looked like at Columbine. And I'll start with my own son!

Benjamin—"Whatever it takes!" was one important attitude that turned the hope of inclusion into the reality. Educators made sure students with disabilities had the assistive technology devices, curriculum modifications, and supports

> LEARN
> BY DOING.
>
> *John Dewey*

they needed. The school provided Benjamin with a laptop computer, software, a standing frame, a wheelchair accessible desk, a desk-top easel, and a used manual wheelchair (which was used as a back-up, in case his chair broke down), as well as other supports and assistance.

I didn't have to "fight" for any of these things. Principal Mike and the teachers were very supportive about whatever a student needed. In some cases, the Principal had to be financially creative to find the money: tapping his building budget, the Special Ed budget, and/or the school district budget. Technically, of course, all these items belonged to the school, but students were allowed to take devices home every day, use them over the summer, and so forth. Providing these devices was a long-term investment: when/if a student no longer needed AT devices, they were given to other students.

Tony—Ten-year-old, "Tony," who has autism, was successfully included in Mrs. W's fifth grade classroom. After enlightening conversations with Tony and his parents, Mrs. W made some simple environmental accommodations to the classroom that were helpful to Tony (masking some of the lights, letting him choose where to sit, etc.). But new experiences routinely came up that required immediate and positive responses. So throughout the year, Tony got the support he needed from his classmates and teacher—he did not need a one-on-one aide (more about the role of paraprofessionals a little later), further modifications were made to the classroom environment, and, of course, Tony received the curriculum modifications he needed so he could learn from the fifth grade curriculum.

In many schools, children with behavior needs are the last to be considered for inclusion in Regular Ed classrooms. *Educators* may be apprehensive, and many *parents* are afraid their children can't be successful in that environment. Principal Mike was proudest of the successful inclusion of children with autism, emotional disabilities, and similar conditions. He once noted, "If a stranger peeked into some of our classrooms, he could pick out many of the children with disabilities—he could see the child who used a wheelchair or the one with Down syndrome. But he wouldn't be able to tell which children had autism or other conditions." This was achieved through the pervasive caring Mike and the staff instituted, which touched every student.

Carter—In a second-grade classroom, "Carter" received the accommodation he needed to learn: the freedom to move. Carter had a sensory integration label, and he learned best through movement. In fact, his mother knew that it was almost impossible for Carter to learn *if he had to sit still*. So in Mrs. M's second grade classroom, Carter—with Mrs. M's blessing—spent much of the day moving around the perimeter of the room, stopping now and then to diddle with a bucket of blocks or dabble with a bin of toys. Carter and Mrs. M had an agreement that he would sit in his seat at specific times during the day, and Carter kept his end of the deal. He also came to his seat when it was time to take tests. And it was obvious that Carter's mom knew what she was talking about: Carter did well on all the tests. While it appeared he wasn't paying

---

—THE REAL CHILD—

Before your child's IEP meeting, invite his Regular Ed teacher to your home, so she can see your child in his natural environment. (Yes, you'll need to clean your house!) In our home, Benjamin is master of his domain—he's powerful and in charge! This is a very different picture than educators have of children based on what's in their files at the school!

A teacher can learn who your child *really is* by spending a few moments with him in his room—as he shows her the toys he plays with, the books he loves, the posters on his wall, etc. This is a much more accurate picture of your child than the negative and deficit-based info in school assessments and reports!

2 STEPS FORWARD 1 STEP BACK

Unfortunately, some educators aren't willing to to invest in the *process of inclusion*. Some say they'll "try" inclusion. But if things don't work out exactly as they thought and/or if difficulties arise, these educators may quickly decide that "inclusion doesn't work." So they go back to the old ways of doing things, and many will become more firmly entrenched in maintaining the status quo.

An emerging practice in some states is the offer of "inclusion grants" by a state's department of education. Money, some feel, is what's needed before a school can become inclusive. But as you heard from Principal Mike, lack of funds does not have to be a barrier.

While some hail these inclusion grants as "the solution," I have concerns about this practice. In general, these grants are awarded to school districts for a specific time period (one year, two years, etc.). So what happens when the money runs out? Do these schools then revert back to segregating students with disabilities in Special Ed classrooms?

attention—since he wasn't sitting at his desk looking at the teacher—he was obviously "taking it all in" while he moved around the room. Did this bother the other students? No, because Mrs. M explained that Carter learned through movement, she respected Carter, and the children modeled her attitude. Carter had friends and was successful!

A Quiet Place—While Carter needed to move, a couple of students in Mrs. T's class needed frequent down-time and/or relief from too much visual or sensory stimulation. The solution? A floor-to-ceiling curtain, strung across a corner of the room (that included a window) provided a refuge. A bean bag chair and pillows were on the floor, and a child could go there whenever she wanted—to sit or lie down, to look at a book, or play with a favorite toy. When she was ready, she rejoined the class, and a teacher or classmate helped with whatever she missed during her self-imposed quiet time.

Peer Support—At Columbine, students were expected to help one another, and many students helped in ways that were unanticipated. Children with and without disabilities may go ballistic, get upset, become angry—in other words, they're fully human! Most of us—including children—don't simply "explode" or "melt down" without giving off cues ahead of time. In several classes, children learned to "read" the signals of their peers (with and without disabilities) and were able to help support one another, which reduced and/or eliminated melt-downs and explosions!

Peer support came in all shapes and sizes. During second grade, my son, Benjamin, was unable to eat his Goldfish and drink his juice box during recess—he was too busy holding onto his walker with both hands. One day when I was volunteering in school, I saw a sight to last a lifetime. I was leaving the school office, on my way to another part of the building when I saw my son's class heading out to recess. I paused, hoping to get a glimpse of my son. When using his walker, he was usually toward the back of the pack. There he was—but what was this? One of his classmates—Amy—was walking backwards in front of him, poking a Goldfish in his mouth, then holding his juice box up to his mouth, then urging, "Come on, Benjamin, we're almost there!"—then she dished out more Goldfish and juice. No *adult* could have thought up such a solution for Benj to enjoy his snacks during recess—it took a seven-year-old, on her own. But Amy, and many other children, were certainly influenced by the teachers who modeled positive, respectful attitudes toward students with disabilities.

Taylor—In Mrs. H's fifth grade classroom, "Taylor" (a ten-year-old with PDD) needed lots of support from the Special Ed teacher and the teacher's aide—or so we thought. One of these supportive teachers was usually pretty close to Taylor, to keep him on track, to keep him calm, and to write his spelling tests (he dictated the answers, and they wrote for him since handwriting was very difficult for him). Principal Mike asked if I would observe in Taylor's room. Taylor didn't like having grown-ups hovering over him, but if someone wasn't close by most of the time, Taylor couldn't stay focused. The Principal thought there must be a better solution—he thought a new pair of eyes (mine) might be helpful. I'm proud to say I did come up with a good idea—a laptop computer. Taylor was entranced—he stayed focused, was able to do his own spelling tests and other writing tasks, and needed much less adult support. It was such an easy solution—why didn't Taylor's teachers figure this out? Because earlier in the year, Taylor's mother told them her son "would *never* be able to use a computer." But I didn't know this bit of information. After watching Taylor for awhile that day, I went to my son's classroom and borrowed his laptop for Taylor to try. Although he had no computer experience, he took to it immediately! Principal Mike used this technique a lot—asking someone who wasn't in the thick of things to observe. Sometimes a new set of eyes *can* see things differently.

Trains and Friends—Here's another story about my son, Benjamin. In kindergarten, Benj wasn't able to "keep up" in math. When he and his classmates were learning one-to-one counting, using beans, buttons, and other small objects, Benjamin was still on "one" or "two" when the teacher was on "eight." The reason? Because of the spasticity in his fingers, Benj had a hard time "letting go" of these very small objects. So I sent a set of his trains to school with him. Thomas the Tank Engine and Friends were "fist-sized" that Benj could easily grasp and release. These became his math counters. Not only could Benj keep up with the counting lesson, but the other little boys in class all wanted to be paired up with Benj for different activities. The trains were a math accommodation *and* a friendship magnet!

Kinder Teachers, Welcoming Classrooms

A teacher's behavior and attitude toward her student(s) with disabilities can make the difference between success and failure. If she ignores these students, so will her other students. If she patronizes them, her other students will do the same. In short, students model the teacher's behavior. At Columbine, teachers saw students with disabilities as "full members" of the classroom, who were expected to participate, learn, be responsible, and more.

The majority of teachers at Columbine were flexible and open-minded, prepared to make changes and willing to try new things—again and again, sometimes—to ensure all their students were successful. In some cases, this meant modifying the environment in ways that were personally beneficial to the student with a disability, and which had little or no impact on other students. In my son's case, the desks in the classroom needed to be rearranged to accommodate his free movement around the room in his wheelchair.

Often, the changes made for Benjamin had a very *positive* effect on other students. When my son was having some difficulties learning to read, we thought the fluorescent lights might be a factor. A private vision specialist suggested diffusing the light by attaching colored tissue paper to the frame surrounding the lights over Benjamin's desk. This seemed to help Benj, and then a number of the students said they'd like the lights over *their* desks diffused, too. Soon, a rainbow of tissue paper (the students chose the colors) "beautified" the entire ceiling grid! This was just one example of teachers learning to listen to *all* their

A CHILD SPEAKS

All children learn differently; some are auditory learners, others learn best visually, and so forth. Teachers, however, may not always be aware of a student's learning style, so it's up to parents and children to educate these educators!

A wonderful mother told me that her son with autism was very much an auditory learner, and was also hypersensitive to too much visual stimulation—he often needed to look away, look down, or even close his eyes. She taught her son to tell his teachers this critically important fact about his learning style: "If I look at you, I can't hear you."

students, and I think this wonderful trait came from Principal Mike. He once told me, "This school belongs to the children. Every adult in the building—including me—is a visitor." So the classrooms belonged to the students, and if they wanted tissue paper over all the lights, it wasn't a big deal to the teacher!

Instructional Strategies—Teachers at Columbine adapted their instructional strategies *and* provided curriculum modifications to meet the needs of students with disabilities, and they recognized these strategies were often helpful to students who did *not* have disabilities. For example, some children with disabilities needed math manipulatives, while the other children used math worksheets. But students without disabilities who struggled with math gravitated to the student with a disability as he worked with manipulatives. Observant teachers recognized that these students would also benefit from similar accommodations.

Other instructional methods included children learning in activity centers and in small groups. When dividing the children into small groups, however, they were placed in "mixed ability" groups, instead of homogenous, ability-based groups. This prevented stratification of the class into the "haves" and the "have nots," and it also enabled students within each group to teach each other (based on the philosophy that the best way to learn something is to teach it).

Multi-age classrooms—My son was in a 1st/2nd continuum class, in which half the children were first-graders and half were second-graders. The students stayed with the same teacher for two years, which enabled her to get to know them well and help them learn better. His teacher once told me she would never go back to teaching only first-graders, noting how much smoother her class went, compared to typical first-grade classes, since the second-graders routinely helped the first-graders.

Teachers moving up with their students—Many fourth grade teachers moved up to fifth with their students. Like the continuum classes, the longer time spent with students enabled teachers to get to know all their students better, which helped them support all students more effectively.

A strong volunteer program—Parent and community volunteers were an integral part of Columbine's success, in the classroom and in the background. In the classroom, the presence of another adult (sometimes more than one) ensured that all students received more help. Other volunteers helped teachers by making copies and doing other tasks throughout the school.

As the years of successful inclusion continued, Mike and the Columbine staff created a Culture of Caring for everyone: students were expected to care for each other *and* their teachers, and teachers needed to care for each other and *all* the students.

New Roles for Teachers

Collaboration between Regular Ed and Special Ed teachers is critically important in inclusive schools, and as you learned from Principal Mike's words,

---

THE CHILD (NOT THE DIAGNOSIS) IS WHAT'S IMPORTANT!

The summer before Benjamin's first grade year, I thought it was very important for his Regular Ed teacher to understand about his disability. So I gave her a book about "children with cerebral palsy." Just before school started, I asked if she had any questions after reading it. "Not really," she said, "I know Benjamin will do such-and-such." I replied, "No, Benjamin doesn't do such-and-such." Confused, she said, "But the book said children with CP do such-and such..." "Well," I explained, *"Some* children with CP might, but Benjamin doesn't."

This wonderful teacher had learned a great deal about CP, but *nothing* about my son. That's when I realized educators (and anyone else) don't need to know about our children's diagnoses; they need to about our *children, as individuals!*

the roles of teachers evolved. In many schools, Regular Ed teachers work autonomously—each may be the only adult in a classroom full of children. In inclusive schools, however, Regular Ed teachers must be willing to share their classrooms with Special Ed teachers, therapists, teacher's aides, and other specialists. Collaboration at Columbine took many forms:

- Regular and Special Ed teachers were co-teachers, with each taking half the classroom. (If a paraprofessional was in the classroom, the students were divided into three groups.) Sometimes, the child with a disability was in the Regular Ed teacher's group; this allowed the Regular Ed teacher to get to know the student and discover how he learned best. Regular Ed and Special Ed teachers worked together to determine the appropriate curriculum modifications, supports, assistive technology needs, and more. Who does what and when was decided by the teachers, so a mutually supportive partnership between the Regular Ed and Special Ed teachers was key.

- Special Ed teachers also become "teachers of teachers." Once a child with a disability was assigned to a Regular Ed classroom, there was no automatic assumption that a Special Ed teacher and/or a paraprofessional was required all day (and more about the role of teacher's aides in a moment). The most critical component of ensuring success is not always another "warm body" in the room, but is, instead, the Regular Ed teacher learning different instructional methods—tricks of the trade—from the Special Ed teacher. If this couldn't be accomplished during their usual planning periods, subs were called in for half a day to enable teachers to accomplish this important task.

- Within a culture of pervasive caring, all educators took responsibility for all students. Teacher's aides helped in different classrooms; they weren't assigned to one child or one teacher, so many people knew how to help many different students. For example, the teacher's aides had the primary responsibility for helping my son go to the bathroom (which involved transferring him to and from his wheelchair to the toilet and everything in between—if you get my drift). If my son needed to use the restroom and a teacher's aide wasn't in the classroom, the classroom teacher used the intercom to call for assistance. And on more than one occasion, different people—*including the principal*—took responsibility for helping my son use the toilet!

The barrier to inclusion in many schools is the Regular Ed teachers' lament, "We weren't trained to teach 'those' kids!" Similarly, some parents are reluctant for their children with disabilities to be in Regular Ed classrooms because *they* feel the classroom teachers aren't trained. But the experiences at my children's school demonstrated that a good teacher is a good teacher. And the most important characteristic is what's *in their hearts, not their heads*. They don't have to be experts in Special Education or experts on a child's disability condition; they can learn valuable information from Special Ed teachers, our children, and ourselves. All they need are good hearts, open minds, a willingness to try new things, and a love of children.

The successful inclusive school really *is* about people's hearts. At Columbine, educators went "beyond" IDEA. In fact, Special Ed law was almost irrelevant.

WERE WE TRAINED?

I have to laugh when I hear Regular Ed teachers say they weren't "trained" to teach children with disabilities. My response to this statement when I'm doing a presentation is this: "Parents weren't trained either! Do you think *I* have a 'cerebral palsy degree' and that's how I got my son? My husband and I get up every day and *learn by doing*. Sometimes things work out OK, and sometimes they don't, so then we try something new. The same is true for educators or others who interact with children or adults who have disabilities or other differences."

An ancient Chinese proverb says:

I hear and I forget.
I see and I remember.
I do and I understand.

Educators helped all children learn *because it was the right thing to do,* not because of any law. I once asked Principal Mike, "How did you get this way? Did you have an epiphany or something?" He was thoughtful for a moment and replied, "I guess I just thought about what I would want if it were *my* child." *That's how easy it can be.*

The Role of Paraprofessionals

In many schools, there's an automatic assumption (by educators and/or parents) that a child with a disability in a Regular Ed classroom must have an aide (also known as a paraprofessional, educational assistant, "shadow," etc.), and this can result in a variety of negative outcomes:

On any given school day, many parents across the country receive the following phone call, very early in the morning: "Don't send your child to school today because the para is home sick." This is almost unbelievable, but it's the reality in many schools!

• The child and the para may sit together in the back of the room (so they don't "disrupt" the rest of the class). The Regular Ed teacher may take little or no responsibility for the child—the para is the "expert." When the para and child always work together, the child may be excluded from group activities, free choice time, and other opportunities to work and learn with other students. The student may be physically integrated in the classroom, but he's not *part* of the classroom, and the other students may actually see him as an "outsider."

• The aide may be more like a "guard" than a helper, working diligently to prevent the child from "doing anything wrong." This is a terrible situation for the child, as he is not given the opportunity to learn self-discipline or self-direction. He learns helplessness.

• At the other end of the spectrum, some paras are more like a child's "guardian angel"—they do too much for the child, including his school work. To some paras, the child becomes an extension of themselves: if the child "looks good" (in his behavior, his school work, etc.), they look good and/or are doing their jobs well. Again, the child learns helplessness.

• In some situations, the intent is to fade the para's help over time. But if this help is faded to nothing, the para will be out of a job! Many are not willing to lose their jobs, so the child is still determined to be "needy." In other situations, a para feels the need to be needed. Thus, she won't allow the child to demonstrate his competency, for then she would no longer be needed.

• When a child is "shadowed" by a para, it's very unlikely he'll become friends with his classmates. Few will approach since kids typically don't feel it's safe or appropriate to "interrupt" when a grown-up is with a child. Few students will offer help since the para is always there.

• Many children who have been assigned a para rebel against the constant presence of an adult. And why not? First, think of the message it sends to the child—no other child in the classroom has an aide (unless one aide is assigned to two children with disabilities, in which case the two children are expected to stick to one another like glue so the aide can handle both!). The message to the child is clear: "You are incompetent." Second, most children do not have a para at home—their moms don't shadow them at home 100 percent of the time. Third, they may not like the para! It's one thing not to like your teacher: students handle this by depending on each other, staying away from the teacher as much as possible, and through other strategies. But if a para is breathing down a child's neck most of the day and he doesn't like her, he'll resist this constant supervision.

Regardless of the *reason* for the child's rebellion, when he rebels (by refusing to do his work, trying to get away from the para, or whatever), his actions are seen not as communication, but as "inappropriate behavior." This, in turn, can lead to the para exerting *even greater control*, which simply exacerbates an already bad situation. In the worst-case scenario, educators determine a child cannot be in a Regular Ed classroom, at which point he's shipped off to a Special Ed classroom. Few recognize that the child was *set up for failure by the presence of too much help*.

Paraprofessionals can be an integral key to the success of teachers and students in inclusive classrooms. Like therapists, we need them—but in a different way! We can learn a great deal from Principal Mike's perspective on the use of paraprofessionals. In my interview with him, I asked his opinion about the commonly held belief that a child with a disability can be included only if he has a one-on-one aide, and Mike replied:

> You have to go back to your basic core beliefs. Why would we assume that every child with a disability needs an adult with him all the time? If you subscribe to the belief that everyone is either "able" or "unable," then you may feel a child with a disability needs an aide. But all of us have a continuum of strengths to needs.
>
> Things aren't black or white! *Who really has a disability?* Research has shown that deciding which students "need" an IEP is a *purely subjective decision.* It's not based on an objective disability category. Instead, it's based on educators deciding to staff a student into special ed because they think that's the best way to help a child with a disability. At that point, the child is turned over to the special ed teachers. This is not a good way to share responsibility.
>
> In our school, we saw it this way: all students would be in regular classrooms, and if a classroom teacher had a student with significant needs, then another set of hands, eyes, or ears were probably needed. And that meant a person would be assigned to assist *the teacher and the classroom,* not just the child. The role of an assistant is to provide services to help a child learn and to level the playing field.
>
> There can be many dangers when an adult is assigned to the child. Kathie, you taught me that "a full-time aide becomes a maid." A one-on-one para doesn't help a child become responsible for himself. A person in this role may actually feel sorry for the child, have low expectations for him, and/or do too much for him. In too many cases, a child actually *learns dependence!*
>
> A para assigned to one child can send a very powerful message that the classroom teacher isn't really responsible for the child—the para is. When one person is assigned to a child, only that person gets to know the child. Kids with disabilities don't "belong" to the special ed department or the one-on-one aides! But this is what often happens if there's not a sense of shared responsibility for all students. In an inclusive school, the para, the classroom teacher, and the special ed teacher all work together in the regular classroom to ensure all kids are supported in their learning. Sometimes the para works directly with a student with a disability, other times the classroom or special ed teacher provides direct instruction. Again,

> "If you subscribe to the belief that everyone is either 'able' or 'unable,' then you may feel a child with a disability needs an aide. But all of us have a continuum of strengths to needs...*Who really has a disability?* Research has shown that deciding which students 'need' an IEP is a *purely subjective decision.*"

it's very important to use a variety of instructional methods that meet the child's individual needs.

We've mistakenly assumed that only adults should help children with disabilities. But children help one another all the time. So we need to make sure peer supports are in place, too. Kathie, I remember something you told us once about Benjamin: that before an adult stepped in to help Benjamin, we should first see if a child couldn't help. We realized Benjamin's classmates could help him with his coat and his backpack, as well as with many other things. Sometimes a peer can help a child learn math *better* than an adult can. We learned to focus on providing the most natural supports in the classroom.

Some needs can only be met by an adult helper; like when a child needs to be physically transferred to the toilet, for example. Even then, this responsibility should be shared among a variety of adults. If only one person knows how to do this, what happens if/when the person isn't there? Classmates can do a great deal. Friends can help a child in the lunchroom, during academics, on the playground, and everywhere else. This informal type of assistance routinely occurs among kids without disabilities. Why shouldn't it happen to kids with disabilities, too?

What about students with "behavior labels"?

The safety of all students is a real concern of teachers and administrators, and there *is* a fear of students who are considered "disruptive." But, again, pervasive caring is what's needed. We looked at what *caused* a child's behavior to escalate, then we worked on *preventing* that by creating an atmosphere in which the child was supported. And that support comes from teachers and other students, in a variety of ways, to meet the child's needs. For example, some children need to be able to physically move around when they're learning, so teachers allowed that. Whether or not a child is "disruptive" is often *subjective,* and it's tied to the classroom environment, the teacher's style, and more. Our teachers used very creative methods of helping children, and sometimes that meant modifying the environment to meet a child's needs. If a child is supported, feels good about himself, and is engaged in something meaningful, "disruptive behaviors" often disappear.

A New Recipe for Providing Help

Providing the child with a disability with too much or too little help, *or* the wrong kind of help, by the wrong person, at the wrong time, can lead to negative outcomes for the child—now and in the future. "Less is more" in this situation. The less an adult helps a child, the more the student will help himself *and* the more other students will help—and this is what's natural in real life.

So I offer a new recipe for help, based on one you might be familiar with. When you make a pot of stew from scratch, do you dump all the ingredients in the pot and hope it tastes OK? Most of us don't. We start with a few basic ingredients, then add a little of this seasoning, and taste. Then we add a little bit of that, and taste. We keep doing this until we get it *just the way we like it.* If we add all the ingredients at one time, and our stew doesn't taste right because we added too much of this-or-that, we can't take this-or-that out!

We can use this recipe in the classroom. Start out with the basics: the Regular Ed teacher, the Special Ed teacher who comes in and out, the child with a disability, and the other students in the classroom, and take a "wait and see" attitude. Allow time for these "ingredients" to blend; give the teacher time to grow, let the natural supports of the students blossom, and see what the child can do for himself. If necessary, add some environmental modifications, assistive technology, or other accommodations. Then let it cook for awhile longer to see how things go. Add a paraprofessional only if it's absolutely necessary, and in small dollops, for specific help, at specific times—*here* and *there,* but not everywhere, all the time.

Imagine how much differently a child will feel about himself in these circumstances—he's competent! Imagine how good the Regular Ed teacher will feel about herself—she's competent! And the other students know they're competent, too! Everybody wins!

Therapies & Specialized Assistance

In a truly inclusive school, students with disabilities are not pulled-out for therapy services and other specialized help; these are, instead, provided to the child in the Regular Ed classroom. Again, collaboration among educators and specialists is the key, and the same techniques for using therapists as consultants, as described in Chapter 6, apply in a school setting.

At Columbine, educators and parents questioned the traditional pull-out method. What are students missing in their classrooms while they're pulled out for therapy? How do the therapeutic activities actually help with the child's overall academic education? How does stacking plastic donuts, riding on a scooter board, or leg stretches help a child in school? How do these and similar activities contribute to his overall success and preparation for a successful adult life, after school?

Many parents (and some educators and specialists) have learned, to their dismay, that children who learn isolated skills in isolated settings may not be able to generalize those skills in other environments. For example, a child may demonstrate improvements in reading while with a reading specialist in a Special Ed room or other "special" environment in the school. But when he returns to the Regular Ed classroom—which is a different environment, with different people—he shows no improvement in reading.

Similarly, an IEP Team may believe that "improving fine motor skills" is a worthy goal, so the OT has the child stack plastic donuts, tie a bow on a wooden shoe, and/or practice other eye-hand coordination activities. These, it's believed, will help him write with a pencil one day. During pull-out therapy, he may successfully whiz through these activities, but they have no effect on his handwriting skills back in the Regular Ed classroom!

When the child is pulled out, the message to the child is clear: he's Presumed Incompetent. In addition, he's not part of the classroom anymore; he's missing academics or other important activities (including, perhaps, recess!), as well as opportunities for social interactions and friendships; he may even get behind in the academics he's missing; the Regular Ed teacher is oblivious to the help he's getting and so she doesn't learn beneficial strategies that can be used throughout the school day; and in the worst-case scenario, the other students see the child as vastly different or as an undesirable acquaintance, since he's taken to the "retard room" or other location. Finally, many children may rebel against pull-out services, by refusing to cooperate or by other means. Some children may quietly go along—they hate being pulled-out, but they've given up trying to fight it. In the process, they may internalize the PRESUMED INCOMPETENT message—a tragic loss to their hearts and minds that may never be undone.

So the solution—with benefits for all—is providing these Services in the Regular Ed classroom, and there are as many ways to do this as there are students, teachers, and specialists! There can be resistance, however, by therapists/specialists who are unaccustomed to this new way of thinking. And like inclusion, itself, learning these new ways is a process for all.

When my son, Benjamin, was in kindergarten, I initially agreed to let the physical therapist pull him out. Then I learned about the activity she planned: helping him walk up the stairs to strengthen his legs. I told her Benjamin would probably do this one time. But when he realized the trip up the stairs *wasn't* for the purpose of going to the library or some other great place, he'd balk. He would not want to go on the "stairs that go nowhere" more than once.

So I proposed an alternative, which would accomplish the same thing, would occur in the natural environment, and would not necessitate pulling Benj out of class, and the PT agreed. She could schedule her time with Benjamin during recess, and could help him climb the ladder on the slide—he would be willing to do this fun activity over and over.

This—and similar activities—was a form of Traditional Therapy, but it did not detract from my son's inclusion in the classroom or typical activities. The following year, we moved to consultative therapeutic services. We believed it would be more helpful for therapists to provide assistance to teachers on strategies to ensure Benjamin benefitted from the Regular Ed environment and curriculum, instead of focusing on therapeutic goals (such as "leg strengthening").

Again, there was some resistance, but once the PT got on board, she really enjoyed her new role! Instead of working directly on Benjamin's *body*, she worked with the PE teacher. Sometimes this collaboration involved the PT helping the PE teacher learn the best way Benjamin could participate in a particular activity, such as modifications to the activity for Benjamin or providing him with a different size ball, etc.

Other times, the PT was Benjamin's "helper." For example, his PE class once spent several weeks learning to swing from a rope, then letting go at the right moment, in order to land safely on the padded mats on the floor. Well, Benjamin could hang on to the rope for dear life. In fact, when his spasticity kicked in and every part of his body tightened up, he would not *be able* to let go of the rope and land safely. So the PT came up with a great accommodation: she brought in a mountain climbing harness and hooked Benj up. He still held on to the rope like the other kids, but the PT held on to the rope attached to the harness. Benj was able to swing back and forth like the other kids (and the PT helped him swing in even bigger arcs!), then on the PE teacher's cue,

I'm always amazed that parents are willing to fight tooth-and-nail to get school therapies for their children, yet most have no clue what they're really fighting for. I've asked parents, "Have you ever *been at school* when your child is receiving therapy?" Most admit they haven't, but they think it's the equivalent of private therapy: 30 minutes of uninterrupted one-on-one time. The reality is usually far different. In some schools, therapists pull kids from different classes and essentially do "group" therapy. In another situation, a therapist was supposed to work with the child during gym class, but she's running late, so she pulls him out of math, instead. And there are many other scenarios. Before you decide to wage war with educators over therapy, observe for yourself so you know if it's worth the fight!

Benjamin let go of his rope, and simultaneously, the PT quickly lowered Benj to the mats with her rope.

In addition to working in the natural environments of a PE class or at recess, the PT provided invaluable assistance to students and teachers in many other ways. She helped with environmental modifications in classrooms; provided information about helpful Assistive Technology devices; and more.

After the school provided a standing frame for Benjamin, the PT showed everyone how to use it. Then we (myself, the PT, the teacher, and Benjamin) decided how best to use it within the typical activities of his inclusive classroom: during small group activities (in science and other subjects), Benj would be placed in the standing frame (which had a large tray attached), and the students in his group gathered around Benj in his standing frame, using the standing frame tray as their work surface.

The OT had more difficulty adjusting to the "consult" model. We told her no more stacking donuts or other typical fine motor activities. Instead, we asked her to schedule her time with Benjamin during writing lessons, so she could help him with keyboarding skills. Writing with a pencil wasn't ever going to be the most efficient way for Benj to write, and the computer was the way to go. The OT bristled at this suggestion, saying, "That's not therapy! *Anyone* could help him with that!" At which point, Benjamin's classroom teacher said, "Well, you're absolutely right about that. Maybe we don't need you in the classroom after all. Why don't you just spend time showing me and the teacher's aide how to best help Benj on the keyboard." And that's what happened.

In the consultant role, the OT provided constructive ideas about handwriting, keyboarding, painting in art class, eating in the cafeteria, etc.; suggested assistive technology devices that might be helpful; recommended modifications in the classroom and other locations in school; and more.

My son did not receive speech therapy in school, but several other students did. A few parents insisted that their children be pulled out for help with articulation and other speech issues. Other parents, however, wanted their children to be helped in the Regular Classroom. In this case, the most sensible time to help children with their speech needs was when students were talking—like during reading time, in music, and/or other times when children were expected to be vocal. For example, during small-group reading activities, the speech therapist was the "teacher" for the group that included the student with a disability. She helped all the children in that group with fun "mouth exercises" and more.

Like Special Ed teachers and paraprofessionals, therapists and other specialists can collaborate with Regular Ed teachers by co-teaching. The PT can co-teach in a PE class; an OT can co-teach a writing lesson or an art lesson; a reading or math specialist can co-teach those lessons with the Regular Ed teacher. In these scenarios, all children in the class benefit, and the specific needs of the child with a disability are met. In addition, when specialists are in the classroom, they're informally *teaching other students* how to provide assistance to the child with a disability.

Pull-out services for *academic* subjects *can* work, if—and it's a big if—this type of help is provided to the whole student body. For example, in some schools up to half the students in any given math class might troop to another room down the hall for "group math tutoring." In this circumstance, a student with a disability isn't singled out. However, there's still a harmful message about competence and belonging of students who are pulled out.

Now here are a few thoughts from Principal Mike about pull-out:

Well, this was something else we learned by doing. At first, therapists *did* pull kids out for the prescribed therapy. But, again, when kids were pulled out, they missed so much in the classroom! And we began to question how relevant "medical-type" therapies were to a child's education. We figured out therapists needed to come into the classroom and provide relevant, meaningful assistance that supported the child's educational goals. In many cases, therapists moved from providing direct service to being consultants: helping teachers learn how to implement beneficial "therapeutic-like" activities throughout the day. Again, it's important that services for kids with disabilities be provided in the natural environment.

In Chapter 6, you met Beth, Rene, and Lorrie, professors at the University of Oklahoma, who are helping Master's level PT/OT students learn new ways of doing things. Following is another excerpt from my interview with them. I asked their opinion about pull-out therapy:

> "We need to stop the pull-out."

RENE: We need to stop the pull-out. We need to become a support to the classroom, to ensure a child's successful participation in the general ed classroom, whether that's during academics, PE, art, music, or whatever. To do this, we must *be* in the same location as the child, and pull-out can't achieve this. If we do our job right, we build relationships with educators and administrators so *all* kids have opportunities. You can't do this by pulling a kid out.

LORRIE: Our focus should be on what's really going to make a difference in that child's school day. A kid might need help learning to get on and off the bus. If so, I must be where the bus is at the right time. And as soon as the child can do it for himself, I'm no longer needed!

BETH: We're also helping our students widen the focus from the individual to the environment. They learn to consider what needs to change in the environment to ensure a child will develop friendships, have successful learning opportunities, and more.

LORRIE: The more you're in the classroom, you become a better helper. Lots of people come into classrooms to help: parents, grandparents, and other volunteers. When you're in the classroom instead of pulling kids out you become just another helper and that's a great thing! I knew this was all working when a couple of kids came up to me and said, "We know whose grandma *you* are!" Well, I'm actually not anyone's grandma! But it was great that the kids saw me that way—they didn't know I was a physical therapist! When you're in the classroom, you're there for the whole classroom, including the teacher.

One challenge was helping a teacher learn new ways of thinking. When she saw me come in the classroom, she automatically said, "You can take him out," because she was accustomed to pull-out. I told her I just wanted to hang out. We're helping our students learn how to "hang out with intent"—and my intent was to see what needed to happen in this classroom so the child and his teacher were successful. I had been told that the child needed this-and-that. But the longer I hung out, the teacher became more comfortable with me and began telling me about other things that could help this student be more successful. This never happens with pull-out!

RENE: When I first started doing stuff in the classroom, I had a bit of an identity crisis when I realized that *anyone* could do what I was doing!

That's what happened to one of the school therapists who worked with my son. How did you resolve this issue?
RENE: By realizing that what I was doing in the classroom was *far more important to a student's success* than anything I could do in pull-out! In many instances, therapists *do* have unique knowledge about assistive technology, modifications, or other strategies to create positive change. In other cases, *others* might be able to do what we do just as well. As a therapist, you *do* need to recognize when you don't need to be there. We need to know when to get out of the way!

And beyond focusing on what the child wants to do, we help students learn about the cultural piece. For example, what is the environment in a school classroom? What are expectations for the child? How can I influence the teacher's expectations of the child in that environment? Sometimes you can best support the child by addressing what's going on in the environment. Developing peer supports, providing information to the teacher, or developing architectural supports are the things that may really make a difference.

> "...what I was doing in the classroom was *far more important to a student's success* than anything I could do in pull-out!"

The Role of Parents and Students

Inclusion cannot happen without real teamwork. The educators at Columbine routinely requested and valued the opinions and experiences of students and their parents.

Benjamin attended his IEP meetings. It was *his* education, and I thought it was very important for everyone to see him as a REAL CHILD. (More about this later.) But it was Benjamin's wonderful 1st/2nd Continuum teacher who shared the importance of Benjamin *participating* in his own IEP meeting. I loved this woman—still do—and she taught me (and my son!) so very much. Midway through his first grade year, Mrs. M told me, "Kathie, we cannot write any more goals for Benjamin unless *he's* involved. You and I wrote his goals—things we believe are important. When you bring him to school every day, it's my job to help him achieve these goals, but he's not interested in many of them! We need to write goals that *he* cares about." *Duh!* She was absolutely right!

During kindergarten, I bought Benjamin a name stamp so he could "write" his name on his papers. In first grade, Benjamin was doing most of his work on the computer, but we *did* think it would be good if he could learn to write his name. Mrs. M and I had talked about this before writing the goal, and our reasoning was that Benj should learn to write his name so when he was an adult he could sign checks, sign papers, etc. Sounds good in theory, doesn't it? In practice, however, it didn't—to Benjamin!

For the first couple of months of first grade, Mrs. M, the Special Ed teacher, and/or the teacher's aide worked with Benj on handwriting—with little success. On one particular day Benj had evidently had enough, and he told Mrs. M he didn't need to write his name—with a pencil on paper—because he already *knew* how to write his name [he'd been doing it for years on the computer]. So Mrs. M told him why this was important: he could sign checks when he was older and so forth. He looked at her for a long while and asked, "What are 'checks'?" Mrs. M realized the example she gave Benj was the wrong one, and she figured this wasn't the right time to launch into an economics discussion with him. She tried a different tactic; suggesting Benj might want to be able to sign birthday cards, to which he replied, "I have a name stamp for that!"

Well, moms and dads, Benj was right. He *didn't* need to learn how to write his name—and he was wiser than we were, because all the time spent trying to get him to write his name could have been spent on other academic goals that were *relevant* and *meaningful* to him! (Memorize those two words and use them when thinking about goals for your child.) We all learned from this experience, and from that time forward, Benjamin and other students with disabilities took a more active role in their own education.

Here are Principal Mike's thoughts on the role of parents:

They need to communicate very clearly about their child's needs and to share the hopes and dreams they have for their child. Also, parents need to tell teachers when they're doing a good job and when they're not, and give them permission and encouragement to do something different or better. Parents need to trust educators, but they also need to advocate for their children. And that's the job of every parent, not just parents of kids with disabilities.

Parents need to be both positive and constructive, and they also need to realize they're probably not going to have it all. For example, if your daughter has Down syndrome, and you want her in an inclusive classroom, don't expect educators to spend hours teaching her functional skills like cooking or tying her shoes! If she's in an inclusive classroom, she'll be part of the school, just like kids without disabilities, and she'll be learning from the regular curriculum. There are trade-offs. If you want educators to focus on teaching your daughter how to cook or tie her shoes, then an inclusive classroom probably isn't the best place for your daughter.

It might not be politically correct to say this, but it's the reality: schools can't do everything for every child. A school is a resource parents can use to help their children become successful. Parents need to consider what they really want the school to do for their children.

I feel it's really important for parents to believe in their children—to see them as learners who have great potential. Do you want your child to acquire only functional abilities, or do you want her to have a real future that includes post-secondary education, a real job, and so forth? Traditionally, we've spent too much time and energy trying to remediate the effects of the disability and/or focusing on a very narrow aspect of a child's development, instead of looking at the child as a whole person.

> EDUCATION BEGINS AT HOME. YOU CAN'T BLAME THE SCHOOL FOR NOT PUTTING INTO YOUR CHILD WHAT YOU DIDN'T PUT INTO HIM. YOU DON'T JUST TAKE YOUR CHILD TO BALLET CLASS. FIRST, YOU DANCE WITH HIM WHEN HE IS A BABY. EVERY FAMILY HAS ITS OWN RHYTHM, AND IF YOU DANCE WITH YOUR CHILDREN, THAT RHYTHM WILL BECOME A PART OF THEM, AND THEY WILL NEVER FORGET IT.
>
> *Geoffrey Holder*

Inclusive education, coupled with positive relationships between parents and educators, creates the opportunity for children with disabilities to learn, grow, and be part of life. Children with disabilities—like all children—can succeed in boundless ways.

Good Strategies Can Work Anywhere

Throughout this section on Columbine's journey to inclusion, I've shared strategies used in an elementary school, but these same strategies can be applied at the middle school and high school levels. In some cases, slight modifications might be necessary. The ideas presented in this chapter are not the only methods that work, and there are a variety of good books on inclusion, some of which focus on primary or secondary schools. But, in the end, a school will experience success only when educators realize inclusion has very little to do with the disabilities of students, and *everything* to do with the attitudes of educators.

Improved Parent/Educator Partnerships

Parents and educators: They're supposed to work together, on behalf of a child. When they do, it's like a sweet symphony, a perfect harmony, a beautiful... OK, enough. When they *don't* work together, it's like a shoot-out at the OK Corral, a guerilla war, or nuclear annihilation with lots and lots of fall-out... I'll stop there.

Parents and educators are equally important in the education of children with disabilities. Both, in theory, are "on the same side"—working on behalf of a child. But, for a variety of reasons, parents and educators often adopt an us/them mentality, and when the dust settles after another scuffle, it's the child who is the ultimate loser.

Later in this chapter, you'll have the opportunity to create an IEP Blueprint that can—hopefully—lead to an inclusive education for your child. But the success of your efforts will depend largely on the strategies you use and your personal relationship with educators.

> PEOPLE WHO FIGHT FIRE WITH FIRE USUALLY END UP WITH ASHES.
> *Abigail Van Buren*

If we want improvements in our children's education, we need to move past the us/them mentality and improve our relationships with educators, because *they touch our children's lives every school day*. As I hope you know by now, we cannot change others, we can only change ourselves. So if we're to have improved relationships, we must change ourselves!

Many years ago, during a brief, but difficult time in my marriage, I went to a counselor, alone. I needed to vent and I wanted "professional" advice. If you're a married woman, you can probably relate very easily to my situation at that time. I complained to the counselor about some of my husband's "bad habits"—little things that, cumulatively, were creating great frustration and anger. I just couldn't see us living this way for the rest of our lives. The counselor asked me if these were "new behaviors" that my husband had just begun. "No," I replied, "he's been doing them the whole time we've been married, and I'm sick of it all!" She pointed out that these behaviors, at one time, must have been acceptable to me, or I wouldn't have married him. Hmmmm—that was

hard to take, but she was right. She then went on to say, "Kathie, when you're in a relationship with someone, it's like you're dancing a slow dance. Your dance steps match. But if one of you changes your dance steps, the other person's dance steps will have to change, too, if you both want to keep dancing." She asked if I wanted to keep "dancing" with my husband—did I want to stay married? Of course I did! So she said, "Then you change your dance steps [change yourself] and his dance steps will change." (I did, and it worked: June 14, 2005 marked 25 years of wedded bliss.)

Remember a couple of quotes from an earlier chapter? Gandhi said, "Be the change you want to see in the world." Leo Tolstoy said, "Everyone thinks of changing the world, but no one thinks of changing himself."

We cannot make educators be a certain way; we cannot make them think a certain way. We can, however, change ourselves, which will, in turn, change the dynamics of our relationships with them.

If you're already at odds with educators, the chances of an inclusive education for your child are slim. Unless the neighborhood school is already inclusive, you're going to be asking educators to change the way they operate. And they're not very likely to do that if—quite frankly—they hate your guts, they think you're a pain to work with, or they see you as a Mother from Hell.

You might be thinking that the educators you have to work with are a pain in the behind and they're the *Educators* from Hell. And they might be. But, for our children's sake, we cannot continue to do battle with one another. Someone has to call a truce, and in most cases, it's up to parents to do this *because it's in our children's best interest.*

In the remainder of this section (and in the IEP Blueprint section) I'm going to ask you to do some things that may make you want to throw this book at me! I'm going to ask you to "play nicely" with educators—and more. You might already be doing this. If so, keep up the good work. If not, your attitude might be something like, "The teachers at my child's school aren't nice to me and they're hard to work with—why should I be nice to them?" *Because it's in your child's best interest to do so.* Tattoo this on your heart to keep your focus on what's really important.

Most of the battles at IEP meetings and disagreements between parents and educators are not really about the child. They might *start out* being about the child and his education, but they quickly degenerate into a battle of wills—and people's egos. We keep score: Educators 2, Parents 0. "OK," thinks the parent, "I'll get 'em next time." And educators may do the same thing. Once our egos are in charge, it's almost impossible to see the forest for the trees (the child and his education, in this case). And many parents have adamantly refused to change their ways: they don't want to lose face—it's too painful to their egos. (And the same might be true for many educators).

But many parents change their tune when they consider this scenario I often share during presentations: if your child was standing in the middle of the street and was about to get run over by a car, would you throw yourself in front of your child to protect him, at the risk of serious bodily harm to yourself—or

Unknown to many parents, much of what goes on at an IEP meeting has little to do with the child, and more to do with the internal politics of the school. For example, if the Special Ed director and the principal are at odds with each other, their poor relationship can impact what happens at your child's IEP meeting! This is why it's even more important for us to have positive relationships with educators who touch our children's lives!

even at the risk of being killed? Every parent I've asked has replied, *"Yes! Of course I would!!!"* And my reply is always, "Then you can change your ways with educators. If you're willing to risk your life for your child, *you can risk your ego.* Isn't your child worth it?" (I'm assuming you'll answer "yes," to this question, so let's get started!)

If you're not on the best of terms with educators, *do whatever it takes to repair these relationships.* If you've said or done things you shouldn't, apologize and make amends. If things have just been tense or stressful, *regardless of who generated the tension,* say something like the following: "I'm sorry we've had difficulty getting along together. I want you to know that I'm willing to do whatever it takes for us to work better together, because I know we both care about my child and his education." Then give the person a big hug. *Yes, a big hug!* Something magical happens with a personal touch. And don't worry if the person is surprised or if she doesn't hug you back. She might think this is a phony act that's a set-up of some kind. Give it time. When she sees this really is the beginning of a "new and improved" relationship, she'll hug you back. You're changing your dance steps, remember?

If you're gritting your teeth at the mere thought of saying the words above or giving the hug, *know this:* many parents who have followed this suggestion have let me know that *saying those words and giving the hug* have improved the relationship immediately. If you feel nervous or are unsure if you'll be able to get nice words to come out of your mouth, role-play with someone—practice until you get it right, then do it.

After you begin the process of repairing the relationship, it's important to *maintain* a positive relationship. (And when establishing new relationships, start off on the right foot, and keep the relationship positive.) We can do this by checking in with educators on a regular basis—personal visits are best, but phone calls will do in a pinch.

> AM I NOT
> DESTROYING MY
> ENEMIES WHEN
> I MAKE FRIENDS
> OF THEM?
> *Abraham Lincoln*

In my son's case, I never wanted to fall back on "calling another IEP meeting" to resolve issues. I preferred to work proactively and anticipate issues before they became big problems. So I asked Benjamin's Regular Ed and Special Ed Teachers and the teacher's aide (along with the PT and the OT, as appropriate) to meet with me (and Benjamin, when appropriate) on the first Monday of the month, for no more than one hour, to talk about how things were going. At some of these meetings, everything was going so great that we were finished in fifteen minutes. At others, we prioritized the issues and handled them quickly to ensure the meeting was over within one hour. And I always brought snacks to these meetings! I deeply appreciated educators taking the time to meet with me on their own time.

There are many different ways to establish and maintain positive relationships with educators—you're limited only by your imagination. And the *more* positive relationships you have, the better. During this process, *you'll also be rehabilitating your image.* If you've been known as the Mother from Hell, the efforts you make to create positive relationships will redefine your persona. And this is more important than you may realize. Some of us (me, at one time) feel proud if educators seem to quake in their boots when they see us coming. We may even brag to others about our power! But some of us have also realized that, while we may sometimes bend others to our will, we have to continually watch over their shoulders. As soon as we're out of sight, they heave a sigh of relief that we're gone, and then *they do what they want!* So what have we really achieved? Furthermore, do we really want people "being scared of us"? *What kind of relationship is based on fear or loathing?*

Moreover, have you ever thought about what effect *our* actions in this regard have on our children? If educators are angry with us or hate our guts, who do you think pays the ultimate price? Our children. No, most educators aren't going to take their frustration with us out on our children by beating them—they're more likely to ignore them and/or not care about them, one way or another.

Here's something I learned years ago that might be news to you: *if educators like you, they'll do right by your child.* Things might not always be perfect, and there might still be issues to resolve, but things will be 100 times better than if educators don't like you. And this is just common sense!

Some parents have complained: "But it shouldn't be like this! Teachers should just follow the law and do what they're supposed to do. How they feel about me should be irrelevant when it comes to my child's education." In theory, that's correct. But real life isn't theoretical. Real life is about human beings—and educators are human beings just like you and me—who have feelings, attitudes, and opinions; who get up on the wrong side of the bed sometimes; who probably respond well to compliments, and poorly to criticism; and who prefer to be around others who treat them well, instead of those who treat them harshly. Yes, in theory, Special Ed law should be enough. But in practice, the law is an abstract, while our children are real.

If we want our children to be treated well by educators, we need to treat those educators well. So get connected, and stay connected to teachers of all kinds, the principal, the secretaries, the librarian, the custodian, and anyone else who might touch your child's life now, or in the future.

You can have an informal face-to-face meeting once a month with your child's teacher(s), as described previously; a brief phone meeting every two weeks; or something similar. If you take your child to school, take a batch of cookies with you once a week: for your child's teacher(s), for the teachers' lounge, for the weekly staff meeting, and/or for the principal and the secretaries. When you pick up your child from school, stick your head in his classroom, or the principal's office, or wherever, to say "Hi" and "Thanks." If your child typically rides the bus, pick her up from school occasionally, and follow the suggestions above—and don't forget to give the school bus driver some cookies, too!

Write educators thank you notes—regularly—for the little things and the big things they do. Take a teacher—or the principal, special ed director, or school board member—to lunch! Amazing things happen when we're on "neutral turf." Keep in mind, of course, that teachers have very short lunch breaks, so plan accordingly! For example, ask what her favorite restaurant dish is, order it "to

WHEN DEALING WITH PEOPLE, REMEMBER YOU ARE NOT DEALING WITH CREATURES OF LOGIC, BUT WITH CREATURES OF EMOTION, CREATURES BRISTLING WITH PREJUDICE, AND MOTIVATED BY PRIDE AND VANITY.

Dale Carnegie

go," then pick the teacher up, and share your take-out meal at a park, where things are calm and beautiful. This is just one example—be creative!

Volunteer at school, in your child's room or elsewhere. (Think long-term, and consider volunteering in classes you might want your child in two or three years down the road!) Be the PTA president—it's hard for educators to tell you "no" when it comes to your child's education if you're a PTA officer, a dedicated volunteer, or provide other help to the school. If you work full-time, find a way to take an afternoon off every so often so you can volunteer. If that's not possible, ask how you can help at home. A friend of mine couldn't spend time at school because of her work schedule, but there were many things teachers needed done that she could do at home.

While you're improving your relationships with educators, take the next step and try to get to know them as individuals. Once you've exchanged your "Angry Mom" hat for the "Cookie Mom" or "Volunteer Mom" hat, do the same thing with educators. If, for example, you take the time to get to know the Special Ed Director (or whomever) as "Fred" who races motorcycles on Sundays, babysits his grandson on a regular basis, and loves tortillas slathered with butter and salt, you'll be changing the dynamics of your relationship. This doesn't automatically mean you'll agree on everything, and there may still be some tension. But knowing him as a *real person*, and letting him know you in the same way, will provide a foundation that will enable you to weather the storms of tension. Imagine seeing Fred at an IEP meeting on Monday and being able to greet him with, "How was your motorcycle race yesterday?" (This example is based in part on my true-life adventures with the Special Ed director in our district. He really *did* race motorcycles on weekends, and he loved the fact that I asked him about it on a regular basis, giving him the opportunity to share his triumphs!)

> WE OFTEN GET IN QUICKER BY THE BACK DOOR THAN BY THE FRONT.
> *Napoleon Bonaparte*

Too often, and whether it's justified or not, many educators feel we come to school only when we're "angry" or we "want something." When we take the time to volunteer, participate in our children's schools, and/or stay in close contact with educators, we create a new image of ourselves, one that says *we care about the people who touch our children's lives.* Remember, this is all about *what's in the best interests of your child!*

Before closing out this section, I need to share another important reason for you to maintain positive relationships with educators, and it's related to your preparation of an IEP Blueprint for your child, later in this chapter. In this Blueprint, you'll be taking a more important role in the Special Ed assessment process, writing goals, and making other significant contributions to the IEP process. In order to successfully complete these activities, you need to be familiar with the Regular Ed classroom(s) you want your child to be in. You're going to need to know something about the curriculum, the atmosphere, and the teacher(s) in those classrooms.

Because many of us have little or no familiarity with Regular Ed classrooms, educators can easily blow us out of the water when we try to have our children included. With the best of intentions, we state our case, but an educator can respond with something like, "But your Johnny can't do [such-and-such], so there's no way he could be in a Regular Ed fifth grade classroom!" If you do not have any familiarity with that classroom, there's little you can say in response, except to fall back on Special Ed law, and we know that's irrelevant to many educators! If, however, you have familiarity with the classroom, you'll be presenting suggested goals, curriculum modifications, and other pertinent information about "how" Johnny can be successful in this classroom. Details about how all this comes together are in the IEP Blueprint section. For now, just know that having great relationships with educators is vitally important so that, when the time is right, you'll be able to go into different classrooms to observe, in preparation for your child's IEP meeting. If your relationships with educators are rocky, opportunities to observe or to visit potential classrooms will be limited.

The Special Ed Evaluation Process

The first step in the IEP process involves Special Ed assessments and evaluations. To clarify, I'm not talking about the statewide assessments mandated by No Child Left Behind (NCLB), but the assessments/evaluations used to determine (1) whether a child qualifies for Special Ed services and later, (2) the student's present levels of achievement.

Historically, many parents haven't been very involved in the evaluation process—we give permission for our children to be tested and the next thing we know, the test results are being discussed at the child's IEP meeting. Sometimes we're very shocked by assessment results; other times we may not agree. But by that time, the genie is out of the bottle and can't be put back in. The results of Special Ed evaluations can have a profound effect on our children's education, so it's important that we know what the law says and become more involved in this part of the IEP process.

IDEA 2004 Part B, Section 614 (b) says the school shall (italics added):

> ...use a variety of assessment tools and strategies to gather relevant functional, developmental, and academic information, *including information provided by the parent*...related to enabling the child to be involved in and progress in the general education curriculum, or, for preschool children, to participate in appropriate activities...The child is assessed in all areas of suspected disability...Assessment tools and strategies [should] provide relevant information...in determining the educational needs of the child...

This part of the law also states the IEP Team shall "...review existing evaluation data on the child, including *evaluations and information provided by the parents, current classroom-based, local, or State assessments, and classroom-based observations, and observations by teachers and related services providers...*" and all of this evaluation data is to be used to determine whether "...any additions or modifications to the special education and related services are needed to enable the child to meet the measurable annual goals...and to participate, as appropriate, *in the general education curriculum.*" [Italics added.]

Educators often use assessments as the *primary* rationale for deciding placement. Once this "decision" has been made (without parental input and prior to the IEP meeting, *contrary to IDEA*), we're put in the position of trying to change something that's already been decided—*we've gotten in the game too late!*

As I detailed in Chapter 5, traditional, standardized assessments/evaluations are frequently used to "prove" what educators already believe to be true about a child. Also, these are often "global" evaluations that are not relative to a child's *involvement and progress in the general curriculum,* and few educators use assessments to determine if modifications are needed to enable a child to participate in a Regular Ed classroom, per IDEA.

Not only should we question how assessments are *used,* we also need to consider the *conditions* under which they're given. How well would *you* do on a test if you were taken out of your natural environment, perhaps without knowing why? What if the person giving you the test is a stranger, or someone you barely know. If you were a child, would you be tense and maybe even frightened? What if you were hungry, thirsty, and/or tired? The *conditions* under which assessments are given are critical factors, which may or may not be of concern to those *giving* the tests—but they should be, if they want accurate results.

So just how accurate are traditional, standardized assessments? How much information do they really provide about a child? And should they be used to determine a child's educational future? Not very, not much, and no!

> EDUCATION IS
> TOO IMPORTANT
> TO BE LEFT
> SOLELY TO
> THE EDUCATORS.
> *Francis Keppel*

There's an alternative: non-standard or informal assessments, which can provide the most useful information about a student with a disability, relative to his *involvement and progress in the general curriculum,* per IDEA. They can also enable the IEP Team to write an effective and appropriate educational program that is truly individualized to the child.

Many educators, however—especially those who routinely do the testing—may balk at informal assessments, and say they're not "legal." But the portions of the law I've shared say otherwise. What specialists may actually be arguing is "school policy"—which may dictate the use of traditional tests. But Federal law trumps school district policy and state educational policies.

Because the idea of informal assessments may be "new" to educators, it's important to proactively and positively explain the benefits and share what the law says. If necessary, negotiate and compromise in order to make informal assessments a reality for your child. Educators, parents, *and students* can work together to design informal, non-standard assessments that:

- take place in a setting that's relevant to the subject being assessed and comfortable for the child, e.g., physical abilities in the gym, on the playground, or in the child's backyard; academic abilities in a classroom setting or at home; communication abilities in reading groups or via conversations, etc.;

- are performed by the appropriate personnel, keeping in mind the language of the law regarding assessing a child relative to his *involvement and progress in the general curriculum*: a PE teacher (assisted by a physical therapist,

"WHAT WILL IT TAKE?"

See yourself as a negotiator. Instead of asking questions that can be answered "yes" or "no," ask "What will it take?" [WWIT] Here's an example of how it works:

Q: WWIT to do ABC?
A: It would take DEF.
Q: So WWIT to do DEF?
A: It would take GHI.
Q: WWIT to do GHI?
A: It would take XYZ.

With every answer, you get another bit of information, which you use in your next question, and every answer tells you more and gets you closer to your objective. It works—try it with educators during the IEP process!

It also works with your husband (or wife), children, and others.

"Honey, what will it take to get the lawn mowed this weekend?"

"It will take me watching the golf tournament first."

"OK, that will work."

This method helps you get what you want or need without nagging, flighting, screaming, begging, or anything else!

if necessary) could assess physical abilities; a classroom teacher from the grade level the child will be going into can assess educational abilities; the classroom teacher, assisted by a speech therapist, if necessary, could assess a child's communication abilities; and so forth;

- are activity-based, designed to provide information on specific areas of concern (e.g., reading and math only, and so forth) relative to the grade level the child will be entering—rather than trying to measure a child's cognitive abilities using global intelligence tests;

- create opportunities to discover the accommodations that will enable a child to be involved in and make progress in the general curriculum;

- measure a child's strengths and competencies, as well as his needs.

Here's one example of an informal assessment strategy: Robby is a nine-year-old who should be in the fourth grade next school year. At the end of the previous school year, he could spend some time in Mrs. T's class, with other fourth-graders. During this time, Mrs. T could encourage Robby to participate in the class activities, and she could observe, relative to math and reading (Robby's greatest needs). During recess time, while the other students are out of the classroom, Mrs. T could sit and talk with Robby about numbers, math, reading, words, etc. to determine what he presently knows. She might decide it's important for Robby to visit the class again; she might want to observe Robby in his current classroom; and she could also give Robby some typical fourth-grade tests on math and reading to see how he does. All this is not to assess Robby for *exclusion*, but to determine his present level of academic achievement *and* to determine what *he will need* to be successful in Mrs. T's classroom.

Robby's mother has also given Mrs. T samples of his work from his current class, and she's invited Mrs. T to visit Robby at home, too—where she can talk to Robby in his natural environment. Robby's parents (and others who know him well), could also share how Robby learns best (through imitation, activities, etc.). Robby's current teacher can contribute assessment data, as well. If Robby has participated in Sunday School or other typical community activities, samples of his work from those settings, if appropriate, could also be shared. Any adults who have worked with Robby (like a Sunday School teacher) could also contribute information about their experiences with Robby.

Mrs. T (and/or others) can include all this information—including her observations—in a report which could become part of Robby's IEP assessment data. Based on her conclusions, the IEP Team might determine that a calculator could help Robby with math, and books on tape would be beneficial in reading, as well as social studies.

This example is just one of the many different ways an informal, non-standard assessment may provide information that is more valuable, accurate, and helpful than traditional, formal assessments. In order for *you* to be a more active and valuable participant in the assessment process, you'll need to visit and observe the Regular Ed classrooms your child may be attending, to become familiar with the general curriculum in those settings, and these visits should take place *before any assessments are done.* Your first-hand experiences, combined with parental expertise and knowledge of your child, will enable you to substantially contribute to the design of informal assessments, as well as to write goals relative to your child's involvement and progress in the general curriculum, determine what related services (including supports and/or assistive technology devices) are needed by the child, and assist educators in the design of curriculum modifications. Your child, with your help as necessary, should contribute to the design of informal assessments. Talk to him about how he could demonstrate his abilities and determine his needs. Also, you could participate in the assessments, as an observer, a "co-tester," or simply to provide additional information.

> LEADERSHIP IS THE ABILITY TO GET PEOPLE TO DO WHAT THEY DON'T WANT TO DO— AND LIKE IT.
> *Harry S. Truman*

As you consider informal assessments, limit them to the "areas of suspected disability" per IDEA. Some testers often test a child in areas beyond what's necessary. In the process, they "find" new "problems." Translated: they find more reasons to justify placement in a segregated classroom!

If educators don't jump for joy over your proposal to use informal assessments, use the "What will it take?" negotiation strategy. You could ask, "What it take to try this once?" Some educators are reluctant to do anything new for fear they'll "set a precedent." So negotiate doing it "just this once." You could also offer a compromise. If your child needs to be tested in four areas, for example, suggest that two of the assessments be informal and two be formal.

As a last resort, you could refuse to give permission for your child to be formally tested. This could turn into a sticky mess, so be cautious. In some school districts, the only parental signature that's considered a "requirement" is the *very first one.* For some parents, that's when their children were three and entered a Special Ed Preschool! Some educators have used that initial signature as "permission" for many things, and for many years! But IDEA 2004 Part B, Section 614 (c) (3) states:

Each local educational agency shall obtain informed parental consent...prior to conducting any reevaluation of a child with a disability, except that such informed parental consent need not be obtained if the local educational agency can demonstrate that it had taken reasonable measures to obtain such consent and the child's parent has failed to respond.

You could consent to only informal, non-standard assessments. Again, educators might argue school policy doesn't allow this, but try, as best to you can, to work out an agreement that doesn't wreck your relationship with educators.

If you're already somewhat familiar with the curriculum of the Regular Ed classroom you want your child to be in (because you've had another child in that grade, etc.), get your journal or a separate sheet of paper and describe how your child could be informally assessed, relative to his "involvement and progress in the general ed curriculum." If you aren't familiar with the curriculum, do what it takes to gain a familiarity as described previously in this section, *then* write some ideas about informal assessments for your child.

The IEP Blueprint

The most effective and appropriate IEP can be written when parents take a more active role throughout the entire IEP process. Typically, educators and parents come to the IEP meeting with specific ideas in mind, but differences in opinions often lead to a breakdown in communications, misunderstandings, confusion, and/or anger. However, if educators and parents are in closer contact *before* the IEP meeting, they can often avoid these dilemmas. And if you draft a proposal (an IEP Blueprint) and share it with educators during pre-IEP meetings, agreement on a variety of items can be achieved prior to the official IEP meeting. The strategies that follow are presented in the hope that the Blueprint will become the model for the actual IEP that's finalized at the IEP meeting.

While you're reading this section, or before going too far in preparing your child's IEP Blueprint, contact the school and request a copy of the blank IEP forms used by your school district. If you have a good relationship with a Special Ed teacher (or if you're rebuilding your relationship with her), she's probably the best source for this. As you write your child's Blueprint, you can ensure it "matches" the official IEP form. Study the district's forms carefully: this will help the IEP meeting go more smoothly and you'll also be able to see if the forms include spaces for all that's required in IDEA. After I distributed an article about curriculum modifications, many parents told me their school district forms had no "place" to write curriculum modifications, thus, the school did not provide them! The Blueprint you create will include these, and other important information critical to your child's success!

The order of the sub-sections that follow closely mirror the order of these topics in the law. Thus, the IEP meeting should begin with a review of your child's "present level." As you review the school district's IEP forms, see how they compare to the law and the order of topics below.

As you read through this section, I'll be asking you to make some lists. You might want to read the entire section before making these lists so the Big Picture will be clear. In addition, you'll need a familiarity with the Regular Ed classroom(s) where you want your child included.

And speaking of the Big Picture, as you think about your child's education, I hope it will be driven by the hopes and dreams you and your child have for the future. If you want your child to become successfully employed (with or without post-secondary education), he needs an academic education, not years spent in segregated Special Ed classrooms!

Reconnaissance

As I mentioned before, you need to be familiar with the Regular Ed classroom(s) which you'd like your child to be in. If your relationships with educators are good, you may not have any difficulty getting permission to observe in the classroom(s). If possible, volunteer in the classroom, so you'll have multiple opportunities to observe. While you're there, visualize your child in the classroom and consider "how" she can *be involved and make progress* in the general curriculum. What supports, accommodations, curriculum modifications, and/or assistive technology devices will she need? What will the teacher(s) need? Will your child's academic goals be similar to those for the students who don't have disabilities, or will they be different, and if so, how? All you learn in this reconnaissance will contribute to the effective IEP Blueprint you'll prepare.

If you're unable to observe, gather information any way you can: talk to your older children about their experiences at that grade level, talk to other parents whose children are currently in that class/grade level, get hold of the books and/or other materials that are used, or find some other method to learn about the classroom(s).

Use your own common sense about whether or not to "announce" your purpose in observing and/or volunteering. If you have established good relationships with educators, but "inclusion" is a dirty word to them, it's probably not a good idea to tell them why you want to observe. They might try to cut you off at the pass. So you'll need to get into the classroom(s) one way or another without divulging why you want to observe. If, on the other hand, inclusion is a possibility, educators might welcome and be appreciative of your efforts to contribute to your child's education.

An Individualized Education and the IEP Team

Before going into the specifics of the IEP Blueprint, I'll share parts of the law parents (and educators) need to know about the content of the IEP.

First, the burden of proof on *why* a child cannot/should not be included in a Regular Ed classroom rests with the *school*. For too long, based on the assumption that a child will automatically be placed in a segregated Special Ed room, parents felt they had to prove why their child *should be* allowed in a Regular Ed classroom, but IDEA states that a child's IEP will include, "...an explanation of the extent, if any, to which the child will not participate with nondisabled children in the regular class and in the activities described..." [Part B, 614, (d) IEPs, (A) (i) (V)]

IDEA 2004 also states:

...the IEP Team...shall consider the strengths of the child; the concerns of the parents for enhancing the education of their child; the results of the initial evaluation or most recent evaluation of the child; and the academic, developmental, and functional needs of the child. [Part B, Sec. 614, (d) (3) (A)]

[An] IEP [is] a written statement for each child with a disability...that includes: (I) a statement of the child's present levels of academic achievement and functional performance—including how the child's disability affects the child's involvement and progress in the general education curriculum...[and] for children with disabilities who take alternate assessments aligned to alternate achievement standards, a description of benchmarks or short-term objectives;

(IV) a statement of the special education and related services and supplementary aids and services...to be provided to [or on behalf of] the child...and a statement of the program modifications or supports for school personnel that will be provided for the child—to advance appropriately toward attaining the annual goals; to be *involved in and make progress in the general education curriculum...*

Has the IEP Team considered your child's strengths and your parental concerns when writing the IEP?

At your child's next IEP meeting, bring a portfolio of your child's work (from previous school years, as well as from home, Sunday School, etc.). You could also bring a videotape that shows your child participating in inclusive activities in the community, doing chores around the house, or in other settings that demonstrate his strengths and abilities.

And during the meeting, remember to use People First Language, reframe "problems" into "needs," and follow other ideas detailed in Chapter 5.

and to *participate in extracurricular and other nonacademic activities;* and to be educated and participate with other children with disabilities and nondisabled children in the activities described in this subparagraph...[italics added]

(VII) the projected date for the beginning of the services and modifications described in subclause (IV), and the anticipated frequency, location, and duration of those services and modifications... [Part B, Section 614, (d) (A) (i)]

Let's look at these a little closer. First, item (I), regarding your child's "present levels of academic achievement and functional performance, including how the child's disability affects the child's involvement and progress in the general education curriculum" should be used—in conjunction with what's in the next paragraph—to determine what he'll need to be successful in a Regular Ed classroom. Some educators use this part of the law as the basis for placing a child in a segregated Special Ed room. In other words, they use IQ scores and/or other assessment data to "prove" that the child could not be successful in a Regular Ed classroom, instead of looking at "what it will take" for the child to be successful in that environment.

Next, item (IV) details several critically important parts of the IEP related to what your *child* will need, and what modifications and supports the *teachers* need, in order for your child to "be involved in and make progress in the general education curriculum" and "participate in extracurricular and other nonacademic activities..." In general, what children with disabilities need can be divided into three broad categories: assistive technology, supports and accommodations (including behavior supports), and curriculum modifications. We'll look at each of these later in this chapter.

Who is on the IEP Team? According to IDEA 2004:

...the IEP Team [is]...composed of the parents of a child with a disability; not less than 1 regular education teacher of such child (if the child is, or may be, participating in the regular education environment); not less than 1 special education teacher...or not less than 1 special education provider of such child; a representative of the local education agency who is qualified to provide, or supervise the provision of, specially designed instruction to meet the unique needs of children with disabilities; is knowledgeable about the general education curriculum; and is knowledgeable about the availability of resources of the local educational agency; an individual who can interpret the instructional implications of evaluation results, who may be a member of the team described [above]; at the discretion of the parent or the agency, other individuals who have knowledge or special expertise regarding the child, including related services personnel, as appropriate; and whenever appropriate, the child with a disability. [Part B, Section 614 (d) (1) (B)]

A regular education teacher of the child, as a member of the IEP Team, shall... participate in the development of the IEP...including the determination of appropriate positive behavioral interventions and supports...other strategies, and ...supplementary aids and services, program modifications, and support for school personnel...[Part B, Section 614 (d) (3) (C)]

> The student
> is the *most*
> *important*
> *member*
> of the
> IEP Team!

Many school staff members who attend IEP meetings may not be directly involved in a student's daily education, so we need to wonder why they're in attendance! On the other hand, there are some people who *should* be at the IEP meeting, and they're not!

Many parents have recognized the following as a valuable guideline: the smaller the Team, the more actually gets done. So let's do away with humongous Teams. Within the parameters of the law, ensure that only those people who have intimate knowledge of your child and/or those who will be working closely with your child on a regular basis, are present at the IEP meeting. And we, as parents, can courteously, but firmly, state our wishes on this subject, and gently "excuse" those who don't really need to be there.

The most important member of the IEP Team is the child—it's *his* education! When the child is present, many wonderful outcomes are possible. First and foremost, he can be involved in writing his goals. I am routinely amazed (but I shouldn't be, after hearing this same story over and over again) when parents and/or educators tell me that the child doesn't know what his goals are! How in the world do we expect him to achieve the goals if he doesn't even know what they are? And, of course, if and when he does *not* achieve the goals, we blame him—when we should blame *ourselves* for setting this child up for failure!

How can we expect our children to be in charge of their lives as adults if we don't give them the opportunity to make decisions about their lives and their education when they're children?

Second, when the child is present, everyone will realize your child is a REAL CHILD, not a diagnosis and/or a laundry list of problems within the stack of reports! Some parents are horrified by the idea of their children attending the meeting, knowing the terrible ways many educators talk about a child. They certainly don't want their children subjected to this awful experience, which can bring parents to tears. And I agree. The solution is not to keep the child out of the meeting, but to have him there, and change the rules: everyone must talk *to* the child, not *about* him. If Team members forget, the parent or the child can offer gentle reminders about the new way of doing things. You and your child can lead the way: focus on your child's strengths, use People First Language, and reframe "problems" into "needs" as described in Chapter 5.

Other parents express their shock at this whole idea by saying something like, "But the meeting usually last four or five hours! I couldn't ask my child to sit for that long in a meeting." And they're right about that. But as I'll detail a little later on, by writing an IEP Blueprint and discussing it with educators ahead of time, you can the cut the IEP meeting in half, or even less!

I trust you and your child to determine the best way to handle this. If your child is in the K-third grade range, it might be better for him to attend the beginning of the meeting, to share his hopes and dreams, and for everyone to be able to spend a little time with the REAL CHILD. On the other hand, it might be best for him to participate toward the end of the meeting, when it's time to write goals. Or, you could consider having your child there at the beginning *and* the end, but not in the middle. Before deciding, finish reading this book!

Children in fourth grade and above—but most especially those in middle school and high school should not only *attend* their own IEP meeting, they should be *running the meeting!* How in the world do we expect our children

GREAT EXPECTATIONS

Did you hear the story about the teacher who asked the principal to p-l-e-a-s-e give her extra-bright students for the next year—she was exhausted from having to deal with average/below average students.

So when the new school year started, she got a list of her students: Mary-126, Steve-118, Emma-130, Taylor-115, and so on. She was delighted, and she and her students had a great year!

Now it was the last day of school. With the students gone, the teacher cleaned out her desk and found the original class list. On her way out of the building, she stopped by the principal's office, waved the list at him, and said, "Thanks for giving me these high- IQ kids—this was the *best and easiest* year of teaching I've had in 20 years!"

The principal had a confused look on his face, snatched the paper out of her hands, took a look at it, and said, "These were their *locker numbers!*"

Badda-Bing!

to be in charge of their lives as adults, if they're never given the opportunity to make decisions for themselves and their education when they're children?

I mentioned this in an earlier chapter, but I'll share more of this story now. My husband worked on a project with "Jan," who had recently retired from the disability services department at a university in Colorado. She told my husband the biggest dilemma facing students with disabilities entering college is their lack of understanding about what they need to be successful in college, especially regarding accommodations, assistive technology, etc. Under Special Ed law, the *school* is responsible for identification and assessment, curriculum modifications, assistive technology, modifications, and so forth. But the reverse is true in higher education: it is the *student's* responsibility to identify himself as a person with a disability, and to state his needs, including modifications, assistive technology, etc. Jan reported that many students who came to her office for help *didn't even know they had a disability!* Others didn't know the name of their condition, and most didn't have a clue about what they needed. This can be a rough beginning for a blossoming college student. Some, near tears, asked Jan or colleagues, "Can you call my mother?" And the reply was, "This is college; we don't call your parents."

I sincerely hope you'll agree that it's important for your child to be at *his own* IEP meeting. But if, for whatever reason, he does not attend and/or does not participate in *writing his own goals,* I hope you'll ensure he knows what the goals are! Now we'll move to preparing an IEP Blueprint for your child.

Present Level: Abilities, Strengths, and Needs

If educators operate from the MEDICAL MODEL (focusing on a child's deficits and trying to remedy them), they, along with parents, may overlook or minimize a child's strengths (abilities, talents, and interests). But strengths constitute an important part of a child's "Present Levels of Educational Performance" (per IDEA), so it's very important to spend time on this issue. A child's *strengths* should be considered when determining placement, as well as when writing goals (as detailed later in this section).

IDEA states that the following areas should be considered when writing the IEP: physical abilities, communication abilities, thinking (cognitive abilities), social and emotional development, developmental or educational growth, as well as other areas specific to the child. Following are examples of strengths and abilities, followed by descriptions of what they represent:

- Susie can add and subtract columns of two digit numbers [cognitive ability; educational growth].
- Kenneth gets along well with others [social and emotional behavior].
- Marta likes to color maps [personal interest/hobby; cognitive ability].
- Jeff likes to read biographies [hobby; educational growth].
- LaToya wants to learn about chemistry [interest; cognitive ability].
- Juan speaks for himself with communication cards [communication and cognitive abilities; social growth].
- Stephanie learns best by imitation [personal strength; developmental growth].

- Mark is a good speller [cognitive ability; visual memory; educational growth].
- Amber has a coin collection [hobby; cognitive ability].

In your journal or on a separate sheet of paper (you started a list in a previous chapter; now you can add to it), list your child's strengths along with *what they represent* (as shown in the examples above). Enlist the help of others (spouse, your other children, people who know your child well, and especially *your child*) to create a comprehensive picture of the "whole child." Include interests, hobbies, and other activities which are important to your child. Your child is multifaceted and multi-talented. Don't try to do this in one sitting—you'll never think of everything at one time! Stick your list on the refrigerator like a grocery list, and add to it on a regular basis.

Affect of the Disability

Per IDEA, the "Present Level of Educational Performance" should include "how the disability affects the child's involvement and progress in the general curriculum." Educators have often used this part of the IEP as justification to segregate a child. But that's not the intent of the law! By following the law and identifying how the disability affects the child, we can discover what a child needs *so he can be involved in and make progress in the general curriculum,* as described in the examples below, and this information can be helpful later when writing goals.

Alyssa's physical disability results in her inability to write legibly. In order for her to be involved and make progress in the general curriculum, she may need any or all of the following: a computer for class work; assistance in learning the computer; worksheets and tests scanned into the computer; a calculator for math; assistance to improve her handwriting skills; oversized pencils, paint brushes, and markers; and shorter tests and/or an extended time frame for taking tests.

Robert has autism and cannot always stay focused on the teacher during lectures, he cannot stay seated for long periods of time, and he frequently becomes upset and wants to run away. To ensure Robert can be involved and make progress in the general curriculum, he may need the following: a rope swing in the classroom or in the adjacent hallway which he can use any time he feels agitated; the freedom to move around the classroom instead of staying seated at all times; hands-on manipulatives and interactive activities to supplement the general curriculum; and small group instruction and extra help during math and science in the regular classroom.

MacKenzie has low vision and she'll be unable to read the written materials used in the general curriculum. In order to be involved and make progress in the regular educational environment, she'll need books and other materials in large print or recorded on audio tape; large print copies of the teacher's overhead transparencies; orientation assistance to learn where things are in the classroom and the locations of other places in the school (art room, music class, library, cafeteria, etc.); and modified curriculum and materials in art and science classes.

In your journal or on a separate sheet of paper, describe how your child's disability affects his involvement and progress in the general curriculum, using the examples above as a guide. Use plain language, not therapeutic or professional jargon. When you prepare your child's Blueprint, you'll create two documents "Educational Abilities and Strengths" and "Affect of the Disability," which constitute the "Present Level of Performance" part of your child's IEP.

Goals and Objectives

According to IDEA 2004, a child's IEP must include:

A statement of measurable annual goals, including academic and functional goals, designed to meet the child's needs that result from the child's disability *to enable the child to be involved in and make progress in the general education curriculum*; and meet each of the child's other educational needs that result from the child's disability...[Part B, Section 614, (d) (A) (i) (II)] [italics added]

Historically, a child's IEP also had to include short-term objectives. But with the 2004 IDEA reauthorization, short-term objectives are only required for students who take alternative assessments.

Think about the goals that have been written for your child in the past. Did the IEP Team follow the law, as described above, and write goals to enable your child to be involved in and make progress in the general ed curriculum? While all parts of the IEP are important, the goals might be considered the most important part, since they're what drives your child's daily experience!

In my travels, I've found a wide disparity among school districts in the area of goals. Some IEP Teams (with or without parent or student input) may recommend (or "enforce") "computer generated goals." Yes, among the wealth of computer programs today, we can find software for IEP goals. The child's disability label is entered, along with other information, and the computer spits out goals. How are these individualized? How do these take into account the concerns of the parents and the child?

Other IEP Teams like to write therapeutic goals focused on isolated skills relative to "normal development," and/or goals related to activities within the segregated classroom. I've seen goals about children learning to tie their shoes, wash their hair, blow their noses, become more organized, and other unusual activities. In general, these types of goals wouldn't be appropriate for Regular Ed classrooms, since they don't reflect the general ed curriculum!

As Principal Mike said, we cannot expect schools to do everything. But more importantly, do we *want* schools to assume responsibility for things that are *our parental* responsibilities? We can and should take responsibility for being our children's first and best teachers. In addition, what opportunities for long-term academic success do our children lose when educators spend time on insignificant and irrelevant activities?

Other IEP Teams may create a long list of a child's "weaknesses" or needs that are related to "functional deficits" caused by the child's disability (can't walk, write, eat, read, and so forth). Then, goals are written to address these perceived deficits. In any of these scenarios, the goals often do not meet the

BE EVER QUESTIONING. IGNORANCE IS NOT BLISS. IT IS OBLIVION. YOU DON'T GO TO HEAVEN IF YOU DIE DUMB. BECOME BETTER INFORMED. LEARN FROM OTHERS' MISTAKES. YOU COULD NOT LIVE LONG ENOUGH TO MAKE THEM ALL YOURSELF.

Admiral Hyman Rickover

criteria established within IDEA (goals relative to a student's involvement and progress in the general curriculum).

When using the strategies detailed here, a list of "weaknesses" or functional needs is both unnecessary and irrelevant. Instead—hopefully—the child's needs (academic and other) will have been identified through non-standard assessments and by determining how the child's disability affects his participation and involvement in the general educational environment. In any setting—inclusive or segregated—writing goals to meet a child's overall *academic* needs is far more important than goals which attempt to "remediate *functional* deficits."

In addition, "therapeutic" goals are generally not appropriate for students included in Regular Ed classrooms, especially if you want your child to move beyond stacking donuts and riding a scooter board. Therapists, who can provide valuable consult services, will be in a position to help your child achieve academic goals, which may include and/or reflect improvements in functional abilities, but which are not solely focused on functional abilities. For example, a goal involving the student doing his work on the computer (instead of by handwriting) might require the consult services of an OT. The achievement of this goal might represent improvements in fine motor skills, but that's not the *focus* of the goal.

A closer look at one example of a "traditional" goal might help you (and educators) think differently about goals. What if "Juanita's" parents believed a goal like: "Juanita will increase her gait speed," is important, in the hope that one day, Juanita can get to her classes on time. First, and before the IEP Team writes such a goal, *Juanita should be consulted*. Is this important to *her*? In addition, the IEP Team can consider whether a *goal* is necessary and appropriate, or if this need could be met through Related Services and/or accommodations.

If Juanita moves slowly because of an awkward gait, is "increasing gait speed" a practical, doable goal? If the PT worked with Juanita in PE class (the natural setting for PT assistance), would this *really* enable Juanita to walk faster? How long would this take? Some students have had a goal like this for years—at what point do we let a child move on with her life?

Instead of trying to get Juanita to walk faster, would it make more sense to provide accommodations? Maybe a friend could carry her books for her, enabling her to walk a little faster between classes. Perhaps Juanita and a friend could leave each class one minute early. Or Juanita might decide she wants a power wheelchair! That would enable her to get to class on time, wouldn't it?

If your next door neighbor—or someone else who knows nothing about Special Education—can read and understand the goals written for your child, they've been written well.

There are many issues to thoughtfully consider when writing your child's goals. We need to focus on (1) what's most important for the child's long-term success and (2) what's really achievable. If we write multitudes of goals, many may never be met simply because there's not enough time in the day! Furthermore, many traditional goals are not appropriate or important to a child's involvement and progress in the Regular Ed environment, per IDEA.

The *way* goals are written can have a profound effect on the child's education and whether the goals are achieved. When they're written in professional jargon, they're often meaningless to everyone except the person who wrote them! How can a Regular Ed teacher make sense of, "Suzanne will [do whatever] four out of five times with 80 percent accuracy, 75 percent of the time."?

At the other end of the spectrum are goals that are senseless because they're so broad. While helping parents with their teenaged son's IEP, I learned educators had written only one goal: "James will improve his behavior." What does this mean? Improve his behavior in what way? To whose standards? How?

Goals need to be relevant and meaningful to the child, and the most effective goals describe *real-life activities* (described next) which your child can master, not isolated behaviors or skills. Writing relevant and appropriate goals is critical: they're the foundation of your child's daily educational experiences. Goals should be written in plain English, so that anyone can understand what they mean. Shouldn't they be written so *your child* can understand them?

Think of IEP goals as a set of instructions for a substitute teacher. If, for example, the classroom teacher is absent one day and she hasn't had the opportunity to review your child's education with the substitute, could the sub review your child's IEP goals (which are contained in a notebook on the teacher's desk, for example) and know what to do? If so, it's a *useful and meaningful living document.* And that's what your child's IEP should be: *a living document,* not a sheaf of senseless gibberish that is filed away as soon as the IEP meeting is over.

> A student's
> IEP should
> be a
> useful and
> meaningful
> *living*
> *document!*

At my children's inclusive elementary school, students with disabilities in Regular Ed classrooms were automatically involved in the general curriculum, so IEP Teams didn't write a ton of academic goals. The assumption was that students would make progress in the general curriculum. There was a greater focus on accommodations, assistive technology, supports, and curriculum modifications which were *the strategies* that enabled the child to make progress.

The following suggestions from The Schools Project of the Specialized Training Program at the University of Oregon, detail valuable ideas for writing effective activity-based goals and objectives:

The purpose of writing an IEP goal is to describe a complete picture of competence by identifying the activity-based outcome that you intend the student to achieve by the end of the school year. First, an effective IEP goal describes something a student will do as an outcome of instruction (i.e., by the end of the school year) that is typical of others the student's age. Second, it describes the parameters under which the student will do the activity (i.e. where, when, how often, or with whom?). Goals describe answers to the following three questions:

1. How will the student's competence change as a result of instruction?
2. When, where, or with whom will the student do the activity?
3. What kind of help or support will the student need?

Each goal should include the following critical features:
*   The goal is an activity.
*   The goal says what the student will do.
*   The goal describes the natural conditions under which the student will do the activity.

A goal is not an activity if it designates performance of isolated skills or behaviors, such as "Sue will read at a 3.5 grade level," or "Bill will learn the value of coins."

A goal does not describe a student's competence if it describes staff behavior rather than student behavior, such as: "Monica will maintain adequate dental hygiene," or "Dianne will have more opportunities to be integrated.

Following are some goals I wrote using the parameters above:

- Dylan will make choices about his lunch selection, his free-choice activities in class, and what games to play at recess using communication cards.

- Emily will read easy-reader books of her choice and will retell the story to her teacher and/or her classmates to demonstrate her comprehension.

- Matt will communicate with his classmates and teachers using words instead of gestures when he's angry, upset, or needs help.

According to The Schools Project, short term objectives need to answer the following questions:
1. What are the specific conditions under which the student will perform the skill? How will the student know to perform the skill? When or what will prompt the student in naturally-occurring situations to perform the skill?
2. What are the specific behaviors the student will perform?
3. How will you measure the student's performance in order to know that she has learned the skill?

Short term objectives should satisfy these critical features:
1. The objectives are driven by the IEP goal.
2. The objectives are observable and measurable and easily understood by everyone.
3. The objectives result in ordinary and individually meaningful outcomes.

Double check objectives by asking:
1. Is the objective related to the IEP goal?
2. Is the objective clear, concise, easily understood, and written in everyday language?
3. Do the objectives represent a broad range of skills that can be taught within the context of the activity, rather than simply being a task analysis of the activity goal?
4. Do all of the objectives say clearly what the student, not the teacher, will do?
5. Do the objectives support the student's positive image and involvement with peers who do not have disabilities?

Remember that short-term objectives are needed only if your child will be taking "alternate" statewide assessment tests.

In addition to activity-based goals, we can also write *strength-based goals.* Earlier, you learned about the importance of sharing your child's strengths during the IEP meeting. Not only are these important in helping everyone see the whole child, but they can also be the basis for meaningful and relevant goals.

If "Stephen" has a collection of baseball cards, his teachers could use this strength in many ways. Stephen could use his collection of cards:

- to learn one-to-one counting (he could count the cards);
- as a way of learning to read or spell (using the players' names, teams, cities);
- to learn higher level math (add, subtract, multiply, and/or divide, using the player's statistics from the cards);
- as a way to learn geography (using the teams' home cities/states).

Do you see how important a child's strengths can be in his education? Don't overlook the important step of identifying and sharing all your child's interests, abilities, hobbies, hopes, and dreams. They can contribute to his success, now and in the future!

Here's one more thing to consider. If you believe you'll have great difficulty convincing educators that your child belongs in a Regular Ed classroom, write goals for your child which can be implemented *only* in a Regular Ed classroom. If, for example, you wrote "functional goals" that focused on an isolated skill ("improved behavior," "writing name," etc.), such goals could be accomplished anywhere, including a segregated Special Ed classroom. But if you write goals related to the general curriculum of a Regular Ed fourth grade classroom, and you make it an activity-based goal, the *only* place that goal can be achieved is in the Regular Ed fourth grade classroom!

In your journal, or on a separate sheet of paper, begin writing goals (and objectives, if you think your child will be taking an alternate statewide assessment) for your child. Make sure to brainstorm these with your child and others who know your child well. *They need to be relevant and meaningful to your child.* As necessary, talk to your child about the grade-level curriculum of the class you hope she'll be in. What goals will enable your child to *be involved and make progress* in the general curriculum of a Regular Ed classroom? Consider goals in any or all of the five relevant areas: physical abilities, communication abilities, thinking (cognitive) abilities, social and emotional development, and educational and developmental growth, as well as other areas specific to your child. Check the goals (and objectives, if necessary) you write against the recommendations from The Schools Project.

Related Services

Related Services can include a variety of components that enable a child to benefit from Special Education services, and they represent *what the school will do.* Related Services can include therapy services (physical, occupational, vision, hearing, speech and language, etc.), transportation, counseling services, assistive technology, interpreters, modifications, accommodations, extra support in the classroom, and more. We'll look at some of these different components, and remember to discuss all of these with your child, and others who know your child well.

THERAPY SERVICES: By now, I fervently hope you'll embrace consult therapy services instead of direct, hands-on, Traditional Therapy for your child. If so, consider what role a therapist will play in your child's education. Will she need to help the Regular Ed, Special Ed, and/or paraprofessional in the classroom learn strategies which will enable your child to achieve his goals? If so, when and how? Should she work in the PE class, to assist your child and/or assist the PE teacher? Would it be helpful for an OT to do the same in art or some other class? Or for a speech therapist to be in your child's class during reading or music? You might have decided your child no longer needs therapeutic services of any kind, and if so, that's terrific!

ASSISTIVE TECHNOLOGY: As described in previous chapters, AT devices can be the linchpin to a child's success. IDEA 2004 says, "...the IEP Team shall consider whether the child needs assistive technology devices and services..." [Part B, Section 614, (d) (3) (B (v)], and it defines assistive technology as:

...any item, piece of equipment, or product system, whether acquired commercially off the shelf, modified, or customized, that is used to increase, maintain, or improve functional capabilities of a child with a disability. [Part A, Section 602 (1)]

What AT devices could increase, maintain, or improve your child's functional capabilities, enable him to achieve his goals, and be involved in and make progress in the general curriculum in a Regular Ed classroom? If necessary, go back to Chapters 6 and 7 to review information about AT devices and strategies for your child to lead a REAL LIFE, for this is what we want to have happen in an inclusive classroom. If you've visited the classroom(s) you want your child in, think about what AT devices could make a difference in your child's success there.

SUPPORTS AND ACCOMMODATIONS (INCLUDING BEHAVIOR SUPPORTS): These can come in many shapes and sizes, and need to be individualized to the child's needs. IDEA 2004 Part A, Section 602 (33) states:

The term "supplementary aids and services" means aids, services, and other supports that are provided in regular education classes or other education-related settings to enable children with disabilities to be educated with nondisabled children to the maximum extent appropriate...

IDEA 2004 Part B, Section 614, (d) (3) (B) details "special factors," such as the need for the IEP Team to consider the language needs of a child with limited English proficiency; the need for Braille for a child with a visual impairment; and the communication needs of a child. This part of the law also states that the IEP Team shall:

...in the case of a child whose behavior impedes the child's learning or that of others, consider the use of positive behavioral interventions and supports, and other strategies, to address that behavior...

Behavior supports can be provided in many different ways. And I hope educators, parents, and students can work together to create accommodations and environmental modifications which support a child's emotional/behavioral needs. It's common for schools to write "positive behavior plans," but in far too many cases, these are be based on rewards and punishments (as Joe Schiappacasse discussed in Chapter 6). If the right supports are put in place to begin with, positive behavior plans won't be necessary! A behavior support might be a peer buddy system, some adult help, or a quiet corner in a classroom and the right to go there whenever the child wants to.

Make sure you share with educators the positive, helpful strategies that work at home, in church, or other environments. If we help children learn to be in charge of their own behavior (internal control), instead of imposing external controls, we'll help them lead successful lives, now and in the future.

CURRICULUM MODIFICATIONS: IDEA '97, Section 300.552 Placements (e) states the following about curriculum modifications (and there's no reason to believe this won't be in the 2004 regulations when they're published after July 2005):

A child with a disability is not removed from education in age-appropriate regular classes solely because of needed modifications in the general curriculum.

What does this mean? Here's one example. A nine-year-old child should be in the fourth grade (depending on when his birthday is). But if he's reading at a second-grade level, this should not be grounds for denying him the opportunity to be in a Regular Ed fourth grade classroom. Instead, the school should provide curriculum modifications (in this case, modifying the reading material to his level) so he can *be involved in and make progress in* the general education environment.

Curriculum modifications (CMs) describe what the school will do to support the goals in a student's IEP. But many parents (as well as many educators) are not familiar with CMs because so many students are still in segregated Special Ed rooms: CMs aren't utilized since the student does not have access to the general ed curriculum!

Writing appropriate CMs is critically important! As I mentioned previously, we didn't write a great number of academic goals for my son; we wrote more CMs to ensure Benjamin had *what he needed* to be involved in and progress in his Regular Ed classrooms.

How do you get started writing CMs? It can be difficult to know what to write until the child is actually in the classroom, because there are many different components, every day, in the curriculum! But in practice, here's what worked for my son's education: his Regular Ed classroom teacher and I (and Benjamin, as he got older) reviewed the teacher's monthly lesson plan in advance. The teacher explained what the overall goal of the lesson, activity, etc. was for the class. With some lessons, we decided Benjamin's academic goal would be the same as his classmates. But he might also need a curriculum modification to achieve that goal. For example, if the lesson involved a worksheet, the CM was for the teacher's aide to scan the worksheet into Benj's computer, so he could answer the questions on the keyboard (since he doesn't write with a pencil). The teacher made a note of this in her lesson plan so the teacher's aide knew what needed to be done and when.

Sometimes, however, the goal for Benj was slightly different than the overall goal for the whole class. For example, if the other children were to write a report

> IN THE LAST ANALYSIS, CIVILIZATION ITSELF IS MEASURED BY THE WAY IN WHICH CHILDREN WILL LIVE AND WHAT CHANCE THEY WILL HAVE IN THE WORLD.
>
> *Mary Heato Vorse*

based on the study of a map or globe, Benjamin would write a report based on what he learned from the geography software program on his computer (since maps and globes were hard for him to use). Again, the teacher made notes in her lesson plan. These were not written into his IEP as they were "on-going" and changed from month to month.

At the beginning of each school year, the initial "lesson-plan review meeting" for the first month of school took about an hour or so. As the year progressed, however, most teachers learned from their own experiences (and Benjamin's), so they were able to create CMs without much help from me or Benjamin, but they always knew they could ask one of us.

Depending on the teacher, your child, and how the IEP Team operates, you may be able to follow a plan similar to what I described. But it might be necessary to be more formal, and include a variety of CMs in your child's IEP.

Following are some examples of Related Services (therapy services, AT, curriculum modifications, accommodations, etc.) which a student might need to *be involved in and make progress in* the general curriculum, and enable him to achieve his IEP goals:

- A child who struggles with math (or who can't write with a pencil) may need a calculator or a computer. This could be an accommodation (AT) as well as a curriculum modification. (This "need" could also become a goal: Tanya will add, subtract, multiply, and divide with a calculator.)

- A child who needs help with reading might benefit from large print books, a reading buddy, and books on tape. In addition, books and other reading material may need to be modified to his reading level.

- A student may need oral tests, shorter tests, or longer time for taking tests.

- Students using mobility devices may need classrooms rearranged to allow easy access; a PT may need to provide technical assistance to the student and/or teachers.

- A child may need behavior supports, such as: a peer buddy system and/or the right to go to a quiet place in the classroom (or the school), without having to ask permission, and to rejoin the class when ready.

- Brailled materials may be needed by a student with a visual disability; a sign language interpreter may be needed by a child with a hearing impairment.

- A student may need adult assistance for toileting or other personal needs.

- Children (1) with hearing or visual impairments, (2) who use wheelchairs, or (3) who are easily distracted may need their desks positioned close to the teacher and/or may need an FM system (the teacher wears a microphone, the student wears a headset).

- A student who cannot write, or one whose writing is illegible or time-consuming may need a computer and/or the student or teacher may need technical assistance from an OT (for keyboarding skills).

- Augmentative communication devices or other types of communication aids may be needed by children who do not have oral communication.

Related Services also include "program modifications or supports for school personnel that will be provided for the child." This can include, for example, assistance for the classroom teacher so she can make curriculum modifications, training of school staff in a student's assistive technology devices, and more. Also consider the "characteristics of service:" *who* will provide it, *when* (day of week, length of time, etc.) will the service(s) be provided, and *where* will the services be provided?

When *thinking* about Related Services, keep your child's needs and goals in mind. But when *describing* them, begin statements with what the school will do, as in the following examples (which are connected to the previous list):

- The school will provide Tanya with a computer and two-digit addition and subtraction computer software.
- The school will enlarge Mario's classroom texts into large print.—or—
  The school will modify fourth-grade reading materials to a second-grade reading level.—or—
  The school will provide second-grade reading level materials that are similar in content to the fourth-grade curriculum.
- The school will provide Riley with oral spelling tests.
- With technical assistance from Mrs. Jones, the physical therapist, the school will rearrange Timothy's classroom to provide wheelchair access.
- With assistance from Mrs. Douglas, the classroom teacher, the school will provide a peer buddy system of behavior supports to Dylan.

In your journal or on a separate sheet of paper, list the Related Services which would enable your child to achieve her IEP goals and *be involved in and make progress* in the general ed curriculum in a Regular Ed classroom. You might want to prepare a worksheet with three columns: (1) your child's daily schedule (the one you hope she'll have) which includes travel to school, arrives at school, math, language arts, recess, lunch, etc.; (2) the Related Services she needs at that time, and (3) the Characteristics of Services.

Write Your Draft

A month or so before your child's scheduled IEP meeting, begin putting all the lists you've created into a polished draft: your child's IEP Blueprint. As you prepare it, make sure it reflects the input of your child, as well as others who know your child well (family members, close friends, former teachers, etc.). Keep it short and sweet: remember, if there are too many goals, they probably won't get done! Focus on what's really important for your child, today and for the long-term. Make the Blueprint easy-to-read and professional looking. Compare the headings of your child's Blueprint with the headings/sections of the school district's IEP forms, just to familiarize yourself with the differences.

Schedule Pre-IEP Meetings

Once your child's IEP Blueprint is completed, begin scheduling pre-IEP meetings with the educators on your child's IEP Team. Remember, you want a small, effective Team.

Here's the Big Picture: you want to meet with *each* IEP Team member, one at a time. Let's say you start with Mrs. A. Call her and say something like, "My child's IEP meeting is coming up next month, and I'd like your opinion on some ideas we have. Could I meet with you for no longer than an hour on [whatever day and time]?" Then, prepare for a great meeting with Mrs. A! I'll leave it to your common sense and intuition to decide whether or not to make Mrs. A a copy of the Blueprint, or if it would be better for the two of you to review your copy. If you feel confident in Mrs. A's discretion—that she won't float her copy to every Tom, Dick, and Harry, you could give her a copy. If, however, you're not sure about this, only take one copy to the meeting and the two of you look over it together. Better to do this, than to ask for her copy back when the meeting is over.

If, for whatever reason, Mrs. A cannot meet with you face-to-face, you can either mail her a copy (assuming you trust her with it, as described above), and you can then have a phone meeting, with each of you reviewing the Blueprint in front of you. In the worst-case scenario, you might have to have a phone meeting, without giving Mrs. A a copy, and you'll just have to share what's in it.

So, one way or another, you have a meeting with Mrs. A. During this time, be upbeat and positive, and share the contents of the Blueprint. Use your own common sense, again, to determine if you have time to share all of it or just parts of it. If the latter, choose the most important parts, from your perspective. During your meeting, ask Mrs. A's opinion, be willing to listen to what she says, and plan on making some changes. Let Mrs. A (and others) know that you're willing to negotiate—you'll be perceived as a reasonable person, which can allow others to be more reasonable, too. But also—and this is very important—decide which items are negotiable and which are not. While meeting with Mrs. A, don't get into any arguments and leave your ego out of it. If there's a serious disagreement over one issue or another, politely drop it and move on to something else.

After your meeting with Mrs. A, make revisions to the Blueprint (those you can live with). Then go on to the next person—Mr. B—and do the same things. At the second meeting, use your common sense to decide if you should tell Mr. B you met with Mrs. A (this might be a moot point—Mrs. A might have alerted others, and this may or may not be a big deal). Continue on until you've met with everyone, revising as you go, making note of which educators have which concerns.

As you meet with each of these Team members, you'll be learning where they stand, what they think is important and why (make sure to ask questions so you'll learn even more), and you'll be negotiating the finer points. After all your meetings, make the final revisions to the Blueprint, and prepare for the "big" meeting. You'll want to make copies of the "final" Blueprint for everyone at the meeting, and hopefully, it will be the basis for the IEP that's written during the meeting. The actual IEP meeting should be a breeze, and it should be a relatively short meeting, because of all the preliminary work you've done.

> WHEN I'M GETTING READY TO REASON WITH A MAN, I SPEND ONE-THIRD OF MY TIME THINKING ABOUT MYSELF AND WHAT I'M GOING TO SAY, AND TWO-THIRDS THINKING ABOUT HIM AND WHAT HE'S GOING TO SAY.
>
> *Abraham Lincoln*

REMEMBER, PEOPLE
SUPPORT THAT
WHICH THEY
HELP CREATE.

ALWAYS GET THE
COMMITMENT
OF OTHERS IN
ANY UNDERTAKING.

HAVE THEM TAKE
A PIECE OF
THE ACTION SO
IT'S THEIR ACTION
AS WELL AS YOURS.

INVOLVEMENT
BEGETS
COMMITMENT.
COMMITMENT
BEGETS POWER.

Herb Cohen

Make the Meeting Fun!

Change the traditional stuffy, tension-filled IEP meeting to an event that's pleasant and productive! Prior to the meeting, share your ideas about a "new and improved" meeting with the person who normally *plans* the meeting (special ed teacher, service coordinator, etc.) Here are some suggestions:

- Move the meeting from the conference room or other "official" place to a location that's friendlier, more relevant, and/or on more neutral turf: the classroom you want your child in, or the library, cafeteria, or gym. How about a grassy spot on the playground if the weather's nice? Or how about your home! Yes, your home! What better way for educators to know more about your child than to see her in her own environment!

- Change the time of the meeting, when possible. If you have the meeting in your home, schedule it for early afternoon and feed everyone a light supper. If your child is a "morning person," have it in the morning.

- Don't sit at a table—it's an artificial barrier you don't need. Pull chairs in a circle and get up close and personal! If your spouse or other family members/friends attend the meeting, intersperse yourselves among educators. Don't set up an us/them seating arrangement.

- Instead of bringing a tape recorder to record the proceedings (and intimidate educators!), use it to play soft, soothing, or inspirational music.

- Your child must be a key player at the meeting—it's his education! He should participate as much as possible. If, for whatever reason, he wouldn't be able to participate in the entire meeting, let him remain in the room (playing, reading, or whatever) in case his opinion or help is needed. Let your child's competence and abilities shine! And don't forget to lay down the new ground rules: while your child is present, Team members need to talk *to* him, not *about* him, using words that make sense to him and which are respectful, like reframing "problems" into "needs" (described in Chapter 5).

- Act as the unofficial host of the meeting. Arrive first, and you and your child can greet the other team members, welcoming them and thanking them for coming. Let your child give them all handshake or a hug when they arrive!

- Don't bring other parents of kids with disabilities or "professional-type" advocates to the meeting. Their presence may inflame an already tense situation. Instead, bring someone who knows your child (T-ball coach, Sunday school teacher, neighbor, etc.). Such a person can bring common sense and calm to the meeting.

- Bring food! How can anyone stay in a bad mood when there's comfort food available! (One mom reported how stern faces turned to smiles when team members approached the meeting room and were met with the aroma of her freshly-baked banana bread!) This works—I promise!

- As host of the meeting, start it off on a positive note by sharing your dreams for your child: "We want Johnny to grow up and go to college [get a job or whatever] just like his brother." Have your child share his dreams, too: "I want to be a fireman when I grow up." Then, ask everyone to share something wonderful about your child. (If this causes one or more people to become speechless, tell them you'll give them a moment to think about it and will return to them when everyone else has finished.) After all the glowing remarks have been shared, begin the meeting!

- Stay calm, cool, and collected during the meeting. If/when things get tense, take a cookie break, tell everyone it's time for a group hug, have everyone do deep-breathing for sixty seconds, or do anything else to break the tension. Compromise and negotiate. Remember, the IEP isn't set in stone. You can always call another meeting in a month or so to renegotiate. Don't make enemies! Pick your battles! Decide if this (whatever it is) is the hill you're ready to die on!

> I'VE A THEORY THAT
> ONE CAN ALWAYS
> GET ANYTING ONE
> WANTS IF ONE WILL
> PAY THE PRICE. AND
> DO YOU KNOW WHAT
> THE PRICE IS, NINE
> TIMES OUT OF TEN?
> COMPROMISE.
>
> *Agatha Christie*

When Benjamin was in kindergarten, we had another meeting a few months after school began. This wasn't an IEP meeting; it was more like a Personal Futures Planning, geared for a child in school. Present were Benjamin; his sister, Emily; my husband and me; Benjamin's teachers; Principal Mike; and several classmates. One "rule" for this type of meeting was that there needed to be as many children present as there were adults! Two facilitators led the meeting: one asked questions of the group; the other recorded the answers with creative artwork on a flip-chart. The purpose of the meeting was to get the input from those who knew Benjamin best—including the classmates he chose to attend—about how to ensure Benjamin's hopes and dreams could become realities, and how to ensure his worst fears would not. The results of this meeting had no official standing, like an IEP report, but the ideas and activities generated were put into place in Benjamin's classroom! You might consider having a similar meeting for your child. Your child's peers will come up with wonderful ideas and strategies!

On-Going Cooperation and Collaboration

Members of the IEP Team can maintain positive relationships with one another and support a child's IEP if they stay in close touch with one another (as previously described), and maintain a "whatever it takes" attitude. Parents and educators can meet, informally, on a regular basis to troubleshoot small issues and prevent them from becoming huge problems.

Parents can and should commit to assisting educators in whatever ways they're needed, and educators can and should welcome and value parental wisdom. When we accept that a child *needs* his parents and teachers to be partners, we can get beyond our differences and cooperate and collaborate with one other. Children are counting on us; let's not let them down.

We can be flexible and open-minded, willing to take the dignity of risk, choosing to trust and respect each other, and being willing to try, try again when things don't work out exactly as planned. Or, we can be rigid and close-minded: unwilling to take risks, trust others, or try new things. The choice is ours. And let's never forget that children's lives are at stake—*and are in our hands.*

Children are counting on us; let's not let them down.

High School and Transition

What will your child do after high school? Are you dreaming Big Dreams that he'll go to college or trade school, enter the workforce (with or without post-secondary education), and be able to move out on his own and support himself at the right time (with or without supports)? If your child is a teen, you'll want to add information from this section into your child's IEP Blueprint.

IDEA requires IEP Teams to write a transition plan for students aged 16 and above, but transition planning *can* begin before age 16, and many parents and students have requested this, since 16 is really a little bit late to start thinking about what a student will do after high school! The transition plan should address what needs to happen so the student can move from public school to post-secondary education, employment, etc., based on the students "strengths, preferences, and interests."

As many parents are aware, IDEA covers students from ages 3 to 22, meaning that a student can choose to receive Special Ed services from the school district until her 22nd birthday. Some parents do choose this for their children (but I often wonder if the *student* has been given a choice in the matter). I really can't imagine any student *wanting* to stay in high school any longer than possible! But many do stay—whether they want to or not. In these situations, young adults with disabilities may be in segregated classrooms and/or they may be working at a job, which was procured for them by the Special Ed department and/or Voc Rehab agency. Some students—believe it or not—are working for free (a.k.a. slave labor)! We need to put a stop to this practice—our teenagers should be paid for their work, the way other teens are.

I have a strong personal bias against students with disabilities remaining in school past the typical age graduation (17-18). Keeping a student in a public school beyond that age seems like an enormous waste of the student's time. But before considering alternatives, it's important for parents and students to investigate the graduation policies of the school district.

I hope you're sitting down when you read this: in many school districts, students who receive Special Ed services, and/or have a modified curriculum, *do not receive a high school diploma!* Instead, they may receive a "certificate of attendance" or "certificate of completion." *Whoopee!*

When I do presentations on inclusive education, I ask parents in the audience if they know the "diploma policy" in their districts. Most don't. One mother *insisted* her daughter would receive a diploma: she was included in Regular Ed classrooms and was on the honor roll. After my presentation, she called the school and was told her daughter would *not* receive a diploma since she was on a modified curriculum and the grades weren't "real."

My recommendation to these parents—and to you—is this: if your child is not going to receive a diploma and/or if high school is not a good place for him to be (if he's not receiving the education he needs, if he's segregated, and/or if he's teased or otherwise made to feel awful about himself), *and* if he's 16 (or has reached the age where he is no longer required to attend public school), *let him leave school and help him get on with his life!* Why make him spend even one more day in a place that's not helping him?

He can study for and take the GED (which he'll need anyway if he's not going to get a diploma from the high school), enroll in college or trade school,

> Do you know the "diploma policy" in your school district for students who receive special ed services? If not, call and find out!

and/or enter the workforce. In many states, students can attend community college at 16, and may be able to enroll *without* a GED, and/or *may be able to earn a GED through a college course.* GED practice tests are available on the Internet (www.gedpractice.com), and your child can study to her heart's content until she's got it mastered. During this time, you and your teen can investigate different options for post-secondary education and/or employment.

At the end of Chapter 7, I provided details about today's Adult Services. Let's work hard and help our young adult children find Real Jobs in the community so they don't need Adult Services and disability welfare! I hope you and your teen will do whatever it takes to make this happen. If necessary, use the strategies described in Chapter 7 to identify your child's strengths and interests and then find the natural supports in the community that will help him with networking to find the job that's right for him. As I mentioned before, I hope we'll think of using the System as a last resort, not the first choice.

NCLB and Assessment Tests

No Child Left Behind (NCLB) mandates the testing of all students in certain grade levels. In the opinion of many, including yours truly, NCLB has created a mess for students *and* teachers. As of this writing, NCLB is being challenged by governors, state departments of education, and Federal legislators from a variety of states, as well as by parent and teacher groups. By the time this book is in your hands, NCLB might be changed, so I won't spend a great deal of time on this subject. You can find accurate, up-to-date information on the Internet or from other sources.

But IDEA 2004 Part B, Section 614, (d) (A) (i) (IV) (aa), states that a child's IEP must include a "statement of individual appropriate modifications" in order for a student to take State and district-wide tests. If the IEP team determines the student should take an alternate assessment, it must include a statement detailing *why,* and identify what the alternate assessment will be.

Because many educators have screamed that students with disabilities are "bringing down test scores," the Federal Department of Education is now allowing school districts to identify up to three percent of all students taking the tests as students with "significant cognitive disabilities," and those students will be given alternate assessments. Also, each state department of education is allowed to *define* "significant cognitive disabilities."

During your child's IEP meeting, make sure to ask lots of questions about this issue. You, along with other parents, might want to do a little investigating to see what's going on in your local school district. What's the definition *your state* decided on for "the most significant cognitive disabilities"? Who created it and what criteria was used? How many students are being classified this way, and what does this mean to their education? Be aware that some educators are already using this change in NCLB as a trigger to place more students in segregated Special Ed classrooms!

Your teen can take the GED test through a university of other educational facility, receive her diploma, and get on with her life! She can study for it on the Internet and when it's time to take the test, she can receive whatever accommodations are necessary. Check with the testing facility for more information. And when her diploma from the state arrives in the mail, it's time to celebrate!

Alternatives to Public Schools

I'm all for inclusive public schools for students with disabilities. When our children are in Regular Ed classrooms, they're learning and growing, making friends, and being prepared for a successful adult life. At the same time, the future (and the present) may be bleak for students with disabilities who are segregated in Special Ed classrooms.

Some parents are determined to hold schools accountable, and they may become Mothers from Hell in the process. While they're rattling their sabers and filing lawsuits, their children are not receiving the education they need. In such cases, the children may become sacrificial lambs.

I'm also all for parents working their tushes off on behalf of their children—I have, many times. And I am ever hopeful that educators will recognize the value of ensuring all students are included and receive the education they need to become successful adults. At the same time, I have great concerns that little progress is being made in many schools, and with the pressures of NCLB, some schools seem to be moving backwards, and more students with disabilities are being segregated.

I am deeply saddened by the stories many parents share about their children being segregated, marginalized, and undereducated in segregated Special Ed classrooms. It's heartbreaking to think about children going through life not having friends at school, not playing with pals at recess, not giggling with friends at lunch, not going to football games or participating in ordinary school activities. And the heartbreak is tinged with anger when I think about students spending 12 or more years receiving Special Education Services, yet all this "special" help has done little to prepare these students for success as adults. So I think we need to be thoughtful about when enough is enough—when it's time to move on and find alternatives to the public school system.

One alternative is a private school. If you can afford it, and can find one that works for your child, go for it! You don't need to make apologies to anyone for taking your child out of public school.

Many parents, however, haven't had much success in this endeavor, even at private religious schools run by the churches they routinely attend! One would think that churches—of all places—would be the most inclusive environments in any community, but they're sometimes the most exclusionary. Still, checking out private schools is certainly an option worth considering. Do your homework and learn what's what as far as the Americans with Disabilities Act (ADA) is concerned. Remember that church-run activities are exempt from the ADA. Private, non-religious schools are covered by the ADA, so they can't discriminate on the basis of disability. But many have enrollment criteria (academic achievement, IQ tests, etc.) which some students with disabilities may not meet.

Another alternative—one that's becoming more and more popular—is homeschooling. As I mentioned previously, my children were homeschooled since middle school. Emily attended one year of middle school (sixth grade)

> LET NO CHILD
> BE DEMEANED,
> NOR HAVE
> HIS WONDER
> DIMINISHED,
> BECAUSE OF OUR
> IGNORANCE OR
> INACTIVITY.
>
> LET NO CHILD
> BE DEPRIVED
> OF DISCOVERY,
> BECAUSE WE LACK
> THE RESOURCES TO
> DISCOVER HIS NEED.
>
> LET NO CHILD
> DOUBT HIMSELF OR
> HIS MIND BECAUSE
> WE ARE UNSURE OF
> OUR COMMITMENT.
> *Allen Martin*

and didn't want to return. I wasn't happy with the school, either, but figured I'd continue trying to work with educators to make things better. There were many things that Emily and I didn't care for. Neither of us liked the social environment, and I was concerned about academics. Emily was on the honor roll, but so were many others; it wasn't hard to make good grades with open book tests and copy-out-of-the-book worksheets!

When Emily said she wanted to be homeschooled, I agreed to give it a try! It worked, and Benjamin followed in his sister's footsteps. So it was my children's choice and I'm glad they made the decision!

Many parents want their children to have a better education, but are reluctant to try homeschooling, for a wide variety of reasons. I was reluctant, too. Like other parents who worry how they'll handle the *summer* when the kids are home, I wondered if we would survive being together *all the time!* But we did—and I loved every minute of it. The fear of being with your children goes away when you *are* with them all the time!

As far as a parent's ability to be a "good teacher," that's not a worry, either! Instead of traditional homeschooling (replicating a school's methods and schedule in your home), we did "unschooling" which involved me following my children's lead and helping them learn what they were interested in. Some days, "learning" took place while on a shopping excursion. Other times, the children worked on their own, and sometimes the three of us played games, read books, and did a variety of other fun activities.

We already had many books in our home that the kids used, but we also made regular trips to the library and used book stores for materials. The games you probably already have in your home are great for learning, too. We often did "math lessons" while following a recipe in a cookbook. Educational videos and computer CDs are available at local libraries, and there's a wealth of great educational programs on cable TV stations! One of the most important things homeschooling taught all of us was that learning goes on all the time, and in any environment. This is in sharp contrast to the widely-held perception that learning goes on between 8:30 AM and 3:30 PM, Monday through Friday, in the school building!

> THE ART OF TEACHING IS THE ART OF ASSISTING DISCOVERY.
> *Mark Van Doren*

Emily "finished" school a year ahead of schedule, took her GED, and went on to community college, where she earned an Associate's degree. She's employed and lives in her own place now. As of this writing, Benjamin is in his last year of "high school," and is studying for his GED. He plans on enrolling in the community college in the fall, then going on to a four-year college to earn a degree in journalism. He wants to be a movie critic (the next Roger Ebert), and he's raring to go!

One of the greatest concerns about homeschooling is "socialization." Parents and others often get up-in-arms thinking children who are homeschooled are isolated. But this is also an overblown concern! First, there are many homeschooling groups that families can join so children can be with other children in organized activities. Second, because homeschooled children are not at school all day and burdened with hours of homework, they have the time to engage in community activities where they can be with other children. But the other consideration is this: some of the problems facing many children in public schools *is* the peer group! How many parents have expressed concern about drugs, sex, and other issues that are peer-group related? Parents of homeschoolers don't have as many concerns in this area—their children are safer! Some researchers, along with many parents, have discovered that children who are homeschooled are generally more mature and more socially-adept than children who attend public school.

I thoroughly enjoyed my time educating our children at home (and in lots of other places in the community). I thought I knew my children well before that time, but I didn't *really* get to know them until we began homeschooling! Many other parents have reported similar experiences.

There are many ways to homeschool, even if you work. Parents can rearrange work schedules, call on other family members, and/or join with a homeschooling co-op. You can investigate the possibilities by reading books on the subject, especially those by John Holt. And I'm working on a booklet on the subject that might also be helpful.

As you think about your child's education, keep the Big Picture in mind: your child as a successful adult. Talk to your child about his dreams—on a regular basis—and let those dreams be the driving force of his education. Remember: there is no magic switch to flip when your child becomes a young adult. If you hope he'll be successful as an adult, he needs to be successful as a child—in school, at home, and in the community.

Our children with disabilities—just like all children—are the future. They deserve the best education, from whatever source, *today*, so they can create the best futures for themselves and our society, tomorrow.

> PARENTS HAVE BECOME SO CONVINCED THAT EDUCATORS KNOW WHAT IS BEST FOR CHILDREN THAT THEY FORGET THAT THEY THEMSELVES ARE REALLY THE EXPERTS.
>
> *Marian Wright Edelman*

Epilogue

I spend a lot of time thinking, talking, and learning about the lives of children and adults with disabilities, and I frequently see parallels to DISABILITY WORLD in non-disability arenas, which can lead to valuable lessons. For example, *The Truman Show,* a movie starring Jim Carrey, is analogous to people with disabilities and family members living in DISABILITY WORLD, but thinking it's the REAL WORLD. When they wake up and realize it's *not* the REAL WORLD, and try to leave it, there can be many obstacles in their path. I won't say more—go rent the movie and see what I mean.

Another valuable lesson recently came from TV. I don't spend a lot of time watching television, but I was aware of the "trading places" shows that seemed to pop up everywhere. That got me thinking about people who both *provide* and *receive* any type of services, and I began playing a little game in my head. I fly a great deal, and "receive services" from flight attendants. Would I be willing to trade places for a day with a flight attendant, and would she be willing to do the same, and become a passenger for a day? Yes. Would I trade places for a day with a clerk at Target? Yes. A cook at Taco Bell? Yes. A telephone repair technician? Yes. A hair stylist? Yes.

I went through many other scenarios in my head, and began sharing this with conference participants who work with children and adults with disabilities in the human services and educational arenas. You probably know where I'm going with this. I found there were only two categories of people that no one was willing to trade places with for a day: inmates in prison and people with disabilities.

A brief discussion with participants reveals why they feel this way: it's not knowing you've committed a crime or the presence of a disability (having to use a wheelchair, for example) that makes people reluctant to trade places with these two groups of people. The overriding factor is the environment: *where and how these groups of people spend their time!* So I wrap up that part of my presentation by asking conference participants to do whatever it takes—to create change—so they *would be* willing to trade places with an adult or a child with a disability for one day.

I ask the same of you: do whatever it takes to make changes in where and how your child spends his time so you would be willing to trade places with him for a day. I would trade places with my son, and I believe many others would, too. Benjamin has a great life, he's always included, and he's master of his destiny. *Your child can do the same.*

> WHEN WE DO THE BEST THAT WE CAN, WE NEVER KNOW WHAT MIRACLE IS WROUGHT IN OUR LIFE, OR IN THE LIFE OF ANOTHER.
>
> *Helen Keller*

When Benjamin was very young, I resolved to live by the following: I wanted to be able to look at myself in the mirror when my son is 30 years old and know that I did everything I could to enable him to live the life of his dreams. He is now 18; so far, so good. I've got 12 more years to go, and I think I'm gonna' make it! And do you know what it's taken to get to this point? Believing in my son and seeing the Big Picture. When we believe in our children and keep the Big Picture in mind, everything falls into place.

> ACT AS THOUGH IT WERE IMPOSSIBLE TO FAIL.
> *Dorothea Brande*

You can do this. If I were a betting woman, I'd bet big bucks that you've already made positive changes or that you're ready to. In the next day or so, go back to Chapter 3 and read what you wrote. Do things already look different to you? Go back to Chapter 5 and add to who your child really is!

I hope you see yourself as a leader. You are. And you and I, along with many other parents, are creating a new future for *our* children with disabilities, *and for those not yet born.* When my daughter, Emily, was about nine, she said, "You know, Mom, if I have a baby with a disability when I grow up, it's gonna' be *no big deal.*" She learned that from her brother, and from me. I learned from my son, and from other children and adults with developmental disabilities, and from parents just like you. Do you see the connections—how we touch each other's lives and we're better for the experience?

With our new attitudes and actions, we're giving birth to a gentle revolution that can change the fabric of our society. When we recognize that disability is natural; when our children are known by their names, instead of their labels; when our children's hopes and dreams—not their diagnoses—are the driving forces in their lives; and when our children proudly take their rightful places in our communities; we will create a society where *disability is irrelevant.*

> I HAD NO CONSCIOUS FAITH, BUT IF I ACTED, THEN FAITH WOULD SURELY FOLLOW. AFTER THAT, I WOULD BELIEVE BECAUSE I HAD ACTED. PERHAPS THAT IS HOW FAITH IS BORN: BY ACTION AND NOT BY CONTEMPLATION. IT WAS WORTH A TRY.
> *John LeCarre*

Imagine a future where the birth of *every baby* is cause for celebration. Imagine a future where a disability diagnosis *generates no tears and no grief.* Imagine a future where *everyone* knows disability is natural, so it's "no big deal." Imagine a future where *all* are included in every environment, and segregated settings are as extinct as the dinosaurs. Imagine a future where *our grown children* are parents, teachers, mail carriers, executives, homeowners, politicians, volunteers, landlords, business owners, doctors, hairdressers, movie stars, plumbers, and leaders. Imagine a future that is influenced by the legacy of *our actions* and our *children's lives.* That future begins today—right now—with us.

I am always inspired by the words of Frances Hodgson Burnett, writing in *The Secret Garden:*

> At first, people refuse to believe
> that a strange new thing *can* be done,
> then they begin to *hope* it can be done,
> then they *see* it can be done,
> then it *is* done,
> and all the world wonders
> why it was not done centuries ago.

I am with you in spirit. Dream big dreams. Lead with a brave heart.

Appendix of Resources

THE PEOPLE YOU MET:

The Educators:
Mike Galvin can be reached at mijoga@aol.com.
Barb Myers (my favorite of all my son's teachers) can be reached at dbmyers@gbronline.com.

The Therapists:
Beth-Degrace@ouhsc.edu, Rene-Daman@ouhsc.edu, Lorraine-Sylvester@ouhsc.edu

Beth shared the following web sites of interest, related to children, therapies, natural environments, and evidence-based practices:

www.poweroftheordinary.org
www.coachinginearlychildhood.org
www.evidencebasedpractices.org

www.otseeker.com
www.pedro.fhs.usyd.edu.au
www.ptwa.org/EBP.htm

SOME HELPFUL BOOKS:

Clear Thinking: A Practical Introduction by Hy Ruchlis with Sandra Oddo
Deconstructing Early Childhood Education: Social Justice and Revolution by Gaile Sloan Cannella
How Children Learn and *How Children Fail* by John Holt (read anything by Holt)
Learned Optimism: How to Change Your Mind and Your Life by Martin E.P. Seligman
Miseducation: Preschoolers at Risk and *The Hurried Child* by David Elkind (read anything by Elkind)
Plato, Not Prozac: Applying Eternal Wisdom to Everyday Problems by Lou Marinoff, Ph.D.
Punished by Rewards and *The Case Against Competition* by Alfie Kohn(read anything by Kohn)
Schooled to Order: A Social History of Public Schooling in the United States by David Nasaw
Teach Your Child to Think by Edward DeBono (read anything by DeBono)
The Art of Living: The Classic Manual on Virtue, Happiness, and Effectiveness by Epictetus, Interpretation
    by Sharon Lebell
The Nurture Assumption: Why Children Turn Out the Way They Do by Judith Rich Harris
*The Myth of the A.D.D. Child: 50 Ways to Improve Your Child's Behavior and Attention Span Without
    Drugs, Labels, or Coercion*, Thomas Armstrong, Ph.D. (read anything by Armstrong)
The Unschooled Mind by Howard Gardner (read anything by Gardner)
What We Owe Children: The Subordination of Teaching to Learning by Caleb Gattegno

Read anything by: William Glasser, Ralph Waldo Emerson, Oliver Sacks, Albert Ellis, and Bernie S. Siegel.

OTHER WEB SITES OF INTEREST:

www.heath.gwu.edu - higher education for students with disabilities.

www.adaportal.org - the Americans with Disabilities Act.

www.moaccessrec.com - inclusive recreation.

www.gedpractice.com - practice test for the GED.

References and Bibliography

Bruer, John T. *The Myth of the First Three Years: A New Understanding of Early Brain Development and Lifelong Learning.* New York: The Free Press, 1999.

Hayakawa, S.I. and Alan R. Hayakawa. *Language in Thought and Action (Fifth Edition).* New York: Harcourt Brace and Company, 1990.

Johnson, Wendell with Dorothy Moeller. *Living with Change: The Semantics of Coping.* New York: Harper and Row, 1972.

Johnson, Wendell. *People in Quandaries: The Semantics of Personal Adjustment.* Concord, CA: International Society for General Semantics, 2002.

Oliver, Michael. *The Politics of Disablement.* New York: St. Martin's Press, 1990.

Rothwell, J. Dan. *Telling It Like It Isn't: Language Misuse and Malpractice/What We Can Do About It.* Englewood Cliffs, NJ: Prentice-Hall, Inc., 1982.

Smith, J. David. *Minds Made Feeble: The Myth and Legacy of the Kallikaks.* Rockville, MD: Aspen Systems Corp.,1975.

Abandoned to Their Fate: A History of Social Policy Toward People Labeled Severely Disabled, videocasette recording from the Specialized Training Program, University of Oregon, 1997.

"Handicapism" by William Henderson, *Equity and Choice,* Vol. 9 No. 2, Winter 1993, 59-60, Corwin Press, Inc., 1993.

Module 1a: The Activity-Based IEP, manual from The Schools Project, The University of Oregon, 1993. Excerpts in "Chapter 9-Inclusive Education," describing activity-based goals and objectives, used with permission.

Parallels in Time CD-ROM, from the MN Governor's Council on Developmental Disabilities, 1998.

Lectures of, and personal conversations with, Rene Daman, Beth DeGrace, Phil Ferguson, Mike Galvin, Ed Roberts, Joe Schiappacasse, Ed Skarnulis, Jopie Smith, Lorrie Sylvester, Tom Tyree, and Colleen Wieck.

www.nces.ed.gov - National Center for Education Statistics

www.va.gov - Veteran's Department